Resource Allocation and Management in Defence

Need for a Framework

RESOURCE ALLOCATION AND MANAGEMENT IN DEFENCE

NEED FOR A FRAMEWORK

AMIYA KUMAR GHOSH

Introduction by
Air Commodore **Jasjit Singh** AVSM, VrC, VM (Retd)

KNOWLEDGE WORLD
KW Publishers Pvt Ltd
New Delhi

in association with

Centre for Air Power Studies
New Delhi

2011 FPBA BEST PUBLISHERS AWARD (ENGLISH)

The Centre for Air Power Studies is an independent, non-profit, academic research institution established in 2002 under a registered Trust to undertake and promote policy-related research, study and discussion on the trends and developments in defence and military issues, especially air power and the aerospace arena, for civil and military purposes. Its publications seek to expand and deepen the understanding of defence, military power, air power and aerospace issues without necessarily reflecting the views of any institution or individuals except those of the authors.

Jasjit Singh
Director General
Centre for Air Power Studies
P-284, Arjan Path
Subroto Park
New Delhi 110010

Tele: (91-11) 25699131
E-mail: diroffice@aerospaceindia.org

KW Publishers Pvt Ltd

Published in India by
Kalpana Shukla
KW Publishers Pvt Ltd
4676/21, First Floor, Ansari Road, Daryaganj, New Delhi 110002
T: +91.11.43528107 E: kw@kwpub.in • www.kwpub.in

ISBN 978-93-81904-45-9

Printed and bound in India

Dedicated in loving memory
of my wife Smt. Dipa Ghosh,
who always stood by me in my semi-academic endeavours,
though at times, it involved difficult decisions

Contents

Preface

This book reflects the work done after the publication of my second book *Defence Budgeting and Planning in India: The Way Forward* (2006). The second book covered some of the major points relating to budgeting and planning processes and their inter-linkages, some major initiatives in India taken regarding decentralised financial management, also touching upon capability-based planning. It evolved out of my first book, *India's Defence Budget and Expenditure Management in a Wider Context* (1996), which was well received.

The present book, among other topics, further explores the concept of capability-based planning and how to link it with budgeting, especially drawing attention to the imperative necessity of introducing programme budgeting in India's defence planning and budgeting. Adding my ten years at the Ministry of Defence, it has been an odyssey lasting two and half decades, exploring various facets relating to defence financial management, planning and budgeting. I have to go still further.

Among other things, this book emphasises the importance of introducing programming in Indian defence to serve as a link between defence planning and budgeting. The responsibility for programming is that of the Services, that need to incorporate weapons and force planning programmes, as part of budgetary proposals, after evaluating alternatives in terms of costs and benefits. The proposed programmes are required to adhere to budgetary guidelines to make them resource constrained. This would enable us to move towards 'output' budgeting.

Force planning has to be an integral part of the budgetary process and should not be done outside the process. This is for two reasons: firstly, the defence budget is more or less determined by the force level and structure, making the obligatory expenditure very high; secondly, force planning itself must be resource constrained, otherwise a mismatch between strategy and resources, as well as between the plan and budget is likely to arise. Capability-based planning has to be based on programmes and, therefore, introduction of programme budgeting and capability-based planning are intimately linked. Capability-based planning cannot be introduced on the basis of input budgeting, which is the present practice of defence budgeting in India. So the mismatch of perspectives between what we want to achieve through defence planning (capability) and defence budgeting (control of expenditure), has already occurred. This needs to be corrected by meaningful introduction of resource constrained programming, having a multi-year perspective. Accordingly, budgeting has also to be on a multi-year basis. It is necessary to have a multi-year framework to link planning (including force planning) and budgeting so that input gets properly linked to output. While attempting this, the issue of linking 'ends' and 'means' has to be addressed, which is one of the basic concerns of strategy, as also economics.

To appreciate the necessity of programme budgeting, as also 'ways' of linking 'means' and 'ends', one has to get acquainted with some of the basic management and economic principles that help in putting them in the proper framework. The first chapter of the book tries to bring these out in the context of the planning, programming and budgeting systems. In the same context, the linkage between economics and strategy is explored. Linking of input to output in defence resource management is not an easy endeavour, as many aspects need to be covered to establish this linkage, which include, among other things, application of economic principles, cost-effectiveness analysis, establishing a capability framework, and scenario-building exercise. The complexity in the endeavour is covered in the second chapter.

Towards the end of 2006, a very important event took place in New Delhi in the shape of the International Seminar on Defence and Economics (November 13-15, 2006) organised by the Finance Division of the Ministry of Defence. This seminar was to acquaint the participants with analytical approaches to contemporary challenges that confront security planners, the core issues in defence economics, and the steps required to reform the budgeting process, including programme/outcome budgeting. However, the impression was that there was inadequate appreciation of the need for understanding the economic aspects of defence resource planning and budgeting and the linkage between economics and strategy. The first two chapters of the book try to cover this gap. Further, a paper entitled "Challenges in Defence Planning" that was contributed by me in this international seminar to highlight the above issues, has been incorporated with some modifications in Chapter 8 of this book.

During 2007-08, I served as a Senior Consultant in the National Institute of Public Finance and Policy (NIPFP) to lead a project on "Strengthening Financial Management Systems" on behalf of the Administrative Reforms Commission (ARC). The project report was finalised in June 2008, followed by a national seminar to discuss the issues raised in the report and deliberate on the course to follow. An important chapter of the report related to "Internal Control and Internal Audit". Presently, many audit findings of the Comptroller and Auditor General (C&AG), relating to shortfall in management of some of the national resources, are coming out in the public domain, leading to debates on policies, and remedying of the deficiencies. However, significantly, absent are discussions about the role of internal audit, its findings, and its efficacy in correcting the deficiencies in resource management. The roles of internal audit and external audit are complementary. Internal audit is to aid management in finding the deficiencies and take timely necessary measures. Internal audit in the government sector is very weak. As a result, it cannot perform the role expected of it as per accepted international practice. In view of the importance of this topic, as highlighted in the report to ARC, Chapter 5 discusses how internal audit can be strengthened to act as the 'eyes' and 'ears' of management, give timely warnings and enable the management to take steps to prevent fraud and mismanagement, enabling it to take timely actions. In my view, prevention of corruption and fraud is an integral part of sound resource management and governance. Therefore, internal audit has to be given much more importance than it is being given today by the Indian government.

In February 2007, the Ministry of Defence (MoD), Government of India, appointed a Review Committee for the Defence Research and Development Organisation (DRDO), in which I was a member. The report of the Review Committee entitled "Redefining DRDO" was submitted in March 2008. After that, it has continued to be deliberated upon in the MoD.

Because of the importance of the findings of the review report which have a great bearing on the modernisation efforts in defence, it is the main basis of a fairly extensive chapter entitled "Modernisation and Challenges before Defence Research and Development" (Chapter 10).

A request was received in April 2009 from the Pakistan Institute of Legislative Development and Transparency (PILDAT), through the Institute for Defence Studies and Analyses (IDSA) to prepare a background paper for Pakistan's Members of Parliament to understand the role played by the Indian Parliamentary Committee (Standing Committee) in reviewing the defence budget over the years. The paper was published by PILDAT entitled "*How to Review the Defence Budget*" in June 2009. In view of its topicality, the paper has been enlarged to include some critical aspects of the review process and incorporated in Chapter 3.

The rest of the topics covered in the book have been presented in other forums, though the shape given to the chapters has undergone modifications.

The book would not have taken the present shape but for the constant encouragement from Air Cmde Jasjit Singh (Retd), Director General, Centre for Air Power Studies (CAPS), for which I am immensely grateful.

Amiya Kumar Ghosh

Resource Allocation and Defence Management:

An Introductory Essay

Jasjit Singh

> *In the year 2054, the entire (US) defence budget will purchase just one aircraft. This aircraft will have to be shared by the Air Force and Navy three-and-a-half day each per week except for leap year, when it will be made available to the Marines for the extra day.*
>
> — Norman R. Augustine[1]

Everyone is telling us that the world is changing; and that is an obvious fact since world events never stand still. Norman Augustine wrote the above three decades ago and we seem to be moving closer to his assessment though few would admit it! The United States is already spending on defence amounts that exceed those of all countries combined! Its Senate kept debating for three years whether the country should acquire 183 or 187 of the latest combat aircraft, the F-22, over 500 of which were originally expected to be acquired because of the Soviet threat. This was the air force that frequently launched "thousand bomber raids" in a single mission against strategic targets. The Royal Air Force, the sword arm of the British Empire in the 20th century, will, sooner than later, possess only 120 combat aircraft—the actual size of the Indian Air Force after independence and the partition of the air force between India and Pakistan!

The obvious question that faces all of us is: what is the way forward: the Revolution in Military Affairs (RMA) and ever more costly military

---

Air Commodore Jasjit Singh, AVSM VrC VM, IAF (Retd), awarded the Padma Bhushan in 2006 by the President of India for a life-time's contribution to national security and defence, is the Director General, Centre for Air Power Studies, New Delhi.

systems, or finding another way to manage defence spending that creates the capability required at affordable costs? How should we look at force modernisation? Is force modernisation only a mix of technology, money and complex systems? The questions are limitless; and the answers not easy to find. It is this dilemma of modern militaries in countries like India, with its hundreds of poor people, that Shri Amiya Kumar Ghosh sets out to explore and answer. And I am not aware of anyone else with credentials better than his to undertake the task of exploring the framework for change in resource allocation and capability building.[2] This is what this book is all about. It explores this and more on how best to allocate resources for management of defence in the new age.

Few economists in India are attracted to defence studies even though a large amount of money is spent on defence. Shri Ghosh, who has an economics background, felt that this lacuna needs to be covered to some extent and he has tried to provide a perspective within which further studies can be made relating to the defence sector by competent people. Some studies can be issue-based, but some have to be of a more general nature so that issues get highlighted for further analyses. Questions of defence policy have economic dimensions, particularly if we treat capital outlay in defence as investments requiring a long-term perspective. This brings in the question of cost-benefit analysis, management of risks, and portfolio analysis towards a balanced investment strategy in capability building. These are some of the issues in which economists should be interested in order to devise how it can be done methodically in an uncertain environment, which is the hallmark of defence.

At the very foundation of his thesis, the author stresses on the need for introducing programme budgeting in defence. This has its roots in economics where the question of choosing alternatives to meet given ends and emphasis on optimal 'output' out of defence spending becomes a more important concern than attention on 'input' aspects for control of expenditure. Choice among alternative means for maximising ends, the basic thought of economics, has wide applicability, including strategic fields. Linking of input to output in defence is not an easy endeavour and it calls for the establishment of a proper framework on analyses, scenario building, and so on.

Mere division of the defence budget into revenue and capital expenditure may be all right for voting purposes, but hardly adequate for rational allocation of resources in defence, particularly when we adopt capability-based planning. While formulating the budget, we tend to give less emphasis to revenue expenditure. Revenue expenditure should be viewed as operating expenses, which are required for meeting the annual operating cost in order to man, operate and maintain a capability. Quite often, the cost of operating a system over its expected life is more important than the investment cost. **It is not right to equate modernisation with the capital budget, particularly if we aim towards capability building,** which has aspects that relate to revenue expenditure. Programme budgeting makes no distinction between revenue and capital expenditure. Only programme budgeting can help in relating resources 'inputs' in terms of manpower, material and installation to 'outputs' like strategic retaliatory forces, airlift capabilities, air defence capabilities, surveillance capabilities, protection of maritime interests, etc.

We have to resuscitate the concept of Budget Centres, which were introduced in the mid-1990s in defence, which involve substantial delegation of financial powers. The concept was to introduce more accountability in defence spending, as also better planning, programming and evaluation in defence expenditure management. In view of these earlier initiatives, which involved introduction of Authority and Responsibility Centres, Accountability Centres and Budget Holders, the basic structure exists to introduce performance budgeting in defence. What is now required is introduction of the programme concept for resource allocation decisions and multi-year budgeting. We also require a high-level institutional mechanism for setting objectives and for taking resource allocation decisions in the light of these objectives. Keeping in view the hierarchical mode of functioning in defence, the concept of Top Level Budget Holders should also be introduced to help in ushering in performance budgeting in defence.

The Long-Term Integrated Perspective Plan (LTIPP) is supposed to be a strategic document. Approving it means endorsing a strategy with objectives laid down as also approving a force structure and capabilities to be aimed at. It cannot, therefore, be adding together of the capital expenditure plans of five-year plans. Five-year plans are required to be derived from it, as also the annual budget. Therefore, the LTIPP has to include all the elements of both revenue and capital expenditure. While drawing up the LTIPP, thought has to be given to the nature of conflict and the type of contingencies for which preparations are to be made, forces are to be positioned and capability is to be developed, keeping in view the conflict scenarios. But all this cannot be undertaken in a vacuum, or on the basis of an "add-on" strategy. **Since the LTIPP is supposed to be an articulation of the national security strategy, the appropriate forum for giving approval to it should be the National Security Council and/or the Cabinet Committee on Security, and not just the Defence Acquisition Council.** As it is an articulation of the national security strategy, it needs to be reviewed and updated at regular intervals in view of the changing security environment. More than once, the Standing Committee of the Parliament for Defence has drawn attention to the requirement of reviewing and updating of long-term plans. A total view is required on force planning, not a piecemeal one, for this can lead to an unbalanced force structure. What is, therefore, required is a high-level empowered committee to review the entire force structure and make appropriate recommendations, which can also be the basis for the LTIPP.

We are now supposed to have introduced Capability-Based Planning (CBP) in defence. The CBP method involves functional analyses of operational requirements. Capabilities are required to be identified based on tasks required to be performed as part of a mission. Capabilities, or the ability to perform a task, provide a common framework for relating disparate elements of defence organisation. CBP relies on scenarios to provide the context against which to measure the level of capability. The concept recognises the interdependence of systems (including material and people), doctrine, organisation and support in delivering military capabilities. Decisions on options and trade-offs are an integral part of CBP, as planning has to be done within the resource constraint and within an economic framework. CBP is concept-led, with stress on innovative concepts.

In the process of modernisation, evaluation of ongoing programmes is an important aspect. There has to be an institutional mechanism to do so as the annual process while deciding upon budgetary submission. The programming process requires proper institutional arrangements, which function in an interactive mode. This will make it more effective towards capability building. For evaluation purposes, the resources of a Service have to be considered within a capability package. The evaluation framework has to ensure trade-off analyses in a consistent manner.

The RMA or transformation is not about acquiring more complex and high-performance weapon systems. The first step in transformation is the transformation of the mind, since more failures are caused by mindsets harping back to earlier experiences. One has to transform from a *platform-based* to a *knowledge-based* military. RMA has to have a significant impact on doctrine, organisation and training related to combat. It is not all about technological innovation. The basic point is: it is the smarter and motivated military that can take maximum advantage of technological innovation. Therefore, the human resource aspects have to be given maximum attention. How to enrich human capital so that is endowed with the necessary skill and aptitude to usher in the transformation process should be the central concern for planners. It is not a question of quantity, but of quality of manpower necessary to bring in the transformation. Financing of transformation in this sense has to be towards investment in human capital for enhancing their skill and aptitude. Since this is the basic requirement for bringing in transformation in defence, there should be no budgetary constraint on this aspect. **RMA is not brought about through weapons and platforms, but involves integration of systems, skills and leadership to produce the desired operational effects.**

Modernisation cannot be treated just as an 'ongoing process' in the sense that schemes once started have to be taken to a conclusion. One of the best ways to generate funds for new modernisation schemes, if RMA is the goal, is to foreclose those that have outlived their utility, so that investment for new modernisation schemes can be generated within an environment of resource constraint. This would call for hard choices and decisions that are to be taken by the higher management in defence. One-to-one replacement of equipment is also not an option in view of the increase in the cost of new equipment by several folds. Induction of new equipment could, therefore, call for reduction in force level. This, again, calls for a comprehensive review of the force structure as an integral part of introducing RMA. Developing the spectrum of capabilities for mitigating various kinds of risks also calls for a balanced investment strategy. The portfolio approach in investment planning is called for. Even from the investment point of view, an in-depth review of the capability requirements in the context of analysis of potential military conflicts and contingencies is a necessity which cannot be avoided any more.

For capability-building, which is a long-term concept, it is necessary to have a longer-term budget plan. It is argued by the author that a ten-year budget plan for defence should be instituted. An 8.5 percent annual rate of growth of the defence budget over a ten-year period could be a sustainable option given the trends in the economy. This would enable long-term investments in crucial capabilities like that of conducting Network-Centric Warfare (NCW). The long-term resource plan, tied to security objectives, would enable the military to set up their priorities and aim at a force structure which is affordable. The long-term financial plan should also be accompanied by a long-term savings plan.

In the context of the long-term budget plan, it is not good enough to confine to the capital outlay of the budget, which may be termed as 'capital budgeting'. There is a likelihood that capital budgeting would take place in the context of the existing strategy with a view to strengthening it, rather than allowing a fresh look at the strategy being pursued. It is also possible that strategy gets formulated through capital budgeting. The aim should be to develop strategy in the sense of setting up of objectives and considering alternatives to achieving them, on the basis of politico-military-economic considerations, which should determine capital acquisition and not vice-versa. Strategy should also determine the budget; and from the budget, the next step is weapon selection.

Long-Term Costing (LTC) for the forces and equipment is a very important concept for long-term planning purposes. We are yet to have such mechanisms. Long-term programmes can be developed only on the basis of LTC. Therefore, long-term budgeting has to be introduced, along with the concept of LTC.

Improving the tooth-to-tail ratio is a major concern of defence management. It is, therefore, important to establish a linkage between defence planning and defence management. In the business world, planning itself is a tool of the management for achieving its goals. Defence has also to be viewed as a giant business and where possible, business practices should be introduced. Logistics is one such area.

The importance of management of the resource allocation decision should call for more emphasis on internal control and internal audit, for which the existing framework is not adequate. Institutional reforms are called for to make it more effective, which also calls for legislative provisions. Internal audit has to act as the 'eyes' and 'ears' of management.

The Defence Research and Development Organisation (DRDO) has to play a crucial role in defence modernisation. The DRDO Review Committee, among other things, has gone critically into the present management structure with a view to making it more user-oriented. The author, who has been a member of the Review Committee, is in a good position to put the recommendations in perspective. One of the aims is towards decentralisation of the functioning of R&D activities by empowering the Directors of the labs with sufficient power to enable them to function in a more autonomous manner. Appointment of a Director General for a cluster of labs has also been recommended to perform many of the functions that are presently done through DRDO headquarters. This is with a view to promoting more accountability and responsibility for R&D work to meet the needs of the users in a given cost-and time-frame. The most important recommendation is towards appointment of a **Defence Technology Commission (DTC)** to provide overall guidance, as also to take crucial decisions regarding induction of critical technologies in defence with a view to ushering in RMA. The committee has also made important recommendations for enhancing its human resource capabilities and for promoting public-private partnerships in R&D activities. The author has given a lot of importance to the immediate setting up of the DTC so that other recommendations get implemented within a reasonable time-frame.

But since aerospace capabilities and technologies not only provide the cutting edge to military (and civil) capabilities, besides being a high resource consumer, it is perhaps more important to expand the concept of the Defence Technology Commission to the Aerospace Technology Commission (ATC) since a vast majority of defence technologies are actually driven and/or managed by aerospace technologies. We have a historic opportunity of large investments being made in the defence arena, along with commitments to offsets which would be the natural expediter of bringing in technology, especially of importance to future design and development. This aspect has been ignored by the DRDO Committee possibly on the assumption that defence would naturally cover aerospace technology development. But that approach would exclude the civil aviation and its vast infrastructure.

Shri Ghosh has produced a masterly volume which every decision-maker, at least in the defence establishment, must read and absorb. For me, it has been a great opportunity to be associated with Amiya for a quarter century and, hence, the pleasure of writing an introduction is a special privilege. His third book in the series, though not planned that way, constitutes a landmark study in defence economics. He has not only brought to bear his enormously sharp intellect to this task, but also his unstinted devotion to a national cause.

Notes

1. Norman R. Augustine, *Augustine's Laws* (New York: Viking Penguin Inc., 1983), p. 183.
2. Amiya Kumar Ghosh was the Secretary, Defence Finance, in the early 1990s when India faced the stark economic-cum-foreign exchange crisis. His early works include *India's Defence Budget and Expenditure* (New Delhi: Lancer Publishers, 1996) and *Defence Budgeting and Planning in India: The Way Forward* (New Delhi: Knowledge World, 2006).

1

Economics and Resource Allocation in Defence

Economists have attempted to apply the principles of economics to policy-making and resource allocation issues in defence from the 1950s onward and had a fair degree of success in bringing reform in the budgetary process, particularly in the USA. This kind of attempt is still to be made in India, though the budgetary allocation to defence in absolute terms and in relation to allocation made for other activities of the government is quite significant.

If we look back to defence budget issues that were being debated in the 1950s in the USA, which ultimately led to the adoption of programme budgeting in defence in the early 1960s (a technique which basically involves application of economic principles to budgeting), we shall find that allocations to defence were not very different from those of India today, though the issue of purchasing power has to be kept in view. The principles underlying programme budgeting subsequently came to be adopted in many countries, particularly for defence, because of the soundness and reasoning behind them.

Therefore, it is necessary to know what these principles are, and under what conditions they are likely to lead to optimum allocation of resources in defence.

The basic nature of economic problems, like the nature of war, remains the same. Therefore, revisiting the issues, particularly in the general context of allocation of resources in the field of defence, is always rewarding, particularly if we are looking for reforms in the budgetary process.

Two fundamental facts provide the foundation for the field of economics. The first is that the 'ends' are unlimited. The second is that economic resources for attaining the 'ends' are limited or scarce. Since the ends are unlimited and the means limited, resources need to be allocated in a manner that would lead to maximisation of attainment of the ends. As George J. Stigler put it, "Economics is the study of principles governing allocation of scarce means among competing ends when the objective of the allocation is to maximise the attainment of the ends."[1]

Thus, economics is basically concerned with allocation of resources among competing ends to maximise attainment of the ends and since the means are limited, it emphasises the necessity for exercising choice in the achievement of goals.

Many of the military problems can be analysed in this conceptual framework. Limited resources mean limited output. Attention gets focussed on 'outputs'. After conceptual clarity about these 'outputs' is achieved, the next point that comes up is that, owing to the limitation of resources, a choice must be made as to what quantities of each 'output' need to be produced to get the 'best value for money'. Therefore, an important field of enquiry is how these choices are being made and on what basis.

An economist naturally analyses military problems in terms of his accustomed framework, using logic of choice. "Military problems can be formulated as economic problems of maximisation, subject to constraints."[2] Constraints, of course, are of resources. We are not talking only of budgetary resources. The nation turns over to the military Services certain resources, some of which are specialised ones—bases, military capital equipment and trained manpower inherited from past periods. Others are general resources like the budget, which, with certain limitations, can be spent on anything

The task of the Services and of the Ministry of Defence (MoD) is to use these resources in such a way that our military power or 'military worth' is maximised. So, when we approach the question of optimum utilisation of resources for maximisation of the military worth, a total look is required at both the 'inherited resources', which are specialised, as also the general resources like the defence budget. "Of course, there is no way of measuring military power or military worth—in the general case—any more than there is a way of measuring an individual's, a family's, or a firm's utility or preference function." But, as Hitch goes on to add, "The conceptual framework helps greatly even if we can't fill all the empty boxes. It tells us how to seek solutions."[3]

This is the basic point: the approach of economics will not enable us to fill the so-called 'empty boxes', but it will help us in determining how to go about in trying to fill them up.

Allocation of Defence Resources: Necessity of Choice

It is not just the issue of allocating budgetary resources. There are several tasks to be performed involving choice and hard decisions, which vitally affect the allocation of resources. The tasks include: choosing of doctrines, force structure, equipment, etc with a view to maximise military worth, *for any given level of available resources.* As Charles Hitch put it, "In this respect, it is essentially a problem of economic choice—of relating military worth or effectiveness to cost in terms of resources and alternative ways of achieving specific, well-defined security objectives."[4] The principal mechanism for allocation of resources is the annual defence budget. But it fails to serve as a mechanism for rational allocation of resources, if it is not linked to defence planning which involves setting up of defence objectives, considering alternative means of achieving the objectives, capabilities to be developed keeping in view the resource constraints and setting up of priorities in terms of resource allocation decisions. Planning, in the context of programme budgeting based on principles of economics, has to perform these functions. Putting together various schemes and projects, ongoing or otherwise, and arriving at an acceptable financial total cannot be called planning, as we must link them to defence objectives in the context of the overall defence strategy which involves hard choices because of limitation of resources, and has, therefore, to be a top-down process.

Here a basic problem is encountered. Planning, in the sense mentioned above, has to be done in terms of missions and tasks to be performed in the context of strategic goals and the weapon systems to be acquired, military units to be raised and maintained in terms of divisions, air wings and ships—the 'outputs' of the Defence Department to achieve the objectives—while budgeting is done through such 'inputs' or intermediate products as personnel, operation and maintenance, procurement, etc.

As we know, defence budgeting in India is prepared in terms of inputs like pay and allowances, stores, works, equipment, etc. It is not possible to link them with defence planning if it is done in terms of missions and tasks and a force structure to successfully carry them out.

If planning is done in terms of schemes and projects with price tags attached to them, then some kind of link in financial terms can be established between planning and budgeting, as we have been attempting to do. But that would not lead to optimal allocation of resources with a view to achieve defence objectives and defence budgeting would not serve the strategic purpose.

This basic problem was faced in the USA in the 1950s in the context of resource allocation in defence to establish the links between planning, which was in terms of missions and objectives, and budgeting which was input-oriented. The RAND Corporation, which was working on this, came up with the concept of 'programming' as a 'bridge' between planning and budgeting. Programming would involve, on the one hand, looking at 'outputs' arising out of various defence activities to link them with planning, and the associated costs of these activities on the other, which would help in linking them with budgeting. The outputs in terms of army divisions, air wings, etc were to be linked to all required inputs of equipment, personnel, supplies, facilities and funds, which are provided in the budget under various heads of appropriation.

The costs of various programmes and programme elements can then be linked to major military missions so that we may know how much defence we are buying, at what cost, as an economist would like to see. This is the advantage of introducing the programme concept in defence budgeting.

In Indian defence budgeting, the concept of programmes is missing. Planning is also not in terms of programmes indicating all the elements of the cost involved in a programme element and how it helps in achieving the stated objectives. Therefore, the link between planning and budgeting does not get established for rational allocation of resources.

Another problem towards rational allocation of resources in India is that military planning is done essentially on a Service basis. The order of priority of forces, weapon systems and activities is based on a long-term plan prepared by each Service on the basis of its doctrine and its strategic perception of the security environment. Long-term planning for the defence establishment as a whole is yet to take final shape.

But the more important point is that the annual budget which is useful for many purposes, does not lend itself very well to the task of rational allocation of resources in the defence field. The fact that " it projects only one year ahead severely limits its usefulness as a means for the allocation of resources within the defence establishment."[5] Without a multi-year budget plan which deals with force planning and costs in a comprehensive manner, it is not possible to arrive at optimal decisions. The implications in budgetary terms of ongoing programmes and future cost implications of decisions made today are required to be linked to the multi-year budget plan to arrive at sound programme decisions. Without this exercise, there cannot be optimal decisions relating to programmes.

While considering the efficacy of the financial management system in defence, it was realised in the early Sixties in the USA, that it must provide among other things the data needed by the top management to make crucial decisions regarding major forces and weapons. In became clear that the financial management system, as it has evolved, could not provide it. Therefore, it was decided that 'programming' which would provide the necessary data in a meaningful way for taking these decisions, should be incorporated in the financial management system. This was not a easy task. The problem here was to sort out all the activities of the defence establishment and regroup them into meaningful programme elements i.e. integrated combination of men, equipment and installation whose effectiveness could be linked to national security objectives.

'Programming' is the economist's conception for improving allocation of resources. It need not be confined to defence as the principles are applicable elsewhere also.

It helps in optimal allocation of resources, stressing three basic principles of economics:

- The concept of trade-off; the classic problem of trade-off is, of course, between 'guns and butter', when we consider the overall resources of the government. But this concept is equally applicable for the lower level of decision-making when, for example, we are considering the necessity of procurement of two systems for strengthening our defence but cannot accommodate both because of limitation of resources, and have to give up one of them, though we might have liked to have both. The same principle would be relevant when we are considering introducing an additional feature into a system, which may involve giving up another, as both cannot be accommodated because of some basic constraint.

- Because of the necessity of trade-off, it is necessary to consider the costs and benefits of alternative courses of action. Here the concept of opportunity cost is important. It is not the cost in the normal sense of the term in terms of input costs. The opportunity cost of an item is what we have to give up to get that item, because of limitation of resources or some other constraint.
- Economists stress the point that a rational decision-maker takes an action only if the marginal benefit of the action exceeds the marginal cost.

For optimisation of decision-making in defence, decisions relating to force structure and budgets should be made together, keeping in view the costs. There has to be explicit acceptance of relevance of costs in defence decision-making.

The other point is effectiveness in meeting the objective. But we should aim at effectiveness not only in one or two areas, but in the entire defence programme. That calls for putting each rupee where it will add the most to total effectiveness. That is why rational allocation of resources is so very important to ensure that marginal cost is equal to marginal benefit for each activity on which defence money is spent.

If rational allocation of resources is the goal, the cost to be considered is not just the procurement cost of weapons and systems, but the cost of the total activity. The costs are both direct and indirect. For example, to deploy one squadron of aircraft, a lot of indirect costs like training base support, logistics, communications, and so on, are required. The costs of these support elements often exceed the investments and direct operating costs of these systems. For rational allocation of resources, the total cost of the activity should be taken into account, not just the direct costs. But more often than not, this kind of cost consciousness is absent, and we are occupied with one or two elements of cost, if at all. What is required is activity costing by trained cost accountants.

The Requirements Approach

Very often, however, cost consciousness is absent in defence and the other approach, which may be called the 'requirements approach' prevails. That is, the requirement of so many divisions, ships, wings of aircraft, and also of the types to meet the objectives or tasks. An integral aspect of the requirements approach is that cost considerations are excluded until after the requirements have been established by military judgement on the basis of needs. Then costs are computed in terms of budget, manpower and specific resource. If the requirements turn out to be feasible, they are adopted; if unfeasible, they are modified in the direction of feasibility.

We are familiar with this approach in the context of formulation of defence plans, where budgetary considerations come last. Where the likely amount that could be made available for the five-year period is subsequently indicated, and there is an obvious mismatch between the 'needs' and the resources available, the plans are modified, to make these feasible.

The requirements are determined on the basis of the military's commitments and 'tasks' to be performed. How are these commitments and tasks determined? The obvious answer would be that these are determined on the basis of military objectives to be attained as per the defence policy of the nation. That could call for an articulated defence policy issued by the government. During the debate on Demands for Grants 1995-96, the Prime Minister stated,[6] "We do not have a document called India's National Defence Policy. But we have got several guidelines which are followed, strictly followed and observed...which are always kept in view while conducting our Defence Policy..." There is a policy but there is no policy document. Commenting on the absence of a policy document, the Standing Committee on Defence stated,[7] "In the absence of any document explaining articulated policy with stated national objectives and national interests, it is not possible *for the policy to be analysed and modified*." This is the crux of the matter. The same policy cannot remain valid for all time to come as there are always new challenges. If a policy cannot be reviewed or changed, it indirectly means that there is no policy. The policy needs to be clearly articulated, with objectives laid down so that, in the allocation of resources, it becomes the guiding factor, and when the policy is modified, its effect on resource allocation also becomes part of the same policy decision. Absence of an articulated defence policy document is a great handicap in optimal resource allocations, as optimality has to be judged by how well it can meet the objectives as laid down in the policy document.

It has to be remembered that policies are articulated in broad terms. To translate them into resource allocation decisions, many intermediate steps are required to be taken, for example, analysis of various threats to our national interest, including 'risk analysis', the level, nature and duration of conflicts that can be visualised, the geographical terrain where conflicts can take place and the type of response that can be contemplated, all of which involve professional judgement.

The next question would be whether the policy document, when articulated, also indicates the availability of resources for developing various military capabilities in the medium and long terms to meet the stated objective? If the answer is 'yes', we have a framework, from the point of view of economics, of commitments, tasks and resources for attempting maximisation of military worth in a given situation. Only such a framework, through the operation of logic of choice, can lead to optimum allocation of resources.

In the absence of such a framework and institutional mechanism for evaluation of costs and effectiveness, the 'requirements' approach prevails, which evaluates options on the basis, perhaps, of some criteria of effectiveness but without considering the costs. It means that the basic approach of economics to develop alternatives and exercise choice to select a cost-effective option is absent in the requirement approach.

Cost-Effectiveness Analysis

By adhering to the requirements approach, we may not be getting the most cost-effective defence. How much is allocated to defence through the defence budget is important, but what is more important, is how we spend the available resources for that will determine the combat power that we actually acquire. The aim, as we have put it, is to maximise 'military worth'. That is why the cost aspect is important. As Kaufmann puts it, *"The ability to reduce the costs of procuring a needed item of equipment can mean either an increase in the amount of equipment purchased or reallocation of resources to the achievement of other important objectives. Cost and effectiveness are intimately related."*[8]

So clarity in objectives to be achieved and consideration of the costs of alternatives are two basic ingredients for exercising choice to maximise military worth.

Cost-effectiveness analysis is another name for systems analysis. Although our national security objectives reflect the composite value judgement of decision-makers, the choice of a particular strategy or military objective cannot be divorced from the cost of achieving it. Systems analysis at the national level involves a continuous cycle of defining military objectives and evaluating these alternatives in terms of effectiveness and cost.

The problem of allocating resources in defence involves choosing of doctrines, weapons, equipment, etc to get the most out of a given level of resources. When resources are not given, one can aim at a certain level of defence at a cost where one has to work in terms of marginal products and marginal costs in order to help the top decision-makers to choose the appropriate level of resources.

Let us remind ourselves, the concept of economic choice is a way of looking at problems and does not necessarily depend on the use of analytical aids or computational devices. This way of looking at problems cannot be confined to economists.

Judgement is always of critical importance in designing the analysis, in choosing the alternatives to be compared and selecting the criterion of choice. But, at the same time, the need for systematic quantitative analysis in defence is much more important than in the private sector of the economy. The main purpose of this kind of analysis is to reduce the uncertainties involved in making a choice among alternatives. Such choices have to be made in many echelons.

Objectives and Consideration of Alternatives

The logic of choice demands that alternatives be costed in some sense *prior to choice.* It tells us that the choices that maximise military power, with the given resources, are the ones that minimise the resource cost of attaining that level of power. Unless alternatives are costed (however approximately) *before* requirements are determined, we cannot know which of the alternatives will contribute most efficiently to military power. It also requires that availability of resources in the medium term is indicated as a budget plan so that choice is exercised, keeping in view the budgetary constraints.

Resources are allocated to achieve specific objectives or to resolve certain problems. In order to allocate and employ resources in an effective and efficient manner, the specific objectives to be attained through the use of these resources must be clearly and succinctly identified. This calls for establishment of a set of programmes oriented primarily towards 'end product' or 'end objective' activities that are meaningful from the planning point of view. This is contrasted with the conventional governmental budgeting, which lays stress on object-class categories.

The concept of programme also means an extended time-horizon. For, the effects and costs of a programme are to be considered over a period of several years or over a sufficiently long period for consideration of its full effects and costs. If a time horizon for consideration of cost (in terms of budgetary appropriation) is only one year, consideration of the total cost of the programme is not possible. If the programme/project concept is missing, it is difficult to relate the expenditure to the end-objectives. To make a rational choice between different projects, it is obviously necessary to take account of the entire costs and benefits of the projects and not that of the first year of the budget.

As stated above, the first requirement for conducting an economic analysis of a programme or a project is to establish the objectives being sought. "The need for this action may appear simple and self-evident, but many analyses have floundered or have been useless because of their failure to clearly establish the objectives of the programme being analysed."[9]

A programme consists, ideally, of a number of different activities aiming at the same objective. The use of the programme concept can, therefore, focus the interest on balancing different means in order to achieve a given objective as efficiently as possible. But the same activity can have multiple objectives. This possibility causes two types of problems. First, there is no obvious way to determine programmes. Second, with a given programme structure, comparison of different activities which also contribute to the objectives of other programmes is possible. All the same, dependence on programmes is often inevitable for determining optimal allocation of resources.

Budgetary issues are a critical part of the domestic policy debate. *"A White Paper must address resource issues, as the availability of funding for capital, operational and personnel expenditure will determine whether or not the defence forces will be able to fulfill their stated objectives."* [10] (Italics mine.)

A Defence White Paper, when issued, becomes the key policy document, which outlines the broad strategic policy framework for defence planning, with a medium term outlook. This may "include an assessment of both traditional and non-traditional security threats and factors. The document highlights issues of greatest priority for that country and provides an overview of how defence policy will be implemented to meet the security challenges. It also describes, in broad *terms, current and planned capabilities and roles of the defence forces."*[11]

As stated above, our Parliamentary Committees (Estimates Committee, Standing Committee on Defence, etc) have recommended the need for a well-articulated document, indicating the defence policy and national security doctrine. However, that demand is yet to be met.

We have, thus, clarified in detail that in the economic framework of analysis of defence problems, defining the 'ends' in terms of objectives, is the most essential step towards efficient allocation of resources. The economists' approach to this problem also leads to consideration of decision-making in stages, since defining the objectives is the first stage of decision-making.

Planning, Programming and Decision-Making

A major step in an economic analysis is the elaboration of primary alternatives available for achieving the objectives. But policy objectives are often imprecise. It is for the next stage of decision-making to make them more precise. This stage, in the context of decision-making, is called 'planning'. This planning is not development of five-year plans but, from the resource allocation point of view, is preparation of alternative plans to further policy objectives, as a part of the decision-making process. As Arthur Smithies put it in his seminal work, "Planning means the preparation of alternative plans that will further the particular policy objectives in varying measures and that are within the bounds of feasibility." [12] Military planners try to design an "array of strategic plans" to further foreign policy objectives."[13]

"Planning" was the first phase of the three-phased McNamara-Hitch financial management system introduced in US defence in 1961. The traditional military function was confined to determination of requirements. Under the new financial management system, the emphasis in the "planning" phase was rather on the review of requirements by the top management.

"Planning" under the new financial management system, was to be done in the context of realistic premises of "scarcity of resources" and "technological proliferation" which opened up many alternatives with their demands of disciplined choice.[14]

Programming is the third stage in decision-making "in the direction of feasibility and may involve selection of alternative plans or a combination of elements from a number of plans."[15] These basic decisions were to greatly influence the size of budgets. The programming decisions were, therefore, based both on relative costs of various alternatives and their efficacy in achieving the objectives.

The programming function was at the heart of the new financial management system installed in the US Department of Defence. This was the most important management technique in the context of the Planning-Programming-Budgeting System (PPBS). It is important to realise that that the need for 'programming' became more evident because of the revolution in military technology, whose effects were reflected in the complex weapon systems which were being planned and inducted at that time. To quote Hitch, "The great technological complexity of modern-day weapons, their lengthy period of development, their tremendous combat power, and their enormous cost have placed extraordinary premium on the sound choice of major weapon systems in relation to the tasks and missions and our national security objectives."[16]

What a modern financial management system in defence must do, above all else, is to 'relate' weapon systems to tasks, and objectives to tasks. The introduction of the programming function into the financial management system would be the means for putting the initiative and decisions in the hands of the top management. The overriding objective of the new financial financial management should be to produce data needed by the top defence management for decision-making on force levels, weapons, and so on, and in the form desired. The programme elements were the basic building blocks for the new decision-making process. So programming became the vital decision-making phase. The budgeting phase was to reflect the decisions taken at the programming phase. Programming is the economist's way of approaching the complicated task of optimal allocation of resources in defence.

In this sense, planning and programming are invariably part of the decision-making process towards efficient resource allocation in defence, as these enable choices to be made. This need not be equated with any budgetary technique like programme budgeting, but these stages of decision-making are of universal application if optimal allocation of resources is the aim. As would be seen, Arthur Smithies developed these points in the context of rational allocation of resources much before the advent of PPBS in defence.

The issue is: how shall we structure these stages so that decisions are made explicitly and deliberately?

Criterion of Measuring Achievement of Objectives

Military objectives may be attained through many different combinations of troops, equipment and tactics. In all the studies, however, there are certain items that the analysts are not permitted to alter and manipulate. Items not subject to change by the analysts are called 'constraints', since they limit the nature of alternatives that can be developed. Constraints may differ from study to study. The items that are classified as variables or constraints depend on the purpose of the study. "The fact that variables and constraints for all alternatives must be determined specifically in terms of the purposes of the study provides another compelling reason for carefully identifying the object of the study. Without clear-cut objectives, the analyst will not know which alternatives to select for analysis or whether items in the study should be considered as variables or constraints."[17]

These studies are in the nature of operational research, which leads to what is called 'sub-optimisation,' or optimisation at a lower level. We have not yet been able to establish a cell consisting of a professional group of operational researchers in the Ministry of Defence to get such studies done that would assist in developing alternatives for decision-making. In fact, in our planning process, we hardly attempt to develop cost-effective alternatives for achieving various defence objectives. When there are no alternatives to choose from, it can hardly be called a planning process.

As we mentioned above, in the decision-making process, the basic function of planning is development of alternatives. If there are no alternatives, then there is no planning. One of the main reasons for absence of alternatives in our decision-making process is the absence of operational analysis in studies for achieving defence objectives in a cost-effective manner. Another is the comparative absence of clear-cut objectives.

Economic analyses are conducted primarily to identify the most efficient means of securing a particular objective from several alternative uses of resources. The efficient use of resources implies either that a specified objective is obtained at the least possible cost or that a specified quantity of resources is used so as to produce the greatest possible benefit.

In the analysis of cost from the point of view of economists, one important point needs to be noted. *Economic analysis is directed towards the future allocation and use of resources.* Money already spent on existing equipment is no longer available for other purposes. Thus, existing equipment represents a 'sunk-cost,' that should not enter into future economic consideration. When analysing alternatives, the only relevant costs in respect of equipment already purchased are the operating and maintenance costs. The costs of new equipment must be included, when analysing alternatives since they represent new expenditures.

While the measurement of achievement may be relatively simple in situations where a criterion like 'targets destroyed' is laid down, most military programmes do not provide such easily measurable results. When a primary objective such as deterring aggression is not susceptible to direct measurement, secondary criteria are required to be developed to measure the efficiencies of alternative methods of attaining the objectives. Such criteria are to facilitate insight into the achievement of the primary objective itself.

Then there is the criterion of effectiveness, which is solely dependent upon the achievement of the primary objective. The difference between efficiency and effectiveness is of great importance in economic analysis.

While it may be held that efficient use of resources is the major consideration of economists and effective use of resources is the primary concern of military decision-makers, economists can help in developing the criterion of effectiveness.

While operational researchers are able to introduce some rational calculus for achieving efficiency in resource allocation decisions, they are faced with the problem of developing a criterion for achieving effectiveness. Operational researchers are prone to choosing criteria which can be tackled through mathematical models. In some cases, they may choose criteria more casually than the occasion demands.

Criteria used by operational researchers have frequently been misleading. Hitch referred to the famous operational research study in World War II relating to German U-boats and convoy losses of the allies.[18] The data revealed that the number of merchant vessels sunk in a U-boat attack was proportional to the number of U-boats with the attacking pack and inversely proportional to the number of destroyer escorts, but independent of the size of the convoy. They also revealed that the number of U-boats sunk per attack was directly proportional both to the number of attacking U-boats and to the number of defending escorts. The criterion was taken to be the maximisation of the 'exchange rate' or ratio of enemy losses (measured in U-boats) to own losses (measured in merchant ships).

The conclusions of the study were:

- The number of ships lost per attack was independent of the size of the convoy.
- The exchange rate seemed to be proportional to the square of the number of escort vessels per convoy. From any point of view, the case of longer convoys was a persuasive one.

On the basis of this study, action was taken to increase the average size of the convoys, thereby also increasing the average number of escort vessels per convoy. Soon it became unprofitable for the Germans to attack North Atlantic convoys and the U-boats went elsewhere. It was contended by the operational analysts that this defeat in the North Atlantic contributed to the turning point in the "Battle of the Atlantic."

The criterion selected can be criticised from the point of view of an economist who looks at the relationship at both the higher and lower levels. "There is no evidence that the researchers stopped to ask: what is the purpose of the convoy business anyway; what are we really trying to achieve by it? ... The function of the convoys was to get across the Atlantic for the supply of England in preparation of the invasion of the Continent." The criterion chosen "completely neglects a dimension of the problem that appears at least as important as those considered—viz., reduced operating efficiency of ships in large convoys and, hence, the *inverse* relation between the size of convoy and capacity of any number of merchant ships to transport men and material across the Atlantic."[19] This is because collecting large convoys takes time. The arrival of large convoys swamps port facilities, which means large turnaround times. Because the speed of a convoy cannot exceed that of the slowest ship, there will be an inverse average relation between its size and speed.

Thus, it was not true that the case for large convoys was persuasive from every point of view. It might well have been worth the loss of a few more ships to ensure timely delivery of supplies required for the Normandy invasion. Thus, a higher level objective was neglected in pursuance of a lower level objective of reducing loss of merchant ships. Another unfortunate tendency of operations researchers in choosing criteria is to prefer *ratios.* "The training, which leads economists to prefer *differences,* is a sound one: it makes sense in any activity to maximise total profits in some sense, not profits per unit.... Ratios are treacherous as operations research criteria because they ignore the absolute magnitudes of both the numerator and the denominator."[20]

The operations research study dealing with strategic air problems ignores the important impacts of bomber deployments on air defence, as well as possibilities of jointly supplying some tactical offensive power along with the strategic bombing.

"Economists are trained to look for external economies and diseconomies, for divergences between private and social products and costs and for the joint products and costs." These are the concepts which are needed for effective defence.

The relationship between attainment of lower level objectives and higher level objectives is extremely important and economic theory is concerned with that. Much of the micro-economics theory is basically concerned with relations between criteria at different levels: usually between criteria of a firm and the consumer at a low level, and of the economy at a high one,

Economists as conceptualisers can help if they do not attempt to generalise too much. Systematic quantitative analysis has its own advantages and economist can learn from that. What we should not be looking for is a perfect solution. One can be satisfied with a good probability of being nearly right in a particular case. This calls for the acceptance of the economic principle of "second best," which is the only way to progress in non-market economies.

Economics and Strategy

Strategic issues involve choosing the most beneficial uses of limited manpower, financial and material resources (in terms of materials, plant and equipment). Proper solutions require one to think through the purpose of the weapon system, formulate valid criteria of effectiveness and then consider alternative systems or mix of systems in terms of their effectiveness and cost. The principal consideration is that cost and effectiveness cannot be considered separately.

Rational economic analysis, aided by the technique of operational analysis, helps in avoiding serious imbalances such as bombers and fighter aircraft without enough air bases and crew, fighter bombers without the required kind of ordnance, divisions without adequate equipment, or lack of aircraft capabilities. Any imbalance will lead to ineffectiveness of the whole system. Economic analysis can help in preventing this.

Another purpose of economic analysis is to discover where an increase in effectiveness is not commensurate with the increase in cost and to avoid further expansion of such programmes. The economic law of diminishing returns has to be kept in view. This general principle applies throughout defence establishments, both in designing weapon systems and the choice of strategies. There comes a point at which small increases in effectiveness can be achieved at a great increase in costs.

Economists do point out that, to a great extent, choice of major weapon systems is a strategic one and such choices should emerge from policy decisions. Not only is the size of the defence budget a function of high level policy, but, to a large extent, so are the decisions about what weapons to purchase. According to Alain Enthoven, the question of the number and type of weapons required is not strictly a military problem but is, in fact, a defence policy problem. Since defence policy also involves political and economic factors, the size and composition of forces have a direct influence on foreign policy and a major impact on domestic policy. As the problem is not merely a military one, it follows that these decisions must be made at a higher level — one where all implications are known and understood. These are national security policy decisions which are based on the interaction of values, on the one hand, and the cost and effectiveness of military forces and weapon systems, on the other.[21]

Other political considerations which are a reality and affect force planning choices are those that involve Service positions, roles and missions and vested interests. Economic considerations play a minimal role in this sphere.

In the end, there is no doubt that economic analysis is only an aid to judgement.

Introduction of systems analysis gave much greater weight to economic analysis in strategic decision-making. Through systems analysis, military propositions can be restated in the terminology and postulates of price theory. Enthoven explained the new economics of national defence as follows: "Estimates of marginal costs and marginal products are provided to the Secretary of Defence so that he and his principal advisers can concentrate their attention not so much on such questions as whether we need a capability to destroy 97 percent of the 100 targets, with the alternatives unspecified, as on such questions as whether the capacity to raise target destruction from 94 to 97 percent is worth the cost of extra 100 missiles."[22]

In their efforts to find optimal solutions, systems analysts also use the "indifference curve" techniques developed in economics. This approach could be used, for example, to determine the best mix of strategic bomber and missile forces to achieve a desired target destruction potential through the expenditure of a given sum. With the aid of a diagram, different curves could depict military worth. Each curve would show different combinations of strategic bombers and missile submarines that promise the same target destruction potential. The task of the analysts is not to show that one weapon system is clearly superior to another. It is to show the unique advantages and disadvantages of each, as well as the respective procurement costs. Essential features of weapon systems analysis include a comparison of all relevant choices as to military worth, and cost and determination of the best alternatives through application of appropriate economics.

The concept of opportunity cost in economics has an important application in the strategic field. When a decision is made to use funds for one purpose, simultaneously, it is decided to exclude the use of those resources for other purposes. For instance, we consider augmenting the airlift-sealift capabilities. In that event, whatever could have been purchased for the cost of airlift-sealift facilities, would have to be foregone. Therefore, it is necessary to consider explicitly what is being sacrificed in order to gain a particular capability and whether the gain is more than the sacrifice that is being made in terms of foregoing additional capabilities elsewhere.

The basic procedure used by economists for estimating relative values and costs is the marginal analysis. Effective use of the concept of marginal analysis requires the decision-makers or the analysts to recognise and apply the law of diminishing marginal utility.

Because of the working of the law of diminishing utility, military analysts must go beyond the determination of total or average benefits to be obtained from total expenditure when analysing a particular mission (e.g. airlift-sealift forces) or weapon systems. The analyst must determine the benefits arising from each increment of expenditure made on a project or programme or weapon system to see whether the benefits are commensurate with the cost.

The principle of diminishing return or diminishing utility, along with another principle of economics—the principle of equi-marginal return—helps us in allocation of scarce resources. What we want to do is to allocate rupees in each category so that any reallocation of this amount does not increase the total military worth achievable. Military worth is a nebulous concept but it helps in understanding the issue. The military worth functions can be drawn in the shape of curves that begin at zero expenditure of rupees and increase as more and more amounts are spent in obtaining a capability. These functions curve downward, implying decreasing marginal returns, i.e. the more we buy of some capability, the less the incremental amount purchased is worth. Interpreting these curves, we have an optimum allocation of rupees when the derivates at all the curves are equal. When the amount expended equals the sums allocated in this manner, for obtaining various defence capabilities, we have maximised the military worth for the allotted amount.[23] This leads to the development of balanced military capabilities.

That the application of these economic principles to strategic issues is not confined to economists can easily be shown by referring to Bernard Brodie, the eminent strategic thinker of the last century, who advocated the application of these economic principles to military strategy. One can refer to his seminal article, "Strategy as Science" (1949) in this context. He said, "In any case, whether we are discussing security policy in the broad sense or more specifically military strategy—or even tactics—we are discussing problems involving economy of means i.e. the most efficient utilisation of potential and available resources to the end of enhancing our security. One might expect to find, therefore, that a substantial part of classical economic theory is directly applicable to analysis of problems in military strategy." He commented that that if the highly developed conceptual framework available in economics were applied in the field of strategy, "some very positive results would follow."[24]

Concept of Balanced Force

In the context of applying economic principles to defence, Brodie makes a very important observation regarding "balanced force," which is one of the basic aims of defence planning. "Almost too obvious to be worth recording, but nevertheless basic and all-to-often forgotten is the point that 'balance' can mean little or nothing except in relation to predictions or expectations concerning circumstances created by one's own strategic plans.

"A force that is well 'balanced' with respect to one set of circumstances is likely to be unbalanced, with respect to another except so far as the balance sought represents a compromise between different sets of possible or probable circumstances."[25]

The balanced force concept entails "establishing orders of probability and of risk for various set of circumstances—in strategy we are always dealing with multiple-contingency analysis—we have a context for resolving the issues of balance according to the well-known concept of *marginal utility*. That is one in which marginal utilities, tactically and strategically considered, of the last increments to each of the existing components were approximately equalised."[26] Brodie adds that to gauge marginal utilities among the components may not be easy, but at least the conceptual basis for "balance" would be clarified.

He comments that it may be "aesthetically abhorrent" to discover gallant admirals and airmen discussing their common problems or get into occasional debate on terms like "marginal utility", "diminishing returns" or "opportunity cost." However, "the advantage of using symbols which are tied to well-thought-out formulations has at least two advantages, besides the obvious one of providing a short-hand intra-disciplinary communication. First, it may help to assure that fundamentals of a problem will not be overlooked. Second, it may offer economies in the process of thinking the problem through."[27]

The air force argument that aircraft carriers are 'vulnerable' and the navy's reply that not a single aircraft carrier was lost in the last three years of World War II are not very illuminating. "The real issue is utility and since every military unit or weapon is expendable, the question of relative vulnerability is significant because it affects utility."[28]

Aircraft carriers are costly to acquire and maintain. But they have distinctive functions. *Costs are comparable only when functions are comparable.* As Brodie puts it, *"The real issue would be the importance of these distinctive functions and characteristics as weighed against their cost. In all this, we could obviously be obliged to tie our analysis to a specific enemy and to a set of conditions which have at least the quality of being conceivable."* (Italics mine.) Again, the concept of utility comes to the forefront. As regards the applicability of the concept of utility in the development of weapon systems, Brodie illustrates this with reference to the case for installing of anti-aircraft guns in ships. The governing dogma, prior to Pearl Harbour, was that offensive strength should not be sacrificed for greater defensive strength. The result was that battleships on the day of attack on Pearl Harbour could not protect themselves from the Japanese fighter planes. It was not until more than a year after that attack that the principle was adopted that the amount of anti-aircraft armament to be installed on an existing ship was to be limited only by the amount it was physically capable of carrying and servicing. "What was belatedly discovered was that the marginal utility of another anti-aircraft gun remained higher than the marginal utility of many other items of comparable weight or space consumption."[29]

The concept of "balanced force" as developed by Bernard Brodie, is of great significance, particularly about the application of the principle of marginal utility and that of calculating the "orders of probability and of risk for various set of circumstances," for resolving the issues of "balance" Evidence of this kind of approach is found even in the recent literature on defence planning and budgeting, which emphasise the basic soundness of Brodie's approach in providing a model for determination of "optimal defence capabilities."

Strategy and Resource Constraint

A step-by-step procedure in developing the strategy and determination of forces required to execute the strategy, without considering resource constraint, would not lead to cost-effective defence. The procedure often followed is: (i) identify national goals and threats to these goals; (ii) determine the strategy to counter the threats; (iii) determine the forces needed to execute the strategy; (iv) determine the budget to build and maintain the forces. The strategy is the key in the chain. It ties goals and threats to forces and budgets. As Franklin C. Spinney points out, this sequential non-adaptive path is intellectually appealing, " but the simplistic assumption that strategy uniquely determines forces and budgets in effect presumes resources (money) are unlimited."[30] In the real world, strategy is the art of the possible. Therefore, strategic decision-making procedure must take into account the internal constraints and more specifically the budgetary constraints.

To give a comparatively recent example, the first Quadrennial Defence Review (QDR) of the USA of 1997, assumed a stable budget of $ 250 billion per year in constant Financial Year (FY) 1997 dollars for planning purposes, for the period 1998-2003 Five-Year Defence Programme (FYDP). The "strategy and force options available to the authors of the QDR were thus to be greatly constrained by the resouces that were assumed to be available."[31]

There were three elements of new strategy : *shaping* the international environment in ways favourable to US interests; *responding* to the full spectrum of crises when directed; and *preparing now* for an uncertain future by *transforming US combat capabilities and support structures* to respond effectively to future challenges. Allocation of resources was made for each element of the strategy to achieve optimality in terms of attainment of strategic objectives. In drawing up its resource allocation plan, the QDR kept in view the shortcomings of previous defence review called Bottom-Up Review (BUR), 1993, which was also shaped in respect of strategy, force structure and modernisations by preexisting budgetary constraints. The main shortcoming of the spending plan of BUR was that it had underestimated operating costs and overestimated savings and, as a result, resources for modernisation got reduced. The QDR tried to allocate the required funds for operating costs and adopted a "selective modernization plan".

It was clarified in QDR 1997, " The fiscal reality did not drive the defence strategy we adopted, but it did affect our choices for its implementation and focused our attention on the need to reform our organisation and methods of conducting business. "[32] *This the main point: the resource constraint should draw as much attention to organisational and procedural reforms as to force structure review.*

Efficiency in resource utilisation implies the most optimal output for any given input, or simply put, the best value for money. This raises the question of how to determine defence value. As defence is concerned with possible future events or threats (defence contingencies), each of which carries an implied risk to the state, defence value could be equated to risk reduction. Each defence contingency carries with it an associated risk. If, therefore, the relative risk value of such contingencies can be determined, this will allow for development of a system of determining the relative defence value.

The term optimal in this context is intended to mean the greatest defence output for any given input or, simply put, the best defence value for money.

The first step in the process is the determination of defence contingencies. This entails describing in some detail the possible future events that the defence forces might have to encounter.

Defence is mostly concerned with possible future events (defence contingencies) and the preparation for successfully countering them when they occur. The probability of occurrence of such contingencies can be statistically determined as well as the potential impact that such a contingency might have on the country. Obviously, contingencies of high probability and major impact carry more risk to the state than those having low probability and carrying minor risk. Risk is, therefore, proportional to the probability of occurrence and potential impact.

Risk, uncertainty and probability calculations are some of the concepts economics deals with in the context of the profit and game theory. Therefore, economists can be of assistance in putting such issues in an analytical framework to aid decision making.

The determination of probability is the most difficult exercise in defence planning as it is the most subjective. It cannot be an exact science as it deals with the future. However, as some experts maintain, without the mind being applied to this factor, it is extremely difficult to plan for the future and to determine the priorities for defence capabilities to be maintained and developed. Under this approach, once the list of contingencies, defence value calculations (relative risk-reduction values) and costs of the elements of force design are available, calculation for achieving best value for money can be attempted. In our defence planning, we do not do this kind of exercise as we are not equipped to do so in the absence of a professional group of defence analysts.

Application of Economic Principles Through Systems Analysis

Resource allocation issues would continue to be the major preoccupations of the Defence Ministry. Systems analysis, carried out under McNamara, appeared to challenge a long-standing attitude that military affairs and economics have little in common. Systems analysts stressed on approaches like qualitative and quantitative analysis, cost-effectiveness studies and development of least-cost solutions. Below the top decision-making level, operations research can blend in, and be coordinated with, systems analysis.

As stated above, through systems analysis, military propositions could be restated in the terminology and postulates of price theory. This enabled analysis to be carried out as in economics. *Analyses were of the highest quality and the work of the systems analysts got reflected in the Draft Presidential Memorandum (DPMs) which were the key features of PPBS, under McNamara, and was the main vehicle for resource allocation decisions in US defence. The aim was to consider the defence programmes as a whole and to look at the large picture.*

For example, if cost was the issue, then the total system cost over the useful life of the system was looked at, not just at the current year's operating or procurement costs. If one was analysing a particular strategic offensive weapon system, one had to start by looking at the total strategic offensive forces. If one was considering nuclear attack submarines, then one should look at the total anti-submarine warfare force, which includes land and sea-based patrol aircraft, destroyers, sonars, and the like. One simply cannot make sense out of costs, or missiles or submarines without looking at totals. The DPMs were the practical result of this principle.

This principle of looking at the larger picture is of abiding importance in force planning and resource allocation decisions for getting the best value for defence money. This looking at the larger picture was possible because of the approach of economists of looking at defence problems by exploring the relationship between the lower and higher levels of optimisation. As Charles Hitch put it, "The only discipline I know, which has made any attempt to explore characteristics of operations criteria and the intimately related question of the relation between lower and higher level of sub-optimisation, is economic theory."[33]

DPMs made it possible to establish the relationship between lower and higher levels of optimisation by bringing in the larger picture. As Enthoven and Smith state, "By 1965, the DPMs had become the principal decision-making documents in the Defence Department. As the DPMs evolved, a workable system for processing the various drafts in DoD was developed and formalised. The resulting DPM system became a unique and highly effective management tool for dealing with controversial issues of military strategy and force planning."[34]

DPMs served as vehicles for orderly investigation and debate in the McNamara period.

The result of all the analytical work done through the application of economic principles in the development of DPMs—combined with modern management techniques of decision-making—led to a tremendous impact on resource allocation decisions, particularly on Strategic Retaliatory Forces, the major concern at that period of time.

As the foreword to the main edition of Enthoven Smith's *How Much is Enough?* brings out, in all, 93 DPMs were prepared in the eight Kennedy-Johnson years. Several have since been been cleared for public release. "The DPMs share five hallmarks on the *definition of objectives,* rather than calculations of precise quantities. They focus on identifying the most *cost-effective* alternatives for achieving the objective. They consider a range of assumptions and offer a range of results, rather than single-point solutions. They also carefully and explicitly state the roles of analysis and judgment."[35]

In other words, DPMs combined everything we have said above, for optimum allocation of resources for defence. The result on force structure decisions was tremendous.

As Dr. Chu and Krieg point out in the foreword, "For example, the Strategic Retaliatory Forces identified the strategy as deterrence (rather than creation of a first strike capability), reviewed the full span of the nation's nuclear forces and adjusted the mix of forces to increase their collective deterrent value, chiefly by enlarging the most expensive and effective ballistic missile submarine force. McNamara's decisions in the DPM shaped the nuclear triad that supported the strategic policy of the United States for the duration of the Cold War. The document itself, which put fully into practice the concept of capability-based planning that has recently received renewed emphasis, is a classic of analysis."[36]

Another important decision emanating from the office of Comptroller of Defence Charles Hitch, pertained to cancellation of the Skybolt missile programme in 1963, which was promised to the British for their bombers and the cancellation of which was to create issues in US-UK relations.

This instance underlines the point that good economic analysis, based on reliable data, on a sound conceptual basis, can lead to very major decisions on force planning. What is the impact of these analyses and decisions on defence budgets? As an eminent economist, surveying the period, puts it, "From 1961 to the Vietnam build-up, the total defence expenditure increased by about 10 percent and defence programs were substantially strengthened in most major areas."[37] Thus, economy in expenditure was clearly in view while increasing the effectiveness of defence. "Since 1961, within a constant total budget, approximately $5 billion has been transferred from strategic forces to various support activities."[38] Since total obligational authority in 1966 was around $51 billion, this was a considerable achievement, based on effective economic analysis and sound judgement.

Economics and Defence Budgeting

The Group of Ministers in India in their recommendations on Reforming the National Security System have, in the chapter on Management of Defence, recommended introduction of programme-based budgeting. To quote, "A need has been felt for review of the form and content of Defence Services Estimates and the expansion of budgetary classification to promote programme-based budgeting, while ensuring compliance with security requirements" (Para 6.52). This is the least discussed recommendation of the Group of Ministers.

As Allen Schick puts it, "Program budgeting (PPB) is planning oriented, its main goal is to rationalize policy-making by providing (1) data on the costs and benefits of alternative ways of attaining the proposed policy objectives; and (2) output measurements to facilitate the effective attainment of chosen objectives."[39] Programme budgeting departs from the simple models of efficiency where objectives are given and the quantities of inputs and outputs are adjusted to obtain an optimal relationship. In programme budgeting, "The objective itself is variable; the analysis itself may lead to a new statement of objectives."[40]

The emergence of programme budgeting in the USA signified dissatisfaction with the bottom up approach in budgeting, when, by the time the budget reaches the top level, most of the decisions have been made. On the micro-economic side, programme budgeting "traces its lineage to the attempts of welfare economists to construct a science of finance predicated on the principle of marginal utility. It was hoped that such a science would furnish objective criteria for determining the optimal allocation of funds among competing uses."[41] It was felt that by appraising marginal costs and benefits of alternatives, it would be possible to determine which combination of expenditure afforded the maximum possible utility.

As Schick points out, stripped of its normative and formal overtones, the principles of welfare economics have been applied to budgeting by economists such as Arthur Smithies. Smithies had formulated a budget rule: "Expenditure proposals should be considered in the light of objectives... and, in general, final decisions should not be made until all claims on the budget can be considered."[42]

Programme budgeting is application of this principle to budgeting. All claims to the budget should be considered in relation to the attainment of objectives by appraising their costs and benefits. The final decision is to be taken after all such claims have been considered. In the incremental budgeting process, we confine our attention to only a small range of issues. The basic advantage of programme budgeting, as pointed out by Schick is, "By structuring expenditures so as to juxtapose substitutive elements within programme categories and by analysing the costs and benefits of the various substitutes, PPB has opened the door to the use of marginal analysis in budgeting."[43]

The reader will recall that we had earlier brought out some of the basic problems in the programme concept. But it does not take away from the basic validity of marginal costs and marginal gains in allocation of resources to attain efficiency in resource allocation decisions.

Limitations of Economic Analysis

The most important contribution of economics to resource allocation is in the realm of costing of alternatives. By making explicit the resources devoted to functions and costing them, the decision-maker has information available to make judgements about whether the costs are 'worth' what they get. It is not the economist's task to decide on what the functions are, how the military capabilities are divided and which of these are relevant. It is the military's task to be explicit on the outputs to be achieved from the resources. As Gavin Kennedy puts it, "Perhaps in the process of specifying the outputs, the military planners will show up inherent contradictions in their earlier thinking."[44]

There may be good military reasons for doing something more expensively. Polito-military judgement will determine whether the resource constraint can be overridden.

Facing up to the reality of bureaucratic politics is, nevertheless, essential. Economic analysts do not decide who makes the decisions or what decisions are made. The decision-maker can interpret a decision differently from his advisers.[45]

Policy decisions are a top level exercise. Economists have to be present if the defence function has to get value from their contribution. Policy planners can be trained to ask the right questions. The problem was put succinctly by Schlesinger, "The obstacles to logical choices are bureaucratic pressures and the proclivity of most human beings to make decisions based on pure intuition rather than adjust one's assessment of the state of the world accordingly... analysis is made to reflect preconceptions."[46]

The aim should be to arrive at policy decisions to the extent possible on the basis of objective analysis. Politico-military judgement will, however, always prevail.

Economics and Modern Defence Management

What could be the most critical input that economists could make to the development of modern defence management? In this regard, we can do no better than to refer to the most important single intellectual contribution to defence management that was made by economists,[47] namely, Charles Hitch and Ronald McKean. As they put it, there are three possible approaches in defence management. The first is the improvement in institutional arrangements within the government to promote efficiency. The second is the increased reliance on systematic quantitative analysis to determine the most efficient alternative allocations and methods. For enunciating the third and most important approach, we shall quote from Hitch and Mckean,

"Increased recognition and awareness that military decisions, whether they specifically involve budgetary decisions or not, are in one of their important aspects, economic decisions, and that unless the right questions are asked, the appropriate alternatives selected for comparison and economic criterion used for choosing the most efficient, military power and national security will suffer. It is our conviction that something can be accomplished by the third approach alone—that is, by understanding of the nature of the problem—even without greater use of systematic quantitative analysis and with no changes in government structure. In formulating policies, it helps to ask the right questions, instead of the wrong ones. If alternatives are arrayed and a serious attempt made to apply sound criteria in choosing the most efficient ones, decisions are likely to be improved even though the considerations that are brought to bear are qualitative and intuitive."[48]

Even then, the challenges are quite a few. These include:

- Developing of appropriate alternatives for comparison.
- Choosing of an economic criterion for making decisions.
- Asking the right questions.

These challenges have to be met to put defence management on a sound footing. But at the end of the process, there should be decision-makers who are inclined to take decisions, including those involving hard choices, through judgement and educated intuition will remain critical inputs. This is because more and more emphasis needs be placed on force integration rather than on individual weapon systems which, in turn, means more dependence on parameters which are only implicitly and subjectively quantifiable.

What we have tried to indicate above is that economics does not accept status quo as the optimum position. Nor does it accept the thesis that change in procedure would bring about improvements. The approach of economics is that of logic of choice on the basis of analysis, keeping in view the larger picture and consideration of alternatives for achieving the 'ends'. The ends are not given but arrived at by an iterative process of considering the availability of means and other constraints.

Economics believes in change to bring about improvements. Changes are to be brought about by in-depth examination of the present position, whether ongoing activities were relevant on the basis of changed circumstances and whether we could not take up something else in view of the new challenges. Whether a change will be an improvement or not, will not be determined by subjective judgement but on the basis of criteria of improvement scientifically arrived at. Therefore, development of criteria of improvement and success is of great importance for economics of defence. That is why it gives so much importance to the development of objectives, to the alternative ways of achieving the objectives and choosing the most effective and economical route to achieve the objectives and measuring the success on the extent of meeting the objectives as the hallmark of optimisation. For economics of defence, the most effective way is also the most economical way.

Economics looks at the future, unencumbered by the past, always believing that if the objectives that have been arrived at through an iterative process are clear, then alternatives are available to meet them in a cost-effective manner. It does not believe that incremental changes will bring about improvement. Incrementalism, it believes, will bring you back where you started from.

Institutional and Other Reforms for Optimal Allocation of Resources

While the right questions may be asked by the economists and limitation of resources and costing of alternatives may be furnished, ultimately, decisions have to made on politico-military considerations. Choices, and difficult choices at that, have to be ultimately made. Decisions on resource allocations on major programmes are the hardest of all.

The choices in resource allocation decisions in defence, which involve commitment to billions of rupees for any one programme to be spent over a number of years, and keeping in view that once committed for a particular programme, the same resources would not be available for other programmes, involve really hard decisions. These decisions have to be made based on explicit criteria of national interests and not by decision-making by compromise among various institutional interests.

Who ultimately is supposed to make these decisions involving choice among alternative programmes in the defence establishment?

The answer should be obvious: it is the Minister for Defence who has to take these decisions on the basis of explicit criteria of national interest. His position is that of a *leader* not a *judge* who ultimately has to make the choice among alternatives after all the parameters and advice are made available to him. If the aim is to optimise the resource allocation decisions, this the is obvious answer, irrespective of the budgetary system being adopted. As Enthoven and Smith indicated the role of the Secretary of Defence in the USA in the context of PPBS, "He must examine proposals from a broader perspective than that of the organisation proposing them, choose among real alternatives, and ascertain at what point further spending on a given military program results in incremental gains so small that it is no longer justified."[49] This we maintain is true for any budgetary system, be it programme budgeting or otherwise if the logic of choices, which is the core of economic principles, is to be applied in resource allocation decisions which are strategic decisions.

This leads to centralisation of decision-making regarding "strategy, force, and financial planning....The revolution in military technology alone almost makes this almost imperative. The great technical complexity of modern weapons, their enormous cost, and their lengthy period of development place an extraordinary premium on sound choices for major weapon systems. For top management of DoD, these choices have become the key decisions around which much of the defence program revolves." These decisions cannot be taken piecemeal lower down the echeleon and they must be related to national security objectives. Decentralised decision-making in strategy and force planning has never worked. " A centralized decision-making authority is needed at the top to attain and exercise the over all perspective necessary to integrate the contributing parts into a coherent goal."[50] Decentralised decision making in strategy and force planning has not worked in the past and will not work in the future. It is the top decision maker who has to choose among alternatives relating to strategy and force structure keeping in view the higher level objectives.

While proposing a new weapon system, one can lose the overall objective. For example, proponents of air defence are eager to have more and better missiles, radars, and interceptors in order to shoot more enemy bombers. But viewed from a higher perspective, the objective of air defence is not merely to shoot down the enemy aircraft but to limit the damage these aircraft can inflict on the population and military facilities, for which there are several alternatives. The decision at the top level may be, for example, to buy long range missiles to strike enemy bases and destroy his bombers before they can be launched. "Or he may decide that it is best to rely on deterrence and not buy active defence."[51]

Keeping in view the importance of major decisions regarding strategy and force structure which will vitally affect resource allocation decisions and the imperative necessity of centralised decision-making, it is not right to just allocate the defence budget to the Services on the basis of a fixed percentage to allow them to spend as they think best. It must be realised that major defence programmes transcend individual Service programmes. More importantly, they depend on national policy with respect to the number and kind of limited war contingencies that a country should be prepared to meet. And the speed and readiness with which it is decided to meet them. The size and readiness of the army must be related to the air force's airlift and navy's sealift capability.[52]

There may be major lacunae in our defence capabilities which might not be addressed if it is left to the Services to decide. In this context, the observation of the Standing Committee of the Parliament in respect of one capability can be made. To quote: "The Committee has also observed that surveillance capabilities of our forces are inadequate. This is primarily due to non-availability of low-level radar systems with the three Services. The Committee feel that all round effort should be undertaken by the Government to ensure that the entire country is covered."[53] Later, the Defence Secretary, in his deposition before the Committee stated that he was also not satisfied "with the level of surveillance either of the air space of the country or surveillance, as protective surveillance for individual installations or individual platforms like a ship... or for that matter cities or industrial establishments of the country..... there has to be a network of radar of various types, which are covering the entire spectrum of various heights at the borders as also within the country."[54] These are the cases where the government has to take the initiative in the resource allocation decisions from an overall strategic perspective, applying the principles of economics of choice. It cannot be left to the Services. The same applies to strategic weapons. Quoting the experience of the USA,

Enthoven and Smith wrote, "Under financial pressure, the Services will seek to keep prestige items—the major combat units and glamorous weapon systems—and cut back the unglamorous support items essential to readiness. The result is the hollow shell of military capability, not substance."[55] This may not be true in our case, but one has to be on guard against this tendency. A passive role adopted by the Defence Minister in resource allocation issues would not help. For various institutional reasons, it is very difficult to reduce the number of major force units though with induction of more capable weapon system, it is possible to do so. This raises the cost of defence without a corresponding increase in capability, as economy gets made elsewhere to stay within the budget. To quote Enthoven and Smith about a universal tendency, "The tendency has been to keep the same number of units and replace older, cheaper equipment on a 1 to 1 basis with more capable and expensive items... The cost to buy and operate an A-6 Navy attack bomber is eight times that of an A-1, so that replacement of A-1's with A-6's means a major cost (and performance) increase, because the Navy proposes that nominal force structure in terms of air wings remain constant. The Services have not emphasized the development of simple, low cost equipment that could be introduced in larger numbers and possibly with far greater effectiveness per dollar."[56]

This is a universal tendency which makes it difficult to arrive at optimal allocation of resources for the force structure. These calls for hard decisions.

Can the Chairman, Chiefs of Staff Committee, aided by the Integrated Defence Staff (IDS) take these hard decisions? Normally, a compromise solution might be arrived at which may not be the best mix of forces from the military point of view. To quote from the report of the Standing Committee on Defence "The Committee further note that the existing structure for higher defence management viz Chiefs of Staff Committee have not been able to optimally perform their role and functions in bringing together and promoting co ordination amongst the Services."[57]

The Committee felt that "to enhance the efficiency and effectiveness of the planning process, there is an imperative need to create the post of Chief of Defence Staff (CDS) to provide a focal point for better coordination among the three Services in the long-term perspective plan in conventional and strategic capabilities, prioritise R&D activities..."[58] In other words, the appointment of a CDS is required for optimal decision-making in resource allocation for major systems for capability-building.

Enthoven and Smith put it years back, *" Rampant technological change is producing not only better weapons of familiar kinds but many new kinds of weapons as well...A similar expansion is taking place in almost every kind of warfare. We have not escaped, however, the ancient necessity for choice arising arising from the scarcity of available resources. "*[59] The revolution in military technology has changed the nature of military programmes; it has also blurred the lines separating various Services. "Is a missile an unmanned aircraft, as the Air Force likes to think, or a piece of long range artillery, which is the Army view? Most major military missions now require the participation of more than one of the Services. Our principal concern must be, therefore, centered on what is required by the defence establishment as a whole for a particular military mission—not on what is required by a particular Service for a part of that mission."[60]

These hard decisions regarding resource allocation for arriving at an optimal force structure are to be taken by the Defence Minister who should have single-point advice from the CDS. The decision regarding the CDS, and giving him a proper mandate relating to resource allocation decisions, should not be postponed any longer if the aim is towards rational allocation of resources.

To aid decision-making involving hard choices, there should be analytical staff attached to the MoD, and to Service Headquarters who should be engaged in systems analysis. Modern-day strategy and force planning has become largely an analytical process. Systems analysis is a reasoned approach to a complicated problem of choice in a context characterised by much uncertainty. It looks at alternative ways of doing a job, and where possible, to identify most effective alternative. Systems analysis is not a panacea for defence but this kind of analysis can be a valuable aid to judgement by defining issues and bringing out alternatives clearly as also to bring out the assumptions involved in a proposal.

The main working premise of systems analysis should be, however, to remember that analysis is the servant of judgement. The aim is to illuminate and inform judgement, which has to play the decisive role as there is important uncertainty in policy issues. Ultimately, defence policies are made and weapons are chosen on the basis of judgement The aim should be to arrive at judgement on the basis of adequate data and well defined issues. The choice of methods used should be on the nature of the problem and availability of data, not vice versa.

A more important thing is, with rapid technological advancements with changes in the nature of warfare, resource allocation in defence faces new challenges. The changes have been so rapid that piecemeal reforms would no longer lead to optimal allocation of resources. More drastic changes are called for. Even restructuring of the armed forces may be required. The Standing Committee of Parliament has rightly observed, in view of the new challenges posed by rapid technological advances and the change in the nature of warfare, *"There is an imperative need to constitute a high level empowered Committee to examine the entire security forces and suggest reforms including re-structuring of the armed forces.... The Committee note there has been no thorough review of the structural set-up of the armed forces since independence, especially of the Army...The need of the hour is to optimally use the available limited resources."*[61]

In other words, without such major reforms involving force structure review and nature of capabilities required to be built up in the light of the technological changes and information revolution, it would not be possible to rationally allocate the defence resources.

Notes

1. George J. Stigler, *The Theory of Price* (New York: Macmillan Company, 1947), p. 12.
2. Charles J. Hitch, "Economics and Military Operations Research", *The Review of Economics & Statistics,* vol. 40, no. 3, August 1958.
3. Ibid.
4. Charles J. Hitch, "Plans, Programs, and Budgets in the Department of Defense", Operations Research, *Journal of Operations Research Society,* vol. 11, no. 1, 1963, pp. 1-17.
5. Ibid.
6. Report of the Standing Committee on Defence "Defence Policy, Planning and Management," March 1996.
7. Ibid.
8. William W. Kaufmann, *The McNamara Strategy* (Harper and Row, 1964), p. 169.
9. Theodore W. Bauer, *Requirements for National Defense* (Washington DC: Industrial

College of the Armed Forces,) p. 71.

10. Committee on Hemispheric Security, Permanent Council of the Organisation of American States, "Draft Guidelines on Developing National Defense Policy and Doctrine Papers White Papers", October 22, 2002; www.oas.org/csh/english/document/cpi0405eou.doc
11. Ibid.
12. Arthur Smithies, *The Budgeting Process in the United States* (New York: McGraw Hill Book Co, 1955), in the chapter "Budgeting and the Decision-Making Process," appearing in R.T. Golembiewski & J. Rabini's *Public Budgeting and Finance*, 2nd Edition (F.E. Peacock Publishers).
13. Ibid.
14. James M. Roherty, *Decisions of Robert S. McNamara* (University of Miami Press, 1970), p. 79.
15. Smithies, n. 12.
16. Hearings, Subcommittee on National Policy Machinery, 1961, quoted by Roherty, n. 14, p. 76.
17. Bauer, n.9, p. 73.
18. Charles Hitch, "Economics and Operational Research", *The Review of Economics and Statistics*, August 1958, p. 205.
19. Ibid.
20. Ibid.
21. Alain C. Enthoven, "Systems Analysis and Decision-Making," *Military Review*, January 1963, pp. 13-15.
22. Ibid.
23. Lt Col Edward Stellini, "Force Structure Planning", *Air University Review,* May-June 1971.
24. Bernard Brodie, "Strategy as Science", *World Politics*, vol. I, no. 4, July 1949.
25. Ibid.
26. Ibid.
27. Ibid.
28. Ibid.
29. Ibid.
30. Franklin C. Spinney, "Quadrennial Defense Review, What Went Wrong and How to Fix it." September 1997, www.d-n-i.net/fcs/pdf/qdr report master doc.pdf.
31. Eric V. Larson et al, *Defense Planning in a Decade of Change* (RAND, 2001), p. 87.
32. US Department of Defense, Report of Quadrennial Defense Review, 1997, p. v.
33. Charles Hitch, "Sub-optimisation in Operations Problems", *Journal of Operations Research Society of America,* May 1953, p. 25.
34. Kenneth J. Krieg and David S.C.Chu, "Foreword to 'How Much is Enough?" June 27, 2005. RAND Edition. Dr Chu is Under-Secretary of Defence for Personnel and

Readiness. Dr Krieg is Under Secretary of Defence for Acquisition, Technology and Logistics.

35. Ibid.
36. Ibid., foreword, p. xi.
37. William A. Niskanen, "The Defense Resource Allocation Process," in Stephen Enke, ed., *Defense Management* (Prentice Hall, 1967), p. 8.
38. Ibid., p. 10.
39. Allen Schick, "The Stages of Budget Reform", *Public Administration Review*, vol. 26, no. 4, December 1966, pp. 243-258.
40. Ibid.
41. Allen Schick, "*The Road to PPB,*"
42. Arthur Smithies, *The Budgeting Process in the United States* (New York, 1955), p. 16, quoted by Schick in Ibid.
43. Ibid.
44. Gavin Kennedy, "The Uses and Limitations of Economic Analysis in Defense Policy Planning," in Lawrence Martin, ed., *The Management of Defense* (The Macmillan Press, 1976), p. 79.
45. Ibid., p. 81.
46. James R. Schlesinger, "The Changing Environment for Systems Analysis," in Stephen Enke, ed., *Defense Management* (Prentice Hall, 1967), p. 110.
47. Charles Hitch and Ronald McKean, *The Economics of Defense in the Nuclear Age* (New York: RAND, 1965).
48. Ibid., p. 107.
49. Alain C. Enthoven and K. Wayne Smith, *How Much is Enough?* (RAND 1971), pp. 33-34.
50. Ibid.
51. Ibid., p. 40.
52. Ibid., p. 335.
53. Report of the Standing Committee on Defence, Demands for Grants 2005-06, para 2.14.
54. Ibid., para 5.10.
55. op cit., p. 336
56. Ibid.
57. Report of the Standing Committee on Defence, Demands for Grants, 2005-06, para 2.21.
58. Ibid., para 2.22.
59. Enthoven and Smith, n. 49.
60. Ibid.
61. Report of the Standing Committee on Defence, Demands for Grants 2006-07, para 1.4.

2

Economics and Strategy: Need for a Framework for Linking Inputs (efforts) to Outputs (results) and Means to Ends

"The central fact about the defense budget is that it is a political problem. The issue is enveloped in the aura of 'national security' and made up of complex and technical military and foreign policy considerations. The effect is to generate among many the impression that it is, and certainly ought to be, far removed from 'politics'. But the defense budget is the very stuff of which politics is made."[1]

The above observation by Schilling is made on the basis of the in-depth analysis he makes of the defence budgeting process for US defence in President Truman's time, particularly that relating to FY 1950 to show how complex the process was . Political intervention at the highest level was required to finalise it. There are very important lessons one can draw, if one studies in detail the formulation of this and subsequent budgets for the next few years, as politics and economics both interacted, but ultimately it is the economic considerations that prevailed, except for the Korean War period. The FY 1950 budget was also significant, as this was the first budget formulated after the position of Secretary of Defence was considerably strengthened for resource allocation decisions.

In the formulation of the budget, there were elements of conflict between the Services and the Secretary of Defence; between the Department of Defence and Bureau of Budget and Department of State; and between the President and his Secretary of Defence. There was divergence of perspectives about the security scenario, and different assumptions were made. Resolution of these conflicts made defence budgeting a political process. These conflicts were in the open. In the normal course of defence budgeting, elements of conflict are always present, because of divergence in points of view and different assumptions made. Reconciling them is not easy, and the practical way out is imposition of a ceiling on the defence budget. There is quite a bit of discretion involved in taking a final view about the level of the defence budget. To that extent, defence budgeting would always be a political process. The element of conflict in the defence budgeting process differs from country to country. In Indian defence budgeting, much conflict is not evidence, but a ceiling is imposed on projections because of fiscal considerations.

There are very important economic factors behind the decisions regarding the defence budget. The existence of a ceiling for the US defence budget was public knowledge by the fall of 1948. President Truman was quoted in September 1948 as saying "...our national security requires that that the total defense program be based on a strong economic system and depend on a *level of expenditure which can be supported in subsequent years.*"[2]

A ceiling of $15 billion was indicated by the President right in the beginning of the budgetary process for FY 1950. The Services felt that this was not enough to maintain the existing force level or achieve the required level of readiness. The Secretary of Defence had his own reservations about this budget ceiling.

The economic reasons for this ceiling were: "Truman was intent on budgets which would avoid deficit financing and would compile, wherever possible, budget surpluses. The tax reduction Bill passed in April 1948 had removed the possibility of a surplus in fiscal 1949 and had assured a deficit."[3] Tax reduction became necessary because of recessionary trends. A deficit budget was expected to create inflationary pressures, so was avoided. Truman, after considering all these economic factors, accepted the recommendation of the Chief of the Bureau of Budget for a ceiling of $15 billion for the defence budget. In spite of pressures from the Services and the recommendation of the Secretary to consider a higher figure, Truman adhered to the ceiling and actually recommended to Congress a figure of $14.4 billion in January 1949. This was notwithstanding the fact that in October 1948, the Russians had placed Berlin in a blockade and the military situation appeared to have deteriorated. Secretary of Defence Forrestal told the President that with a

$14.4 billion budget, the Services would have only the capacity to conduct an air offensive from Britain and control of the Mediterranean would be ruled out. Therefore, Forrestal argued for two budgets , one within the ceiling of $15 billion and a higher budget in the vicinity of $18.5 billion, predicated on the attainment of a capability exploiting the holding of the Mediterranean Line of Communication (LOC).[4] Thus, it became clear that the levels of defence budget have important strategic connotation. It also brings out that if budgeting involves hard decisions then there is no difference between budgeting and strategy-making. That is why top-level decisions are required to decide about the level at which the budget would be fixed.

Truman was not receptive to the idea of receiving alternative budgets. He wanted the higher budget to be "held in reserve" as the presentation of a higher budget "would be interpreted as a step toward preparation for war." The higher budget could be kept as "supplemental", to be presented if the situation became more dangerous. Risk management in determining the defence budget was done at the highest level. Truman often held that defence budgeting was equal to strategy making.

For FY 1951, the ceiling indicated by Truman was $13 billion, which was supposed to represent a careful "balance between the security needs in the light of our foreign policy and economic and fiscal problems facing us domestically."[5] Truman also rejected the proposal of the Secretary to increase the air force budget significantly on the ground that it would mean vastly increased appropriations in future years.

This brought in an important principle that is, in determining a budget, its effect on future budgets, because of additional commitments, needs to be kept in view. In Indian budgeting, we only keep in view the current year's commitment of expenditure; the future year's commitment in terms of the budget is not a major concern.

The Russians exploded the atomic bomb in August 1949 (much earlier than expected), but the ceiling remained. The reason for a lower ceiling in FY 1951 was again economic, reinforcing the earlier arguments for the ceiling for FY 1950. As a result of the 1949 recession, the prospects of revenue were lower, the size of deficits loomed larger and the opportunity for new taxation remained the same. Before, however, the US Congress took a final view on the FY 1951 budget, the North Korean Army crossed the 38th parallel. The Korean War changed the picture and in calendar year 1950, the US defence spending was $19 billion which was 6 percent of the GNP. In the first half of 1953, it went up to $51 billion and constituted 14 percent of the GNP. This brings out the important point that defence spending is discretionary in nature: when the situation warrants, it can go up; it can be brought down after the situation stabilises.

Following his nomination for the Presidential campaign, Eisenhower asserted that overall government spending, especially defence spending, must be drastically reduced. The goal was both 'security and solvency'. The most urgent problem facing the new Administration was, therefore, to end the Korean War quickly, which they did. This enabled them to revise downward the Truman Administration's budget for fiscal 1954.The Korean War had ended. Each Department was given an 'assumed' expenditure ceiling for approaching a balanced budget in fiscal 1954 and achieving it in fiscal 1955; for the Department of Defence these were $41.2 billion for fiscal 1954 and $34.6 billion for fiscal 1955. This compared with the $45.4 billion which had been projected by the Truman Administration.[6]

The Department of Defence was directed to submit to the National Security Council a statement of programme revisions which would be necessary to reduce expenditure to these levels. The Joint Chiefs of Staff (JCS) were required to make a study and present it to the National Security Council. The gist of their presentations was that the proposed fiscal limit would seriously constrain the rate of build-up of military capability and would dangerously affect national security. The Joint Chiefs of Staff were then directed to make a further study of how much reduction could be made in the existing programmes without affecting the security of the country.

The additional study of the JCS warned against any reduction in the existing force levels, particularly as the Soviet Union was going to have substantial stockpiles of atomic weapons and the means of delivering them during this period. As the aim was reduction of the defence budget, and Joint Chiefs were not prepared to provide the rationale for it, the budget experts in the Defence Department initiated this exercise. To achieve the required reduction in the budget, they focussed their attention on supporting activities , lead times and avoiding all those expenditures which could be postponed to the next year (FY 1955).

The result of this review, which was submitted to Congress, called for a reduction from $41.2 billion (assumed 'ceiling) to $36 billion in the request for new appropriations and a cut-back in planned expenditures from $45.4 billion (for FY1954) to $43.2 billion.

The new Republican Administration announced the concept of "long haul" which assumed that the Soviet threat was of an indefinite duration and, therefore, called for the maintenance of a reasonably sturdy military posture over a long period of time. For this, no peaking of expenditure was called for as the 'crisis year' concept was dropped.

The famous strategic policy joint-study document NSC-68 authorised by President Truman, which outlined the policy of containment, was finalised in 1950. The document estimated that within four years, the Soviet Union would have enough nuclear bombs and a sufficient capability for delivering them to offset substantially the deterrent capability of American nuclear weapons. In comparison, it emphasised the inadequacy of the Western capability to meet limited military challenges due to lack of conventional forces, shortcomings in the Western alliance system, and the military and economic weaknesses of Western Europe.[7] The paper rejected the possibility of negotiation with the Soviet Union except on the basis of political considerations.

This policy paper was a radical departure from the economy policies followed in formulation of the defence budget. Secretary of Defence Johnson, who agreed with the conclusions of the study report, assigned to the Chief of JCS, the responsibility to see that NSC-68 was programmed and priced. 'Programming' for it, was handled in the budget planning process. The aim was that the costing of these programmes would be the basis for the FY 1952 defence budget.

Events in Korea in June 1950 changed the whole frame of reference for the Defence Department budgeting. When the Korean War began, NSC-68 remained unprogrammed and unapproved.[8] NSC-68 had major limitations in that "it was a general statement of policy without a definite settlement of its meaning in terms of tangible decisions about budgets, procurement, and forces."[9] President Truman did not question the validity of NSC-68, "but he wanted to know what the cost would be to implement it before deciding what to do about it...Truman rejected the proposal implicit in NSC-68 to choose without prices. All that he committed himself to was, in effect, that may be he would decide what to do about NSC-68 later, when he could see what it would cost."[10] But all the same, the quality of military build-up during the Korean War was facilitated by the existence of NSC-68, which depicted the larger picture of the strategic challenge and was referred to as a policy paper. At the same time, Truman's stand brought home the point that strategies have costs, which can be worked out in terms of their programme content, and one can choose on the basis of what is affordable. This continues to be the basic problem of defence budgeting in India. In the absence of the programme concept, costs cannot be linked to strategy.

What is to be noted is that the concept of 'programming', that is, considering alternative ways of spending the defence money for capability building, with reference to their cost and benefits, has to be there if we want the defence budget to meet strategic objectives.

The costs of strategies have to be worked out to link the means and ends. General statements on strategic matters hardly serve much purpose. A strategy should be so formulated that the cost of each element of the strategy can be worked out so that the link between the strategy and the budget can be easily established, may be through costing of relevant programmes. If there is no programme concept, the cost of a strategy cannot be worked out.

President Eisenhower also made a thorough reexamination of the politico-military strategy of the United States . This became famous as Project 'Solarium'. The process adopted in developing the grand strategy for the United States in Project 'Solarium' is now being referred to in US defence strategic literature as the ideal process to develop a grand strategy for the 21st century. The Joint Chiefs of Staff were intimately involved with the process and gave their report to the President and Secretary of Defence. Although no specific forces were recommended, the new Chiefs "did discuss alternative levels of manpower and dollars—mostly lower than currently in force—and related those to the capabilities and strategy which they could support. These figures were generated by the Chiefs themselves and represented their attempt to carry out the President's directive to keep in mind the economic capacity of the country in formulating their program."[11] Even a super-power has to keep in view its economic capacity while formulating defence programmes. This programme, called the Sequira programme was based on certain assumptions, principally that international relations would not deteriorate. This brings out the point that the assumptions behind a strategy need to be spelt out.

The Korean War terminated in July 1953 with the signing of the armistice. Of major importance was the explosion of the hydrogen bomb by the Soviet Union on August 12, 1953—less than ten months after the United States' first thermonuclear explosion. But this did not affect the US defence budget.

In parallel, preparation for FY 1955 started in 1953. President Eisenhower approved a National Security Council paper which established a projected level of defence expenditure for 1955 of $40 billion, which, at the level of existing tax rates, would have involved a budgetary deficit. It was clear on further analysis that a deficit could not be avoided in FY1955 without reducing the defence budget by another $4 to 5 billion. This was not acceptable to the President as it would have meant taking more security risks than he was willing to take.

Thus, while deficit reduction is an important goal in budgetary planning and resource allocation, the risk involved in reducing the expenditure beyond a point needs to be clearly assessed and judgment exercised about the prudent level of expenditure. This has to be done at the highest political level.

The paper also established military personnel ceilings for the armed forces to be reached by the end June 1954. These figures represented a reduction of about 145,000 from the active manpower in the beginning of calendar year 1953, to be further reduced if the Korean War were to end during 1953.

This brought into focus another important issue in the formulation of the defence budget.

Amounts to be allocated to defence budgets ultimately depend on the force levels they have to support. The debate that ensued was about the level upto which forces could be reduced from fiscal 1955 onwards, keeping in view the security requirements and the need for adhering to fiscal 'targets' which were suggested. Ultimately , the Chiefs developed a military strategy based on certain assumptions and recommended the force levels for the 'long pull', to be reached by the end of fiscal 1957. "In terms of manpower, the level-off strength was set at 2,815,000, approximately 540,000 less than the total personnel strength scheduled for June 1954, with the Army absorbing about 420,000 of the reduction. The Army was to have one million men, the Navy, 650,000, the Marine Corps, 190,000, and the Air Force, 975,000."[12]

Budget planning and force planning are intimately linked. Therefore, in deciding about the appropriate level of the budget to be approved, the force structure required to implement the strategy has to be clearly kept in view. The approach adopted for determining the ceiling on the defence budget is very important and could be emulated when the aim is to bring down the budget deficits, as in the case of India.

In an economic annex, the Joint Chiefs of Staff outlined the fiscal considerations which guided their thinking. These were the same projections of federal receipts and expenditure through fiscal 1957 which the Everest Committee, set up by the Joint Chiefs, had worked out with the assistance of a group of economists. At the request of this Committee, economists from various agencies were asked to calculate the tentative defence budgets for three years. The methodology adopted was simple and interesting . To quote Snyder, " The economic calculation which was then performed had two steps : first, a combination of the estimates of the gross national product with the assumed tax rates to obtain an estimate of governmental revenue for the fiscal years 1955, 1956, and 1957; then, a subtraction of the projected expenditures of the other agencies from the estimated revenue to find out the 'remainder' available for the military budget. The remainder turned out to be $34.5 billion for 1955, $32.8 billion for 1956, and $33.8 billion for 1957. The controlling figure was for the 'level-off' year of 1957."[13]

To work out the force level requirements, these figures were used with the "remainder" figure of $33.8 billion for the Department of Defence in fiscal 1957.[14] Some further cuts were made by the Bureau of Budget and army was asked for more rapid reduction. With these additional cuts, the army was to shrink in manpower by about 24 per cent during the two fiscal years 1954 and 1955.

The strategic precepts of New Look , with the force levels for 1955, 1956, and 1957 and the outline budget for 1955, were given formal and definite approval by President Eisenhower at a meeting of the Security Council in December 1953. This was the strategy of "Long Haul".

The basic approach of the concept of 'Long Haul' needs to be seen in the proper perspective. It deemphasised the external and emphasised the internal criteria for determining the military preparedness policy. Thus, "it minimized the importance of traditional bases for the requirements by the military: enemy capabilities and the United States commitments."[15] More important than the military 'requirement' of force level, was the question of what the country could 'afford'. This approach was also to lead to balance in procurement which was not to be externally determined.

In terms of action policy, the New Look policy included a determination to use nuclear weapons, especially nuclear air power in a wider range of contingencies than before. The policy highlighted the objective of 'deterrence' and played down the objective of 'defence at minimum cost.' It, thus, accepted the risk of greater costs in war in return for reduction in the costs of preparing *for* war.[16]

It becomes obvious that the key to the whole issue was to what extent defence manpower could be reduced in the four Services to be within fiscal targets which were externally determined. Strategy could be adjusted on the basis of affordable force level . The important point to note is that it was not the strategy which determined the force levels, which determined the budget. It was the suggested budgetary limits for defence, calculated by economists on the basis of likely GDP growth determining the increase in revenue, and competing budgetary needs of other departments and agencies, which led the process of determining the force level and the strategy to be adopted. This became possible as the Joint Chiefs of Staff became partners in developing a security strategy where achievement of economic security became the most important goal.

In Indian defence budgeting, imposition of ceilings by the Ministry of Finance, does not lead to hard decisions as the cuts imposed hardly exceed 10 percent of projected amounts (which always have some padding) and has hardly any effect on force levels and modernisation efforts. There is also the stage of revised estimates where a fresh look can be given to the budget on the basis of trends of expenditure. The revised estimates stage has become so important that one can conclude that soft budgeting options are followed while deciding upon the budget estimates for initial budget allocations. Because of the 'soft' budgeting regime, hard decisions regarding strategy and force structure are avoided.

Another important point came to be established in the process described above for deciding upon US defence budgets in the mid-Fifties. For proper *force planning, be it for reduction or for increase , it has to be conceived on a multi-year basis, as these take time.* Therefore, budgeting has also to be in the multi-year mode. That would ensure that force planning is in conformity with budgets available for the years covered under multi-year planning. Achieving fiscal targets like doing away with fiscal deficits or bringing them down to a predetermined level, calls for a multi-year fiscal planning, keeping in view likely GDP growth and expected growth in revenue by additional taxes or even without any increase if the economy is in a recession mode. The fiscal situation and the competing demands for expenditure made it obvious to the Eisenhower Administration towards the end of 1953 that though the Korean War had ended, it was not possible to achieve a balanced budget in FY 1955 as other challenges remained. If properly planned, it could be achieved in FY 1957. That was how the expenditure plan was drawn up and the level of budget availability for defence for three years was indicated for force planning purposes. Force planning was done accordingly under the leadership of the Joint Chiefs of Staff and the strategy was drawn up in conformity with the force planning, making appropriate assumptions. This involved taking of risks which higher management is supposed to do after considering probabilities. This was done. Presidential approval was obtained when all these exercises were tied together in a coherent force and budget plan.

Imposition of 'ceilings' on the defence budget right in the beginning of the planning process was the procedure adopted under the Truman Administration until the Korean War broke out. The cost aspects were the main consideration for acceptance of a defence strategy. Truman did not indicate his approval to NSC-68 as programmes required under it and their costs were yet to be worked out. He declared that the US national security required that the total defence programme be based on a strong economic system.

But the important point to note is that if likely budget ceilings are to be used for defence planning purposes , *then the ceiling is required to be indicated right in the beginning of the process and not at the end as we tend to do.* If it is put at the end of the process, then a mismatch is likely to occur between force planning assumptions and fiscal planning assumptions.

This is an important point for Indian defence budgeting. The above model of decision-making for defence continues to have its relevance if achievement of economic security becomes the primary goal at any stage of national development. Without it, national security conceived in a bigger perspective, gets threatened.

As would be seen, the above approach concentrated more on the *input* aspect, that is, the amount to be provided in the defence budget in a political process of decision-making and less on how it should be spent to get best results or the 'output' aspect, which the economists would be concerned with. In other words , instead of conceiving defence budgeting as a 'political problem', as in the quotation of Schilling with which we began, can we bring in some 'economic rationality' to it apart from the 'affordability' aspect?

This question takes us to the next level of budgetary theory and practice of recent years: attempting to link input to output.

II

For central government Departments in India, the attempt has been made in recent years, in accordance with the practice all over the world, to bring performance orientation(or 'output' orientation) into their functioning. Performance budgeting has been put into operation during the last five years, indicating that they have to set down goals, objectives and performance parameters, while formulating the budget, which are required to be achieved while implementing the budget. The performances are to be reviewed while formulating the next year's budget, referred to as 'Outcome Budgeting,' for example, the Outcome Budget of the Department of Agriculture and Cooperation 2009-10 indicated the physical dimensions of the financial budget as also actual physical performances in 2007-08 and 2008-09 and targets of physical performance for 2009-10. As per the Ministry of Finance, the outcome budget is intended as a policy tool to establish effective linkages with allocation and disbursement of public funds on the basis of measurable performance.

This development is in keeping with the evolution of budgeting theory for the public sector. It has taken its time for introduction in government budgeting in India, though the first Administrative Reforms Commission (ARC), in its report towards the end of the 1960s made a strong recommendation for the introduction of performance budgeting in India. They were influenced by the introduction of the Planning, Programming and Budgeting System (PPBS) in all federal government departments in the USA in 1965 following its success in the Defence Department where it was introduced in 1961.

Theoretically, it is difficult to distinguish between performance budgeting and programme budgeting. Under the budgetary theory, it was developed in the 1950s with the concept of programmes to link input with output. This was an effort to quantify and evaluate the output of the public sector. Both performance budgeting and programme budgeting involve linking input to output. In both cases, the linkage has to be through programmes.

The Defence Ministry is yet to become part of this exercise. This is a position which is difficult to accept. As stated above, PPBS was first introduced in US defence in 1961. This was the best example of output budgeting.

Therefore, absence of this concept in defence management in India is inexplicable, except for the fact, that we are unable to define the 'ouputs' in defence. In its absence, we cannot also introduce performance budgeting in defence as there can be no criteria of efficiency and effectiveness in defence spending.

Today, the planning remains with the Services and the Ministry of Defence is concerned only with control of expenditure for which budgetary ceilings are imposed as communicated by the Ministry of Finance. That control of expenditure was the main objective of expenditure management in defence, was made clear by the Ministry in the mid-Seventies of the last century, when the Ministry of Finance was keen to introduce performance budgeting in the wake of the ARC recommendation, in the entire Government of India. A Committee of the government headed by the Dy. CAG recommended codification of expenditure on the basis of programmes, sub-programmes and activities to provide an accounting structure to introduce performance budgeting, which was accepted by all Departments other than defence, which decided to stick to object-based accounting budgeting as it facilitated control of expenditure.

The government, apparently following the same philosophy, has exempted defence from the present wave of budgetary reforms followed from 2004-05 onwards, though the defence budget today has crossed $ 40 billion. In effect, it means following the practice followed by the US government till 1960, as depicted above, with the notable exception that ceilings are not indicated in the beginning of the process and force planning is not made an integral part of the budgetary process. The basic aim is control of expenditure. There is no attempt to link inputs as represented by various allocations in the defence budget to the 'outputs' of defence. This was also the deficiency in defence budgeting in the USA in the 1950s, as depicted above.

Apart from military leaders, defence analysts, researchers and economists working in the field of defence, this deficiency was noticed also by important members of the US Congress. For example, the Chairman of the House Defence Appropriations Committee, in a letter to the Secretary of Defence in 1959, stressed the importance of looking at defence programmes and budgets in terms of major military missions, by grouping programmes and their cost by missions. He also emphasised the need for practical means to link costs to missions.[17]

Concept of Programmes: 'Importance of Programme Budgeting'

The mission and output concept become all the more important because of the need for joint missions and joint operations, made essential under the new military technical revolution brought about by the advent of the nuclear and missile era. That is why relevant 'outputs' in defence had to be defined through a centralised planning process on a unified basis through *planning and execution of programmes* which cut across the Services.

Programmes are the basis though the output concept gets clarified, as also provides a basis for linking cost and output . "Tasks" and "Missions" became the central concepts in defence, to give meaning to programmes, which *cannot be laid down on single Service basis.* To quote Charles Hitch, "The *revolution in military technology has not only changed the character of our military program, it has also blurred the line of demarcation among the various services.* ...Therefore, our principal concern must now be centered on what is required by the defense establishment as a whole to perform a particular *mission* – not on what is required by a particular Service to perform its part of that mission. This is not only true with regard to planning of our military forces and programs, but also with respect to the development of new major weapon systems."[18]

The revolution in military technology that he was referring to was in the context of the *nuclear and missile age.*

This has changed the character of military programmes which can no longer be conceived in terms of single Service tasks. India became a military nuclear power in 1998, and we have inducted missiles as part of the military forces, but we continue to think in terms of single Service programmes; tasks and mission concepts are missing from our planning. We are now in the midst of another Revolution in Military Affairs (RMA) which is enabled by information technologies. This has brought in the concept of Network-Centric Warfare (NCW), precision strikes from a distance and other capabilities, changing once again the character of warfare. We have, however, not appreciated it implications. The networked command and control elements are best exploited by a joint and integrated effort of three Services. The need for jointness and joint operations is obvious to successfully exploit the potentialities of RMA, which our likely adversary is attempting to do in a big way.

Outputs can also be defined, as brought out above, by specific capabilities. For example, McNamara wanted to manage the defence effort in terms of meaningful programme entities—"of 'outputs' like the B-52 force, the Polaris force, the army airborne division force, etc associating with each output all the inputs of equipment, personnel, supplies, facilities, and funds, regardless of the appropriation account in which each was financed."[19] It was necessary for him to know, "to optimize allocation of resources, the cost of, for example, a B-52 wing—not *only the cost of equipping the wing but also of the cost of manning and operating it for its lifetime or at least for a reasonable period of years in the futur*e. *Only then, he would be in a position to assess the cost and effectiveness of a B-52 wing as compared to other systems designed to perform the same or similar tasks."*[20] In other words , cost and effectiveness between alternatives were required to be considered in terms of performance of *tasks*, and the *cost* of the system, apart from the procurement cost, has to include the costs of manning, operating and maintaining it over a reasonable period of time. This, for force planning purposes, as a practical device, was taken as seven years and cost was projected on a multi-year basis. It became "clear that a new function which we call programming would have to be incorporated in the financial management system."[21] The programming was to provide the link between input and output.

Programming tried to link output in terms of goals of force structure to costs on a multi-year basis. In other words, without this multi-year planning and jointness in approach towards capability planning and operational planning, we cannot define defence outputs nor link them with inputs.

The PPB as developed in the US Department of Defence differs from the concepts of performance budgeting in two significant ways. First is the "emphasis on choices among programs, where such choices are grounded in systems analysis. Second , PPB is a centralizing decision process, not a technique for improving the effectiveness of program operation. Any benefits that accrue to the latter are of the nature of incidental spin-offs."[22]

Programme budgeting injects into the decision process a new set of actors—the analytical staff. "The political scientists who view government budgeting as essentially a bargaining technique in the general setting of conflict resolution are appropriately concerned lest the systems approach substitute an apparent economic rationality for political rationality."[23]

As far as defence budgeting in India is concerned, this kind of 'bargaining' has never been there, nor has the budget process been viewed as a mechanism of 'conflict resolution'. The defence budget as presented by the Ministry of Finance gets all round support. Therefore, what is required is to bring in 'economic rationality' by connecting input to output by bringing in programme budgeting.

Programme budgeting is the product of two general strands of influences. One is the effort to improve the techniques of evaluation. Another, more importantly is, "introduction into contemporary budget-making of the concepts and methods of economic analysis, along with the latter's offspring, systems analysis."[24]

Programme budgeting has three objectives The first is taxonomic , that is the classification of government activity by goals and objectives. This was achieved by us by the end of the 1970s. The second objective of programme budgeting is analytical, that is, comparison of costs with outputs and exploration of alternative means of achieving outcomes. This is the difficult part and is yet to be attempted in the Indian government budgeting. The third objective is long range planning of government programmes. We are yet to take a meaningful step in this regard, though the defence Services have for a long time drawn up perspective plans to give effect to their procurement plans.

Traditionally, government budgeting has been prepared, reviewed and executed on the basis of line item classification or object classification. The expenditure side of the budget has been described as the things the government buys. The object classification was developed primarily for expenditure control and accountability. This is the continued relevance in government departments for financial control and audit. Defence budgeting in India is confined to object classification of expenditure. But object classification is necessarily restricted to the measurement of *inputs*. It does not describe the activities of government agencies or their *outputs*. "Activities are the implementing link between inputs and outputs; they are the intermediate step in the sequence inputs—activities—outputs. The activities of a government agency are the things that it does."[25]

Programmes are a collection of activities aimed toward the same objective. The conception of output relevant to programme budgeting is one which encompasses the whole range of objectives of the operating agency.

There are fundamental issues in programme budgeting which go beyond classification of expenditure programme-wise or activity-wise. It involves restructuring of decision-making within the government. Programme budgeting raises further issues in the relationship of analysis to policy.

The present process of resource management in defence in the USA for linking input to output, has been renamed as the PPBE process. The addition of 'E', refers to the execution review phase of the process. Execution review occurs simultaneously with the programme and budget reviews. The purpose of the execution review is to provide feedback to the senior leadership concerning the effectiveness of the current and prior resource allocations. This is like the performance review as it has been defined for other departments in India now. But this is a feedback process and would be meaningless unless performance goals are properly set. These goals under the PPBE process are laid down through what is designated as the 'planning' phase. This phase consists of two steps: one is *resource informed* articulation of defence policies and military strategy known as Strategic Planning Guidance, on the basis of which a planning process known as the Enhanced Planning Process is initiated. This process results in *fiscally constrained* guidance and priorities for military forces, modernisation, readiness and sustainability, supporting activities and infrastructure activities. This leads to the issuance of the Joint Programming Guidance.[26]

This guidance is the link between the planning phase and programming phase. This phase, resulting in a document called POM by each DoD component, provides detailed descriptions of proposed programmes, including time-phased allocation of resources(forces, funding and manpower), programme-wise projected six years into the future. The POMs are reviewed at a higher leadership level to evolve a coherent defence programme.

Unlike earlier, the budgeting phase of PPBE occurs concurrently with the programming phase; each DoD component submits its proposed budget estimates. The budget *converts* the programmatic view into the format of the Congressional appropriation structure.

The changes from the earlier process are noteworthy. We have already mentioned incorporation of the 'budget execution phase' in the process to have a performance review of the programmes, as a feedback process for decision-making in resource allocation.

The most important point is that the Programming Guidance is *resource-constrained* and *not just resource-informed.* This means the programmes to be developed or modified within the resource limits indicated in the guidance document. *In this way, the budget ceiling concept gets incorporated in the PPBE process*. This is a major reform in the process where the ceiling got imposed later through the budgeting phase with the decision taken at the level of Secretary of Defence.

The basic point is that to establish a clear link between strategy and budget, programmes need to be devised to implement the strategy, and the programmes need not only to be costed, but also be resource constrained. If at the programme formulation stage, the programmes are not resource constrained, the link between strategy and budget would be most tenuous.

Making the programme guidance "resource-constrained" allows it to make the budgeting phase concurrent with the programming phase, and not another phase of decision-making, as used to happen earlier. This shortens the time required for the whole process. Programming is now for six years instead of five. Issuance of the strategic and programming guidance takes place every two years, and the budget is prepared for two years, though the budget is approved by Congress on an annual basis.

The input-output concept provides an intellectual framework for achieving an effective defence by allowing linking of costs to benefits or 'utility'.

Defence costs are not static. Both personnel and equipment costs are rising inexorably. Equipment replacement costs are doubling every five years. This point cannot be shirked even though the security environment has not undergone a change.

'Utility' of defence spending in various directions has to be assessed considering both the 'value' and 'cost' aspects. Because of the inexorable rise in cost, the existing force level becomes unaffordable in a few years' time as the budget can increase only in a limited way which would not be sufficient to maintain the existing force level. Force levels determine in a big way the defence output , technology being another determinant. Therefore, in-depth defence reviews are required to determine what force level is affordable in the context of higher cost and what changes can be made in the light of new technologies so that defence output does not fall. This is necessary even if the security environment has not undergone any change.

'Utility' of spending for various defence activities undergoes change, with change in the security environment.

In the endeavour to fit these concepts together i.e 'input', 'output', 'cost' and 'value', in a dynamic environment, when neither the costs nor values of outputs are undergoing change, it is helpful to conceive of defence as an *enterprise,* instead of just another government department.

Investment Decisions

Looking at defence as an enterprise has led to imbibing many of the practices of the business world in defence since the early 1960s, in US defence and elsewhere. This has also led to clarification of the output aspects.

It started with the Planning, Programming Budgeting System (PPBS). It was followed by various reviews to ensure that there are adequate processes to link input to output, organisational reforms undertaken to link strategy to resource management. Now techniques of Scorecards (to look at performance aspects) and Spreadsheets and other computer models to aid decision-making in defence, are adopted as in a big business enterprise.

Because of the enterprise concept, procurement decisions are seen as *investment decisions* for the future, which are required to be made on the basis of cost, benefits and risk analysis, keeping in view a likely conflict scenario. In other words, the same considerations and analyses apply as for a big business where market competition and likely future market conditions determine how it is to be organised and what investments are to be made, taking into the account the competitors' reactions.

We have noted in an earlier chapter that in the Quadrennial Defence Review (QDR) of the USA of 1997, fiscal reality made the defence establishment focus their attention on the need to reform the organisation and methods of conducting business. How to conduct the defence business in an efficient way should be the concern of higher management. This would also call for better risk management in allocation of resources.

As per the QDR of the US Department of Defence of 2001, the "management of risks" in taking "investment" decisions, has become the central concern of the higher level of defence management, as in the case of the business world in an uncertain environment. Management's chief concern is to decide about which risks can be taken and which cannot, on the basis of analysis of security challenges and the probability of their taking place. "Risks" also should be properly "balanced" in taking investment decisions. Procurement decisions would be determined by what extent a particular procurement decision would mitigate an identified risk. This is necessary as resources are limited , therefore, all risks cannot be covered. The hallmark of good management of defence is the best management of risk within given resources. This calls for more sophisticated tools of analysis and techniques than used currently.

The concept of 'hedging' in investment, as in the business world, has come in a big way in decision-making in defence to meet various kinds of risks and keeping possibilities open for adjustments , instead of being committed to meeting only one kind of risks. When we talk of meeting the challenges of a 'spectrum of conflict', and 'planning under uncertainty' as the hallmarks of the present-day security environment, we have to think in terms of, 'management of risk', 'hedging of investments' and exploratory analysis. One or two sharply defined conflict scenarios, would not be right way of meeting the need for planning under uncertainty. These challenges cannot be subsumed under the overall concept of 'modernisation'. The questions to be answered are 'what is to be modernised', 'in what way' and 'for what'? We have to rather focus on capabilities for missions potentially *important in many contexts.*

Accordingly, modernisation in defence would mean how well it is able to manage the 'risks'(to be defined), by getting properly equipped and organised to effectively meet the risks which are defined through in-depth analysis, scenario building and high level decision-making as to which risks are to be covered and to what extent and which risks are already adequately covered , so that no further investments are required in that direction, and which risk is required to be covered by non-military means. Acquisition is only one aspect of it, flowing out of decisions regarding strategy of risk management in the short , medium and long terms. For the medium term risk management, we require the tool of five-year plans, and for the long term, of perspective plans.

We have all these but these are basically procurement plans, not plans for investments for management of risks in security.

Defence as a Business Enterprise

To conceive defence as a business enterprise is not a new way of looking at it. In fact, many of the tools used in defence for resource allocation decisions emanates from conceiving defence as a business enterprise. And this perception has been prevalent for quite some time, except that in India, we are still to think of defence as an enterprise.

The prevalence of the concept of defence as an enterprise in the US defence (and other Western countries' Defence Departments) would be corroborated by the continued use of the Planning, Programming and Budgeting System (PPBS) for strategic planning, as well as a tool for decision-making for resource management. That the enterprise concept, with the top leadership responsible for strategy making for resource allocation decisions and with its hierarchical structure of management, is more relevant for defence than most of the other activities of the government, is established by the fact that PPBS (now PPBES) continues to be used in US defence, while it was given up after a few years in other federal government departments of the USA (by 1971). The enterprise concept gets further established by the fact that now 'E' has been added to PPBS (in 2002) to emphasise execution and monitoring of plans that are crucial for the success of a business.

Most of the government Departments cannot function like an enterprise with centralised control and strategic guidelines; goals, missions and tasks cannot be defined except in a very general way. Defence was, and is, different. Here, missions and tasks are required to be laid down with sufficient clarity as force planning and resource allocation have to be done on that basis. *Therefore, if it does not function in an enterprise mode, it just cannot deliver.*

The entire field of defence logistics, which accounts for a major portion of defence expenditure has been viewed in Western nations as a 'business' for a long time, using the concepts and tools of the business world, not only for inventory management, but in all its aspects. *Logistics is expanded to include procurement and training*. The entire 'output' of logistics can be treated as 'input' for the 'output' of 'combat' effectiveness of the military forces. This would call for a critical look at how efficiently the inputs are combined and delivered to generate the desired output. Incidentally, PPBS did not pay attention to logistics, and was one of its principal shortcomings. This weakness of PPBS is now being overcome; the addition of 'E' is indicative of that fact, apart from other organisational reforms to make logistics more cost-effective.

That we have not been able to bring in the enterprise concept in defence would be evident from the routine way we deal with logistics. We attempt to confine logistics to in-house efforts, irrespective of costs. In fact, cost accounting of supporting and maintenance activities is totally absent. The most important step of having a cost-effective defence with proper linking of input to output would be to conceive of the entire logistics area as a business enterprise and bring in reforms to make it cost-effective.

An analyst with an economist's bent of mind could go further and conceive of defence as a giant firm with a corporate structure, in the business of production of national security, in an effective manner. It has monopoly position in providing security to the country from external aggression. The Raksha Mantri (RM) is the corporate head. The military Services are extraordinarily important partners in this enterprise.

This may be a mechanistic way of looking at this great enterprise, which may keep certain important factors out of the reckoning, but does help in focussing attention on other important aspects of defence, which can be helped by an analytical framework, whose ambit can be gradually expanded.

This way of viewing defence has three important implications:

- As it is in a monopoly position, from a social point of view, it has a heavy responsibility in interpreting threats, analysing alternative ways of meeting them and deciding upon cost-effective options within the resource limitations. Its shareholders are the common citizens of the country.

  Shareholders in all private corporations play a passive role; it is the priorities of managers that prevail.[27] Therefore, for defence which may be viewed as a corporation, political guidelines are necessary so that the defence manager's priorities are in conformity with the national security policy.

- The military Services, as the most important partners in this enterprise, and the Ministry of Defence, have joint responsibility in maintaining the morale of this enterprise for which true professionalism has to be encouraged . The human dimension of management is very important for sustaining morale, giving a boost to innovative spirit and achievement, and inculcating integrity among managers. The financial crisis in the USA, beginning in 2007, has led to existing management theories being given a critical look, drawn attention to incorporation of 'values' in the work life of managers as also to the liberal arts for a more fruitful management science.[28]
- The bureaucracy, both in the civil and military, is there to assist the RM in taking important decisions. Among other things, given the very high cost of defence which is the result of policy choices in the past, they have to pay major attention to policy choices, so that costs incurred in the foreseeable future are, in their judgement, commensurate with the returns. Even before the advent of programme budgeting , the Secretary of Defence in the USA had to play a crucial role in making annual force level recommendations. To quote Samuel Huntington regarding the position in 1950s, "The most important duty of the Secretary is to make the annual force level recommendations to the President. This includes advice as to: (1) the strength of forces; how many divisions, ships, wings; (2) the level of forces: percentage strength of divisions, etc.; (3) the readiness dates of forces; and (4) and deployment of forces. The translation of this advice into dollar terms furnishes the basis of the military budget recommendations."[29]

Force planning and likely deployment was supposed to be an annual exercise along with the annual budgetary exercise. That is how the linkage between input and output was established, though in a limited way. In this process, the Secretary of Defence had to play a most crucial role in giving final shape to the budget and advising the President of the USA in this regard. If the Secretary of Defence can play this role effectively with the assistance of the bureaucratic and analytical staff responsible to him, then the "Planning" aspect of PPB or the big "P", the most vital aspect of the process, is taken care of. There has been a lacuna in this regard in the PPBS process for which the QDR process had to be instituted to guide the PPBE process.

We do not have any such exercise, though it is accepted that it is the force level and force structure which determine the defence budget in every country. "The responsibility for force level recommendation is one which the Secretary cannot avoid. *It is the basic element of military policy*. If he attempts to escape this duty, he is only delegating it to someone else and tacitly approving his conclusions."[30] He has three options in this regard: "He may simply endorse the views of his military advisers and pay little heed to demands for economy and efficiency. In this event, he is only acting as a military spokesman. He may listen to fiscal experts, and adopt their recommendations without reference to strategic implications. Here he functions as a business manager. He may attempt to integrate military and economic considerations into an overall defense policy. In this case, he acts as a *policy strategist*."[31] We expect the RM to play the role of policy strategist. As Huntington puts it, the interest which the Secretary defends before the legislature is greater and the people should be broader than mere military interest. If the Secretary is to play the role of policy strategist, he should have the support of a 'combined military-civilian staff' responsible to him alone. "This staff should aid him in resolving disputes among the Services, distributing shortages among them, and helping him formulate policies on the budget, procurement, logistics, manpower , personnel, and intelligence…Only if the Secretary had a civil-military policy staff would it be possible to confine the Chiefs to their proper concern with war plans."[32] What is needed is the institutionalisation of the Secretariat viewpoint: "A small, competent corporate body to aid the Secretary in developing interests and advice surrounding him into a comprehensive military program."[33]

This is achievable even if we do not go though various reforms in the process and procedure, by instituting this kind of body to assist the RM to play the role of policy-strategist. This he is unable to do today because of lack of institutional support, and lack of correct perception of his role as a leader.

Strategic Objectives Lead to Programme Objectives

The defence enterprise, like any enterprise, is required to be conceived in terms of two main aspects: one aspect is the *cost* of defence, which in an imperfect sense can be equated with total defence expenditure, which has to be borne by the national exchequer; the other aspect is the *outputs* that help in providing external security to the nation.

As in the business world, the defence enterprise has to be conceived of consisting of various programmes for meeting specific objectives. A programme will have various sub-programmes and each sub-programme can be divided into various activities. Activities are to be categorised in such a manner that they meet the overall objectives of the programme. For each activity, which has to have an output, orientation should be linked to resource allocation for that activity, to know the cost of that activity. The costs of all the elements for a particular activity, irrespective of the budget category they come under, have to be considered to make a proper assessment of the cost and benefit of that activity, and to what extent it meets the objective of the programme or sub-programme. This objective has to be derived from the higher level objective of the programme. Programme level objectives are derived from the strategic objectives set up at a higher level.

Thus, there has to be a cascade of objectives from the higher to the lower level: a 'hierarchy of objectives'. There is no point in looking at output at a lower level of functioning (unlike other government organisations where it can be done), except to see to what extent it helps in meeting the higher level performance goals. Contribution to the achievement of the programme objective by each programme element (or activity) could be treated as a benefit, whose 'value' can be measured in terms of performance criteria laid down. Thus, the programme concept in resource allocation decisions, helps in linking costs to benefits(utility). Output can be seen in terms of the utility it provides for achieving effective defence.

Without the programme concept, there can be no performance evaluation.

When Robert McNamara, who was earlier President of Ford Motor Company, took over as US Defence Secretary in 1961, he brought with him the programme concept from the business world. President Kennedy gave him the twin task of achieving an effective defence force under a new defence strategy ('flexible response'),which would call for increase in the conventional force level and also of achieving the objective as economically as possible.

The strategic context determines what components the programmes should have, with what emphasis and objective. Therefore, programme decisions cannot be taken in a routine way, and call for high level deliberation.

Concentrating on the input aspects or the means alone, would not enable us to make a choice. But choice is the heart of decision-making. As Charles J. Hitch put the issue squarely, "Surely this choice is made by seeking the most efficient way of carrying out end products, such as achieving a nuclear deterrence force. And efficiency *within* programs can and should be sought more carefully than by pondering over proposed expenditures for total personnel, procurement, and construction. *Indeed, the use of these categories is likely to cause inefficiency.*"[34]

The most important step in linking input to output in an efficient way is to recategorise the expenditure on inputs in terms of programme categories that correspond more closely to '*end-product missions*'. He adds, "Officials can make more perceptive judgments about the importance to the nation of these missions than they can make about the worth of the categories." as listed in traditional input categories. He goes on to add, "If activities are grouped into more meaningful missions, however, it seems likely that better subjective appraisals of output can be made and also that better indicators of performance can be provided. There is no hope, of course, of measuring the ultimate worth of defense." Achievement of a particular force structure or changes in it, cannot be treated as output. The enemy's probable reaction has to be taken into account. The pertinent question is whether we are buying sufficient strength relative to that of the enemy. Thus, considering programme increments, we have to take into account the *enemy's probable response and the strategy he is likely to adopt. How would it counter our increased capability?* For these simple performance measurements, including change in the force structure would not reveal much . It is possible to make an analysis comparing alternative ways of carrying out broad missions, taking into account the enemy responses. That is where systems analysis comes in to establish a more scientific approach towards achieving the goals.

In India, we continue to view the costs of defence as composed of the costs of personnel, stores, travelling, equipment, etc., use them for formulation of the budget and for being approved by the Parliament. It does not serve any purpose in rational allocation of resources in defence. It is the accountant's budget, formulated on the basis of trend of expenditure and overall ceiling.

As the programme concept is yet to be adopted in resource allocation, we not only ignore the cost connotation of defence activities but also lose sight of the output aspect of each activity.

The Annual Procurement Plan (APP), the only plan that gets formulated today, involves attention to only the capital budget. Procurement decisions are subsidiary decisions which require to be guided by policy decisions as incorporated in programme decisions.

Confining attention to procurement as the main content of defence policy, as seems to be the case today, involves attention to only the capital budget, which represents 40 percent of the defence budget. What happens to the rest 60 percent of the defence budget, which represents a major portion of the defence cost? This portion of the defence budget has a major role in 'defence preparedness' which has to be treated as part of capability building integrated in the programme concept.

If we are not looking at the 'inputs' in their totality, how can we look for 'outputs'? Procurement of equipment also comprises inputs, which get their value from the outputs they are expected to produce. If we are not clear about 'outputs' in terms of missions and tasks to be performed, which are politically validated, then it is quite likely that we may not be making the right kind of procurement decisions. The concept of defence as an enterprise with its' input-output' concept is missing, and it gets reduced to functioning as another type of bureaucracy.

Looking at the concept of 'input-output' also makes us aware of what input is missing to achieve the right 'output-mix'. For example, the intelligence 'input' in the strategic context, is a most vital input in defence planning, for making the defence 'output' more relevant in terms of the evolving threat scenario. This would lead to formulation of strategic guidance.

In the competitive environment of the business world, the importance of market surveys and market intelligence, as inputs for management decision-making, to decide about what to produce and at what price, needs no emphasis. In defence, however, we do not have a proper mechanism for formulating strategic guidance on the basis of actionable intelligence and net assessment of our strength for our defence planning, to decide what should be the priorities in resource allocation decisions, keeping in view the *tasks and missions* to be performed.

Today, we have to plan for defence under uncertainty about likely future threats and their nature, unlike other government activities. It has to be understood that today's uncertainty is *strategic* in nature, and has to be addressed at the highest level to guide defence planning. Defence planning, to be relevant, can no longer be undertaken as a routine process nor can modernisation be treated as an 'on-going' process. For, this is an era of discontinuity, both in terms of the military-technical revolution that is taking place, and due to the profound change in international politics after the end of the Cold War, as a result of which the security scenario can no longer be extrapolated from the past.

So firm guidance from the top is absolutely essential for defence planning in the present world. "Strategic guidance" from the top becomes the most important 'Input', with a capital 'I', instead of a 'way' of linking 'means, and 'ends' or of linking of input to output, as traditionally thought. Strategic guidance would help in defining the outputs and broadly how to achieve them.

'Capability-based planning', by which as we tend to describe our defence planning today, using the US defence planning lexicon, would involve looking at all the aspects of defence activities to achieve defence objectives. What is, however, required is 'a sense of direction' which would be derived by our national strategic goals: how we define our position in the world; do we take a role in shaping our strategic environment in keeping with our *national security objectives*, the immediate strategic environment and the resource constraints. Relevant capabilities are to be defined in the context of these objectives. Can we have a framework here?

Strategy-To-Task Framework

An influencial framework for defence planning developed more than a decade ago by eminent US defence analysts in the above context, is called the *"strategy to task" framework.* Its theme is quite simple –there should be a coherent and visible set of relationships all the way from national military strategy down to operational objectives, tasks, and force employment concepts for accomplishing them.

This is aimed at by integrating strategic, programme and operational planning. To quote Glenn Kent and William Simons, the authors of this framework, "The first step in defense planning is to define a clear sense of direction that can be followed consistently and, thus, set the stage for providing the most relevant military capabilities within the constraints imposed. The challenge is to link the processes of developing and acquiring military equipment, and of organizing, training and equipping more closely to national security objectives."[35]

The point to note is that the aim should be to develop 'relevant' military capabilities, which means a combination of 'acquiring military equipment', 'organising' and 'training' to achieve defined national security objectives.

It is most important to have a strategy at the highest level (National Security Council) to give a sense of direction to defence planning. At the next level, of the ministry, to develop a strategy as a plan to achieve specific strategic objectives through programming. Strategy exists at all levels. The budget is also a strategic plan, but we, of course, do not recognise it as such. This problem exists elsewhere also. The "spending plans usually lack a *coherent audit trail* of how allocating resources in this manner achieves national security objectives."[36] There should be a hierarchy of defence planning objectives – from national security objectives down to specific military tasks – to establish the *necessary audit trail.*

Tasks are to be undertaken in pursuit of operational strategy. Military tasks are refined through the concepts of *employment of resources* by the commanders in the field on the basis of resources they expect to have at their disposal in pursuing specified operational objectives. "These concepts of employment indicate the possible allocation of effort among tasks: where, how frequently, for what scope and duration force elements would be applied to the accomplishment of various tasks."[37]

In this framework of strategy-to-task, 'objectives' rather than the context of 'conflicts' becomes the organising theme. It also reflects the fundamental relationship between strategy and objectives. A plan is a strategy of attaining objectives. As the authors put it, "Outlining a plan or strategy to attain stated goals at one level of organization simultaneously defines objectives to be achieved at the next level of implementation".[38]

An important advantage afforded by attention to this pattern of subordinate objectives "is its utility in supplying a clear audit trail from a higher level of policy articulation down through successive levels of administration"[39] Tasks will determine what programmes are to be given attention to. Without programmes to serve as a link, the audit trail between input and output cannot be established.

We can have other frameworks with other organising themes for linking input to output, keeping in mind the basic point that there must be a strategy for setting goals as also for attaining them and there has to be an audit trail down to the functional units to link strategy to operational planning.

A framework like this can be a powerful unifying device for the strategic community. It would help many players in the field to know how their tasks and responsibilities relate to one another.

Another framework for linking input to ouput, which has been under discussion for several years now, is called Effects-Based Operations (EBO). EBO is not just an operational concept. EBO operations need to be conceived and planned in a *systems framework* that considers the full range of direct, indirect, and effects that may be achieved by the application of military, diplomatic, psychological and economic instruments.[40] That is why linkages are important.

An important concept in EBO, in operational planning, is the 'centres of gravity', which if successfully attacked, would have enormous effect on the whole campaign. As Paul Davis points out, a fundamental problem is that in many conflicts, there may be no vulnerable centre of gravity to attack. For example, much of the enemy's support may come from outside its own borders or this may be distributed in such a way that it may be difficult to attack.[41] It may involve the entire population or the opinion of civil population could be decisive for continuing the war efforts.

The track record of EBO includes many failures or unintended consequences. The primary reason for this is that war and many contingency operations short of war, generally occur in an environment—which Paul Davis calls the *Complex Adaptive System* (CAS). A defining feature of CAS is that in some variables may behave in unpredictable ways.

Some principles have been identified to guide effective application of EBO-based planning. The following principles can be emphasised:

- Defence planning should focus on *mission-system capability*.
- Analysis pertaining to EBO should deal explicitly with probability and randomness. This may require application of *models and games*. Efforts should go into quantitative modelling.
- Use should be made of *exploratory analysis* that paves the way for innovative thinking for linking input to output
- Use should be made of *empirical information*, including that obtainable from history

For developing mission-system capability, mission-system analysis is required. "Mission-system analysis (MSA) is undertaken to guide mission-system planning (MSP), the purpose of which is to develop mission-system capabilities (MSC). The first tenet of MSA is that one organizes *thinking around output*."[42]

The reason for talking of MSA is that it has much in common with the 'strategies-to-task' approach, discussed above.

The linking of input to output, in the above context, has to be done through application of quantitative modelling and games and exploratory analysis to take care of the uncertainties of the likely effects of a given action.

The point also comes in that we cannot just talk of increasing 'capabilities' without taking seriously notions about how they would be employed or precisely how much of that capability would be needed. That would help in identifying 'capability gaps' for standard and non-standard contingencies. This approach would draw more attention to operational aspects in defence planning than has been the practice under PPBS. Of course, there has to be more realism in threat assessment so that attention is focussed on the right kind of capabilities.

Capability Framework and Investment Strategy

The focus of capability-based planning is not just on capability building by identifying 'gaps' . By what process are the 'gaps' identified? Presently, the individual Services determine what 'gaps' exist and formulate procurement proposals.

The essence of capabilities-based planning has been brought out in the Quadrennial Defence Review (QDR) Report 2006 of the US Department of Defence, which stressed on developing joint war-fighting capability. To quote, "The essence of capabilities-based planning is to identify capabilities that adversaries could employ and the capabilities that could be available to the United States, *then evaluate their interaction,* rather than overoptimize the joint force for a limited set of threat scenarios."[43]

Evaluation of likely interaction in a conflict scenario with an adversary, which would also involve analysis of what capabilities that adversary is likely to employ and to what extent joint capabilities can match them, should determine what defence planning should aim at.

This is where the input of intelligence is essential. It is in this context that QDR 2006 stressed two essential needs :

- "Need for considerably better fusion of intelligence and operations to produce action plans that can be executed in real-time."
- "Realization that everything done in this Department must contribute to joint warfighting capability."[44]
- On the basis of these, QDR 2006, called for *shift in emphasis* on various points, most of which are relevant for our defence planning:
    - "From separate military Service concepts of operation—to joint and combined operations."
    - "From single Service acquisition systems—to joint portfolio management."
    - "From an emphasis on ships, guns, tanks and planes—to focus on information, knowledge and timely actionable intelligence."[45]
    - "From single Service acquisition systems—to joint portfolio management."
    - " From an emphasis on ships, guns, tanks and planes—to focus on information, knowledge and timely actionable intelligence."[46]

Among the inputs, *'actionable intelligence'* becomes the most important input in capabilities-based planning, as it helps in identifying what capabilities the adversaries could employ, the likely interaction, and planning our capabilities to counter them in a cost-effective manner.

Assumptions behind the intelligence assessment have to be spelt out, so that these can be critically examined, before these can be treated as 'actionable'. The overwhelming importance of this input for decision-making is very clear in the context of Operation Iraqi Freedom. This related to the assessment of intelligence about possession of Weapons of Mass Destruction (WMD) by Iraq, before the launching of the operation. As George W. Bush states, "The conclusion that Saddam had WMD was nearly a universal consensus."[47]

But as it became subsequently clear, though there was a "widespread assumption" about the possession of WMD by Iraq, there was an intelligence failure in this regard.[48]

Bush observes, "In retrospect, of course, we all should have pushed harder on the intelligence and revisited our assumptions."[49]

The QDR 2006 defined *two fundamental imperatives* for the US Department of Defence:

- "To prepare for wider asymmetric challenges and to hedge against uncertainty over the next 20 years."
- "Implementing *enterprise-wide* changes to ensure that organizational structures, processes and procedures effectively support its strategic direction."[50]

The first point related to the investment strategy to be followed in capability building is to 'hedge' against an uncertain future. That would call for a long-term vision, with analysis of trends and then to decide about the likely scenario that would emerge, and prepare on that basis.

The second point that is equally important is the organisational dimension of strategy – it should be an enterprise-wide approach so that 'inputs'(efforts) may be more efficiently linked to 'outputs' (results) in the context of the strategic requirement.[51]

Let us briefly cover the investment aspect, with which defence procurement is concerned. Since the end of the Cold War, the information-led revolution in military affairs has brought about *discontinuous changes in the security environment*, adding to further uncertainty. "During periods of discontinuous change, defence planners are confronted with the need to affect large scale changes in military capabilities, doctrine and structure i.e. to transform the military. This need to transform must be balanced with the need to maintain sufficient capabilities to address immediate challenges to national security."[52]

"Transformation" does not just relate to acquisition of more capable equipment, as we tend to interpret it. It refers to a *process* by which military organisations affect large scale changes in capabilities, doctrine and organisation in response to discontinuities.[53]

The question is: what investment strategy is to be followed in the context of discontinuous change? This calls for more difficult choices than before, involving trade-offs. For example, in the context of US defence "the concept of 'investment' can be viewed as sacrificing current consumption (i.e. buying more of capital currently in production, such as the F/A-18E/F or maintaining the current force structure) in order to acquire a greater military advantage at some future point in time (e.g. by updating the national training infrastructure; improving military education; or increasing funding for research and development—to include developing the industrial capacity for new systems and capabilities)."[54]

This is how defence investment can be viewed in a period of discontinuous changes brought about by the revolution in military affairs, leading to a process of transformation of the military in various countries, in response to fast changing technologies and change in the security scenario.

What should be the investment strategy in such an environment? One important point would be the ability to *"identify those capabilities that stand to lose much of their value once major shifts occurs in a strategic environment, and those that will grow rapidly in value."* [55] *Another, would be the ability to minimise the costs imposed on investments by risk and uncertainty.* Investors typically develop strategies to hedge against risk and uncertainty. One such hedging strategy is mentioned above.

The QDR process starts with the Strategic Planning Guidance(SPG) which is issued by the US Secretary of Defence, a classified document right at the beginning of the process which lays down the objectives of the next defence plan. For QDR 2006, which was to cover the period 2006-11, guidance was issued one year earlier, which was supposed reflect the Pentagon thinking that traditional warfare capabilities must go hand in hand with a broader set of skills to deal with new security challenges presented by the global war on terrorism. The strategy was intended to guide the Services in preparing the defence budget and the accompanying six-year spending plan. This was expected to lead to a reexamination of earlier "priorities for weapon system modernization, many of which are designed largely to deal with conventional military threats."[56]

The important point is, it marked a shift away from earlier transformational ideas. Earlier transformational ideas were built on the basis that it would be a decade or longer, before the US military would face a formidable foe in the post-Cold War era. This was the notion of 'strategic pause', which gave rise to long-term projects with 'leap ahead ' capabilities.

But Afghanistan and the Iraq War led to reconsideration of how to transform the military.

The draft strategic guidance called for improved tactical airlift, a larger stable of non-lethal weapons, development of a sea base and shallow-draft, high-speed ships and better intelligence delivery to war-fighting units.[57]

There was also growing concern about the 'catastrophic' threat to high value targets. The other challenge was about development of 'disruptive technologies.

How to adjust to the new strategy became the main challenge for defence planning. It became necessary to look at important programmes to see where they fit in the context of new challenges. New planning goals were to be set to deal with irregular, catastrophic and disruptive threats. New priorities were to be set for programmes. This became possible because defence spending was on the basis of programmes which linked inputs to outputs. For 'each threat category', defence planning and policy staff had to "hone a strategic objective and link it to a policy goal" and the Secretary also wanted the policy staff to "quantify different kinds of major missions and strategy objectives to which the military will need to respond."[58] The new threat categories required "new joint concepts that set a new intellectual framework for response".[59]

The biggest transformation for the US was the concept of homeland defence developed after 9/11. This should be treated as a most significant part of the US defence. It is the Secretary of Defence who issues the guidelines for planning for homeland defence. The same concepts of capability planning are used as for US defence. That they are an integral part of each other would be evident from the fact that that the draft strategy directed the combatant commanders and senior Pentagon civilian officers to work out how a new focus on homeland defence "would change the needs for force structure, technology and management."[60] The strategy for homeland defence described a layered defence that improves the surveillance near the US borders and intelligence gathering overseas. This vision required vast constellations of air, land and sea sensors and better battle management systems and communication gear.

These capabilities are relevant also for US defence, therefore, they have to be seen in an integrated manner.

But decisions need to be made: choices are getting made and resources *are* being allocated. Therefore, a very critical component to any investment strategy is a clear statement by the Defence Ministry leadership describing its vision of the future competitive environment, the objectives to be achieved and the *tasks to be accomplished.* This means that investment planners in defence must have some understanding of "both the key strategic and operational challenges confronted by the armed forces, as well as the point-of-departure operational concepts for dealing with these challenges."[61]

The emphasis should be on tasks to be accomplished, which will determine what investments are to be made. Focus should not be just on capability building or acquiring technology, in a discontinuous environment. Introducing higher technology cannot be the central goal of defence planning and procurement. *The central focus should be on the tasks to be accomplished or the goals to be achieved.*

This change in focus can be put in terms of how economists often view change in emphasis in analysis and policy in the macro-economic context. For example , Jeremy Black's explanation in the context of military history that places emphasis on *tasks* rather than *technology*, can be viewed in this way. To quote, "Displacing technology, means in part, moving from a *supply side account* of military history, one that is focused on capability and its impact on warfare. Focus on tasking or setting the goals.., in turn, directs attention to a *demand-led* account."[62]

The *task* cannot be defined as just achieving victory as this is of limited value, "for the very nature of victory is dependent on the purpose of the military and its particular objectives, and, thus, on the *process of tasking*; which in narrow terms helps address the issue of prioritization between conflicting requirements. The selection of goals is also important to the issue of costs, as the constraints posed by the latter are made more or less serious by the needs to be addressed."[63]

Absence of the programme concept in our defence management means the link between inputs and tasks cannot be established. It also hinders issue of proper strategic guidelines, which can be meaningfully given only in terms of priorities to be assigned to various programmes in the context of tasks to be achieved and the costs that could be incurred.

As no strategic guideline in the above sense can be issued, the bureaucratic approach serves the purpose of controlling the cost of defence without reference to goals or tasks and linkage between input and output.

Emphasis on 'tasks to be accomplished' also helps us in determining the military capability to be built up in a robust manner. Stephen Biddle refers to a requirement of a "more robust conception of military capability".[64] . In this endeavour, three things are required. First, "analysis must disaggregate "capability' into separate dimensions of ability to control territory, ability to inflict casualties, and ability to control duration, and specify causal effects with respect to these dimensions directly rather than conflating them."[65]

Second, analyses must distinguish between offensive and defensive capability; a unidimensional 'capability' as a variable to "arbitrarily exclude politically important possibilities."[66]

Third , it should be an empirical analysis that must reflect force employment in the measures of capability, that is, how the forces would actually be used.

The implication is quite clear. The tasks to be accomplished should be the defining theme for capability-based planning. The concept of disaggregation of capability is a 'must', if we focus on tasks to be accomplished.

The essence of development of military capability cannot be captured by the level of the defence budget, by the rate it is growing or by concentrating on the capital budget.

One can draw an analogy in the field of economic analysis in distinguishing between the 'growth' and 'development' of an economy. The concept of growth relates to growth of national income indicated by GNP and GDP. 'Development' has a wider connotation referring to not only increase in national income, but also to aspects which lead to mutually reinforcing comprehensive effects to meet the social challenges, which include improving the capability of the people(through better health and education), improving their living standard up to a modest level in keeping with accepted criteria, maintaining social harmony, etc. In other words, the concept of 'development' has socio-economic dimensions that are missing in the concept of GNP which is taken *as a single undifferentiated total without a thought about their composition or pattern and associated socio-economic relations.* [67]

The concept of military capability on a similar analogy has to be viewed not as a total concept, but by disaggregating it into several aspects of capability which are interconnected and reinforce each other, to lead to an effective military power to meet the security challenges. The concept of sub-programmes, under programme budgeting, would help in disaggregating several aspects of a capability in a meaningful way.

For strategic decisions at the highest political level, the military capabilities can be treated as the 'means' for achieving the 'ends'. Ends at this level can be described broadly as the 'value positions' in determination of which political, economic, psychological and military factors overlap.

The aim should be to maximise the 'ends' or 'values' arrived at through well defined interaction among top level institutions. For an apt quotation in this regard, one can cite from the important book of Glenn Snyder, "*Rationality may be defined as choosing to act in a manner which gives the best promise of maximizing one's value position on the basis of a sober calculation of potential gains and losses, and probability of enemy action.*"[68]

It also follows from the above way of looking at strategy-making that the term *rational is applied to the process of achieving a goal or value rather than to the goal itself.*[69]

This is appropriately to be attended to at the Ministry level which would be concerned with setting strategic goals in conformity with policy goals which are to be set up at the highest political level .

Goals, however, are not given once for all time. There have been *historical transformations of goals. "The techniques of combat and production* change and, thereby modify the strategic value of positions."[70]

Effect of Changes in the Way of Production and Distribution of Commodities

There are also fundamental changes in the way production and distribution of commodities and services are getting organised in the world today, with the potency of seriously influencing economic relations between nations and thereby the strategic value positions to be aspired for. *For example, a major portion of our GDP is contributed by the service sector, which is a source of our strength as well as vulnerability.* Strength because of its contribution to the GDP and its growth, vulnerability because it depends on international demands, which may not endure in a conflict environment. This aspect has been dramatically brought out by Thomas L. Friedman, in his best seller, *The World is Flat*. Prevention of conflict among nations would be a major aim of international diplomacy, as the world would become flatter. With tongue slightly in cheek, he propounds the "Dell Theory of Conflict Prevention" which stipulates, "No two countries that are part of a major global supply chain, like Dell's, will ever fight a war against each other as long as they are part of the same global chain...They want to make just-in-time deliveries of goods and services—and enjoy the rising standards of living that come with it. One of the people with the best feel for the logic behind this theory is Michael Dell, the founder and chairman of Dell."[71]

He goes on to add, on the basis of the interview with Dell, that countries whose workers and industries *"are woven into a major global supply chain know that they cannot take an hour, a week, or a month off for war without disrupting industries and economies around the world and thereby risking the loss of their place in the supply chain for a long time, which would be extremely costly."* [72]

No strategic expert can ignore this aspect, that is, the importance today of much closer international interdependence in the generation of the national income of each nation than at any time in the past, making cooperation between nations an important component of the pursuit of national interest.

Mention is also made by Friedman , by way of illustration in support of his thesis, of the Indo-Pak crisis of 2002, which did not escalate beyond a point. While there were important factors like the deterrent effect of Pakistan's nuclear arsenal, Freidman adds, "India's role in global services was an important additional source of restraint on its behavior, and it was taken into account by New Delhi."[73] He refers to the worry expressed by software firms in Bangalore regarding the developments, which seem to have been explained to the government through the Confederation of Indian Industries (CII), "that providing a stable, predictable operating environment is now key to economic development."[74] As he notes, today "India is to the world's knowledge and service supply chain what China and Taiwan are to the manufacturing ones... General Electric's biggest research center outside the United States is in Bangalore, with seventeen hundred Indian engineers, designers and scientists."[75]

Similarly, significant increase in bilateral trade between neighbouring countries, aided by official policies, leads to increase in stakeholders on both sides who are interested in maintaining peace and a cooperative atmosphere.

These may be restraining factors, but are not deterrent factors. The conflict situation in the world, because of the scramble for limited resources (oil, water, minerals), may become more acute. Or, these may become a basis of broad understanding between nations and setting up of international norms as a conflict may aggravate the situation, affecting all countries adversely. The Indo-Pak Indus Water Treaty of 1960 is a shining example of cooperation for the distribution of the most scarce resource i.e. water.

The present oil price, which has jumped during the last decade, is a glaring example of what a conflict can do. The earlier jump in 1973 is also attributed to conflict in the Middle East.

Going by history, aggression is not always determined by a rational calculation of costs. Or many of the wars would not have taken place. There are also problems of perception and misperception between adversaries which affect strategic policy-making, and may aggravate the situation, beyond control.

Therefore, preparing for countering probable aggressive behaviour of adversaries, by developing suitable capabilities and doctrine, would continue to be prime objective for the defence business.

At the top level of strategy-making, political, economic, cultural and military factors play interacting roles in determining the 'ends' to pursue.

The issues of strategy-making at the highest level have an enduring quality of their own. One still learns from Thucidides who saw an intimate connection between internal and external politics, his stressing on uncertainty, chance and friction in the conduct of warfare; from Clausewitz, who considered the notion of conflict as the 'collision of two living forces', and from Sun Tzu who described the 'art of war' and what can be called, the 'indirect approach'.

What is, however, to be emphasised is that it is the element of *force* which distinguishes defence strategy and planning from purposeful planning in other branches of human activity.

Next Level of Strategy: Linking 'Means' to 'Ends'

At the next level of strategy-making in linking 'means' and 'ends', management tools, technological factors, and consideration of cost factors play key roles in the development of alternatives and decisions are made on the basis of how best to reconcile the ends and means. Various management tools can be used to achieve cost-effective solutions to problems. The Ministry of Defence and Service Headquarters are primarily concerned at this level of strategy-making.

But, can the national strategy and military strategy be differentiated in such a way that national strategy determines military strategy and military strategy in turn determines operational strategy?

This is how it is generally presented, as a classic model of hierarchy of functions. It is the generally accepted view that "political decisions and military implementation are discrete functions, sequential and independent..."[76] Such an approach eases civil-military friction, but has other risks. This can leave the gap between policy objectives and military operations unfilled, as well as that between capabilities and their *purpose,* in terms of attaining policy objectives. This kind of division of responsibility can leave the 'strategic gap' unfilled. "To keep concepts clear, it is less useful to think of the three realms—policy, strategy, and operations—than to think of strategy as a *bridge* between policy and operations. A bridge allows elements on either side to move to the other. As a plan that bridges the realms of policy and operations, effective strategy must integrate political and military criteria rather than separate them."[77]

There are basic challenges in developing strategy. The first is how to use force to achieve political objectives. The second is how to do it at an acceptable cost. The first, while daunting, is easier for a superpower than for most countries. So what is relevant for others? This issue was not addressed, *but presumably it is the cost considerations which will be the overwhelming factor in determining what objectives would be set and how to achieve them within an acceptable cost.*

Betts was essentially analysing the relationship between ends and means in war conditions and what could be a good example of strategy-making in a conflict situation and how to integrate political aims and military requirements. The linear model does not work and "straight line thinking puts the operational cart before the political horse."[78]

But what could be an integrating factor in peace-time conditions when one is to prepare for likely challenges and cost considerations become the most important consideration in strategy-making? Formulating tasks, keeping in view political, economic and operational considerations, at the decision-making level in the Ministry of Defence, would provide the basis for integrating political aims and operational requirements.

Linking input to output is facilitated by the economist's concept of the short run and long run in analysing the equilibrium conditions.

In the longer run, all factors become variable. "Some are variables subject to our control, some are variables subject to the enemy's control, some are subject to nobody's contol. But all are variables. Moreover, they are interdependent."[79] Military force composition and development decisions which are the 'output' aspects take two or three to ten years or more to fructify. This fact alone vastly increases the number of interdependent variables which are to be considered. As a practical measure, one has to factor out those variables which are especially important and 'suppress' the rest.

Decision-making becomes somewhat easier if there is a long-term view of availability of resources. In the medium and long terms, the provision in defence budgets would provide resources for various types of infrastructure, manpower planning, training needs and building leadership at the subordinate level which are treated as 'inherited resources' in the short run and take care of most of the 'intangibles'. *Thus, a medium term (say five years) view of availability of defence resources makes it possible to link defence inputs to outputs in a more meaningful way than confining attention to annual budgets and annual plans. Defence capability building is a long-term business.*

Without the framework of a medium and long-term plan, annual defence budgets cannot be linked to defence outputs. Defence outputs need to be modified to meet changing situations, which may call for modification of some of the on-going programmes, annually. Therefore, we cannot talk of fixed five-year plans and fixed programmes. Investments made in the past are generating output now and investments made now will generate output in the future. That is why we should have a rolling five or six-year defence plan and correspondingly a rolling five or six-year budget. It has to be a dynamic plan as modifications in programmes may have to be made in view of changed circumstances. So planning and programming become year round activity.

We confine our attention to annual plans. By doing so, at best, we can link the defence budget to annual plans, but not to the defence output. And, by formulation of defence plans for fixed five years and long-term plans for fixed fifteen years as a backdrop of the annual plans, we rob the plans of their dynamic elements, with the basic risk that the outputs, when they get generated out of on-going investments, may lose their relevance and value.

On the basis of the analogy of a firm's option in the short run, while most of the costs are *fixed* in nature (cost of existing force structure), others are variable(additional expenditure on men and material for additional activities), it is the variable expenditure which gets managerial attention as it can be controlled and can produce additional output. Ninety per cent of the defence budget gets spent on the existing force structure and, therefore, in the nature of fixed cost viewed in the short run perspective of one year, for which the annual budget is provided. It is viewed as 'obligational' expenditure, whose cost is automatically provided in the budgetary process. In the short run perspective, the cost of the existing force structure is taken as given; it is the budget that is left after meeting the obligatory amount that gets attention as to how to spend it, which is not more than 10 percent of the budget.

But a firm in the competitive world does not confine its attention to the short run. It focusses its attention equally on the long run as it has to produce its output at the lowest possible cost, maintaining its quality while striving to expand its business. In the long run, all the costs are treated as variable and one can go in for a more efficient plant and equipment, organise production in a more efficient way. That is why in microeconomics, the long-term cost curve is shown to be lower than the short-term cost curve, showing evidence of better planning, better utilisation of resources and a more efficient plant. Therefore, from the point of long-term cost, the major driving force of the defence cost, which is the force structure and its level, should get major attention to make it affordable as also relevant in a future conflict scenario. The monopoly position of defence enables it to disregard the cost aspect.

If we have to bring in cost-consciousness, we have to simulate some of the conditions of a competitive world in carrying out its activities. We have already mentioned about logistics being treated as inputs which should deliver in a cost-effective manner, as in the business world, where the customer-supplier relationship should be established. This should be the obvious step in simulating the competitive conditions of the business world. We have done it in a limited way for the ordnance factories. This should cover the entire field of logistics by introducing customer-supplier relations where the price aspect should be given major consideration to decide about alternative ways and sources of supply. Conceiving defence as a business would generate this attitude.

There should also be explicit constraints on the resources that would be made available in the medium term to the Services for each of their programmes, so that decisions on trade-offs get made, to achieve the outputs in an economical manner. In the business world, enterprises have to generate their own resources by earning them which makes it necessary for them to look critically at all aspects of their activities to achieve economy, and risk management becomes a central concern.

If budgets are available to defence on the basis of trend of expenditure and ability to spend, then the business outlook cannot develop, nor is it necessary. For, whatever money is required, would be provided. The so-called annual 'ceiling' on the defence budget is no ceiling as the phenomenon of returning unspent money from the budget is a continuing feature of defence budgeting in India. There has to be a budget ceiling for every year for a five-year period, *in a multi-year budgeting framework. This is necessary for control of obligations as also for generating a long-term view in investment making. A longer term view has to be generated by putting in long-term budget constraints programme-wise, so that priorities get maintained.*

Not instituting a multi-year budgeting framework for strict adherence was a major failure of the PPBS framework in US defence.

In India, institution of the five-year defence plan has become an exception rather than a rule. Multi-year budgeting is yet to be accepted as a tool of expenditure management. Parliament, by sanctioning the annual budget, puts an overall limit to the cost of defence and annual appropriation accounts are put up, indicating how the amounts sanctioned have been spent. As the budget is totally input oriented, not much light is shed on what kind of returns become available for spending the sanctioned annual amount. So, in effect, outputs do not get linked to inputs as there is no framework of medium-term plans nor concept of programmes, which itself is a multi-year concept.

Cost of Defence and Choice of Strategy

Each strategy has a cost, in terms of forces required to implement it, operations and maintenance expenses and equipment. The choice of the relevant strategy has to be made by the policy-makers, after balancing various needs, keeping in view the ability to bear the cost by imposing additional taxes and the possibility of deficit spending.

The choice of financing has to be prudently done keeping in view the state of the economy. In the 1960s, S.S. Khera (retired Cabinet Secretary), in an important book, *Problems in Defence*, drew attention in an important chapter entitled "Cost of Defence" to its various components and how they should be related to national policies, keeping in view the various challenges facing developing countries like India. He stated that they "must trim their policies, their international postures, their domestic economic effort, their military plans and strategies, to their resources."[80] In other words, the defence policy and strategy to be followed in a developing nation is constrained by the availability of resources and meeting of competing needs.

The overall cost factor cannot be disregarded too long, as it will be detrimental to the fiscal health of a country and its economy. If development gets neglected, then, in the long run, the resources available for defence would be adversely affected.

Khera also raised some basic questions in the mid-Sixties when the defence budget had touched a figure of Rs 1,000 crore. To quote, "A nation that is spending Rs 1,000 crore a year on defence needs to ask itself as to the kind of security it obtains for the money. Does the defence strategy devised by those in charge of the defence apparatus conform to the realities of the situation, the nature and extent of the threat, and the prospective ways in which the threat is likely to develop? Is the defence apparatus, including particularly the army divisions and their equipment, and the air force, designed and developed as a suitable instrument of that policy?"[81]

We have to add the Navy, along with the Army and the Air Force, as it is consuming now 18 percent of the defence budget, as against 5 per cent when Khera wrote the above piece. As against Rs 1,000 crore, we are now spending close to Rs 2 lakh crore. The questions raised by Khera still remain valid, and more so.

The point is: how do we attempt to answer these valid questions? What kind of management and analytical apparatus have we developed since then to answer such questions? The answer would probably be: not much.

In this context, operational analysis becomes important, to bring some clarity to ends which are achievable, and the alternatives available in this regard. For example, in the *Statement on Defence Estimates,* of the UK,

1973, it is stated that operational analysis studies have been increasingly applied to solve this problem, "...concerned with objective choice between alternative options...have been increasingly applied to questions of defence strategy and to the major policy decisions which face NATO. They continue to help in solving problems of resource allocation within the defence budget, particularly in the equipment field."[82]

The political dimensions of strategy are no doubt the most important in the pursuit of a grand strategy. But as the strategy of 'long haul' of President Eisenhower showed, the economic aspects are equally important even for a developed country. The defence strategy, according to him, should be such that resources allocated to defence do not jeopardise the economic growth of the American economy. Economic security was the basis of military security, therefore, military spending had to be contained within acceptable limits as per fiscal prudence. The security policy was framed accordingly.

He also warned that the nexus of the *military-industrial complex* harms the nation's interest by influencing policy-making in defence procurement. This threat is always present in the procurement field for all major powers.

As far as arms sellers are concerned, they are in what the economist calls a monopolistic competition situation, as each sells a differentiated product in the market relating to a weapon system meeting the same goal. The products are similar in that they broadly meet the operational requirements, but, at the same time, are somewhat differentiated in the sense that each has a feature or two which differentiates one from the other.

As the requirements cannot be laid down in great detail, the choice would ultimately depend on which of the features, which differentiate the products, are given importance by the user, from the operational point of view, apart from the price aspect. Price may or may not be the determining factor, depending on the importance assigned to the feature differentiating the product from others. Here there is lot of scope for discretion and judgement.

Keeping the defence budget around 2.5 percent of the GDP (keeping the size of the GDP in view) as in our case, has its own connotation for the *force level* one can maintain.

Colin Gray, while bringing out the importance of various other dimensions of strategy, highlights the importance of the level of the defence budget in adopting a strategic posture, "This matter of sheer quantity is of utmost importance because it is the defense budget that transforms strategic ideas into steel, high explosive, and plutonium."[83]

The USA, being a superpower, can determine its strategy with greater flexibility than others. For others, particularly for a developing nation, 'ends' have to be more closely attuned to the 'means' available. Limitation of means in determination of the strategic posture becomes the dominant consideration. Therefore, the tools for achieving economy and efficiency in defence expenditure have to receive more, not less, attention than for a developed nation.

In this connection, one can refer to Raymond Aron's distinction between two terms, *security* and *force*. Maximisation of resources for development of forces and other indices of power does not necessarily involve maximisation of security. "In any system, there exists an *optimum of forces*; to exceed it will produce a dialectical reversal. Additional force involves relative weakening by a shift of allies to neutrality or neutrals to the enemy camp."[84] One could also add that it may lead to joining up of enemies.

And he adds, "If security were, by evidence and necessity, the preferential objective, it would be possible to determine rational behavior *theoretically*. It would be necessary, in each circumstance, to determine the optimum of force and to act in consequence."[85]

The achieving and maintaining of an optimum force level politically determined should be one of the basic goals of the security policy to maintain peace.

Apart from security, the objectives of *power, glory and idea* have also shaped the diplomatic-strategic behaviour of nations. In this context, the pursuit of "national interest" is often invoked as an objective of diplomatic–strategic policy and, consequently, in determination of the defence policy. It is argued that force level and structure should be determined by a broadly defined national interest.

As Aron points out, security, power, glory, ideas are essentially heterogeneous concepts which cannot be reduced to a single term like national interest. "If the rivalry of states is comparable to a game, what is 'at stake' cannot be designated by a single concept, valid for all civilizations for all time...The plurality of concrete objectives and of ultimate objectives forbids a rational definition of 'national interest' even if the latter did not involve, in itself, the ambiguity that attaches to collective interest in economic science."[86]

The economist has no other definition of *interest* than the scale of preferences, variable from individual to individual, or the maximisation of *utility* measured by monetary quantities. It is very difficult to shift from *individual interest* to *collective interest.* The concept of the Pareto optimum in welfare economics has its own limitations.

It is equally difficult to reduce national interest to collective interest, except in a very limited sense to remind the leaders that the security and greatness of the state must be the objective of diplomacy .[87]

Kenneth Boulding in his classic work, *Conflict and Defense* commented forcefully, "What must be emphasized is that national interest is not a clearly defined quantity like a physical magnitude; it is a psychological magnitude that may be drastically changed by internal shifts in power or changes in philosophy or value systems within the ruling hierarchy or even of the mass of people."[88]

One essential element in the national interest concept is that it is "vague and ill defined or defined at certain salient points", therefore, it can hardly be the proper basis for military posture or force planning.

But the overall cost of defence cannot be ignored too long by any country, however well-endowed it is with resources. We have already mentioned about Eisenhower's strategy to reduce defence expenditure from the high level of the Korean War. Economy in defence expenditure was the main goal and the strategy was formulated accordingly.

The Vietnam War took defence expenditure to an unsustainable level from the mid-Sixties onward, because of a larger commitment of US forces there.

There was growing opposition to the war and the efforts had to be scaled down by the end of the 1960s. During the Nixon era, the US troops were reduced from Vietnam in stages before the final withdrawal in the 1970s.

The cumulative cost of war and inability to bear the overall cost in terms of both human and material, led to change in the grand strategy. The Vietnam War also brought out that the 'centre of gravity' in a modern democracy is public opinion, which is the psychological dimension of war-fighting. This also affects the doctrine to be adopted. This is more evident in asymmetric warfare. With this dimension, it becomes more difficult to link input to output, but the economic concept of 'means' and 'ends' remains as relevant as in other circumstances.

President Nixon shifted the defence planning strategy from the 2½- war scenario (Russia, China, and one smaller confrontation) to a 1½-war scenario (Russia and one smaller confrontation).[89] Diplomatic initiatives were taken to come closer to China. Costs determined the strategic planning.

In the UK, right from the beginning of the 1980s and even earlier, economic factors tended to dominate strategic thinking, which led to questioning of the basic assumptions and the possibility of maintaining the existing force structure. It was clearly recognised that economic factors limited the freedom of choice on alternative defence postures.[90]

One of the factors to take note of in the context of assessing defence cost, is the factor of 'defence inflation', that is, the annual growth in the cost of personnel and equipment. This is an abiding feature in defence. This feature of defence makes it difficult to reduce the defence budget even if the economy passes through a difficult period.

For example, Morarji Desai, the Indian Finance Minister who was always keen to present a balanced budget, and always very concerned about rising defence expenditure, expressed his inability to reduce the expenditure. In presenting the central government budget as Finance Minister for 1967-68, (when the country was passing through a difficult economic period), he stated that the hoped for "levelling off, leave alone reduction in defence expenditure" could not be achieved, since the cost of maintaining the defence Services and supplies had gone up "during the past twelve months as a result of both the internal price rise and change in exchange rate."[91]

Since that period, the annual increase in the price of new equipment, which as per available estimates goes up by at least 10 per cent per annum, has become the most important factor for 'defence inflation'. This is a universal feature.

This factor alone, the world over, makes it imperative to review the force structure from time to time, even if the fiscal picture of a country is not dismal. The replacement costs of existing equipment, which, on the average, has an expected life of 25 to 30 years or more, could be ten times more than the existing cost. To quote John Baylis regarding the experience in the UK, "With the cost growth, especially in equipment, considerably outstripping the general level of inflation, even the annual 3 per cent increases in real terms in the defence budget were not sufficient to allow the government even to implement the reduced defence plans of its predecessors. There was also the associated problem that more and more of the overall defence budget was being taken up with equipment purchases."[92]

The 1981 UK White Paper recognised the change in the defence environment, which every strategic review should do, particularly the ability of "modern weapons to find targets accurately and hit them hard at long ranges…increasing the vulnerability of major platforms such as aircraft and surface ships." To meet this and indeed to exploit it, the White Paper argued that the balance of investment between platforms and weapons needed to be altered "so as to maximise real combat capability."[93]

In view of the problems associated with rising costs and effectiveness analysis, the economic concept of *balance of investments,* is invoked to get proper returns for the investment made. The concept of diminishing marginal returns for investments made in a particular direction of capability building becomes helpful in deciding where to reduce investment. Any change in the security environment has to be taken into account in assessing the returns.

The overall conclusion of the 1981 review was that Britain could not go on as before and "substantial and uncomfortable changes" were necessary. Thus, economic factors became a predominant factor in strategy-making as they vitally affected the *'affordability'* aspect.

As nuclear capability was not to be disturbed in view of the Cold War compulsions, the effect had to be on conventional forces. The idea of 'defensive deterrence' as a strategic posture came to be advocated in some quarters. It implied a different emphasis in force structure than before. As Greenwood points out, " Action would include enhancing the home base's coastal, territorial and air defences. On the naval side, that would mean great stress on mine-hunters and fast patrol boats at the expense of provision of bigger ocean-going warships."[94]

This is not to indicate what actually needed to be done, but to make the point that economic factors, particularly the cost factors, make the existing force structure, because of cost inflation, unaffordable, over time, making it necessary to look at various options for change in the strategic posture, and to choose the force structure that would support the new strategy, which could, at the same time, be cost-effective.

Drawing attention to this UK review is important for two reasons: (a) it was done in the midst of the Cold War when strategic challenges were quite acute and the UK was an important partner in NATO; (b) the US defence budget, during the same period (Reagan Administration) got a surge as it interpreted the threat scenario differently, and fiscal stability was not regarded as a concern. The overall effect was a big rise in defence costs without a significant impact on the force structure.

Correct interpretation of threats is the basic ingredient of a defence policy as also achievement of cost-effective solutions.

In the case of the UK, analysts clearly saw that commitment to real annual increases in military spending of 3 percent or thereabouts would have to be abandoned if the government had to control overall expenditure, which was essential at that time.

In this circumstance, the appropriate policy of the UK government was, as David Greenwood suggested, *"to set a budget ceiling at the existing expenditure level and cut the nation's military coat according to this amount of cloth."*[95]

Cutting the nation's military coat according to the cloth available is an abiding concern as continuous high fiscal deficits have their own security implications. If allowed to linger for long, this would call for drastic change in the strategic posture.

Economic factors make it imperative to control the cost of defence. Control of cost involves a review of force structure which is the main driving force of defence costs; which, in turn, affects the strategic posture. As John Baylis pointed out, for the UK, even with continuation of the 3 percent real increase per annum in defence spending (inherited from the previous government) it was still not possible to sustain the then existing defence programme. To quote the UK, government's Defence White Paper of 1981, "even the increased resources we plan to allocate cannot adequately fund all the force structures and all the plans for their improvement we now have."[96]

We are not attempting an historical analysis, but trying to show from instances in the past and present how economic factors contribute to shaping the strategic posture. As also what steps are taken to reconcile the cost of defence and the objectives to be achieved through periodic strategic reviews. Objectives get modified because of the inability to bear costs. If the threat is defined in a more alarming way, on the basis of certain perceptions, then defence expenditure can surge without comparable benefits in terms of security or capability building, as happened in the Reagan Administration. Perceptions got modified subsequently on the basis of more objective assessments, but defence expenditure continues to surge, as it has its own momentum. Strict limitation of defence expenditure came through legislative intervention in 1986. After the end of the Cold War, deliberate efforts were made by several force and strategy reviews i.e. Base Force Review, Bottom-Up Review, to bring down the cost of defence in the USA.

In the present century, from 2004 onwards, in the Bush era, the high costs of the Iraq War as also the war in Afghanistan, and following of the strategy of Global War on Terror (GWOT), have led to major increases in defence costs in the USA. At the initiation of the war, Defence Secretary Rumsfeld and the Office of Management and Budget estimated the costs to be in the range of $50-$60 billion.[97] There is Congressional Research Service (CRS) Report for Congress, which brought out that with the enactment of the FY 2010 Defense Appropriation Act, the US Congress had approved a total of $1.086 trillion for carrying out the wars. Out of this amount, it was estimated that the Iraq War accounted for $748 billion.[98]

Among the factors driving the costs of war was the increased cost of personnel. The estimates did not take into account the long-term costs like the disability costs for veterans and the cost of replacing the equipment used in the war. A very important factor has been the rise in the price of fuel. Stiglitz points out, “The world price of oil has risen from around $25 per barrel when the war started to close to $100 per barrel as this book goes to press”[99]

The Iraq War had the most far-reaching global consequence in terms of rise in the fuel price. “In global terms, the jump in oil prices since the start of the war dwarfs all other costs. The higher oil prices assumed in our moderate scenario represent a direct cost to the world economy of approximately \$1.1trillion, taking into account the macroeconomic repercussions."[100] Since this estimation, the fuel price has stabilised around \$115 per barrel, affecting adversely the economies all over the world. In the Indian context, the prices of food articles are also influenced by oil prices, leading to food inflation. "High oil prices push prices of fertilizers upward, raise transportation cost and also lead to increased diversion of agricultural production towards bio-fuels."[101] The cost of food production is going up year after year, while the returns are not adequate, making it an increasingly unprofitable venture.

The 1973 Yom Kippur War also led to a surge in oil prices which almost brought to an end the era of planning for economic development in India. Thus, any war anywhere in the world, because of interdependence between economies, can have extremely adverse effects on economic stability in the developed countries and growth in the developing countries.

When the strategy for Operation Iraqi Freedom was formulated, as stated above, it was anticipated that it would mean an inexpensive conflict. "Instead", as Joseph Stiglitz (while making the cost assessment in 2008) states, "We have a war that is costing more than anyone could have imagined. The cost of direct military operations – not even including long-term costs such as taking care of wounded veterans—already exceeds the cost of the twelve-year war in Vietnam and more than double the Korean War. And, even in the best case scenario, these costs are projected to be almost ten times the cost of the first Gulf War, almost a third more than the cost of the Vietnam War, and twice that of World War I."[102]

Many questions get raised in hindsight about the objectives. But decisions had to be made at that time, when after 9/11, decision-makers in the USA were more concerned to ensure that such attacks did not recur. But why was the cost aspect not kept in view?

For providing some sort of general answer to such questions which may recur, we may draw upon the observations made by Richard Betts (written before Operation Iraqi Freedom) in the article quoted above relating how to bridge the gap between policy and operations. Citing the strategy followed in 'Operation Desert Storm', he observes that if the attention was confined after August 1990, and the assumption was made that the objectives of the operation "were to expel Iraq from Kuwait and cripple Baghdad's ability to undertake aggression again, the Bush strategy worked effectively and efficiently. Iraq was routed at the minimum cost to Washington... American military partnership worked well together in integrating political aims and military requirements."[103]

Many believed that the strategy should have aimed at the ouster of Saddam. But this would have ignored other elements of the strategy, namely, risk and costs. "A strategy that would have guaranteed the ouster of Saddam would have been far riskier. Its costs would have risen as the odds of success fell. The American forces would have had to take Baghdad, which, in turn, would have dramatically raised the probability of overtaking the *culminating point of victory.*"[104] This concept of 'culminating point of victory', is important in deciding about the cost and benefit. In the Korean War in 1950, "the culminating point was probably the Inchon landing and restoration of South Korea upto the 38th Parallel, before the march to Yalu and the Chinese intervention. In Iraq in 1991, it was not far beyond where policymakers decided it was."[105]

What about the culminating point for Operation Iraqi Freedom? One can only speculate. But if regime change was the main objective, then probably the culminating point was reached when President George W. Bush declared aboard the USS *Abraham Lincoln* on May 1, 2003, "Major operations in Iraq have ended..."[106] It was also declared that the mission in Iraq had been accomplished.

But "the transition from dictatorship to democracy" which subsequently became an objective, took a lot more time as the insurgency broke out.

Here also, the cost aspect is only one dimension and more relevant in the short-term context. The long-term perspective of security from the US perspective, by bringing in a democratic form of government in that troubled region, can be more relevant than the short-term cost calculations.

How to pay for the war is another abiding concern of economists. In the case of operations in Iraq and Afghaistan, the cost had been financed by borrowing. Taxes were not raised to pay for the war.

To quote Stiglitz again, "Deficit spending gives the illusion that the laws of economics can be repealed, that we can have both guns and butter. But, of course, the laws are not repealed. The costs of war are real even if they have been deferred, possibly to another generation."[107] Even a superpower is not above these laws.

As per estimates by the Congressional Budget Office (CBO) made in 2008, to carry on with the existing strategy would have meant for the Obama Administration for the period 2008-13, an average annual increase in the defence budget by about 24 percent over that estimated by the earlier Administration. It was argued, "With a large increase in funding unlikely, it seems reasonable that President Barack Obama will attempt to solve the Pentagon's financial problems by seeking a *closer match of budgetary resources with the overall defense and national security strategy.*"[108]

But since budgetary priorities change rather slowly, it was argued that the aim should be to integrate at least "some of the hard budgetary choices into a coherent strategic framework that truly connects means with ends ..."[109]

But then President Obama had also agreed to a surge in force level in Afghanistan, as the security conditions demanded it. The additional cost has to be seen in the context of longer term reduction in cost if it allows speedy withdrawal of US forces afterwards.

The strategy-resource gap has, however, brought about renewed debates about the grand strategy to be followed by the United States in the next decade, as was done under the Eisenhower Administration, so that strategic choices are dictated by economic realities and a grand strategy is put in place to reconcile various aspects of the nation's long-term interest.

The US Congress passed the Budget Control Act (BCA) in 2011 to address its unsustainable long-term finances, particularly, high costs in its discretionary spending. Under the BCA, adjustments fall in the discretionary portion of the federal budget (constituting 38 percent of the US federal budget). Expenditure for security programmes in the Defence Department and its partners, accounts for half of discretionary federal spending. This means that the security sector will shoulder the major share of adjustment.

It was indicated that the Department of Defence would soon submit plans for $450 billion of spending reductions over 10 years from the Five-Year Defence Plans (FYDP).[110]

There are other challenges that make a strategic review necessary as was done several decades ago under the Truman and Eisenhower Administrations. The diffusion of military technologies and the substantial increase in anti-access/ area denial capabilities in the potential adversaries may make it more difficult for the USA to project military power across the globe, than earlier. There are also challenges of home security, for which significant resources have to be allocated.

These challenges have important implications for two important activities, namely, 'investment' in military assets and creation of 'value' in terms of war-fighting capabilities. The investment in traditional capabilities — ships, aircraft and tanks — provide utilities for a long time by increasing war-fighting capabilities. But increase in the enemy's counter-measure capabilities directed against these assets tends to decrease their utility. One can take counter-counter-measures to protect the value of these assets. Depending on the progress of technology, progress in enemy counter-measures may lead to significant decline in the value of traditional assets, bringing in the phenomenon of what can best be described as *'wasting assets'*. This brings out the urgent necessity of rebalancing the investments in assets, particularly as today, the technology of counter-measures has advanced a lot, nullifying the value of many traditional assets. Keeping in view these challenges , US Secretary of Defence Robert Gates, pointed out the need for a more 'balanced' military. As Andrew F. Krepinevich argued, "What is needed is nothing short of a fundamental strategic review of the United States' position in the world—one similar in depth and scope to those undertaken in the early days of the Cold War."[111] The strategy must recognise "two wasting assets of the non-military kind: the erosion of the United States' financial position and the reality that the United States' allies will no longer shoulder a larger share of the collective- security burden… . All this suggests that the United States must pursue a more modest strategy than that advanced by the Bush Administration in the wake of 9/11—one that reflects a better balance between goals and resources, features a reduced emphasis on *wasting military assets,* and involves vigorous identification , development and exploitation of new areas of advantage."

The kind of warfare that one is likely to be engaged in or a strategic combination of both symmetrical and asymmetric warfare, would determine the parameters to value the military assets. How the enemies would deploy their capabilities to make strategic gains would have to be studied in detail, keeping in view their history, their culture and their strategic outlook.

Therefore, probable conflict scenarios need to be drawn out, a number of them, with a lot of interaction with intelligence agencies, diplomats and the strategic community.

In a situation of uncertain future , drawing up of threat scenarios and meeting them in conceptual terms, language, methodology and tools of economics can be used. 'Landscapes' can be drawn incorporating threats and their likelihood and the probability of the army getting involved in it. This landscape can be generated using various inputs: guidance from leaders, national intelligence estimates and strategic planning guidance. This landscape can be called the Threat and Likelihood or L&T scenario. In the model, as a given circumstance becomes more *likely,* the threat to national interest becomes more severe, the *utility* of investment actions that provide required army capability to address the circumstance is greater than the *utility* of investing against circumstances that are not at this level of threat or likelihood.

The results of this analysis can be combined with an analysis of the existing budget and investment categories to produce *a portfolio of investments that provides a mix of material capability for the army.*[112]

The L&T plot then can provide a useful tool for prioritising the circumstances for budgeting purposes. *The prioritisation is accomplished using a utility function.* It is possible to use a famous model in economics used in discussing distribution of income, called the Cobb-Douglas utility function for this kind of analysis. In this formulation, the marginal utility of a change in threat is the inverse of marginal utility of a change in likelihood.[113] Increasing budget priority is given to alternative circumstances that are rated more highly in this utility plot.

As costs considerations (and resource availability) become the determining factor for overall strategy-making, the concepts of marginal costs and marginal benefits in allocation of resources become an important exercise in arriving at a more balanced military.

Because of the diffusion of technologies and development of anti-access/area denial capabilities, the value of many of the traditional military assets have the character of 'wasting assets', and all major powers have to make a strategic review to 'balance' the capabilities.

An in-depth military review has to bring out which assets are declining in value,and which are increasing in value, in terms of operational environment, so that a proper balance may be struck. Investments in assets like Unmanned Aerial Vehicles (UAVs), submarines with anti-submarine capabilities, advanced ammunition, missiles with more and more precision, cyber and space capability, would continue to give higher and higher returns as joint warfare becomes a reality. These investments have to be balanced by investment in those assets whose value has declined in relation to both cost of investment and cost of their maintenance.

Marginal Cost and Marginal Benefit

How do you achieve a more 'balanced' military? Naturally, by more balanced investment in various capabilities, which Bernard Brody talked about. Here the concepts of marginal cost and marginal benefit becomes important .

It is held by some analysts that the techniques of marginal analysis developed by economic theory are not operable in the top level of decision-making.[114] But suppose we take a broader view and marginal cost in terms of specific capability building which involves billions of dollars? Capability building can only be thought of in incremental terms of costs and benefits over time. Benefits have to be computed in military terms on the basis of 'net assessment'

Further, as the defence budget is formulated in an incremental way, we have to look at the relationship between the additional budget and additional capabilities. The additional spending in the budget can be termed as marginal cost, a very important concept in economics. To quote Samuelson, "Marginal cost is one the most important concepts in all of economics. **Marginal cost** denotes the additional cost of producing 1 extra unit of output."[115] In defence, we cannot directly relate to 'output', we have to relate to an intermediate product called 'capabilities. How best we can relate has been a challenging task for the economist, for which he had to establish tools of analysis like linking the bundle of inputs to the elements of capabilities.

In trying to see a parallel between the two in terms of approach, and provide some insight ,one can do no better than quote from Bernard Brodie's famous article "Science and Strategy" in *World Politics* in 1949: "That strategic theory is reducible to a few common-sense propositions does not distinguish it from other social sciences, including the science of economics, which has undoubtedly enjoyed the most systematic development among the social sciences and which, I shall shortly point out, bears other and significant parallels to strategy."[116] Economics can also be reduced to a few simple propositions. The comparison between economics and strategy is fruitful in view of the similarity of objectives between the two fields. The task of economics is fundamentally efficiency in allocation of resources. "It is the study of the efficient allocation of the national (or other community) resources for economic ends set by the community... Strategy by comparison, is devoted to discovering how the resources of the nation, material and human, can be developed and utilized for the end of maximizing the total effectiveness of the nation in war."[117] The point, thus stated, is subject to various qualifications. During peace-time we are more interested in avoiding a war than in winning one when it comes to it and, accordingly, our military preparations get affected. Security is, after all, as Brodie points out, a derivative value, meaningful to the extent it promotes other values. "But in any case we are dealing with problems of efficiency in the allocation of limited resources and with measuring means against policies and vice versa."[118]

In a military sense, strategy deals only with mobilised resources but strategy must also anticipate the trials of war and by anticipation, seek where possible to increase one's advantage without jeopardising maintenance of peace and pursuit of other values. This broader objective is referred to by Brodie as 'security policy', which is sometimes called 'grand strategy'. The security policy has to deal with political, social, economic as well as military matters.

Security policy, thus, defined, " can hardly be the province primarily of the soldier, though he should be able to offer pertinent advice....the question of offsetting costs, political or otherwise, and the consequent determination of net profit or loss is not only a question of civilian responsibility but actually involves skills with which the soldier is not normally equipped, though it is desirable that he appreciates the limitations in freedom of maneuver which beset the politician and diplomatist....He should be able to provide us with a rational plan for the allocation of whatever sums are accorded him, but the determination of how large these sums should be, depends on a large number of factors, many of which lie entirely outside his usual realm of discourse."[119]

But coming back to our main theme of applicability of economic principles in security policy, we would like to again quote Brodie, "Whether we are discussing security policy in the broad sense or more specifically military strategy—or even tactics—we are discussing problems involving economy of means i.e. the most efficient utilization of potential and available resources to the end of enhancing our security. One might expect to find, therefore, that a substantial part of classical economic theory is directly applicable to the analysis of the problems of military strategy."[120] We have earlier referred to his application of economic principles in supporting the military concept of 'balanced force'.

Addition to capabilities is conceptually related to incremental budgeting, in the practice followed in India . To give a relevant quotation from Paul K. Davis, one of the most important advocates of Capability-Based Planning (CBP) and an authority on defence planning , "In capabilities planning, one seeks to identify the mix of force elements and systems that maximizes capability for different levels of the budget, and to keep track of how rapidly needed capability is rising with additional expenditures. *Since significant reforms with big pay-offs often require a buy-in expense, this analysis should be based on 'chunky marginal analysis'. That is, the question is not how best to spend the marginal dollar, but the marginal billion or ten billion dollars.*"[121]

Keeping in view the level of one defence budget, we should speak of marginal millions rather than billions. But the importance of marginal analysis comes out in CBP. *Davis also illustrates this conceptual approach diagrammatically, with a kind of 'utility function' for additional expenditures and relating them to threat estimates and capability obtained for each level of budget expenditure.*

So the concept of marginal utility or military worth can, in a broad sense, be applied even under capability planning , if we confine our attention to how much additional capability gets generated by spending the extra amount allocated under the defence budget, to enable us to decide about the budget level.

Action-Reaction Phenomenon

In the defence business, the existence of the phenomenon of action-reaction between two adversaries to counter the other's capabilities, sometimes makes it difficult to apply simple principles of marginal cost and marginal returns in developing an optimal level of capabilities. In a monopoly business, the principles of marginal cost and marginal returns do not apply in determining the point of maximum profit. In the defence business, the phenomenon of action–reaction between adversary countries becomes a major determinant in strategy making and consequent resource allocation. A monopoly has no rivals. Rivalry plays a major role in resource allocation decisions in an oligopoly . Firms which are monopolies in their own country, get into rival situations in the quest for dominance over each other.

In an oligopolistic situation, since the firms choose their strategy simultaneously, each firm selects a strategy that it believes will maximise its gain *given what it believes the other firm will do.* The firms play what is described in economics as a *non-cooperative game of imperfect information.* This also leads to misperceptions about each other's intentions.

Let us , in developing this point, refer to Robert McNamara's retrospective analysis of the expansion of nuclear forces by the United States and the erstwhile Soviet Union .

The prevalent argument in the United States was that it must continue to expand the nuclear forces merely to catch up with the Soviet Union. McNamara observes, "The reality of the matter is much more complex than such *misperceptions* suggest. Soviet decisions about the forces that they will build are not simply the result of an internally motivated drive for power and superiority. *Many of their force increases over the past twenty years can best be understood as reactions to American developments. In reverse, the same applies to many American developments. I have referred to this as the 'action-reaction phenomenon.' It is a fundamental force driving the nuclear arms race.*"[122]

This phenomenon was restricted not only to nuclear weapons but involved force development in general ,as McNamara confesses, "While serving as Secretary, I was repeatedly forced to take decisions about the forces we would begin to build today to balance Soviet forces that we believed might exist tomorrow. *Such decisions were speculative, based on incomplete, often contradictory, and constantly changing information.*"[123]

Weapons development decisions take time to translate into operational forces. Therefore, in taking production and development decisions, the US was forced to *guess* what Soviet forces would look like five or ten years hence. As they had limited knowledge of Soviet capabilities, they tended to make "*worst-case assumptions*".

In the process of catching up with the other, by the end of 1985, the United Stated had a total of 11,200 warheads and the Soviet Union had 9,900 consisting of both atomic bombs and missile warheads.

To describe this kind of situation, economists, borrowing from the analysis of the oligopoly, applied the *theory of games*. The games theory leads to the use of a set of tools to analyse conflicts and cooperation between firms, when they have to take account of each other's action and probable reaction. Why do not the firms cooperate and come to an agreement which is mutually beneficial? This is because of lack of trust in each other. This leads to a situation described in strategic literature as the *prisoner's dilemma.* Cooperation between the two 'prisoners' is difficult to maintain because cooperation is individually irrational.

Some analysts now look at past wars on the basis of perceptions developed by the theory of games. For example , Eric Hobsbaum the most eminent historian of the 20th century, asks a basic question about World War I, keeping in view its disastrous results for the European civilisation, as to why some sensible statesmen did not decide to settle the war "by some compromise before it destroyed the world of 1914." Most wars of the past were not fought to total exhaustion as in the case of World War I. There was no basic ideological divide between the two sides at that time, and there were statesmen who recommended some compromise settlement during the course of war. "Why, then, was the First World War waged by the leading powers on both sides *as a zero-sum game, i.e. as a war which could only be totally won or totally lost?*"[124]

A zero-sum game, in game theory, is defined as a game in which the sum of the pay-offs is always zero. In other games, total pay-offs depend on the strategies the players choose. The smallest and largest of these pay-offs are, respectively, the minimum and maximum pay-offs associated with that strategy. The strategy that gives the biggest minimum is the **maximin strategy**. The strategy that gives the smallest maximum is the **minimax strategy.**

The question is: when there were many strategies to choose from on the basis of game theory, why was World War I played as a zero-sum game? This point is important as the consequences of this war were disastrous, with the loss of lives of ten million human beings and tortured emotional lives of millions more. No less important is the fact, as John Keegan writes, "The Second World War, five times more destructive of human lives and incalculably more costly in material terms, was the direct outcome of the First."[125]

Hobsbaum, in trying to find the reason for it, writes, "....that this war, unlike the earlier wars , which were limited and specifiable objects, was waged for unlimited ends. In the Age of Empire, politics and economics had fused. International political rivalry was modeled on economic growth and competition, but the characteristic feature of this was precisely that it had no limit." For the two main contestants, Germany and Britain, it was an 'either/ or' situation. Compromise was not acceptable. The only war aim that counted was 'total victory'. In World War II, it was called "unconditional surrender".[126] No party was mindful of the cost of the war, in either war. It was again, from one point of view, a zero-sum game as Federal Germany after World War II lost its status as an independent military power and Britain and France "were forced ... however reluctantly, to accept their relegation to second rank status..."[127]

The concepts of competition and conflict, mentioned above, can be seen in the games theory perspective. Competition is a broader concept than conflict. Competition in its broadest sense exists when the potential positions of two behaviour units are mutually incompatible. How do we define a 'conflict' position? As Boulding puts it, " Conflict may be defined as a situation of competition in which parties are *aware* of the incompatibility of potential future positions in which each party *wishes* to occupy a position that is incompatible with the wishes of the other."[128] All cases of conflict involve competition, but not all cases of competition involve conflict. In an actual conflict situation, there must be awareness, and there must be incompatible wishes and desires. "Even where people are aware of potential conflict, there may be no actual conflict if there is no desire of one party to occupy a region of its behavior space from which it is excluded by the other."[129]

We have to have an introspective view of whether, in the above sense, a conflict exists between two countries, whether there is basically an incompatibility of future positions for both the countries or whether they are compatible.

From the above static model, we can go to a more dynamic model, which takes into account the action-reaction phenomenon. Most extensive theoretical treatment has been carried out in this regard by Lewis Richardson along the lines of classical physics which has been adopted by economists, and partial equilibrium analysis applied. The Richardson model has been used to describe the phenomenon of the arms race. But it can be used more broadly to explain the conflict situation between two parties by the action-reaction phenomenon.

In explaining the action-reaction phenomenon, the concept of "reaction coefficient" was used by Kenneth Boulding to develop the Richardson model. He defined the reaction coefficient "as the amount by which the equilibrium level of hostility of the one increases per unit increase in the hostility of the other. The reaction coefficient, therefore, measures the touchiness of the parties."[130]

While one can assume the reaction function to be a given and draw reaction curves on that basis to arrive at an equilibrium position, one can remove this limitation. We can suppose that each party has some control over his reaction function. This means the reaction function is chosen over a certain range of possibilities. "This implies a certain distinction between shortsighted and longsighted equilibria. The equilibrium of a simple Richardson process is shortsighted in the sense that it assumes for each party a simple reaction to the perception of the current position of the other. If, however, we take into account the possibility of longsightedness, that is, the possible deliberate shift of the reaction functions themselves, the results of the analysis may be very different."[131]

The "action-reaction phenomenon," described by McNamara as the "fundamental force driving the nuclear arms race", seen on the basis of the Richardson model as analysed by Boulding, can only be described as a phenomenon where reaction functions are a given, and 'reaction co-efficient' is such that there is no equilibrium position. Clearly, there was absence of longsightedness aiming at a deliberate shift in the reaction curve emanating at a policy review.

Though the game theory operates at a level of abstraction, can this be applied to the conflict situation? As we have mentioned above, there is a concept of pay-off in the game theory. In a general situation of decision making under uncertainty, there is uncertainty about the pay-offs themselves. Any decision, however, involves some image of alternative pay-offs. To quote Boulding again, "The pay-off matrix is a useful analytical device and, frequently, can be used to clarify a conflict situation; the notion of minimax as an equilibrium of mutual choice is important, as it does not involve any assumptions about the behavior beyond a certain shortsightedness in maximization. The real world is, however, much more complicated..."[132]

Thomas Schelling, the economist, became famous in applying the theory of games in conflict situations. The arms race phenomenon was explained by Schelling by a process which he called the "dynamic feedback" process. To quote, "There is a feedback between our military forces and conflicts that they simultaneously reflect and influence."[133] It follows that the chances of successfully managing strategic interaction depend on participants *being aware that such a feedback process is at work.*

His important concept of "threat that leaves something to chance," also evolved out of the game theory. This is where risk manipulation comes in.

Schelling defined the concept of stability in the nuclear age in terms of "balance of deterrence". The classic statement in this regard had been that of William Kaufmann, stating that states were deterred from undertaking certain acts "when the costs and risks are of sufficient magnitude to outweigh prospective gain".[134]

A balance of deterrence does not mean symmetry in striking power, but is the reciprocal ability to retaliate. The idea of 'even' distribution of forces is not a sufficient condition for stability in this case. The situation is stable when either side can destroy the other, whether it strikes first or second.[135]

Schelling also called into question the usefulness of dichotomy between *conflict* and *cooperation* in the theory of international relations. He showed " that most ,if not all international political situations involved mixtures of both conflictual and cooperative elements. Although zero-sum games and games of pure cooperation might be useful ways to define the ends of a continuum, neither was likely to describe a real world situation. Even war...was shown by Schelling to involve a cooperative dimension."[136] This is particularly true of limited wars. In conflict situations where both 'hostility' and cooperation is present, coercive bargaining is of central importance.

Schelling's emphasis on the importance of communications between potential adversaries so as to be able to manage crises and similar incidents was a major stimulus for the installation of the famous hotline communication link between the US and Soviet leadership.[137]

The theory of games, extensively applied in economics, allows us insights into the strategic field, which would not have been otherwise possible. We will take the model of the Prisoners' Dilemma.

Prisoners' Dilemma and Cooperation

In the Prisoners' Dilemma model, each person has a 'dominant' strategy, in the sense that no matter what others do, each person's own goals are better served by following that dominant strategy. At the same time, everyone's goals would have been respectively better served had they followed a more cooperative strategy. There is now fairly extensive game theory literature in dealing with the prevalence of cooperative behaviour in finitely repeated Prisoners' Dilemma games. Emergence of cooperation in the formal literature of the game theory is sometimes explained by introducing some kind of a 'defect' in either the knowledge or reasoning of the players.

But need it always be so in real life? What about *one-off* real life situation? As Amartya Sen points out, "It is also possible that people clearly understand their goals, wish to maximize them, but nevertheless take note of other people's goals, due to a recognition of the nature of mutual interdependence of the achievements of different people in these situations."[138]

Behaviour is ultimately a social matter as well. What we should do in a given situation or what should be our strategy "may reflect a sense of identity involving recognition of other people's goals and the mutual interdependencies involved."[139] What a person can be seen as maximizing "depends on a certain reading of what he or she takes to be the appropriate control variables and what variations are seen as the right means of control exercised by each player."[140]

In the above game, if we substitute 'player' by leader, we get a cooperative strategy in the world politics. Recognition by the leaders of interdependencies among nations and economies is the key point leading to cooperation rather than conflict. As referred to earlier Thomas L. Friedman in *The World is Flat* has forcefully indicated how prevention of conflict among nations would be a major aim of international diplomacy, *as the world becomes flatter*. Therefore, the Prisoners' Dilemma model may be less applicable in the future in the conduct of world diplomacy than in the past.

Importance of Tools of Analysis for Cost-Effectiveness

Introduction of the Planning, Programming and Budgeting System (PPBS) in 1961,in the Kennedy-Johnson era, is of importance to us, not as a budgetary system, but because of the tools it introduced for an effective defence within the limitation of resources. PPBS was, in effect, a management decision-making system to achieve, economy, efficiency and effectiveness in defence expenditure management.

The concept of achieving *cost-effectiveness* in defence resource management came to the forefront. In this effort, systems analysis was introduced as a tool of higher defence management, particularly in the choice of weapon system. McNamara's perception was that the choice of weapon system had become the main ingredient of defence policy and strategy-making.

Systems analysis drew attention to the following factors:

- total system cost over the useful life of the system;
- looking at the total force, in determining the additional capability required;
- looking at the larger picture, in its endeavour to reconcile lower level and higher level objectives in operational planning;
- clearly defining objectives and identifying the most cost-effective alternative for achieving the objectives.

We also noted earlier that McNamara introduced the instrument of Draft Presidential Memorandums (DPMs) for orderly debate on applying the above principles in resource allocation decisions and strategy. The DPMs were drafted by the systems analysis office under Enthoven , who was elevated to the level of Assistant Secretary (Systems Analysis) in the Department of Defence.

Through the approach of systems analysis, economic principles came to have a direct bearing on strategy formulation by affecting the choice of weapon systems.

The importance given to systems analysis by McNamara has been subject to debate in the post -McNamara period.

What is required is a balanced view regarding the scope of application of these principles. Bernard Brodie, the eminent strategic thinker of the last century (whom we have quoted earlier from his famous article "Strategy as Science" which appeared in 1949), drew attention to the importance of applying economic principles in strategic matters, much before systems analysis made its debut.

Brodie, while dealing with issues relating to war and politics and this interaction, also dealt with the role of systems analysis in defence management in an incisive manner, in *War and Politics* (1975). It is worth dwelling upon it, as it brings out the issues involved in an authoritative manner. He thought that systems analysis was the "outstanding contribution of RAND to modern strategic thinking". [141]

Systems analysis was designed "especially to choose new weapon systems for the future.. This technique requires estimating or projecting costs for elements in each system as also calculating the effectiveness of each system for its assigned task...Systems analysis is not primarily a matter of reducing overall defense costs. The goal is to get the most tactical and strategic effectiveness for one's money, but if the results also help keep down overall defense costs, that is not an end to be despised. "[142]

It is also to be remembered that systems analysis is primarily devoted to the comparison of systems to accomplish the same or similar missions. *It is not equipped to answer whether the mission to be undertaken is worth the cost or effort.*

Brodie points out, "The question of ends is usually a much more important question than of optimum means, and the systems analyst is not only without any special equipment for handling the latter, but may even be negatively equipped, that is , he may have a trained incapacity for giving due weight to political and social imponderables. So too, for that matter, may be, the military officer."[143]

Brodie made these comments apparently keeping in view the experience of the USA in conducting the Vietnam War and the inability of systems analysis to make any worthwhile contribution in taking the strategically correct course of action. Let us not forget that systems analysis was not designed to answer such questions. The ability of the enemy to bear the losses in the battles and the motivation provided by intense nationalism is in the realm of imponderables.

Let us, however, go back to the more limited issue of decisions regarding weapon systems.

McNamara believed that individual Services could not be depended upon to make wise decisions concerning their own major weapon systems. The record seemed to show "that they were too eager to expend large sums in pursuit of some extra margins of speed or other characteristics of performance concerning their ships, aircraft or tanks—margins that might indeed have a tactical or strategic advantage but sometimes a very modest one that seems hardly proportionate to the extra cost. It was not only a matter of buying the better but more costly of two types offered(which might or might not make good sense), but also premature phasing out of an entire system of, say, fighter planes in favor of another system that promised too little advantage to justify the shift."[144]

McNamara appointed Alain C. Enthoven, the economist, to direct such projects. As the impact of such studies in systems analysis on the weapon procurement decisions became more and more evident and significant, the opposition of the Services grew.

Let us take the proposal for nuclear-powered warships in the mid-1960s. In this case, it was about the propulsion system of the ship *John F. Kennedy*, whether it should be nuclear-powered or not. Spokesmen of the navy made the case entirely in terms of superior performance, but not of the extra cost.

Enthoven, soon thereafter, in a forum, stated that everybody was in agreement that nuclear–powered warships were tactically superior to their conventionally powered counterparts, and implied that this would be true of aircraft carriers as well as submarines. His point, however, was that the navy had not made any attempt to *quantify* the added tactical and strategic superiority in order that it might be compared with the added cost.

Brodie brings out succinctly the issue about the validity of this type of questions, though *prima facie* , it might seem rather out of context, "This may seem to the layman like a bizarre request : How can and why should one quantify a superiority of tactical performance? Actually , no one is asking for precise figures, but rather for some idea of whether the nuclear carrier is twice as good, or one-and-one half times as good. If it is twice as good, would the navy be willing to do with half the number of carriers, or would it prefer to have the presently authorized numbers even if they be conventionally powered? These are not unreasonable questions, and faced with them, the navy may tend to become more measured in its advocacy and perhaps remember that the whole concept of carrier- borne aviation has long been under fire and it would, therefore, not do to have individual carriers become astronomically costly."[145]

In this instance, though, the navy got its way, with the next or Nimitz class of carriers laid down, which were projected for nuclear propulsion. Thus, it is not the analysis that often determines the decision, but also how strongly the Service concerned feels about the case.

From the analysis point of view, the basic point is that that some quantification of relative advantage or performance of new proposals for modernisation has to be made. Which is to be related to their relative cost because the budget is limited. Overall fighting capability is determined by force structure and how it is effectively combined . In the quest for modernisation, the force structure should not be adversely affected. In the economist's way of looking at it, total utility should increase; additional marginal utility in one direction should not be negated by reduction in utility elsewhere.

The concept of utility can be taken to a higher level of conceptualisation in terms of utility of military power.

One should resist the idea of thinking of utility as a subjective pleasure or usefulness a person derives from consuming a good or service. As Samuelson and Nordhaus in their most famous text-book on economics point out, "*Rather, utility is a scientific construct that economists use to understand how rational consumers divide their limited resources among the commodities that provide them with satisfaction.*"[146]

In the context of national military power, Klaus Knorr, in an important work , used the concept of 'utility' for analytical purposes and to give a conceptual structure to policy issues in a general way. He accepts, "Utility is a matter of perception and values. It is essentially subjective and this fact precludes computation and comparison between countries over time."[147] But it helps us to give the problem a "conceptual structure". He began with a simple formula, clearly stating that the realities involved are not capable of quantification.

$$U = V - C = (V1 + V2 + \ldots Vn) - (C1 + C2 + \ldots . Cn)$$

The utility (U) which a nation (or its leaders) derives from military power—that is, from its maintenance and use—depends on the satisfaction of certain values (V) and accrual of certain costs (C). Utility depends on the difference between aggregate values and aggregate costs."[148]

The important point to note is that in this framework, 'utility' is not independently arrived at. Values are independently arrived at, and utility is arrived at after determining the 'costs' of achieving the values. Utility is not independent of 'cost'. While there are financial costs in terms of manpower, materials, land and capital, the "real economic costs are the use of these resources for other purposes—private and public consumption and investment—that are foregone when they are expended on military efforts. The foregone uses represent a value loss."[149] In other words, Knorr uses the concept of 'opportunity cost', which an economist understands as cost to be concerned with.

There are various kinds of values and costs. The study of the behaviour of states shows a variety of foreign policy purposes for which military power has been utilised. "Most, if not all, of these purposes can be reduced to two classes: defensive or non-acquisitive goals, and offensive or acquisitive goals...Foremost among the defensive goals has been the preservation of physical security from external aggression since...territorial integrity has been, and still is, the indispensable basis for a high degree of self-determination."[150]

Defensive goals include the undisturbed satisfaction of established interests that can be threatened and that are capable of being defended by military means. These may include foreign trade, free passage through seas, protection of nationals abroad, etc "In brief, defensive goals involve protection of various assets and advantages that are part of status quo."[151]

What about offensive goals? "In short, offensive goals involve acquisition of various assets and advantages in a way that, through the employment of military power, revises the the international status quo."[152]

It is clear from this conceptual formula that the utility of war and military power is subject to change. Such changes occur if shifts occur in the values derived from, or the costs incurred by, the maintenance and use of national military power. "On the value side, there may occur a diminution or augmentation of the value objects for the attainment of which military power can be applied; or these objects may rise or fall in value. On the cost side, there may occur a reduction or enlargement of costs in terms of kind or magnitude; or their costs may become subjectively more or less appreciated in terms of magnitude."[153]

At any one time, variations in values and costs expected from maintenance of military power in part account for differences among nations in their attitude towards maintaining military power, and towards its aggressive or defensive employment. The most important point Knorr makes in this context is, however, that *changes take place in utility of military power over time*. There are also non-military means of international influence that have their own utility and are also subject to change. The utility of military power depends to some extent on the utility of non-military means of international influence. Knorr observes, two decades after the end of World War II, "We strongly suspect that, during the past two decades, some means of international influence other than military power have –relative to the exertion of military strength—appreciated in value."[154]

This analysis indicates that the utility of military power cannot be assessed independently without conisdering foreign policy objectives and their utility in the emerging environment.

Let us now go to the next level of analysis in terms of military capability building where resources are taken as given.

One point that comes out from the Knorr formula is that whenever we consider acquiring something of military value, say A, we have to consider the cost involved and if the cost of A exceeds the cost of acquiring that value, then total utility in terms of military power would go down. The opportunity cost of acquiring A could then be considered as the value B that is given up.

From total utility, we have to go to the concept of marginal utility. The marginal utility concept can be conceptually seen as a broad indicator of additional benefit in terms of gain of additional military capability for spending the defence budget (again considered in the margin) beyond what is already committed or obligated. This can be treated as marginal cost. We can compare marginal cost and marginal benefit, to see whether there is a net benefit. This way of looking at the problem of resource allocation gets lot of validity under the emerging concept of Capability-Based Planning (CBP), which we have adopted for defence planning.

It needs to be remembered in that India's defence budget, almost 90 percent, stands committed on the existing force structure as 'obligational' expenditure and earlier capital purchase commitments. It is only a marginal 10 percent of the defence budget or even less, that is available for new commitments and investment decision-making. Every year, a 'ceiling' is imposed on the defence budget while finalising the Budget Estimates (BE).

This means that any additional expenditure out of the incremental budgetary amount, which does not generate commensurate marginal utility , can only be at the expense of some other utility which is sacrificed, affecting adversely the total utility of defence expenditure.

Therefore, assessing marginal cost and marginal benefit of spending the extra rupee would be the most important means of increasing total capability or utility within the budgetary ceiling imposed. Comparative analysis of the utility and costs of different weapon systems, but meeting the same objective, leads also to the concept of "trade-offs" in the efforts toward modernisation of the defence forces.

Commenting on India's current effort at military modernisation in this particular regard, Stephen Cohen and Sunil Dasgupta observe, "It is hard to find systematic public analysis of the trade-offs between aircraft and missiles. No country chooses one exclusively over the other, but understanding the trade-off is important to balance investment."[155]

If the aim is to 'balance the investments" across various capability options, comparison of utilities and costs of various options would be necessary.

The first priority in CBP is addressing the existing 'Capability Gaps'. This is because it is presumed that when these 'gaps' are closed, there would be increasing returns, to be measured not only by the additional utility to be generated by the new system, but also the increased utility of existing systems from which full benefit could not be obtained earlier because of the capability gaps.

An assessment of the importance of closing the 'gaps' and to the priority to be given to each in spending from the budget, can only be done by systems analysis.

The aim should be to identify the mix of force elements and systems that maximises capability within a given budget. Here simple utility analysis would not do. As Paul Davis pointed out, in capabilities planning, one has to identify the *mix of force elements* and *systems* that maximises capability for different levels of the budget, to enable one to keep track of how the needed capability is rising with additional expenditures in a given timeframe. "Since significant reforms with big payoffs often require a buy-in expense, the analysis should be based on 'chunky marginal analysis'. That is, the question is not how to spend the marginal dollar but the marginal billion or ten billion dollars."[156]

There is another important point in the context of capability planning which goes beyond simple utility analysis. "Another feature of capabilities analysis is that it strongly encourages measuring the value of additional expenditures with multiple measures of effectiveness (e.g. measures recognizing substantially different contingencies or contingency details, problems of sustainability and all-weather suppression of air defenses, the potential need for vertical development and armored offensives."[157] By contrast, "requirements analysis" is aimed at finding out "the least-cost way to accomplish a particular set of requirements... and may yield a force that is ill suited to other cases....When planning against uncertain potential threats of uncertain capability in uncertain contingencies, it is wise to keep track of how much one is paying to decrease risk."[158] In such an uncertain environment, management of risks becomes the central concern of defence planning.

Both these points of relating marginal cost to marginal benefit through 'chunky marginal analysis' and to meet the need of 'multiple measures of effectiveness' call for systems analysis for getting value for money. This kind of analysis is totally absent in our investment decisions relating to modernisation, which needs to be urgently rectified.

Seeking cost-effective alternatives for procurement of weapon systems is the main object of systems analysis which we referred to above. In this endeavour, application of economic principles is of the utmost importance, including relating lower objectives to higher level objectives which economists are trained to do.

Bernard Brodie, whom we have quoted above, puts two important conditions for undertaking effective systems analysis:

- "Systems analysis, being absolutely necessary for certain kinds of choice, is best done by those who are appropriately trained for it and who, by dint of great diligence have acquired a scarce and valuable experience in their art.
- "It is likely to be more effective if it is done under an authority who has no difficulty in subordinating Service interests to other interests of the nation."[159]

The above points need to be remembered. The techniques of systems analysis is no doubt indispensable for the choice of the weapon system but the choice of the weapon system is not the whole of strategy, nor the most important part of it. Brodie raises the point of what influence systems analysis had in the fighting in Vietnam and states, "Practically none—and not as some have said , because it was not tried. It simply was not relevant."[160]

McNamara did get avidly involved in the Vietnam War like other members of the US Administration.

But one has to remember Clausewitz's concept of "fog of war", which makes it difficult to apply analytical techniques in warfare. Added to that, there will often be 'misperceptions' because of wrong interpretation of intelligence gathered, no less due to the fact of one's proclivity to believe what one wants to believe. The post mortem of the Vietnam War brought this out, as would be the case in recent and past wars.

On the question of applying economic and managerial principles, Edward Luttwak, another important expert on strategic matters, in his book *Pentagon and the Art of War*, brings out a totally different point of view. While giving importance to cost-effectiveness aspects in designing weapons, he states that "conflict is not like civilian business and efficiency is the wrong goal to pursue."[161] He emphasises the importance of "intangibles". This aspect is ignored in the approach of economists. The most important intangible is the quality of operational methods and tactics embodied in the plans of the armed forces. He also stresses the importance of organisational quality, its structural appropriateness or lack of it. He feels that the organisational structure of forces greatly influences their war-effectiveness.[162]

In 'intangibles', Luttwak gives maximum importance to what he calls "quality of strategy", which is not just a top-level function. "The first of intangibles standing between the inputs we pay for and the outputs of military capability that we actually obtain is the quality of strategy at all levels. If we make a wrong choice between different forms of military power in shaping our national military strategy, such as overfunding the navy at the expense of the army, then we spend a great deal and yet remain weaker than we should be. If we make a wrong choice in our force strategy, such as overstressing armor and artillery at the expense of light infantry, then our ground forces may be strong by some abstract measures of firepower and yet weak in fighting the small wars that actually come our way."[163]

More problems would occur if were to make a wrong choice in the theatre strategy.

In each of its levels, the quality of strategy determines the 'outputs' of deterrence and fighting strength that we can actually obtain from the inputs we pay for. This important point has to be constantly kept in view while trying to apply cost-effectiveness analysis on strategic issues. This also draws attention to devoting sufficient attention to training and developing leadership qualities among soldiers and officers, so that some of the 'intangibles' in converting inputs to outputs are taken care of.

Other important point is the 'uncertainty' factor which besets defence policy-making. This makes linking of input to output in defence quite problematic. Can systems analysis help in this endeavour?

We would like to quote Alain Enthoven in this regard, the most prominent expert in this field. "Even when uncertainties are present, it is better to use numbers than to avoid them. Quantitative analysis is possible even if there are uncertainties...there are simple techniques for dealing with uncertainties which make it possible to point out the major ones for the decision-maker and indicate their significance. In fact, rather than conceal uncertainties , a good analysis would bring them out and clarify them.[164]

The basic criticism, as we have seen above , against systems analysis is that it tends to overemphasise factors that can be reduced to numbers, and underemphasise factors that cannot. As Enthoven points out, "The tendency to ignore important factors, quantitative or non-quantitative, is a failing that is less likely to occur under the systems analysis approach than under alternative approaches. For it is the vital part of systems analysis to bring to bear the best of relevant, modern analytic techniques for organising data and summarizing important aspects. If an individual must lay out clearly all his assumptions, objectives and calculations, both his critics and the decision-maker can see what was done and whether analysis overemphasized quantitative factors, if indeed it did."[165]

It is also true that the intuitive judgement of an experienced personnel in any complex field may often rest on oversimplification of important aspects.

This may put at rest reservations about the introduction of systems analysis in defence.

It is a painstaking endeavour, which often proceeds through successive approximations, and in the process, often clarifies the strategic objectives to be pursued which might have been rather hazy in the beginning of the process.

Thus, systems analysis, should be viewed as a process which should be scientifically designed, depending on the nature of the problem being addressed. While embarking on it, an analyst has to decide upon the data to have a fair idea about the options that could be considered. The aim is that the outcome of analysis would help in making the final choice.

Carried out in a scientific way, using quantification where required, systems analysis can help in clarification of ends or objectives to pursue in the achievement of higher strategic goals. In the process, it can also help the decision-maker in the choice of appropriate means to attain the objectives in a cost-effective manner.

Asking fruitful questions, intelligently designing alternative systems to be compared , skillfully interpreting the results of calculations and relating them to the problem being explored, are the most critical phases of systems analysis.

Conceived this way, instead of thinking about it in terms of building mathematical models and manipulating them, systems analysis should be viewed as "an attempt to discern and answer questions of importance in the choice of policy."[166]

Often, there are no final 'solutions' to the most important strategic questions. But they can be made more manageable. The systematic and explicit character of systems study widens the possibilities of criticising it and, thus, reduces the possibility of error.

'Requirements' are set at the top as a policy level decision. Then comes procurement. As Wohlstetter puts it, then requirements "come down to the procurement officer from higher up, but not from On High. The scrutiny of constraints is one of the most fruitful aspects of a thoughtful systems study. To conclude then, goals set down in the course of policy decisions are never final. Ends are means to further ends and on occasion must themselves be evaluated. One man's means is another man's objective."[167]

Certain basic points in this regard need to kept in mind. First, the authoritatively received objectives "are likely to be not merely broad, but extremely thin and rarified".

Second, "the authorities, so far as they say anything definite, even where they don't , are likely to conflict".

Finally, "the attractiveness of an objective depends on its cost. The game may not be worth the candle."[168] Determination of costs requires close study.

The aim should be to make several goals compatible, which depends on the means used and, in fact, leads to invention of new means.

The above points suggest "the necessity of looking back down again from ends to means, to evaluate ends. *In fact, we are always in the process of choosing and modifying both means and ends. We appraise the end in terms of the means required, as well as the reverse, in short, we look at them together.*"[169]

It is also necessary to point out that even where systems analysis doesn't set out primarily to affect objectives, it is likely to do so. As Wohlstetter indicated, the instance of choosing among alternative 'basing systems' in the US strategic defence.

An analysis was done of the interplay among target objectives, bases and bomber performance and the principal outcome of the study "was to clarify the aim of deterrence and display the possibility of divergence between a capacity for destroying an enemy's strategic force under some circumstances and the ability to deter the attack."[170]

Systems study involves, as stated above , extended empirical work. In the course of such a study, which involves a method of successive approximations, objectives get clarified. In the nuclear strategy field, Wohlstetter points out, the vital difference between the objective of getting a first strike capability and the objective of getting the second strike capability did emerge in the course of extended empirical work. In this study, it successively introduced obstacles, measures and counter-measures. "The analysis then not only was affected by the objectives considered, it affected them."[171] There is, of course, a difference between the systems approach or study and systems analysis, the former being a broader approach.

Selection of proper criteria of choice is the central problem in the design of systems analysis, which also bring to the fore the basic problem determining cost and objectives in military decision-making at the *operational level,* in our view the most important level. "Objectives are likely to be such things as enemy targets destroyed, enemy planes shot down, the probability that the war will be deterred. Costs may be crew lost, aircraft lost, millions of budget dollars expended. Frequently, we can find common denominators, especially on the cost side. But also frequently, especially in the objective side, things just won't add up."[172]

A decision on force composition of the air force involves optimising for the air force as a whole. This is the decision at the highest level which will require criteria based on complex factors, which cannot be attempted through systems analysis.

But many decisions at lower levels, including relating to force composition, can be made by factoring out the variables which are of first order importance and aim to 'sub-optimise' for some sub-element of it. Here systems analysis aided by good judgment can help a lot.

But the basic thing to remember is that systems analysis is the methodology for solving problems based on the *notion of systems.* It involves looking at interdependence of factors, to balance one against the other so that the objectives are achieved effectively. The most important aspect of systems analysis is the *process of solving the problem.*

The final conclusion : even if systems analysis cannot determine the 'best', it has been demonstrated from various instances that it can find an option distinctly 'better' than those likely to be accepted otherwise.

The systems approach has a broader connotation than systems analysis which involves :

(i)looking at objectives, particularly the performance measures of the whole system; (ii) the system's environment, i.e. factors which are outside its control, including the budgetary constraint; (iii) resources, i.e *those which are inside the system, which it can control and change within its advantage (e.g. quality of personnel, training, educational requirements, leadership capabilities, imbibing technological advances)*; (iv) the components of the system, their goals and performance measures; (v) the management of the system

Management in the systems approach involves *inter alia* looking at basic *missions, tasks and activities* that the system would perform rather than at departments, divisions, offices into which the organisation is divided. Only by analysing tasks and activities, can management estimate their the worth for the total system, whereas there is no feasible way of estimating the worth of a department's performance.

The systems approach is the only scientific way of developing capability -based planning in defence, which we are supposed to have adopted. Unfortunately, no analytical basis has been established for ushering in capability-based planning.

Michael Howard, in his famous article , identified various dimensions of strategy , designed to demonstrate an unwise focus on weaponry in the American strategic debate.[173]

Howard's dimensions were the social, logistical, operational and technological. His emphasis on the human dimension of strategy was so basic and obvious that it often escapes the attention of scholars with a theoretical approach. As Colin Gray puts it, "At all relevant levels of analysis , strategy is done by *individuals*. Strategy is 'done' by tactics; tactics is 'done' by combat forces, *inter alia*; and the most important element in combat and support is people. And to be yet more precise, the people in question come down to individuals."[174] He adds that the master concept in Clausewitz's theory of war, is not strategy; rather it is the remarkable trinity, composed of primordial violence, hatred and enmity. Clausewitz associated these three elements with people. This was also contained in Clausewitz's concept of 'friction'. Friction is the gap between planning and operations. Each part of the military is "composed of individuals, each one of whom retains his potential for friction."

These aspects *prima facie* make it difficult to apply managerial and economic principles in the conduct of war. But there are important lessons too.

The importance of 'individuals' draws attention to leadership qualities in the conduct of war.

For example, reflecting on the lack of a decisive outcome in favour of India in the 1965 India-Pakistan War, the official history published by the Ministry of Defence does not reflect on any material deficiency, but draws attention to the leadership failure in some of the sectors where the war was fought. At many places, powerful assaults were not launched by commanders because of lack of initiative. "On occasions, senior commanders wavered and failed to lead their men from the front. In some cases, they did not visit the frontline and communicate with junior officers to direct the course of war." Because of this "some great opportunities were allowed to be wasted."[175]

It comments, "Poor performance of some commanders can perhaps be ascribed to the flaws in the selection, education and training system. The qualities of leadership, courage, initiative and aggression, which stand commanders in good stead during a war, have to be nurtured in peace-time assiduously."[176]

Intelligence was also lacking , which is a great contributory factor in the outcome of war, not often given the importance it deserves. For example, 'Operation Grand Slam' launched by Pakistan on September 1, 1965, came as complete surprise to the Indian Army.

When asked by the Prime Minister, towards the end of the war, whether India could have won if the war was prolonged by some days more, a General of the Indian Army was reported to have replied that most of India's frontline ammunition had been used up and there had been considerable losses in tanks. The war account records that by then only about 14 percent of India's frontline ammunition had been fired and the number of tanks still held by India was twice the number Pakistan had. To quote K. Subrahmanyam who drew attention to the above, "Here is a valuable lesson on logistics, intelligence assessment and management. If India had continued the war for a few days more, a victory could be achieved."[177]

The importance and necessity of joint operations in today's warfare,is getting increasingly highlighted. Ignoring this aspect may lead to strategic failure.

In the 1965 Indo-Pak War, according to Air Chief Marshal P.C. Lal, the then Army Chief and his commanders were wedded to the idea that military operations were principally an Army affair. The necessity of joint operations was, however, brought home during the battle of Chhamb, when the Army needed air defence and tactical support.[178]

Some integration among the three Services has since been achieved. But it is also held that the ideal set-up for conducting a modern war is yet to emerge. As Gen V.P. Singh(Retd COAS) points out, "Our existing Higher Defence Control Structure perpetuates single Service thinking. It is not conducive for the desired level of jointmanship and synergy in defence or operational planning."[179]

This organisational dimension of strategy is yet to be given sufficient importance. It is this aspect which, when properly addressed, leads to increasing returns, without consuming much resources, and may be the most critical factor in determining the outcome in today's warfare.

Rationalisation of resource allocation for logistics where a lot of resources get used up but often not efficiently, depends on application of economic and management principles. In logistics, both economics and strategy play interactive roles. Logistics is often a neglected aspect of strategy. As Colin Gray points out, "Strategy requires the use or development of scarce economic resources. *It rests completely upon economic activity, and entirely upon logistical performance, i.e. the supply and movement of armed forces. In short, strategy has an economic-logistical dimension that is fundamental , enduring, comprehensive, and inescapable . There is much more to strategy than economics and logistics , but strategy attempted heedless of their discipline is wont to founder at operational and tactical levels of war...* The economic and logistical dimensions of strategy have a subordinate but enabling role *vis-à-vis* the political and operational military dimensions.... almost every campaign and war is shaped in its course and at least influenced in its outcome by the economic–logistical dimension."[180]

Gray also goes on to quote Field Marshal Lord Wavell, who stressed upon the need for sound knowledge of what he calls the "mechanism of war" i.e topography, movement and supply. These are the real foundations of military knowledge, not strategy and tactics, as most people think."[181]

It is also to be noted that the cost involved in the support structure and infrastructure was neglected under PPBS. There was hardly much cost-effectiveness study in this regard under PPBS. To quote Paul Davis, , *"The PPBS has no agreed basis for how to analyze the how-much-is-enough question with respect to support structure and infrastructure—even though increasingly, that is where the money is."*[182]

This is a great omission for those engaged in cost-effectiveness analysis. The improvement brought about in the private sector in logistic management needs to be closely studied in improving military logistics to improve the quality of service levels. Information technology will play a key role. In the Indian context, public-private partnership in providing logistic support is almost a neglected area. But operational effectiveness has to be a key concern for effective logistic management. There would be two countervailing pressures, namely, demands for increased efficiency and lower cost, on the one hand, and effective maintenance of combat capabilities and training, on the other. Training needs are to be considered as part of support systems and adequate amounts provided for it. The logistics aspect of strategy also has to be seen in the context of the enemy's war-fighting capability. As our own combat effectiveness can be increased by proper management of logistics, similarly, the enemy's combat effectiveness can be diminished in a cost-effective manner by targeting his vulnerability in this regard . Therefore, paying attention to logistics has to be one of most important aspects of strategy-making.

As regards application of management principles, the Measures of Performance (MoPs) and Measures of Effectiveness (MoE) need to be developed for various aspects of logistic support. We are yet to introduce these concepts.

There is sufficient degree of decentralisation in terms of financial powers in Indian defence financial management. The concepts of Budget Centres and Budget Holders has been regarded as part of our reformed budgetary management in logistic areas for more than a decade and a half. What is lacking is performance orientation. These metrics need to be developed to move toward performance oriented budget management. Incentives need to be provided for optimal performance.

For this, a monitoring agency for evaluating performance is required. There should be cost reduction targets for maintenance activities, which would call for introduction of an effective costing system to measure performance.

To provide direction, a logistics organisation needs to institute a roadmap or plan to identify the specific effects it must accomplish to attain its objectives. It has to set individual agendas for its subordinate agencies' action. Almost always, planners will need to balance multiple effects across all plans to select the preferred plan. This may also call for trade-offs among alternatives. Therefore, there is a big challenge in putting together cost-effective supporting services, which would be hastened by the application of economic and management principles in getting the best value for money.

The Material Support System (MSS) can be viewed as supply chain management. It should include maintenance activities, not only in the bases and depots, but also sustaining engineering, equipment modernisation and modification processes at depots, bases, ordnance factories and contractors, including the contractor support and defence organisations that supply transportation and distribution services. Every link in the chain has to perform effectively to maintain the military capabilities. This call for an integrated logistics management system.

As an expert in the context of the Indian Army puts it, "We find our Divisions saddled with the vast and unwieldy logistic establishments grouped under the ASC, EME and Ordnance in the main, as also Engineering Services (MES), medical and postal. Accordingly, separate overheads are maintained for each of these services down to the level of divisional headquarters."[183]

Tactical operations are expected to take place close to our borders and a war can last only for a short duration. So the experience of World War II, in maintaining that kind of logistics structure where divisions were to function away from Indian shores, are not relevant. "Thus, to continue maintaining a vast logistical establishment is proving uneconomical and more of an addendum to the revenue expenditure. A review, therefore, is long overdue and there is a convincing case for an Army Logistic Corps (ALC) that integrates in its fold the ASC, AOC and EME."[184] The British Army, has already opted for a united logistics corps.[185] On this integrated basis, restructuring of logistics can be done right upto the divisional and independent brigade levels. In the field formations, on the basis of the restructuring proposed, the strength of the personnel gets reduced in a significant way, leading to a saving of 25,000 men.[186] As regards total personnel, the ratio between field and non-field segments works out to 12:10 which the author points out is not a "productive balance for the organisation as a whole."[187] The EME uses one-sixth of the manpower authorised for the Army.

There is also scope for economy through rationalisation of regimental training centres. When a review was carried out, some of the infantry regimental training centres were found to be training only a few recruits at a time. There is a huge overhead cost in running a training centre, therefore, these should be productively used by training adequate numbers. The number of regimental centres can be significantly reduced if this concept is used. Similar economies can be made even in Category. A training establishments.

Savings made by reorganisation of logistics can be used to augment the number of field forces, for which there is pressing demand because of the threat scenario in the northeast. Thus, economy in manpower through restructuring of logistics, given the ceiling on manpower and the limitation of the defence budget, should be treated as part of the strategic review.

If for no other reason, a high level strategic review should be made by the government to restructure the logistics, using the integrating concept to effect both economy and efficiency, with a view to augmenting the strength of the fighting forces in all the three Services at the same time for more effective operational purposes.

The other important concept of economics , which is of wide applicability in logistics, but is not applied in the quest for empire building and using the command principles , is the concept of *transaction costs*. A firm which requires a specialised service has two options: either it can do it by itself—by providing the service itself—or it can buy it from outside from some other firm. How will it decide? The answer was provided by Ronald Coase, the economist (who received the Nobel Prize in economics in 1991). His analysis is based on the concept of *transaction costs*, which are the costs associated with all market transactions. This concept is succinctly brought out by Lipsey and Chrystal. For example, when a firm purchases some good or service, it must identify the market and then find out what different quantities and qualities are available at different prices. That takes time and money , and it usually involves some uncertainty. These are the market transaction costs. "When the firm decides to do the job itself, 'in house', it uses the *command principle* : it orders the product to be made, or the service to be performed, to its desired specifications. The market transaction costs are avoided, but the advantages of buying in a competitive market are lost. Furthermore, as the firm gets larger, the inefficiencies of the command system tend to rise relative to efficiencies involved in decentralising decision-taking through the market system."[188]

The Indian defence organisation, viewed from an economist's point of view, is a very gigantic 'firm', and is complex in its structure. Efforts toward making it more cost-effective would involve streamlining the logistics, keeping in view the concept of transaction costs, so that adequate funds are available for ensuring the fighting capability of the frontline forces. All the savings made through cost–effectiveness studies of logistics and implementing them in the Army, which has the most elaborate logistics organisation, should be made available for improving the fighting capability of the infantry, armoured forces and artillery. After all, about 45 percent of the defence budget gets spent on the Army, and the defence budget is quite large. It has now to be ensured that not more money than necessary should be spent in providing support services and overheads. It may mean privatising many of the support services which are now provided in-house.

When services are provided in-house, cost considerations of providing the service and maintaining huge overheads are lost sight of. In the case of ordnance factories, cost considerations were not getting the appropriate consideration in providing ordnance stores earlier and the Army had to bear the additional expenses, as it was part of the Army budget. The budgetary reform was made in the late 1980s by introducing the 'customer and producer' relationship between the Army and ordnance factories and introducing the concept of 'net budgeting'. This led to adopton of more commercial practices like negotiating the prices in advance, putting together a long-term plan, and introduction of an improved cost accounting system. The customer-producer relationship can and should be established in providing services to the Army, Navy and Air Force.

Providing cost-effective logistic services with a view to generate savings for spending more for improving fighting capability within the existing budget, should be the most important part of a long-pending strategic review in India.

Economics of Defence Strategy

As we have tried to portray above, the economics of the defence strategy involves looking at two broad aspects, namely, cost and return. The cost of defence is one aspect which one can easily ascertain, the return one cannot. Various efforts have been made to relate the two, as pointed out above.

The economics of strategy lays stress on formulating a five-year defence plan on the basis of the programme concept for capability building, with yearly evaluation and mid-course correction where the returns are not commensurate with the cost incurred or better alternatives available.

The mechanism for programme evaluation has to be immediately set up under the Defence Secretary in the Ministry of Defence. This in-depth on-going evaluation of on-going programmes should be treated as the most crucial component of ensuring that costs are commensurate with returns. It should not be just an expenditure plan, as in the past. It has to be programme-based; programmes are to be approved at no less than the level of Defence Minister, who in a sense is not just the political head but a corporate head.

S.S. Khera writing (in 1967) when there was a defence plan (which, keeping in view its achievement in terms of capability build-up, was quite successful, as the results of the 1971 War showed), being concerned with the appropriate returns to the defence cost, made the following points:

- Scientific methods should be applied "to achieve effectiveness and economy throughout the defence apparatus. In terms of defence costs, major economies could be achieved, with greater reliance on modern methods of management in production and maintenance".[189]
- "Modern methods of inventory control can achieve dramatic results in avoiding waste and achieving efficiency…It has been estimated on good authority that a 10 per cent cut in defence expenditure could be achieved simply through the modern methods of inventory control, better handling of production resources, and imports of spares and equipment."[190]
- "In terms of value for money spent, the effective introduction of even a moderate degree of scientific management and administration throughout

the armed forces on the lines introduced during Lord Mounbatten's period as Chief of Defence Staff in Britain, and by the Americans in several sectors of their military formations , would probably yield a saving of anything up to 20 per cent or more in the defence budget."[191]

Khera laid emphasis on change in attitude as a prerequisite to bring in the above changes.

" The prerequisite for this is a change in attitudes, at the top levels of command, and of *willingness and ability to introduce scientific methods, especially by way of operational research systems analysis,* and communication and control systems in as many sectors and at as many levels throughout the defence apparatus".[192]

We are not dealing here with the communication and control systems which are the most important aspects of defence management. We are concerned with what is referred to as scientific methods.

Introduction of the scientific method in defence management is still the crying need to make returns commensurate with the heavy cost the country is bearing in defence.

We also drew attention to the strategic aspects of linking means to ends.

An emerging view in defence literature in the context of choice among alternative strategies, keeping in view their cost and effectiveness, is to draw heavily from the analogy of the business world. In a commercial enterprise, a business strategy is developed and resources are allocated to the *operating units.* These units, which are in the frontline of implementing the strategy, are held responsible for delivering results. To quote from a comparatively recent publication from RAND authored by eminent defence analysts, "In the 1970s and 1980s, businesses learned the value of organizing their strategic planning around operating units rather than production units. Doing so permitted a better alignment of allocated resources and responsibilities. It was a substantial aid in improving productivity of the enterprises…The operating unit has become, for a wide spectrum of enterprises, the fulcrum for linking objectives and costs."[193]

In a like manner, the US Department of Defence looks to the Combatant

Commands (COCOMs) to execute its strategy. These commands can be viewed as operating units.

The authors observe that though great strides have been made since the passage of the Goldwater Nichols Act towards "joint" military planning and operations, this has proved to be difficult. The authors suggest that while the objectives of each COCOM get established, the objectives should be analysed for each of them and the needed capability stated clearly in *output* terms . This will determine what resources are to be allocated to each CCOCOM. With an assessment of the capabilities needed for each of them, "force planners can identify the program and force shifts that they believe will effectively, and cost-effectively, deliver those capabilities..."[194] The authors then elaborate on the methodology to implement this approach to defence resource management and outline the components of some of the strategies.

The important point is that, to apply this methodology, we have to have a theatre concept in organising our forces to ensure jointness in force planning and capability building. Each theatre would have its strategic challenge as the adversary would be different, the terrain would be different and the enemy would use different kinds of capabilities. Therefore, the strategic objectives would be different in each theatre. The capabilities required for different theatres have to have different emphasis. The theatre commanders take the entire responsibility to achieve the strategic objectives. We are yet to accept this concept in organisation of our forces (except for the Andaman Command).

Therefore, aligning the costs to strategy—in our case—is, to that extent, difficult, as also achieving rational allocation of defence resources for optimum combat capability.

Attempt to Set up a New Analytical Architecture to Define Defence Output

We have been motivated by the recent US approach in defence planning (QDR, 2001), and have indicated that capability-based planning would be our approach. Our procurement planning procedure has apparently been influenced by it in taking decisions about procurement necessity on the twin requirements of "operational requirements" and meeting the existing "capability gaps."

But there are quite a few basic challenges in adopting capability-based planning. Briefly put, it needs what is called a new analytical architecture and a new definition of defence *output.*[195]

The capability–based approach *implies* a modular, building block approach to force design and operations. A new analytical architecture is called for which briefly involves the following steps:

- The starting point would be drawing up 'plausible' conflict scenarios.
- Only those scenarios should be selected which are relevant for force planning.
- Operational challenges are required to be identified for each scenario: these decisions are to be taken at Service Headquarters level to be coordinated by the ministry.
- Operational challenges in terms of *mission goal*s are to be assigned to *theatre commanders,* if these are established *to ensure 'joint' operations.*
- Metrics are to be identified to achieve the mission goal.

The Secretary of Defence or Defence Minister should mainly focus on "operational challenges", which have to receive top level attention which would transcend individual detailed scenarios.[196] In other words, focussing on 'military outputs' has to be defined in terms of accomplishment of operational missions and capabilities to achieve them. "This is in contrast to planning for more platforms or communication bandwidth which are merely inputs from a top-down DoD perspective. It is also in contrast to listing 'activity areas', such as improving precision fires or improving collaborative planning. The operational challenges provide the context and lead to valid metrics."[197]

The next step for each operational challenge is to develop alternative concepts of operations and to identify forces programmes. This step is designated as the "mission system description" in which potentially critical components of capability are identified so that the planners may address them effectively.

In this context, the most important point in the above "architecture," in fact, the pivotal point, as far we are concerned, is introduction of the concept of *theatre commanders*, which would lead to integrated planning and joint operation. In achieving the mission goal i.e output, this is the most important organisational improvement that can enhance it most significantly.

This would logically lead to the establishment of the Chief of Defence Staff. In India, we have the Andaman and Nicobar and Strategic Forces Command as a model of jointmanship. There are other places which have posed operational challenges in the past and joint operations have not taken place, leading to less than successful results. Theatre command concepts need to be introduced in these operational areas for better *military output.*

The next step would involve the creation and assessment of options and suggestion of alternatives. "The appropriate paradigm is *mission systems analysis*.."[198]

This step can be meaningfully taken by the introduction of the concept of the theatre commander, who would have to be an integral part of defence planning. Managing transformation, another key concept in defence modernisation, would require synthesis of top-down and bottom-up activities. This can be facilitated by the institution of theatre commanders, for what would be necessary is "to decompose the operational challenges and identify subordinate challenges and responsibilities consistent with statutory operational challenges and unified commander missions. The goal here will be functional/technical and operational integration—rather than mere coordination—of capabilities for future joint operations."[199]

The transformation of forces that we are aiming at, cannot be achieved without transformation of the *architecture for capability building.* This would call for a systems approach for meeting the objectives of the mission.

Thus, from *systems analysis*, as discussed above, under capability-based planning, we transcend to *mission systems analysis.* This would help in linking *inputs to outputs* in a dynamic context i.e., the operational context, with reference to mission objectives. In the systems approach, the inputs which would include various capabilities (viewed in a static context), enter the system and get into the process; modified by the internal capacity of the process, they get converted into outputs and the 'feedback mechanism' modifies the inputs. The 'feedback' process conflicts with the tendency to equilibrium within the organisation, and the system configuration and its boundaries are in a constant process of change. This is the dynamic process of converting input to output. The 'feedback' reflecting the imperfect integration of inputs, regarding the system's environment and the individual interests, fulfilled or not fulfilled, may lead to changes in goals and other corrective actions.

When several actions are required to attain goals, rationality requires *co-ordination* . When defence is concerned, coordination is not a good enough concept to attain goals—what is required is *joint* action and organisational restructuring to achieve the goals and ensure a feedback process through a bottom–up approach.

Why the change in emphasis to *mission systems analysis*? It is because by analysing missions, one can estimate the worth of an activity for the total system.

To implement capabilities-based planning, the Ministry of Defence will need a new analytical architecture, which can be on the above lines or a more sophisticated one. This makes linking *inputs to outputs* in defence quite a complex task as the inputs get modifieds affecting the outputs, and then both the inputs and outputs get modified through the feedback mechanism. But this complexity has to be addressed through a proper analytical architecture and design system for exploring various alternatives and solutions.

The force structure needs to be reviewed after debating on the strategic goals in each theatre of operation, the environment in which it would function, and what would be the metrics of operation and capabilities which need to be enhanced by readjustment of resources within the theatres. Thus, as a logical step, after identifying the 'capability needs', there should be a 'capability audit' to identify where there is surplus and where there is a deficiency, before identifying the 'capability gaps'. The approach has to be 'joint' in capability audit and capability advancement.

The question also arises of how much we should worry about the so-called 'capability gaps', in our defence planning? This would to a great extent depend on our defence strategy which would be dictated by the resources that can be made available for defence. If the operational doctrine is defensive in nature, then the 'capability gap' would be assessed one way. There would be a different assessment if the strategy is what is euphemistically called 'active defence', which has an offensive element in it. Assessment of 'capability gaps' for an overtly offensive-oriented strategy would be still more different.

The extent of concern for these gaps would depend on how seriously the adopted operational doctrine is being activated and how much political backing it has.

For example, during the Cold War, the capability gaps in Western Europe vis-a-vis the Warsaw Pact countries were enormous. The bulk of the Western European states were able to provide forces only for linear defence against a feared Soviet attack. In terms of strategic air power, or airlift capacity and aircraft carriers, most of these states were weak or had no strength. This was even more true in terms of nuclear weapons and missiles.[200] From the American point of view, this was not an insuperable problem. And for the Western European countries also, it was not much of a concern as they had basically a defensive doctrine. As Jeremy Black points out, "However, concerns developed as the Americans advanced the concept of Air-Land Battle in the early 1980s, because its requirements for mobility in attack and defence, and for air-ground coordination, required a weaponry, a command and control system, and an operational doctrine that most of the Europeans lacked and.... no sign of acquiring....in essence, the emphasis in Western Europe has not been on high spectrum warfare." During the Cold War "these were mostly *garrison* states, very different from the USA, the *expeditionary* state."[201]

An expeditionary oriented state will view capability needs in a different way from a defence oriented state. This point cannot be over-emphasised. This difference in orientation would be seen in contrasting military capability, force structure and doctrine, which would be reflected in different tasking of military forces among states.

To quote Black on this very important point on devising a theory of capability building:

> The goals set for the military vary greatly, inviting attention to the problem of how best to classify and account for tasks. These are far from easy. A cultural interpretation of tasking, which employs the notion of strategic culture and focuses on reasons for conquest, or alternatively, for the avoidance of aggressive warfare, directs attention to the concepts and moods that help frame the formulation of tasks, as well as to the moments when

decisions are taken: ideological factors, as well as the political and military contingencies. Such an interpretation *directs attention to variety between states, and thus, diversity within the international system, and accentuates the methodological difficulties of devising a general theory of military capability and change, one that is valid across several cultures.*[202]

The question of affordability is also there. Even an expeditionary state has to weigh the cost of building a capability for a particular challenge against the cost of capabilities to meet other challenges, as the resources are limited. For example, the United States, towards the end of 1979, in the wake of the Soviet invasion of Afghanistan, declared the Persian Gulf as a zone of vital interest to America (under the Carter Doctrine), but in terms of capability-building in that zone, hardly anything was done. Clearly, the cost factor dominated and more time was taken to build up the capability when resources permitted it.

After the end of the Cold War, a major force structure review was undertaken in 1990, which yielded the 'Base Force' which was 25 percent smaller than the Cold War level. In 1993, there was another review called the Bottom-Up Review (BUR) of the defence-strategy programme. The important point is that the BUR did not change US defence strategy in major ways, but it cut US force levels by about 15 percent from their Base Force targets. The question of affordability was the main concern. The same concern was uppermost in the 1997 Quadrennial Defense Review (QDR), though the modernisation programme had suffered for several years. US defence at that time was spending about $245 billion annually, down from $350 billion (in 1996 dollars) in 1989 which was considered insufficient to support the BUR force structure. All the same, a limit of $250 billion for annual spending on defence for the next four years was laid down under QDR. But the strategy of having the ability to fight two nearly simultaneous Major Regional Conflicts (MRCs) conflicts on the scale of Operation Desert Storm, as laid down under Base Force and BUR, was retained with some cosmetic changes.

This showed that in strategy-making the perceptions of other countries matter. As two eminent analysts prior to the finalisation QDR 1997 wrote, on why it was essential for the USA to retain 'two MRC" capability, "This 'two MRC' capability has become synonymous with the level of military capability viewed necessary to support the US position as the world's sole remaining superpower. Both the terms 'superpower' and 'two MRC force' are gross characterisations of the US' status in the post-Cold War world and the forces that it has opted to maintain...perceptions matter and labels have much to do with shaping perceptions."[203]

So we have identified two important factors: cultural aspects and perceptions in force planning and capability building. This major limitation of the input-output model of defence planning should be kept in view.

To bring the model back, we shall bring in the concept of scenario building. We have mentioned above, in the context of 'Analytical Architecture for Capabilities- Based Planning', that only those scenarios should be selected which are relevant for force planning. Here we focus on the *process* aspect of the input-output model of defence planning.

"To have the right force requires an examination of the right scenarios. Good defence planning appreciates the degree to which the scenarios employed in the planning process can determine the outcome of that process."[204] The 'surprise' element has to be part of the scenario building exercise.

Economists always draw attention to the importance of assumptions for a particular model in the economic world. Many elegant models have been built on the basis of 'heroic' assumptions. This aspect should be given particular attention in the scenario-building exercise. These should not be optimistic assumptions. Nor should the scenarios be crafted only to accommodate the concerns of major participants in the force planning process—intelligence, the projections of future enemy behaviour, should be an important ingredient. Khalilzad and Ochmanek warn against use of large and complex computer models to simulate battles built upon a set of equations designed to make an estimate of a combat, for presentation purposes. These presentations often do not state the assumptions behind these models, which are of great importance to the decision-maker.

As the authors point out, the theatre-simulation models have become more of an obstacle to understanding than a tool for enhancing it. These models are complex, multi-dimensional and opaque. *"Without masses of information about intermediate products from a model run... it is impossible to audit the process by which the model turned inputs into outputs.*"[205]

One way out of this problem is to disaggregate military operations into smaller pieces for the purposes of analysis. "If one wants to know the probable value of a new anti-tank weapon, for example, it is probably better to focus on the analysis of what it takes to stop armoured units under a possible range of circumstances than it is to use a theatre model that tries to capture everything from air-to-air combat to the relative quality of allied and enemy units."

The general conclusion is that more transparent assessment tools can be employed if analyses are focussed at the operational level. The decision makers can decide whether key assumptions used in the analysis are credible and how much value is to be placed on the conclusions.

The main point is that if the aim is to introduce capability-based planning then accepted models and assumptions should not be used just to support existing mindsets and interests.

Notes

1. Warner R. Schilling, Paul Y. Hammond, Glenn H. Snyder, *Strategy, Politics, and Defense Budgets* (Columbia University Press, 1962), p. 216
2. Quoted by Schilling, Ibid., p. 47.
3. Ibid., p. 154.
4. Ibid., p. 181.
5. Ibid., p. 206.
6. Glenn H. Snyder, "The 'New Look' of 1953", in Schilling, et. al, p. 394.
7. Paul Y. Hammond, "Drafting NSC-68", in Schilling, et. al, p. 306.
8. Ibid., pp. 340-345.
9. Ibid., p. 362.
10. Ibid., p. 372.
11. Snyder, et. al., op.cit, p. 414.
12. Snyder, et. al., op. cit, p. 454.
13. Snyder, et. al., op. cit, p. 441.
14. Ibid., p. 454.
15. Snyder, et. al., op. cit, p. 475.
16. Snyder, et. al., op. cit, p. 493.
17. Quoted by Charles J. Hitch, 'Planning-Programming-Budgeting', *Decision-Making in Defense* (University of California Press, 1965), H. Rowan Gaither lecture series,

p. 26.

18. Charles J. Hitch, 'Planning-Programming-Budgeting', *Decision-Making in Defense*, (University of California Press, 1965), H. Rowan Gaither lecture series (italics mine).
19. Ibid.
20. Ibid.
21. Ibid.
22. Jesse Burkhead and Milner, *Public Expenditure*, p. 184.
23. Ibid., Jesse Burkhead quoting Mosher, p. 202.
24. Jesse Burkhead and Milner, *Public Expenditure,* p. 174.
25. Ibid., p. 175.
26. *Joint Programming Guidance*, http://akss.dau.mil/dag/Guidebook/IG_cl.2.asp
27. A. Berle and Gardiner C. Means, *The Modern Corporation and Private Property*, Harcourt, Brace and World, 1932.
28. Joshep A. Maciariello and Karen E. Linkletter, *Drucker's Lost Art of Management*, Tata-Mcgraw Hill, 2011, p. 90.
29. Samuel P. Huntington, *The Soldier and the State*, Nataraj Publishers, originally published in 1954, p. 440.
30. Ibid.
31. Ibid., p. 441.
32. Ibid., p. 448.
33. Ibid., p. 450.
34. Charles J. Hitch and Ronald N. McKean, *The Economics of Defense in the Nuclear Age* (Harvard University Press, RAND, 1960), p. 54.
35. Glenn A. Kent and William E. Simons, "Objective-Based Planning", in Paul K. Davis ed., *New Challenges in Defense Planning* (RAND, chapter 3, 1994).
36. Ibid., p. 61.
37. Ibid., p. 67.
38. Ibid., p. 62.
39. Ibid.
40. Paul K. Davis, *Effects-Based Operations* (RAND, 2001), p. 7.
41. Ibid., p. 24.
42. Ibid., p. 30.
43. *Quadrennial Defense Review Report*, Department of Defence, USA, February 6, 2006, p. 4.
44. "Preface", *Quadrennial Defense Review Report*, Department of Defence, USA, February 6, 2006, p. vi.
45. Ibid., p. vii.
46. Ibid., p. vii.
47. George W. Bush, *Decision Points*, Virgin Books, 2010, p. 242.
48. Ibid., pp. 268-269.

49. Ibid., p. 242.
50. QDR, n. 43, p. 1.
51. QDR, n. 44, p. vii.
52. Andrew Krepinevich, "Executive Summary", *Defense Investment Strategies In An Uncertain World* (Center for the Strategic and Budgetary Assessment, 2008).
53. Ibid., "Introduction", Note 1.
54. Ibid., p. 52.
55. Ibid., "Executive Summary", p. ix.
56. Jason Sherman, "Facing a New Reality", *Armed Forces Journal*, December 21, 2004.
57. Ibid.
58. Ibid.
59. Ibid.
60. Ibid.
61. Ibid.
62. Jeremy Black, *Rethinking Military History* (Routledge, 2004), p. 126 [italics mine]
63. Ibid.
64. Stephen Biddle, *Military Power, Explaining Victory and Defeat in Modern Battle* (Princeton University Press, 2004), p. 194.
65. Ibid.
66. Ibid.
67. Jean Roberts, in W. Sachs, ed., "Development Dictionary", 1997, quoted by Kamal Nayan Kabra, *Economic Growth and Development in India: Deepening Divergence*; Alternative Economic Survey, India, 2011 (Yuva Sambad Prakashan, 2012), p. 7.
68. G.H. Snyder, *Deterrence and Defense* (Princeton University Press, 1961), p. 25.
69. John Garnett, "Strategic Studies and Its Assumptions", in John Baylis, ed., *Contemporary Strategy* (London: Croom Helm, 1987), p. 17.
70. Raymond Aron, *Peace and War, A Theory of International Relations* (Transaction Publishers, 1966), p. 80.
71. Thomas L. Friedman, *The World is Flat* (Penguin Books, 2006), p. 587.
72. Ibid., [Italics mine].
73. Ibid., pp. 592-593.
74. Ibid.
75. Ibid., p. 591.
76. Richard K. Betts, "The Trouble with Strategy: Bridging Policy and Operations", *Joint Force Quarterly*, 2001-02, Autumn/Winter, p. 23.
77. Ibid., p. 24.
78. Ibid., p. 26.
79. Charles Hitch, *An Appreciation of Systems Analysis* (RAND Corporation, 1955).
80. S.S. Khera, *Problems in Defence* (Orient Longmans, 1968), p. 246.

81. Ibid., p. 246.
82. Quoted by J. W. Gibson, "Systems Analysis in British Defence Policy Making: Some Achievements and Limitations", in Lawrence Martin, ed., *Management of Defence* (MACMILLAN Press, 1976), p. 88.
83. Colin S. Gray, "Strategy in the Nuclear Age: The United States, 1945-1991", in Williamson Murray, ed., *The Making of Strategy* (Cambridge University Press, 1995), p. 584.
84. Aron, n. 70, p. 72.
85. Ibid.
86. Ibid., pp. 91-92.
87. Ibid.
88. Kenneth E. Boulding, *Conflict and Defense* (Harper and Row, 1963), p. 276.
89. Richard A. Stubbing and Richard A Mendel, *The Defense Game* (Harper and Row, 1986), p. 60.
90. David Greenwood, "Economic Constraints and Political Preferences", in Baylis ed., n. 69, p. 31.
91. Khera, n. 80.
92. "Introduction", John Baylis, ed., *Alternative Approaches to British Defence Policy*, p. 5.
93. Ibid.
94. Greenwood, n. 90, p. 54.
95. Ibid., p. 53
96. *The Way Forward,* 1981, UK Government, cmnd 8288
97. Joshep E. Stiglitz and Linda J. Bilmes, *The Trillion Dollar War* (Allen Lane, 2008), p. 7.
98. Congressional Research Service, 7-5700, www.crs.gov- RL33110
99. Stiglitz and Bilmes, n. 97.
100. Ibid., p. 132.
101. V. Upadhyay, "Inflation and Food Security", *Alternative Economic Survey*, India 2011, Alternative Survey Group (Yuvasambad Prakashan, January 2012), p. 73.
102. Stiglitz and Bilmes, n.97, pp. 5-6.
103. Betts, n.76, p. 28.
104. Ibid.
105. Ibid.
106. Bush, n. 47, p. 257.
107. Stiglitz and Bilmes, n.97, p. 7.
108. Ionut C. Popescu, "Strategy-Resources Gap", *Joint Forces Quarterly*, 2nd Quarter, 2009, pp. 85-86 [italics mine].
109. Ibid.
110. Mark D. Toutman, *Making Tough Choices Tougher*, *AFJ*, Jan/Feb 2012.

111. Andrew F. Krepinevich, Jr., "The Pentagon's Wasting Assets," *Foreign Affairs*, July/August 2009.
112. John Peters et al., *A Methodology for Developing Army Acquisition Strategies for an Uncertain Future* (RAND ARROYO Center, 2007), pp. 15-16.
113. Ibid., p. 26.
114. Gavin Kennedy, "The Uses and Limitations of Economic Analysis for Defence Policy Making", in Laurence Martin, ed., *The Management of Defence*, p. 78.
115. Paul A. Samuelson and William D. Nordhaus, *Economics*, 18th Edition. p. 125, 2005.
116. Bernard Brodie, *Strategy as Science*, Vol. 1, No. 4, July 1949, pp. 467-488.
117. Ibid., p. 476.
118. Ibid., p. 477.
119. Ibid.
120. Ibid., p. 478.
121. Paul K. Davis, "Planning Under Uncertainty Then and Now: Paradigm Lost and Paradigms Emerging", Paul K. Davis, ed., *New Challenges in Defense Planning* (RAND, 1994), p. 44 [italics mine].
122. Robert McNamara, *Blundering into Disaster* (Bloomsbury, 1986), p. 53 [italics mine].
123. Ibid., [italics mine].
124. Eric Hobsbaum , *The Age of Extremes, 1914-1991* (Abacus, 1994), p-29 [italics mine].
125. John Keegan, *The First World War* (Vintage Books, 2000), p. 3.
126. Hobsbaum, n.124, p. 30.
127. Ibid., p. 5.
128. Boulding, n.88, p. 5.
129. Ibid.
130. Ibid., p. 26.
131. Ibid., p. 37.
132. Ibid., p. 57.
133. Thomas C. Schelling and Morton H. Halperin, *Strategy and Arms Control* (Pergammon-Brassey's, 1985), p. 4.
134. William W. Kaufmann, "The Requirements of Deterrence", in W.W. Kaufmann ed., *Military Policy and National Security* (Kennikat Press, 1956), p. 16.
135. Thomas Schelling, *The Strategy of Conflict* (Harvard University Press), p. 232; also the analysis made by Robert Ayson, *Thomas Schelling and the Nuclear Age* (Frank Cass, 2004), p. 60.
136. David A. Baldwin, "Power Analysis and World Politics", in Klaus Knorr, ed., *Power, Strategy and Security* (Princeton University Press, 1983), p. 28.
137. Ayson, n.135, p. 32.

138. Amartya Sen, *On Ethics and Economics* (Oxford University Press, 1987), p. 85.
139. Ibid.
140. Ibid.
141. Bernard Brodie, *War and Politics* (Macmillan Company, 1975), pp. 460-461.
142. Ibid.
143. Ibid.
144. Ibid.
145. Ibid., pp. 469-470.
146. Paul A. Samuelson and William D. Nordhaus, *Economics*, 18th Edition, 2005, p. 84, [italics in original].
147. Klaus Knorr, *On the Uses of Military Power in the Nuclear Age* (Princeton University Press, 1966), pp. 8-12.
148. Ibid.
149. Ibid., p. 11.
150. Ibid.
151. Ibid., p. 10.
152. Ibid.
153. Ibid., p. 13.
154. Ibid., p. 16.
155. Stephen Cohen and Sunil Dasgupta, *Arming without Aiming* (Brookings Institution Press), p. 27.
156. Davis, n.44, p. 44.
157. Ibid.
158. Ibid.
159. Brodie, n.141, p. 471.
160. Ibid., p. 479.
161. Edward Luttwak, *The Pentagon and the Art of War* (1985), p. 138.
162. Ibid., p. 141.
163. Ibid., p. 140.
164. Alain C. Enthoven and K.Wayne Smith, *How Much is Enough* (Harper and Row, 1971), pp. 70-71.
165. Ibid.
166. Albert Wohlstetter, "Analysis and Design of Conflict Systems", in E.S. Quade, ed., *Analysis for Military Decisions* (RAND, November 1964), p. 103.
167. Ibid., p. 117.
168. ibid., p. 121.
169. Ibid., p. 122.
170. Ibid., p.127.
171. Ibid., p. 126.
172. Hitch, n. 79.

173. Michael Howard, "The Forgotten Dimensions of Strategy", *Foreign Affairs*, 1979, pp. 976-986.
174. Colin S. Gray, *Modern Strategy* (Oxford University Press, 1999), p. 23.
175. S. N. Prasad and U.P. Thapliyal, eds., *The India-Pakistan War of 1965: A History* (Copyright of Ministry of Defence, Government of India, Nataraj Publishers, 2011), pp. 313-314.
176. Ibid.
177. K. Subrahmaniyam, *The Times of India*, September 7, 2000, quoted by Prasad and Thapliyal, Ibid., p. 315.
178. Air Chief Marshal P. C. Lal (Retd.), *My Years with IAF* (New Delhi,1986), Quoted by Prasad and Thapliyal, n.175, p. 311.
179. General V.P. Malik (Retd.), *The Indian Express*, September 16, 2000, quoted by Prasad and Thapliyal, n.175, p.311.
180. Gray, n.174, p. 31-32 [italics mine].
181. Archibald Wavell, *Generals and Generalship* (New York, 1943), p. 10.
182 Davis, n.44, p. 48.
183. Brig. Jaspal Singh (Retd.), *India's Land Forces, Structural Imperatives,* USI project, (Manas Publications, 2003), p. 61.
184. Ibid.
185. Brig. Pramod Sarin (Retd.), *Military Logistics: The Third Dimension* (Manas, 2000), p. 362, quoted by Singh, n.183.
186. Ibid., p. 70.
187. Singh, n.183, p. 72.
188. Richard Lipsey and Alec Chrystal, *Economics* (Oxford University Press, Eleventh edition, 2007), p. 116.
189. Khera, n.80, p. 252.
190. Ibid.
191. Ibid.
192. Ibid., [italics mine].
193. Paul K. Davis, Stuart E. Johnson, Duncan Long, David C. Gompert, *Developing Resource-Informed Strategic Assessments and Recommendations* (RAND, 2008), p. 9.
194. Ibid., p. 21.
195. Paul K. Davis, *Analytical Architecture for Capabilities-Based Planning, Mission-Systems Analysis and Transformation*" (RAND, 2002).
196. Ibid, "Summary", p. xiii.
197. Ibid.
198. Ibid., p. xviii.
199. Paul K. Davis, James H. Bigelow and Jimmie McEver, "Analytical Methods for Studies and Experiments on Transformation of the Force" (RAND, 1999), p. vii.

200. Jeremy Black, *Rethinking Military History*, 2004, Routledge, p. 143.
201. Ibid., p. 144.
202. Ibid., p. 129 [italics mine].
203. Zalmay Khalilzad and David Ochmanek, "Rethinking Defence Planning," *Survival*, Vol. 39, Spring 1997, p. 44.
204. Ibid., p. 46.
205. Ibid.

3

Review of the Defence Budget

Under India's parliamentary system of governance, making of budgets is the exclusive responsibility of the Executive. However, the overall budget is to be approved by the Parliament each year as a Money Bill. The Parliament can approve or reject the budget or any of its demands but cannot modify them. The system, thus, differs significantly from the American one, where Congress has the authority to modify the budget. The parliamentary review of the budget undertaken in India should be seen in this context.

A brief description of the defence budgeting process may be in order.

The defence budgeting process in India starts along with the budgeting process of other Ministries and Departments of the Government of India, on the basis of the Budget Circular issued by the Budget Division of the Ministry of Finance (MoF) in the middle of September each year, containing instructions and guidance for the preparation of the Revised Estimates (RE) of the current year and Budget Estimates (BE) of the next year. The budgets are finalised by the end of December.

The Budget Circular is accompanied by various instructions issued in the past by the Department of Expenditure regarding economy measures, rationalisation of expenditure, and measures for augmentation of revenues, for being kept in view while preparing estimates. Particular attention is drawn to the instruction regarding the exchequer control system introduced from April 1, 2006, known as the Modified Cash Management System whose main aim is to obtain greater evenness in budget expenditure and reduce the rush of expenditure in the last quarter of the financial year. Under this, monthly expenditure plans are to be worked out, and in the last quarter, not more than 33 percent of the budgetary provisions can be spent.

On receipt of the Budget Circular, the Budget Division of the Ministry of Defence (Finance), in turn, issues circular to the Service Headquarters

(HQ), Defence Research and Development Organisation (DRDO) and Department of Defence Production for their budget projections for the RE for the current year and the BE for the next year, keeping in view various parameters, including trends of expenditure.

The defence budget in India, is mainly composed of the budgets of the three Services, which represent 92 percent of the total budget. Projections are made by the Services on the basis of (i) expenditure pattern of past years and current trend of expenditure; (ii) prevailing inflationary trends; (iii) committed liabilities; (iv) anticipated requirement of stores; (iv) annual acquisition plan; (v) requirements on account of new units/formations/ establishments; (vi) annual works programmes, etc. The projections by the Services and Departments are consolidated and estimates are projected to the Ministry of Finance after approval of the RM. This is the first stage in budget preparation.

These estimates are discussed in the MoF with the Financial Advisers of Ministries/Departments in October/November. After the pre-budget meetings are over, approved ceilings of expenditure, as finalised in these meetings, are communicated to the Ministries / Departments, on the basis of which Financial Advisers are to prepare the final Budget Estimates.

So, in effect, the budget takes its final shape after the Ministry of Finance imposes its "ceilings" keeping in view competing demands and overall constraint of resources.[1]

The ceiling indicated by the MoF is not the overall ceiling on the defence budget but is indicated demand-wise.

The entire defence expenditure is treated as non-plan expenditure, which gives the Ministry of Defence more autonomy in the preparation of the budget than other Ministries/Departments, whose budgets are divided between plan and non-plan segments.

The departmentally related Standing Committee system, was inaugurated by the Vice President and Chairman of the Rajya Sabha (Upper House) on March 31, 1993. The Committees were constituted soon thereafter. It was a historical landmark in the evolution of the Committee system in the Indian Parliament.

Each of the Standing Committees consists of not more than 45 members—30 to be nominated by the Speaker from among the members of the Lok Sabha and 15 to be nominated by the Chairman, Rajya Sabha, from among the members of the Rajya Sabha. The term of the members of these Committees is not to exceed one year.

After the general discussion on the budget is over, the Lok Sabha (Lower House) adjourns for a fixed period and the Standing Committee considers the Demands for Grants during the recess. The demands are thereafter considered by the Lok Sabha in the light of the reports of the Committee.

As would be seen, the Standing Committee has no role in the preparation of the budget of the Department concerned. Its role is confined to undertaking a review of the Demands for Grants for the Ministry/Department concerned. Its recommendations on the basis of review, if they pertain to certain allocations made are, however, given due weightage in the preparation of the next year's budget.

The budgetary requirements for the defence Services are included in the following six Demands for Grants presented to Parliament:

- Demand No.21, Defence Services – Army
- Demand No.22, Defence Services – Navy
- Demand No.23, Defence Services – Air Force
- Demand No. 24, Defence Services – Defence Ordnance Factories
- Demand No.25, Defence Services – Research and Development Organisation
- Demand No. 26, Capital Outlay on Defence Service

The first five Demands for Grants (Demands 21 to 25) are categorised as Revenue Expenditure of the defence budget. Revenue Expenditure includes expenditure on pay and allowances, transportation, revenue stores like ordnance stores, revenue works, expenditure on Petroleum, Oil, Lubricants (POL), etc.

Requirements for Capital Expenditure are contained in the Capital Outlay (Demand No. 26), which caters to the requirements of capital expenditure of all the Services, ordnance factories, Research and Development (R&D) organisation. It includes expenditure on land, construction works, plants and machinery, equipments, tanks, naval vessels, aircraft and aeroengines, dockyards, etc.

The defence budget is formulated on the basis of the structure mentioned above, making it a totally input oriented budget. Control of expenditure is the main theme of defence budgeting in India, for which an input oriented budget is well suited.

The fundamental rule on which the system of budgetary control may be said to rest is that no item of public expenditure may be incurred, unless provisions exist to meet it in the sanctioned BE of the year concerned. This rule applies to the nature of expenditure as well as the amount.

While analysing various points made by the Standing Committee on Defence while scrutinising defence budgets year after year, it may be worthwhile to look into the perspectives from which the defence budget, as it stands, can be analysed.

The key ingredients of the defence budget can be looked at from the "requirements" as projected by the three Services, going into their reasonableness.

But it can take us only up to a point, for in the final stage of the budgetary process, as per the laid down procedure, there is a "ceiling" which is imposed by the MoF.

Secondly, the "requirements" are projected by the Services on the basis of their respective perspective plans and annual plans, which are not open to scrutiny. So, for the reasonableness of the "requirements" which form the basis of their respective budget projections, one has to depend to a large extent on the analyses and judgement of the Services which have their financial planning wing and control mechanism.

There is another approach towards scrutiny of the defence budget from the "cost" angle i.e. by treating it as composed of various *costs* that the defence Services have to incur or the *prices* they have to pay, from their respective budgets, to maintain the forces and supporting staff, to achieve an acceptable level of defence preparedness and build up the necessary capability.

The basic ingredients of the defence budget, from this point of view, are the *costs* which are to be incurred to meet the *requirements,* and many requirements cannot be met because the costs of other items exhaust the total budgetary resources made available to a Service. Prioritisation is the only answer, but that keeps many requirements unsatisfied.

Thus, the defence budget of India can be scrutinised from two perspectives: from the perspective of requirements and from the perspective of costs. One could also add another perspective, that is, requirements, keeping in view the costs. That would mean the introduction of the programme concept in defence budgeting which would enable both requirements and costs to be seen in the context of specific programmes. That would mean introducing an output orientation in defence budgeting.

But since our defence budget, as explained above, is an input oriented budget and is not formulated in terms of programmes, it is difficult to analyse the budget as at present, simultaneously from the requirement and cost points of view, nor is it possible to link the budget to the end objectives of defence spending.

Accepting the present limitation from an analytical point of view of an input oriented budget, the main aim while scrutinising the defence budget from the "cost" point of view is that these costs, which are the ingredients of the defence budget, are not more than what is reasonable and should be reflective of good management practices. Cost consciousness should prevail all along the line so that costs borne by the defence budget in carrying out various defence related activities are not more than what is fair and reasonable.

Some of these costs are controllable and some are not. The manpower costs, infrastructure costs, inventory costs and many other costs are controllable by adopting proper manpower policies and good management practices.

Costs, as reflected in the budget, are to be looked into with a view to economise on them without reducing efficiency, so that public money is not wasted and we get cost-effective defence.

The aim, for example, should be to eliminate inefficiencies in support processes and to ensure that the quality of maintenance does not suffer. Cost-effectiveness in support areas also helps in better allocation of resources to maximise military capability available to the front line.

It should be the endeavour of any critical scrutiny of the process of defence budgeting to see whether, among other things, it ensures that the front line receives the logistic support needed within the framework that provides the best balance between operational effectiveness and efficiency. Overenthusiastic effort to cut down the maintenance expenditure to increase the allocation for capital acquisition should not lead to reduction in operational efficiency and impairing readiness.

In defence budgetary literature in India, most of the costs are often treated as "obligatory," for which it is held that budgetary provisions, in any case, are to be made. These are treated as policy related costs, determined by the "*strength and composition of armed forces maintained for the defence of the country.*"[2]

But these costs are also controllable through a periodic review of force structure which should be both strategy driven and resource driven.

Some of the infrastructure costs are controllable in the medium term, by taking effective measures from now on so that future defence budgets are less burdened by these costs. For this, a longer-term view regarding cost control is necessary.

This also underlines the need for both medium and long-term planning and linking defence budgeting with it, so that savings can be generated for modernisation efforts. Defence planning and linking it with budgeting is, therefore, not a luxury, but a necessity for evolving an affordable and effective defence. Planning should be regarded as a necessary ingredient of defence, which has often been emphasised by the Standing Committees by expressing their anxiety in timely approval of defence plans.

As would be seen from the discussion which follows, the general approach adopted by India's Parliamentary Committee on Defence (Standing Committee) on the defence budget was that they looked mainly into the cost aspects in the first few years of their scrutiny of the defence budget, as the general environment for public finance was of expenditure control and economy in expenditure. In the subsequent years, however, with easing of financial stringency and higher rate of economic growth, they have looked into the requirements aspects more intensively.

As per the first report on the Demands for Grants 1993-94, the scrutiny of the demands was conducted on the basis of the following information:

- policy/programmes/activities brought out by the Ministry of Defence (MoD) in the Annual Report;
- past commitments carried over in the current year i.e. 1993-94;
- anticipated liabilities for the current year; and
- increase over the previous year's estimates.

The above documents were consulted by the Committee while scrutinising the demands for grants for subsequent years also. This reflected the concern regarding the "requirement" aspects of the defence budget.

In the first two years of its review of the Demands for Grants for the Ministry of Defence, the Standing Committee, went into the aspect of "reasonableness" of the increase sought in the Revised Estimates of the previous year's budget as also that for the budget of the current year over the Revised Estimates. It went into the reasons for the increases, and found the increases given as reasonable and modest.

The Committee also looked into allocations which had been provided for modernisation schemes in the budget of 1993-94 in both the Capital and Revenue accounts. It was noted that the term "modernisation" was not a classification for budgetary purposes. The Committee were informed that the budgetary constraints had an impact on the modernisation programmes.

The Committee came to the conclusion, keeping in view the overall constraint in resources, that the best way to generate funds for modernisation of the armed forces was through generating internal savings by taking well considered economy measures.

The Committee took particular interest in various measures of economy being undertaken by the Services and the Ministry. It gave special emphasis to these in its reports on the defence budgets of 1993-94 and 1995-96. Apparently, it succeeded in conveying an effective message to the Ministry of Defence and the armed forces to manage defence expenditure in a cost-effective way.

The Standing Committee referred to the earlier recommendations of the Committee on Defence Expenditure (CDE) set up in June 1990 regarding achieving economies in specific areas of defence expenditure. In response, the Ministry of Defence explained that action had already been taken to reduce expenditure relating to manpower, petrol, oil, transportation, inventory management, etc. The Standing Committee expressed the hope that the economies will be suitably reflected in the Demands for Grants of the future years.

The Committee also went into the specific details relating to the economy measures initiated by the Services. In response, the Ministry explained that in the army, savings were achieved through reduction in the authorisation of equipment, one-time reduction in the inventory in the Army Ordnance Corps, reduction of land norms, introduction of fuel efficient vehicles, introduction of transportation model, etc. These had resulted in a saving of about Rs. 1,000 crore per annum. These savings were envisaged in the budget and had been observed in practice. Similarly, the economy measures initiated by the Navy were likely to result in an annual savings of Rs. 49.93 crore and economy measures initiated by the Indian Air Force (IAF) were to result in a saving of Rs. 67.19 crore. The Committee recommended that the measures regarding conserving of petroleum products should be undertaken by all organisations under the Ministry of Defence, more vigorously.

The Committee made very significant recommendations for achieving economy in the inventory of ordnance stores. Similarly, personnel requirement of the manpower for non-combat duties, the Committee felt, needed constant review for all the Services.

By emphasising that money saved by a particular Service should be available for modernisation (presumably for the same Service that effected the saving), the Committee was enunciating an important principle. It was : economy achieved by these measures by a particular Service which required efforts and sacrifice should not lead to reduction in the overall allocation of the budget, but should be redistributed to increase the allocation under the capital head, for expenditure on modernisation. This is an important principle. If this kind of incentive is not provided, the Services may not be enthusiastic in achieving economy in areas where it is possible.

The report pertaining to the Demands for Grants 1994-95 also looked into the economy aspects with a lot of attention. Some of the important steps taken and consequent savings per annum, which the Committee was informed about by the Ministry, were: (i) rationalisation of the non-combatant manpower in the army (Rs. 200 crore); (ii) rationalisation of authorisation of tanks per regiment (Rs. 60 crore); (iii) modernisation of inventory management and introduction of the Central Inventory Control Point System (Rs. 100 crore); (iv) off-loading of the requirements hitherto met by the Electrical and Mechanical Engineers (EME) and other units of the Army to the civil market (Rs. 20 crore); (v) introduction of a new transportation model including decentralisation of the supply system (Rs. 12 crore); (vi) use of simulators for training (Rs. 300 crore); and (vii) the rationalisation of plinth area for residential accommodation for officers and men (Rs. 8 crore).

The Committee observed that measures regarding conservation of petroleum products as recommended by its first report had not led to reduction in allocation under the POL head. It noted that the Budget Estimates under these items for 1993-94 was revised at a higher figure and a still higher amount was planned to be spent in 1994-95. It was explained by the Ministry in its Action Taken Note that the increase was due to increase in the prices of POL, and in actual terms, there was no increase in consumption of POL.

The Standing Committee also reiterated the need for the report of the Committee on Defence Expenditure to be made public as early as possible.

The Committee was of the view "that a little more openness even in the matters relating to defence will not militate against the national interest. ..."[3] This is an important point for a democratic system of government. Reports dealing with the efficacy with which public money is spent and how this could be improved upon should be made public, as also measures taken by the government to implement the recommendations, as the taxpayers should be satisfied that public money was well spent.

The Committee was concerned at the fact that there had been an increase of 10.87 percent in the Budget Estimates of 1995-96 as compared to that of 1994-95 whereas the rate of inflation during 1994-95 was 11.41 percent, allowing no increase in real terms in the defence budget, 1995-96. The Committee also noted that the Gross Capital Expenditure which was 29.45 percent in 1994-95 (RE) declined in 1995-96 (BE) to 28.84 percent, indicating a deceleration of the modernisation effort.

As per the next report, the increase in the BE for 1996-97 over the previous year's RE worked out to 3.2 percent only as against the existing rate of inflation of about 4.5 percent. In other words, there had been no increase in real terms in the defence budget for 1996-97 at all.

The Committee, in its report for 1996-97, gave a table showing how defence expenditure as a percentage of Central Government Expenditure had fallen from 17.55 percent in 1986-87 to 13.58 percent in 1996-97. It also indicated that defence expenditure as a percentage of Gross Domestic Product (GDP) had fallen from 3.58 percent in 1986-87 to 2.72 percent in 1994-95.

Referring to the budget provision for 1997-98 which represented 20.75 percent increase over that of the previous year, the Committee observed that if the amount required for implementation of the Fifth Pay Commission was excluded, the actual budgetary hike would only be 8.5 percent over the RE 1996-97 against the existing inflation rate of about 7.8 percent "Thus, in real terms, the hike in the Defence Service Estimates for 1997-98 is only notional."[4]

The inadequacy of the increase in the defence budget was again commented upon by the Committee while reviewing the Demands for Grants 1998-99 when it observed that the hike in the defence budget was just about enough to meet the outflow of the Fifth Pay Commission's recommendations and general inflation. The rupee devaluation had further eroded budget capacity. "Thus, in real terms, the provision for items other than salary in the defence budget remains static, if not reduced. In terms of percentage of GDP also, the defence budget has stagnated at 2.4 percent over the last decade. This low level of funding is totally insufficient to meet crucial requirements, including modernisation of the armed forces," it observed. The Committee emphasised that in the interest of the security of the country, defence spending should be raised at least to the level of 3 percent of the GDP.[5]

The same kind of comments were made while examining the Demands for Grants 1999-2000. In real terms, the hike in defence outlay for the year 1999-2000, appeared to the Committee as "notional."[6]

In a table presented in the report, it was shown that the recommendations made by the MoD for the budget were much lower than the projections made by the Services/Departments and allocations made by the MoF were still less. In effect, the amount allocated by the MoF by imposing a ceiling was about 18 percent less than the amount projected by the Services/Departments.

In scrutinising the Demands for Grants for 2001-02, a similar table was presented, which showed that the amount allocated as per ceiling made by the MoF was about 16 percent less than the amount projected by the Services/Departments.[7]

In the Action Taken Notes, the government, in their replies relating to the Committee's observations on the inadequacy of the increases in the defence budget, have all along stated that the observations had been communicated to the Ministry of Finance for their consideration and necessary action. In one of the replies, the government categorically stated, "As already brought to the notice of the Committee, the Ministry of Finance make final allocations for defence taking into consideration all relevant factors."[8]

The recommendations of the Standing Committee of the presentation of the budget do not result in any increase for defence allocations. As per India's system of financial administration and governance, this really should be accepted as a final point. Reiteration of this point leads to needless discussions, points and counterpoints, without any tangible result.

Therefore, it is felt that discussing the adequacy or otherwise of the overall defence budget after it is finalised, is not a very productive exercise and the Committee should rather look into other aspects which relate to economy and efficiency of defence expenditure. This point was appreciated by the Committee while scrutinising the Demands for Grants 2001-02 when it stated, "The Committee is of the view that effective security cannot be had by merely presenting a bigger defence budget. It requires effective defence finance procedures which, in turn, needs an integrated defence planning organisation."[9] The reason for this observation was that an analysis of the figures showed that an amount of Rs. 4,100 crore of the allocated defence budget remained unspent during the year 2000-01. The Committee felt that the tedious and time consuming procedures had led to delay in defence spending, particularly that relating to procurement. The Committee desired that the procedure should be streamlined. While scrutinising the Demands for Grants 2002-03, the Committee again took note of unspent funds amounting to Rs. 5,000 crore, the major portion of which related to capital expenditure. This story of surrender of funds from the allotted budget, year after year, has been a recurring one.

The Committee in its report on the Demands for Grants 2004-05 noted that the Budget Estimates for the defence Services for the year 2004-05 showed an increase of 17.92 percent over the Budget Estimates of the year 2003-04 and an increase of 27.69 percent over the Revised Estimates for the year 2003-04. The increase was mainly in capital expenditure (Para 30 of the Report on Demands for Grants for 2004-05). Notwithstanding the higher allocation, the Committee noted that the MoD might have to seek additional funds from the MoF because almost the entire amount allocated for capital expenditure would be spent on committed liabilities. The Committee suggested that the MoD might approach the MoF after reassessing the situation.[10]

The Committee also noted that during the previous five years i.e. from 1999-2000 to 2003-04, substantial funds amounting to Rs. 32,740.26 crore for capital expenditure had lapsed due to non-fructification of modernisation schemes. In their earlier reports, they had recommended creation of a Defence Modernisation Fund (DMF). The Committee noted that the MoF had in principle agreed to the creation of the DMF,which would be available for utilisation during the next three years and that the then Finance Minister, while presenting the Interim Budget, 2004-05, announced the setting up of a non-lapsable Defence Modernisation Fund with a corpus of Rs. 25,000 crore. The Committee was, however, surprised to note that no allocation was made for this fund in the General Budget 2004-05 and was dismayed at the policy reversal.[11]

In the report on the Demands for Grants for 2006-07, a table has been furnished indicating provisions in the Budget Estimates, Revised Estimates, Actuals and Shortfall. The figures shown in the table indicated that there was reduction of allocation from BE to RE and from RE to actual amount spent since 2000-01, except in the year 2004-05. These again indicated shortfall/ underutilisation of budgetary allocations. What bothered the Committee was reduction of the amounts allocated at the RE stage compared to BE provisions. It was stated by the Ministry of Defence that the Ministry of Finance reduced the amount at the RE stage based on the progress of expenditure and their assessment of requirements of funds during the remaining part of the financial year.

The MoF also stated that in all these years, during the course of the mid-year review, it was found that the capital expenditure of the MoD was much below the amount provided in the budget. The Revised Estimates was arrived at keeping the pace of expenditure and absorptive capacity of the

MoD in the next two months in view. The MoD indicated that streamlining the acquisition procedures through the procurement manual would help reduce the time between various stages of acquisition proceedings. The Committee was not satisfied with the explanation. To quote, "Expressing strong displeasure, the Committee feel that there is a need for better financial planning and management in the Ministry of Defence."[12]

The Committee, as mentioned above, in its earlier reports had recommended creation of a non-lapsable DMF to ensure timely availability of funds for acquisition of defence equipment.

It was brought out by the MoF, that it would not help matters as parliamentary approval would be required for utilising the money from the fund. But the Standing Committee reiterated its recommendation regarding creation of the DMF for better budgetary management of defence procurement.

The position taken by the MoF has been that as adequate funds were made available in the beginning of each financial year for meeting the requirements of capital expenditure, there appeared "to be no need for sequestering scarce public resources in a Fund."[13]

The attention of the Committee while examining the Demands for Grants for 2008-09 was focussed on "Curbing of Wasteful Expenditure." The Committee's attention was drawn to various studies that have been undertaken by the Services "in-house" and by the Integrated Defence Staff (IDS) to identify wasteful expenditure. Reference was also made to findings of the IDS that (1) optimisation of defence resources could be achieved, for example, by amalgamation of assets in several areas through promotion of tri-Service institutions; (2) by a pragmatic review of reserve levels which fall in the realm of overassurance; (3) effective exploitation of the Information Technology (IT) revolution backed up by a sound networking system and in other ways.

The Committee has all along emphasised in its reports the need for achieving self-reliance in defence acquisitions and in this context, recommended a higher percentage of allocation of the budget to defence R&D which was about 4.5 percent of the defence budget in 1994-95, so that R&D programmes are completed on schedule. Its reports also drew attention to the Ten-Year-Self-Reliance Plan to achieve a self-reliance index of 0.7 percent.

Following the Standing Committee's recommendations, the percentage of allocation of defence R&D has gone up gradually to 6 percent of the defence budget.

For better management of the defence budget, the Committee had desired that the 9th Defence Plan for the period 1997-2002 be finalised on time. It also wanted that a firm commitment be made by the government for allocation of resources for five years rather than year to year.

In the Action Taken Note submitted in 1998, the Ministry of Defence had said that the 9th Defence Plan was approved by the Cabinet Committee on Security in December 1997 for which a firm commitment of funds for five years was given.

In fact, this became possible because of the combined efforts made by the MoD, Minister of Finance, Service Chiefs, the Cabinet and the then Principal Secretary to the Prime Minister. The yearly budgetary allocations made from 1997-98 to 2001 to 2002 to defence i.e. in the 9th Plan period and the expenditure made, broadly conformed to the figures originally approved in the beginning of the plan period.

But this could not be repeated for the 10th Defence Plan (2002-07), in spite of the concern shown by the Standing Committee in several of its reports. The same problem continues for the 11th Plan. It only shows that a well formulated Defence Plan can get approved in time only when concerted efforts are made at the higher level of decision-making in the government, though Standing Committees could help by repeatedly referring to its need, in their reports.

Although legally and technically, the recommendations of the Standing Committees are not binding, the government generally accepts most of them. For example, in its report on the Demands for Grants 2008-09, in the very first chapter, a reference is made to the Action Taken Report on the recommendations relating to the Demands for Grants 2007-08. It contained 76 observations/recommendations of which 57 were accepted. For reasons put forth by the government, in respect of 10 recommendations, the Committee did not wish to pursue Action Taken replies. One of the recommendations referred to allotment of 3 percent of the GDP for the defence budget, another related to a separate Pay Commission for the armed forces. In the case of four recommendations, it did not accept the replies of the government, one of which related to the need for increasing the budgetary allocation to the Navy. In five cases, the replies of the government were awaited.

One should not forget the limits within which the Parliamentary Committees are required to function. They have to function as per the rules of procedures. The Standing Committee can express its views and make recommendations in the form of a report, but it does not fall within its purview to direct any authority or government to do or not to do any particular act or do it in a certain way. Its main function would be to influence the government for taking such action which it considers desirable.

The Standing Committee, through its reports, has succeeded in putting defence budgeting in the proper perspective. Today, through the medium of its published reports, there is a wealth of information in the public domain about the defence budgeting process, trends in budgetary allocation and various considerations which go into defence budgeting. By inviting representatives of the Finance Ministry in its deliberations and asking them to put their point of view before the Committee regarding budgetary allocations, alternative points of view and putting them on record, the reports have succeeded in making the analysts, decision-makers and the public aware of various issues that are relevant in defence budget-making and managing.

The Standing Committees on Defence have gradually expanded the scope of examination of defence related activities to gain better insight into defence expenditure management. They have furnished reports on Defence Public Sector Undertakings, Defence Research and Development—Major Projects, Welfare of Servicemen and Ex-Servicemen, Upgradation and Modernisation of Naval Fleet, Manpower Planning and Management Policy in Defence.

The report rendered in 2001 pertaining to Manpower Planning is of particular importance as 35 percent of defence expenditure is manpower related. The Committee noted that the army had formulated a plan for effecting underposting of 50,000 soldiers over a period of financial years till 31.3.1999, covering all types of units and formations. The basic aim was to cut down on manpower cost so as to release resources for more investment in higher technology weaponry. The Committee wanted it to be done in a time-bound manner. [14]

The Committee also expressed its unhappiness about the deficiencies in the cadre strength of officers in the army and advised the government for taking necessary steps to fill up the vacancies. The Committee noted that about 50,000 Service personnel who constitute a rich source of trained and disciplined manpower, retired or were released from active service every year. The Committee recommended that more ex-armed forces personnel should be retrained and absorbed in the paramilitary forces.[15]

In this connection, it supported the recommendation of the Fifth Pay Commission regarding engagement of one-third of the annual intake into the combat and combat support arms of the Army Personnel Below Officer Rank (PBOR) on a shorter term of seven years, with the provision of their remustering into the other supporting arms and services within the army. The Committee did not understand the reasons for the government not considering favourably any proposal to reduce the colour service. Reduction in colour service would reduce the pension bill of the Service personnel.[16]

The Committee also stressed the need for improving the "teeth to tail" ratio to reduce manpower cost by economising on support staff in the army.[17] Eminent experts from outside were also invited to present their point of view in this respect. One expert commented that the manning strength in the IAF in certain activities was more than the standard adopted abroad for similar activities. These affected the teeth to tail ratio in the IAF.[18]

The Committee, in this context, reviewed the functioning of the Standing Establishment Committees of the three Services which are the expert bodies to examine the staffing strength of various units, with a view to optimise the manpower strength. The Committee expressed unhappiness on the functioning of one of the Standing Establishment Committees.

By giving a very detailed report on manpower planning in defence, the Committee not only provided very useful information relating to manpower in the Indian Army, Navy and Air Force but also put the issues in proper perspective to enable defence analysts and decision-makers to arrive at the correct conclusions.

The reports of the Standing Committee on Defence have been a great help in focussing attention on important aspects of defence budgeting, on the necessity for cost control and curbing of wasteful expenditure, as also the need for early approval of Defence Plans so that money for defence is spent efficiently for achieving the strategic objectives in a cost-effective way.

Control of defence expenditure is, no doubt, a very important aspect of defence budgeting. But the problem facing defence budgeting from the late Nineties onwards has been, paradoxically, the inability to spend the allotted amounts, particularly under the capital outlay account.

In every report of the Standing Committee in recent years, both the unfulfilled requirements for various schemes and projects of the Services and the extent of surrender of budgetary allotments have been brought out. The Finance Ministry has also been frequently criticised for allotting less than the projected amounts in the Plan and for the annual budget, as also for reduction of the budget at the RE stage.

One wonders, however, what the surrenders would have been like from the budgetary provisions, if the projected amounts had been allotted.

The phenomenon of surrendering funds has become more pronounced since 2000-01. Since then, every year, barring 2004-05, substantial funds have been surrendered at the RE stage and at the end of the financial year, in spite of all the efforts made to spend the allotted amounts by frequent monitoring of expenditure. Up to 2008-09, upwards of Rs. 40,000 crore have been surrendered in this way, because of inability to spend the allotted amount.

The Standing Committee in its several reports has criticised this aspect of defence budgeting and attributed it basically to bad financial management and cumbersome procurement procedure.

The Committee's repeated insistence for the creation of the Defence Modernisation Fund (DMF) emanates from this phenomenon of surrender of funds under the capital head year after year, though there is a huge requirement of funds for modernisation.

The MoF has not agreed to the DMF (as per their deposition before the Standing Committee) because, they say:

- funds have never been denied to defence whenever a scheme has matured for implementation and provision for a supplementary budget is always there;
- every year, the Ministry of Defence has surrendered funds at the RE

stage, because of inability to spend the allotted amount on the basis of trends of expenditure;

- even if the DMF is created, for drawing money from it, supplementary budgets would have to be prepared as Parliament's approval has to be obtained, therefore, there is hardly any benefit.

For these reasons, the MoF feels that there is no necessity to keep aside so much funds for future spending in defence, as there are many competing demands for other activities for which funds are required now. In other words, if money cannot be spent, it should be surrendered.

It is not the question only of somehow spending the allotted amounts by any means, but also securing efficiency in spending the amounts. The Standing Committee itself, in its reports, has drawn attention to wastages and the need for economy and efficiency in defence spending so that more money can be spared for modernisation. This kind of economy cannot be brought about by ad hoc measures, as these economies have be enduring ones. So control of expenditure has to be emphasised but the "control" has to be defined in a wider context of achieving planned targets within the resources made available.

Economy in defence expenditure should always be the desired goal of expenditure management. But it cannot be achieved by ad hoc measures.

Effective measures for achieving economy in defence spending have to be properly planned for on the basis of specific studies. It takes time to fructify, as it may involve restructuring of support areas, introducing economical models of logistic support and even closure of establishments which have lost their utility, and achieving economy in manpower by rationalisation of activities. Achieving this kind of economy requires multi-year focus, with performance measures and clear targets for achieving savings for each year.

Then there is the basic issue of prioritisation of expenditure among competing programmes because of scarcity of resources. We often mention its need without realising that the annual budgetary exercise is hardly conducive to a prioritisation exercise, as it provides for all ongoing activities and existing commitments in a routine manner, as the reports of the Standing Committee show.

Expenditure prioritisation is about choices between alternative policies and the fiscal impact of specific policy choices on future budgets.. This cannot be done when attention is confined to one year of the budget, as the fiscal impact of the choice would be felt in the subsequent budgets. A prioritisation exercise has to be an integral part of the budgetary process.

So, for prioritisation of expenditure decisions, keeping in view the impact of present decisions on future budgets, multi-year budgeting is essential. As Marc Robinson puts it, international experience proves that for being effective, "*expenditure prioritisation needs to be conducted as a systematic routine integrated with the budgetary process*" and that "*expenditure prioritisation tends to work best when the budget is put on a multi-annual basis, either through multi-year allocations or a system of rolling forward expenditure estimates*....fiscal impact of specific policy choices can often not be measured in the prospective budget year. This point has long been recognized by performance budgeting advocates, well before the recent resurgence of interest in medium-term budgeting. The original US program budgeting system (PPBS), for example, aimed to plan expenditure over at least a five-year plan horizon."[19]

So when we aim to introduce prioritisation in expenditure decisions which is a must in expenditure management in defence, there is an imperative necessity to introduce multi-year budgeting, for optimal allocation of resources.

The other very important aspect in defence budgeting in India which calls for immediate introduction of multi-year budgeting, is that allotments of funds for capital expenditure, in both absolute and percentage terms, have gone up significantly in the defence budget in recent years. The percentage in recent years has been above 40 percent which is very high by all standards. Only a decade ago, the capital budget used to be 28-29 percent of the defence budget.

Many of the projects/schemes under consideration, are 'big ticket' items where huge expenditure is involved over several years. These are all in the nature of investments for future capability building, where careful analyses of costs/benefits are involved.

These investments should not be made in a hurry, without proper cost-benefit analysis. It may be prudent in some cases to deliberately wait before taking a decision, as various alternatives are required to be assessed and new opportunities continue to arise due to rapid technological changes.

For building of capabilities under the concept of the Revolution in Military Affairs (RMA) which is getting incorporated in the doctrines of the armed forces, investments for items categorised as force multipliers, have to take place over a period of several years, as considerable R&D activities are involved. Many of these investments are interlinked.

Planning for such investments also underlines the *need for multi-year budgeting in defence*.

It is also to be remembered that in defence procurement cases, to ensure transparency, fairness, proper evaluation and assessment of all aspects of the proposed investment, the laid down procurement procedure has to be followed strictly. It cannot be curtailed to fit a given time-frame. Issues arise which have to be sorted out after due deliberation. In urgent cases, a fast track procedure can always be followed but that should be the exception.

So there are four aspects in the defence budgeting process which need to be attended to:

- ensuring economy and efficiency in defence spending in a planned manner;
- prioritisation of expenditure between competing programmes;
- avoiding surrender of funds under the capital account in the defence budget;
- supporting multi-year investment planning and expenditure planning for optimum allocation of resources.

All the four aspects mentioned above lead to only to one conclusion: that is there is an urgent need for budgetary reform in defence, giving particular attention to the budgetary process for optimal utilisation of resources. We have to introduce output oriented budgeting. Defence budgeting has till now avoided performance budgeting. Already, outcome budgeting has been introduced in the civil side.

We have to introduce performance budgeting, with the programme concept in defence budgeting. The programme concept is necessary so that one can meaningfully talk of output or objectives and relating output to relevant costs.

This variant of performance budgeting, we may also call *programme budgeting*.

"Programme budgeting is the performance budgeting mechanism which has had the most enduring influence."[20]

Basically, programme budgeting comprises (a) the objective-based ("programme") classification of expenditure; and (b) use of performance information in a systematic way for taking decisions about budgetary priorities between competing programmes.

For defence, keeping in view the heavy investments in weapons and systems where investments have to be spread over a number of years, performance budgeting has to be more in the nature of the Planning-Programming-Budgeting System (PPBS) which is aimed at moving "planning from the periphery to the center of budget operations"[21] rather than its simpler version, where performance budgeting is concerned only with the use *of performance measures* in the budget.

In fact, *"performance information"* that we mentioned above, goes beyond *performance measure* to include performance evaluation and cost/ benefit analysis.[22] Using performance information, in this sense, makes performance budgeting indistinguishable from programme budgeting.

Without the abovementioned reforms in budgeting, the review of the defence budget by the Standing Committee is not likely to be effective and the Committee is apparently aware of this.

This point can be illustrated by reference to some of the points which have emerged in the Committee's budget review reports so far.

Share Between Revenue and Capital in Defence Budget

While scrutinising the defence budget for 2007-08, the issue of what should be the proper allocation between revenue and capital expenditure in the defence budget, came up for lot of discussion in the deliberations of the Standing Committee.

It was brought out by the representative of the MoD that in the 8th Plan period, overall 70 percent of the budgetary allocation was for revenue spending and 30 percent was for capital expenditure. In the 9th Plan, it was 74 percent for revenue expenditure and 26 percent for capital; while in the 10th Plan period, the percentage of revenue expenditure came down to 64 percent and the percentage for capital expenditure went up to 36 percent. This showed greater emphasis on modernisation than before. In 2007-08, as per budgetary allocation, 56 percent was for revenue expenditure and 44 percent for capital expenditure.

The Defence Secretary, however, added a word of caution, saying that beyond a certain point, the revenue expenditure cannot be brought down.[23] He also added that keeping in view the inflationary trend, the amounts projected by the Services for revenue expenditure in the 11th Plan period might be inadequate. "The revenue spending, which goes into their budget, is very essential for ensuring the readiness level of various weapon platforms that they have. If they have to maintain70, 80 or 85 percent level of serviceability, all those spares are needed. All the ammunition gets funded through the revenue budget. *So, if we have to have enough ammunition to fire from various types of weapons that we have, revenue spending has to remain at a reasonable level.*"[24]

The Committee stated, " During evidence, the representative of the Ministry of Defence also admitted that beyond a point, revenue expenditure cannot be curtailed as that may hamper defence preparedness and the allocation for revenue expenditure for the year 2007-08 is inadequate." The Committee also felt that "due precaution should be taken in the matter so as not to adversely affect the defence preparedness of the country."[25]

These depositions raise several points. What is the "reasonable level" of allocation for revenue expenditure in the defence budget? What is the point below which revenue expenditure cannot be allowed to fall, so that defence preparedness is not affected? As is evident from the deposition of the Defence Secretary before the Committee, he was apprehensive that projections made by the Services for revenue expenditure for the 11th Plan were inadequate, indicating that probably more than necessary emphasis was being given on allocation for the capital budget. The same predilection can be there while projecting requirements for the annual budget. In any case, allocation of 44 percent for the capital budget is unsustainable. It could lead to a situation, as in the past, where weapon systems would be acquired but there may not be enough resources to operationalise or maintain them

Secondly, the Committee itself noted that the bulk of the expenditure of the army was on the revenue account and "*there is a huge gap between the revenue expenditure and capital expenditure of the army, due to different kind of requirement and work performed by it. The Committee endorse the views of the Ministry of Defence that revenue expenditure cannot be curtailed beyond a certain point and that any reduction in revenue expenditure should not be at the expense of the army's readiness/preparedness.*"[26]

The Committee also expressed its concern about "the declining trend in the share of the army in the defence budget, which was 57 percent in the year 2002-03 and has now come down to 47 percent in the current year."[27]

So, what it makes clear is that behind the issue of allotment of the defence budget between the revenue and capital budgets, there is a much bigger issue of the respective roles of the three Services and the tasks they have to perform in ensuring the security of the country.

There is now, of course, the concept of jointness and the doctrine is evolving in this direction. This puts emphasis on mission and task orientation in resource allocation decisions, rather than on Service-wise allocation, though that issue cannot be avoided in taking a macro view of the matter on the basis of technological changes and new concepts of warfare.

In fact, mere division of the defence budget into revenue and capital expenditure may be all right for voting purposes, but hardly adequate for rational allocation of resources in defence; in fact, it is a means of hiding the real issues.

For rational allocation of resources, we have to introduce programme budgeting, in which all elements of cost would be included in a programme for achieving an approved mission. Whether the allocation for the revenue expenditure is adequate or not has to be ascertained programme by programme and on the basis of its specific requirements. To quote Charles Hitch who was the main architect in introducing programme budgeting in US defence under Robert McNamara, indicating the importance of allocating for operating expenses which is catered for what is categorised as revenue expenditure in our budget, "The operating costs are the annual operating costs required to man, operate, and maintain the capability. Quite often, the cost of operating a system over its expected life is more important than investment costs. For example, it costs as much to operate and maintain an infantry division for one year as it does to equip it in the first place. Thus, operating costs can be crucial to the initial management decision to produce and deploy one weapon system as compared with another."[28]

It is not enough to equate the capital budget with modernisation; we must know what the modernisation is composed of, and how it is helping in building capability for meeting the emerging threats; in other words, what is the output of the defence budget, keeping in view both the revenue and capital expenditure.

Only programme budgeting can help in relating resources "inputs"—manpower, material and installations—together with their costs, to military "outputs"—strategic retaliatory forces, general power forces, airlift capabilities, air defence capabilities, surveillance capabilities, protection of maritime interests, etc—which cannot be done by merely distinguishing between revenue and capital expenditure.

Outcome Budget: How to Move Towards it

In its report on the Demands for Grants 2008-09, the Committee showed its interest in the formulation of an "Outcome Budget" in defence. In this context, it stated, "The Committee desired from the Ministry of Defence, brief particulars of all major schemes/ projects under implementation and project-wise achievement against the targets (both physical and financial) during the last two years in the Ministry of Defence. The Ministry of Defence have not furnished any information thereon." [29]

If the aim is to examine the outcome, going through the schemes and projects may not be very illuminating, unless one is able to link them with the budgetary allocations, on the one hand, and the objectives they are supposed to serve, on the other. The outcome can be assessed only in relation to the programme, of which the scheme/project under review, is a part.

Output budgeting is the basic step towards outcome budgeting, for which we require a well-conceived programme structure, keeping end objectives in view as also the decision-making mechanism at the apex level for major resource allocation decisions.

Incidentally, the Ministry of Defence is one of those Departments/ Ministries that have been exempted from presentation of an Outcome Budget by the MoF. However, even those that have been exempted, have been requested by the MoF to carry out this exercise for internal use and voluntarily decide to place it in the public domain, fully or partially. The desire of the Committee was indicated in this background.

The Defence Secretary clarified during the evidence that the Ministry was trying to develop an infrastructure for this exercise. He also stated, "In the Ministry of Defence, because of the nature of its functioning and the nature of expenditure, we could not produce the outcome budget. But if you feel it should be submitted, we will try to do it for certain areas."[30]

There is nothing in the nature of the functioning of defence or in the nature of defence expenditure to prevent it from introducing output budgeting which will help in assessing the outcome. In fact, programme budgeting, which is the other name for output budgeting, was first introduced in the Department of Defence in the USA in 1962 and on its overwhelming success there, it was introduced in the rest of the federal government in 1965 which is referred to as PPB. The basic aim of PPB was to establish a firm linkage between programme planning and budgeting. Without such a linkage, planners can easily lose touch with the constraints imposed by scarce resources, while budgeters can easily be divorced from the contents of plans and programmes.

It was not just as a budgeting technique—it was an aid to higher management decisions. The basic aim was, as McNamara put it, "We must ensure that the Army is balanced to the Air Force, that the Navy is balanced to the requirements of the Army, that the financial budget is balanced to the military force structure required as a foundation for our foreign policy.

"It is this type of decisions that come up to my level, and until we translate this basic policy into a *balanced force structure*, I know of no other way to follow."[31] The method which McNamara adopted in assisting him in making these decisions was the planning-programming-budgeting system.

In this context, it is worth recalling that the Group of Ministers on Security Management in their report in 2001 had recommended that steps to be taken toward programme-based budgeting in defence.

The Task Force on Management of Defence (set up by the Group of Ministers) constituted a Study Group on Budgetary Reform in August 2001 to overcome the deficiencies in the existing input-based budgeting.

Among the terms of reference of the Study Group was expansion of classification of expenditure to promote programme budgeting. The Study Group made recommendations in this regard to enable introduction of programme budgeting.

But programme budgeting involves facets other than detailed classification of expenditure. The basic building block of this system is classification of expenditure into programmes i.e. objective oriented classification so that activities with common objectives are considered together, where the objective of each programme is explicitly defined. Therefore, it requires a well conceived framework of programmes/sub-programmes/activities to facilitate allocation of resources keeping in view the intended output.

The primary objective of programme budgeting was improved allocative efficiency and better expenditure prioritisation. To achieve this, it requires (a) a decision-making structure in the MoD to decide about priorities in the allocation of resources among programmes, as also reallocation on the basis of evaluation of ongoing programmes and strategic considerations ; (b) a longer time-frame for budgeting than what the annual budget provides as costs and benefits are to be considered in a longer time-frame; and (c) introduction of systems analysis for evaluation of alternatives before deciding upon a programme from the cost-effectiveness point of view.

All three elements are essential for the introduction of programme budgeting in defence. So mere introduction of more classification heads of expenditure would not do. In any case, the starting point is introduction of an objective oriented programme structure.

Why do we require a longer time-frame for budgeting under this concept? As McNamara, testifying in 1962, explaining the reasons for a longer time horizon, stated, "Sound choices of major weapon systems in relation to military tasks and missions have become the key decisions around which much else of the defense program revolves. But the full cost implications of these decisions cannot be ascertained unless both the programs and their cost are projected over a period of years, ideally over the entire life cycle of the weapon system. Since such long-term projections are very difficult to make with any degree of accuracy, we have fixed on a 5-year period..."[32]

This requirement puts the need for multi-year budgeting in defence in the proper perspective. With the introduction of programme budgeting, the introduction of multi-year budgeting becomes necessary.

The Study Group that set up the Task Force on the Management of Defence did not recommend introduction of multi-year budgeting as it was not in its terms of reference.

It, however, recommended introduction of Vol II of the Defence Services Estimates (DSE) to show where money is allocated, on what it is spent and by whom.

The DSE Vol II was introduced in 2002-03. While it was the right step, it did not show programme/activity-wise allocation; as such, a framework is still to evolve. But the principle that we have to focus on, in activities and outputs in defence, has been accepted by the introduction of DSE Vol II, whatever be its present limitations.

It also resuscitated the concept of Budget Centres, which was introduced in the early Nineties in defence for better management of resources. The concept was supposed to introduce planning, programming, evaluation and accountability in defence expenditure management. This concept is important as it led to substantial delegation of financial powers to Service Headquarters and subordinate formations. In view of these earlier initiatives which involved the introduction of Authority and Responsibility Centres, Accountability Centres, Budget Holders and substantial delegation of powers, the basic structure exists to introduce performance budgeting in defence. What is required is introduction of the programme concept for resource allocation decisions, multi-year budgeting and a higher level institutional mechanism for setting objectives and taking resource allocation decisions keeping in view the objectives.

Outputs in government are services, that is, these are service outputs. Service outputs consist of a bundle of activities for which resources are to be allocated. These constituent activities cannot be considered as outputs in their own right because only when they are combined with other activities that an intended outcome can be potentially achieved. This important distinction has to be kept in view.

Introduction of the concept of capability planning enables easier introduction of the concept of outcome budgeting, as is evident from its fairly successful use in Australian defence budgeting.

Input budgeting has hardly any utility in achieving efficiency and effectiveness in defence expenditure management. It cannot even achieve economy in the real sense of the term, as it is formulated on an incremental basis, without conscious resource allocation decisions.

By properly implementing the Budget Holder and Budget Centre concepts which were introduced in the mid-Nineties in defence for better budgetary management in support of the concept known as the New Management Strategy, it is possible to easily introduce performance orientation in the defence budget.

This is because substantial delegation of powers has been made for implementing the concept of Authority and Responsibility Centres which were introduced as part of the New Management Strategy.

Keeping in view the hierarchical mode of functioning in defence, the concept of Top Level Budget Holder should also be introduced to facilitate introduction of performance budgeting in defence.

The Standing Committee, while reviewing the defence budget, may like to enquire about implementation of the ideas contained in the New Management Strategy or New Financial Strategy as it was called in the Army, and to what extent performance budgeting has been or is being introduced in the context of large delegation of powers for implementing the concepts of authority, responsibility and accountability. It should be remembered that these concepts emanated from Service Headquarters, precisely because they became aware of the limitations of the existing input oriented budgeting and wanted to give the defence budget an output orientation by bringing in the concepts of authority and responsibility.

Therefore, with a decade and a half long pioneering background of implementation of these concepts in the defence budget (which were not thought of in the civil Ministries/Departments), which have also been formally introduced in Vol II of the DSE, with performance budgeting and outcome budgeting being adopted in the civil Ministries/Departments, there is no reason why performance budgeting should not be introduced in defence without delay.

The review of input-based defence budgets, as at present, cannot reveal much, as it is designed only for control of expenditure. The control aspect has lost much of its relevance with the inability to spend the allotted amounts year after year.

What is worthwhile to concentrate upon is what is the 'output' of this massive expenditure, for which a programme-based budget is essential, both for rational decision-making in resource allocation as also for review of the defence budget by the Standing Committee of the Parliament.

Defence Budgeting in a Strategic Framework

We have noted above that under the existing budgeting system, much of the allocations in the defence budget are treated as "obligatory" in nature, which is determined by the "strength and composition" of the armed forces. Most of the defence expenditure falls in this category, being policy driven expenditure, for which allocations have to be automatically made in the defence budget every year.

From time to time, however, restructuring of the armed forces may be required for strategic reasons. Being aware of this fact, the Standing Committee made the following observation while scrutinising the Demands for Grants for Defence 2006-07, "The Committee are aware of the *rapid technological advancements and changes taking place globally in the warfare technology and feel there is an imperative need to constitute a high level empowered Committee* to examine the entire security gamut and suggest *reforms, including restructuring of the armed forces,* as may be necessary to meet any eventuality in future."[33]

The Committee noted that there has been no thorough review of the structural set-up of the armed forces since independence, especially of the

Army whose strength constitutes almost 90 percent of our defence forces. "The need of the hour is to optimally use the available limited resources... *The proposed Committee should be given the mandate to suggest suitable manpower restructuring by trimming the force size (teeth to tail ratio) with corresponding increase in the use of advanced and sophisticated technology in our armed forces*; review the authorisation of the peace and war establishments which are existing since the Second World War... *It is high time to effect substantial savings within the available defence budget for restructuring and modernising our forces*" (emphasis mine).[34]

Such a review would have a major impact on the resource allocation decisions and would have helped in developing the right capabilities for future conflicts. In fact, the future conflict scenario has to be clearly visualised in such a review, as force restructuring has to be done on that basis. Another benefit of such a review would have been that it would have to indicate availability of funds on a long-term basis so that capability planning could be done in a meaningful way. Further, if savings are to be generated, it would have to indicate the areas where it was to be done and what should be the extent of savings.

In the next report pertaining to the Demands for Grants 2007-08, the issue came up in a different way in the context of drawing up the Long-Term Integrated Perspective Plan (LTIPP) 2007- 22. The earlier LTIPP 2002-17 did not get approved as the 10th Plan did not get approved and had to be revised for covering the 11th, 12th and 13th Five-Year Plans. Since the 11th Plan is yet to be approved, though three years have passed, it is clear that the LTIPP would again be revised.

The Ministry of Defence in a written reply indicated, "The revised LTIPP (2007-22) is being prepared following a deliberate and integrated 'Top Down' approach by articulating National Security Strategy, National Military Strategy, National Military Objectives, and so on. Such an exercise has been undertaken for the first time and is an extremely involved process with inputs from three Services, MoD, NSA and various other agencies. The document is expected to be ready by December 2009."[35]

On the above basis, the Committee noted "that an integrated Perspective Plan covering three Plan periods from 11th to 13th Plan, i.e. from 2007-2022 will be approved by the Defence Acquisition Council by 31st October 2009." It is also added that this long-term plan would be different from earlier plans in that there will be a "shift from *equipment-based* approach to *capacity-based* approach."[36]

There are a few points here which add to the confusion.

The minor one is about the dates. While the document was expected to be ready by December 2009,[37] the Defence Acquisition Council was supposed to approve it by October 31. Secondly, about the sequence of events: since the LTIPP is supposed to be a strategic document following a top-down approach involving a major shift in planning procedure from an equipment-based approach to a capability-based approach, its approval has to precede the preparation of the Plans. But the 11th Plan (2007-12) had already been prepared on the usual basis as in the past by taking into account "committed liabilities, prioritised modernisation schemes, obligatory charges and maintenance requirements of the defence services and departments"[38] and projected to the Ministry of Finance in July 2006.[39]

There was no indication in the deposition before the Committee whether any strategic thought had been given regarding objectives to be attained in the plan period, the nature of conflicts for which preparation was being made, the capabilities that are required to be developed in view of likely threats, etc. It apparently is not derived from the LTIPP 2002-17 which was already available, and which was supposed to have an articulated strategy adopting a top-down approach. As is evident from the way the 11th Plan is stated to be put together, it is not very different from the annual budgetary exercise in which the same inputs are taken into account. *In other words, the Five-Year Plan basically boils down to five annual budgets and nothing more than that.*

It is no wonder it is treated as such by the MoF, as is evident from the following response, as indicated in the report of the Committee: "The proposals of the Ministry of Defence were examined and the views of the Ministry of Finance were conveyed… indicating therein that it would be realistic to assume year on year increase in defence allocations in the range of 8-10 percent for the purpose of the planning exercise for the 11th Plan as against the annual average growth rate of 12.35 percent per year indicated by the Ministry of Defence." [40]

Interestingly, the reply of the MoF also refers to certain suggestions being made by it on the 11th Plan regarding "certain operational aspects having substantial financial implications with the request that the Ministry of Defence review the same with the objective of rationalising expenditure while, at the same time, not compromising on modernisation plans." [41]

In other words, the MoF is no longer prepared to look at the projected plans only from the financial affordability point of view, and would be going into the operational and strategic aspects of the plan. This provides a new challenge to the DoD, which has to go into these aspects independently, so that these aspects are gone into from a systems analysis point of view, so that the MoF feels assured that all aspects of "rationalising expenditure," including from the operational and strategic angles, have been examined in the MoD before finalising the plan.

In any case, as indicated by the MoF, the 11th Plan should be redrawn, keeping in view financial realities, and the entire effort in preparing the plan has apparently gone waste. The position is not different from other plan periods. So we are back to square one. And the LTIPP is still to be approved.

The third point is: how is the LTIPP supposed to be articulating the National Security Strategy or even for that matter, National Military Strategy? Is it not a matter of political decision-making where the National Security Council and Cabinet Committee on Security would deliberate, and the Indian Parliament give its approval? How can the Defence Acquisition Council give approval to such a document without first getting approval for the National Security Strategy?

The Standing Committee did not raise these issues. But what it said is also very relevant. It stated, "The Committee are of the view that in the changing paradigm of the security scenario, threat perception and fast changing scientific and technological field, the long-term plan needs a regular and sustained review of its content and thrust. Therefore, the Committee wish to recommend that the long-term plan should be reviewed and updated from time to time well in advance, in order to make it realistic..." [42]

This recommendation is in keeping with the earlier recommendation made while scrutinising the 2006-07 budget for review of the structure of the armed forces. Since the LTIPP is prepared on the basis of Perspective Plans of the three Services, this kind of proposal of restructuring cannot emanate from the LTIPP. This point will be evident from the following paragraph in the report of the Committee. Referring to the status of the revision of the Perspective Plan, the Ministry indicated, "*The process of revision has already been completed by the Navy in terms of the Maritime Capability Perspective Plan,which covers the period 2007-22.* The other two Services are in the process of completing this exercise, updating the LTIPP from 2002-17 to 2007-22. Once these individual plans are ready, these will be integrated into one Long-Term Perspective Plan and after necessary approvals within the Ministry of Defence, it will be taken up with the Ministry of Finance for approval in principle..."[43] So much for the top-down approach in preparation of the LTIPP 2007-22, deriving it from National Military Strategy, etc.

From the deposition before the Committee, it seems the navy is pushing ahead in implementing its perspective plan. There is stated to be a directive by the Defence Acquisition Council that the total number of ships should not fall below 140. The Committee noted that "in pursuance of this directive, a 10-year (upto 2012) ship building plan was envisaged for induction of 83 vessels of various categories...19 ships are presently under construction (excluding *Admiral Gorshkov*) and cases for acquisition of 24 new ships and 6 submarines and 11 aircraft are being processed."[44] The Committee went on to add that it "earnestly desires that the Ministry should take effective steps in order to strictly adhere to the directives of the Defence Acquisitions Council that the total number of ships does not fall below 140."[45]

The Committee also noted that there have been shortfalls in certain critical areas of the Navy like surveillance, mainly in terms of long range aircraft, and acquisition of submarines, and desired that "immediate steps should be taken to meet the above requirements of the Navy in a time- bound manner." Sufficient funds should be made available for it.[46]

Elsewhere, the Committee takes note of the manpower shortage in the navy. "The Navy has also highlighted the shortage of manpower in critical areas. This is a matter of crucial importance." The Committee recommended that the navy should be allowed to make additional recruitment.[47] So the mismatch between capital acquisition and manpower has started in the navy which will adversely affect its combat capability.

In the above context, the Ministry assured the Committee, "In order to ensure that naval preparedness is not adversely affected, the progress of the Navy's expenditure and status of ongoing/new schemes would be constantly reviewed during the fiscal year and plan period. *If need be, Ministry of Finance would be approached for additional allocation of funds.*" [48]

This is the issue. What are the long-term cost implications of the new force structure of the navy as envisaged in their Perspective Plan? We have to include in it both the acquisition cost and operational cost of the *Admiral Gorshkov* and the other aircraft carrier being built indigenously, not to talk of the third one which is being recommended by the Committee.

What if the Ministry of Finance does not allot additional funds? They have already stated that the LTIPP should be drawn up assuming an average budgetary increase between 8-10 percent per annum.

If the planned naval force structure containing 140 ships with two aircraft carriers is given effect to, and other deficiencies are to be met, can it be contained within 18 percent of the defence budgetary allocation as it is at present? Or would it need to go up to a higher percentage of allocation, say 21 to 22 percent of the defence budget? In that case, the percentage of allocation for which Service should go down? The Committee has also expressed its apprehension about the falling percentage share of the Army in the defence budget.

It has also strongly recommended that the government should accord highest priority to "ensure that squadron strength (of the Indian Air Force) at any time should not fall below 39.5 and strive to achieve the ideal requirement of 44 squadrons."[49]

All these requirements, given that unit cost of weapon systems is increasing at a rate approaching 10 percent or so per annum, (in other words, a modern weapon system can double in cost every seven years or so), mean a rate of increase no defence budget can be expected to match.[50] There has, therefore, to be a trade-off, even within a Service, in planning for force structure, keeping in view very limited growth in the budget in real terms, about which the Standing Committee itself has shown concern from time to time.

With the fiscal deficit being now much higher than was contemplated in the FRBM Act, and the government's attempt to contain the deficit, the chances of substantial increase in the defence budget in future years are not very bright.

In this background, a piecemeal approach to force planning can only lead to an unbalanced force structure which will mean a less capable military than could be achieved with the resources made available. What is required is a strategic defence review by a high level empowered committee, as recommended by the Committee in its report on the Demands for Grants 2006-07, which will "examine the entire security gamut" and go into the whole issue of "restructuring of the armed forces" within the given budget, and make recommendations "to make substantial savings for restructuring and modernising our forces." [51]

Such a report, containing recommendations regarding the restructuring of forces, capability to be built, readiness and preparedness to be achieved and resources likely to be made available for the next five years, on being accepted by the government, shall become the basis for defence planning and budgeting for the next five years.

Otherwise, we may land up with an unbalanced force structure and/or inadequate balance between defence preparedness and modernisation.

It may be mentioned that the major and medium powers of the world have all carried out such strategic reviews during the last decade and half in view of the change in the conflict scenario, rapid advances in technology and the process of innovation brought about by the notion of RMA.

For example, in the UK, the Strategic Defence Review (SDR) was conducted in 1997-98 and the report came out in July 1998. It was regarded for a long time as a model of defence planning. It aimed at bringing foreign policy and defence policy together in an affordable manner. The major organisational change as a result of the SDR was the combination of single Service logistics through the creation of the tri-Service Defence Logistics Organisation (DLO). Since its creation, it has sought to rationalise logistic provisions. This is how a defence review helps in achieving economy and efficiency through organisational changes. Recently, the DLO was combined with the Defence Procurement Agency (DPA) and is now collectively known as Defence Equipment and Support (DE&S), creating the largest Top Level Budget Holder in the Department. Though we have in our budgetary management partially introduced the concept of High Level Budget Holder, we are yet to introduce the concept of Top Level Budget Holder, which is essential if we want to introduce performance budgeting in defence where the objectives are set at the very top of the hierarchy and then 'cascaded' down through various levels.

Force structuring issues are addressed though these reviews on the basis of strategic guidance. The experience with these strategic reviews shows that because of limitation of resources, each Service has to accept trade-offs in force structure decisions, otherwise it would lead to an unbalanced force structure. Further, the strategic posture should keep in view the resource position.

For example, the centrepiece in terms of procurement requirements resulting from the SDR was the decision to focus on expeditionary warfare with two large aircraft carriers at the heart of the new capability.

The major casualty in the last decade as per an informed commentator has been the surface fleet of the Royal Navy. It has come down to 26 surface ships and some 16 minehunters, much below the force level envisaged in the SDR. This became necessary to protect the funding for the future aircraft carriers.[52] In the view of many experts, the expeditionary strategy adopted by the UK government was never affordable.

It is reported that the British government may be about to move to a system of regular reviews as in the case of the Quadrennial Defence Review (QDR, the first of which was conducted in 1997.[53]

The QDR is mandated by the US Congress. It is performed every four years. When the process for the Defence Department's 2010 QDR started, the US Defence Secretary, in April 2009, announced some major moves affecting the US Air Force and proposed retirement of 250 tactical aircraft. The move was supposed to allow the air force to instead buy things like modern ammunition, unmanned aircraft and other surveillance and other reconnaissance enablers. They also decided to reduce purchase of F-22 stealth fighters to 187 as more were not affordable, and cancel a next generation bomber programme.[54]

The aim, in other words, of such reviews is to increase the combat and operational capabilities to meet the strategic requirements, within the likely available resources. This requires the trade-off between squadron strength and gaining overall combat capability.

In making these reviews, the defence planners today have to keep in view the challenges posed by RMA.

Defence planners of important military powers in Asia have acknowledged the potential of RMA, particularly Information Technology (IT) in adopting a more cost-effective force structure. RMA calls for changes in organisational structure, resource allocation, doctrine and strategy.

For the Chinese political and military leaders, RMA is regarded as the major area of great power competition that will determine China's position in the world in the next 20 years. The Chinese military has accorded IT the highest priority in its modernisation programme. Advocates of RMA in the People's Liberation Army (PLA) feel that superiority in information technology leads to superiority in combat operations. Information technology makes possible small-sized battle formations without compromising strength and outcome, if they are suitably equipped with high- tech weapons.[55] China is stated to be studying the offensive employment of IW against foreign economic, logistics, and C4I systems…"[56]

Japan has gone in for the IT-RMA with a defensive posture in consonance with its defence policy, "The Japanese Perception of Information Technology-Revolution in Military Affairs."[57]

This bring out the point that RMA concepts would have different applications depending on the defence policy and strategy. It would be different for a country adopting an 'offensive' operation oriented policy from a country adopting RMA for defensive purposes. Countries facing different strategic conditions will choose alternate paths. As Takahashi puts it, "Unless it is strategically relevant, even highly advanced weapon systems will not support national security."[58]

Society is moving from an industrial to an information age. The defence strategists feel that military power would in future flow from information technology and strongly argue for pushing information down to the tactical level and for more widely distributed operations. Advances in technology led to the concept of "network-centric warfare". Forces at tactical and operational levels can make use of it and take quick decisions in operational matters. This may call for major restructuring of forces. In the Navy, for example, network-centric operations can allow spreading the capabilities now lodged in big ships among more numerous, faster and stealthier ships.

IT has led to developing a new kind of warfare like cyber warfare. Press reports quoted the UK's Security Minister's warning of a cyber threat from Al Qaeda, confirming that the UK had already faced cyber attacks from some foreign countries. The UK government published its new Cyber Security Strategy to combat these threats.[59] Both China and Pakistan are reported to be bolstering cyber warfare capability at a rapid rate. The Indian Army, as per reports in the Press, has set up some institutions to guard against this kind of warfare.[60] But these steps may not be enough as the threat can be widespread, affecting financial markets, power grids, air traffic control and other facets of public life. A debate is needed as to whether cyber warfare should become an important component of India's security doctrine or not.

Then there are space-based programmes.

The point is that, ultimately, the challenge is that we have to fit in all these programmes when the allocation for the defence budget is only around 2.4 percent of the GDP. The question is: how to evolve a balanced force structure which would be affordable, keeping in view what would be the strategies of adversaries? What would be the use of each of the high cost systems in the strategic environment we are placed in? What would be the defence policy that would guide the acquisitions ?

It is seen from the experience of other countries that any long-term defence capability plan is soon likely to get outdated because of the change in the security environment. The capability priorities are likely to change every few years.

The threats to national security today are emanating from many sources from state and non-state agencies. The character of the national security environment has changed totally, with threats emanating from many sources, particularly terrorist threats and other threats to internal security, which are taking larger dimensions, in terms of national concern, than threats from external aggression. Various agencies would be engaged in the assessment of threats in their arena of activity, which may vary in approach and quality. What is really required is strategic planning for national security which is inclusive and deliberative in order to come up, among other things, with policy priorities for resource allocation decisions across the agencies to develop different capabilities for meeting the spectrum of threats to national security, in an integrated manner. This calls for capacity for long range planning at the highest level of the government.

For getting a true example of such an inclusive and integrated process of strategic planning, one has to go back to the initiation of "Project Solarium" in the USA under the leadership of President Eisenhower.[61] This kind of inclusive and integrative strategic planning is missing even in the USA today.

What is required today is the conducting of a National Security Review to develop a national security strategy through an inter-agency process, which may be led by the National Security Adviser to the Prime Minister to identify various capabilities required to meet the full spectrum of threats to national security. Such a review should logically precede the Defence Review suggested above.

In the above background, the Standing Committee on Defence can play an important role in influencing the decision-makers in the government through its deliberations and reports:

- in instituting a comprehensive strategic review at the national level to be followed by defence reviews at periodic intervals;
- defence reviews should be the basis of defence plans which, in turn, should be the basis for defence budgets;
- adopting performance budgeting on the basis of programmes; the programmes to be based on end objectives in view and should be costed on the basis of activities to be performed;

- adopting multi-year budgeting and long-term costing of ongoing programmes to ensure that ongoing programmes are affordable.

As explained above, only when the defence budgets become programme-based as also performance oriented, would it be possible to review these on the basis of their costs and benefits as also evaluate their progress on the basis of appropriate benchmarks.

Programmes with end objectives in view and criteria of performance would be the basis for introducing output and outcome budgeting in defence. It cannot simply be done on the basis of input budgeting.

Therefore, immediate efforts should be made to introduce programme budgeting in defence on the basis of the framework mentioned above, reactivating the concepts of Budget Centres and Budget Holders who should be provided with indicative budgets for the next few years, with a view to plan their expenditure. The objectives to be achieved and performance parameters, however, should flow from the top, which would make it necessary to introduce the concept of Top Level Budget Holders. This concept has helped in the introduction of cost-effective expenditure management in defence in the UK.

The defence budget should reflect the defence strategy and decisions of higher management regarding force structure and capability. Today's budgeting process which is a summation of the budgetary projections of the three Services and two Departments of Defence, subject to imposition of a ceiling by the Ministry of Finance, is a totally inadequate tool for higher level decision-making for optimal allocation of resources in defence. The budgetary process in defence has to be streamlined to incorporate the resource allocation decisions emanating from higher management, for which there has to be required institutional support in the Ministry of Defence. As already stated, a comprehensive Defence Review should provide the basis for defence plans and annual defence budgets.

If the defence budget is formulated on the above basis, deriving from a strategic review and showing allocations on programme basis, with performance orientation, it would provide a proper basis for scrutiny by the Standing Committee as to whether it is achieving optimal allocation of resources for effectively meeting the goals and objectives of national security.

Notes

1. Report of the Standing Committee on Defence on Demands for Grants 2008-09, Lok Sabha Secretariat, Para 2.27, p. 13, April 2008.
2. Defence Services Estimates, 2008-2009. Procedure followed in regard to budgetary control over defence expenditure, Appendix C, Para 3.
3. Report of the Standing Committee on Demands for Grants 1994-95, Para 37 of the report.
4. Report of the Standing Committee on Demands for Grants 1997-98, Para 23.
5. Report of the Standing Committee on Demands for Grants 1998-99, Para 24.
6. Report of the Standing Committee on Demands for Grants 1999-2000, Para 26.
7. Report of the Standing Committee on Demands for Grants 2001-02, Para 23.
8. Report of Standing Committee 1998-99, Action taken on recommendations on Demands for Grants, MoD 1997-98, p. 7.
9. Report of the Standing Committee on Demands for Grants 2001-02, Para 27.
10. Report of the Standing Committee on Demands for Grants, 2004-05, Paras 31 and 33.
11. Report of Standing Committee on Demands for Grants, 2004-05, Paras 40 to 43, pp. 19-20.
12. Report of the Standing Committee on Demands for Grants, 2006-07, Para 1.43.
13. Report of the Standing Committee on Demands for Grants, 2006-07, Para 1.58 and Demands for Grants, 2008-09, Para 2.33, p.16.
14. Twelfth Report, Standing Committee on Defence (2001) Manpower Planning and Management Policy in Defence, Para 13.
15. Ibid., Para 40.
16. Ibid., Para 42.
17. Ibid., Para 88 to 90.
18. Ibid., Para 98.
19. Marc Robinson, "Making Performance Budgeting Work," in Marc Robinson, ed., *Performance Budgeting, Linking Funds and Results* (Palgrave Macmillan, IMF, 2007), p. 115.
20. Marc Robinson, "Performance Budgeting Models and Mechanism,“ in Ibid., p. 4.
21. A. Schick, *Budget Innovation in the States* (Brookings Institution, 1971).
22. Robinson, n. 20.
23. Report of the Standing Committee on Demands for Grants 2007-08 para 2.31.
24. Ibid., Para 2.35.
25. Ibid., Para 2.36.
26. Report of the Standing Committee on Demands for Grants, 2007-08, Para 4.10, pp. 40-41.
27. Ibid., Para 4.8.

28. Quoted by William W. Kaufmann in *McNamara Strategy* (Harper and Row, 1964), p. 176.
29. Report of the Standing Committee on Demands for Grants 2008-09, Para 2.40.
30. Ibid., Para 2.43.
31. Quoted by Kaufmann, n. 28, p. 172.
32. Ibid., p. 175.
33. Report of the Standing Committee on Demands for Grants 2006-07, Para 1.4, p. 2.
34. Ibid.
35. Report of the Standing Committee on Demands for Grants 2007-08, Para 3.4.
36. Ibid., Para 3.5.
37. Ibid., Para 3.4.
38. Ibid., Para 3.12.
39. Ibid., Para 3.16.
40. Ibid., Para 3.16, p. 35.
41. Ibid., Para 3.16, p. 35.
42. Ibid., Para 3-7, p. 31.
43. Report of the Standing Committee on Demands for Grants, 2007-08, Para 3.2, p. 30.
44. Report of the Standing Committee on Demands for Grants 2005-06, Para 4.16 pp. 49-50.
45. Ibid., Para 4.21.
46. Ibid., Para 4.18.
47. Ibid.,Para 4.20.
48. Ibid, Para 4.10.
49. Report of the Standing Committee on Demands for Grants, 2006-07, Para 5.12, P. 63.
50. David Karpatrick,"Is Defence Inflation Really as High as Claimed ?", *RUSI Defence Systems*, October 2008, pp. 66-71.
51. Report of the Standing Committee on Demands for Grants, 2006-07, Para 1.4.
52. Dr Jeffrey Bradford, "Contrasting Efforts: The British Strategic Defence Review and the United States Quadrennial Defense Review Processes," *RUSI Defence Systems*, October 2008, p. 83.
53. Andrew Chuter, "UK Preps 1st Strategic Review in 11 Years," *Defense News,* June 15, 2009.
54. *Defense Daily,* May 15, 2009, The Daily of Aerospace and Defense, USA, report by Marina Malenic.
55. You Ji, "Learning and Catching Up: China's Revolution in Military Affairs, "in Emily O. Goldman and Thomas G. Mahnken, eds., *The Information Revolution in Military Affairs in Asia* (Palgrave 2004) pp. 97, 103.
56. Mahnken, in concluding article, Ibid., p. 216.

57. Sugio Takahashi, in Ibid., p. 85.
58. Ibid., p. 92.
59. Report in *Business Standard,* July 5, 2009.
60. *The Times of India* News Report on May 2, 2008.
61. Michele A. Flournoy and Shawn W. Brimley, "Strategic Planning for National Security, A New Project Solarium," *JFQ*, Issue 41, 2nd quarter 2006, pp. 80-86.

4

Financing Transformation of Military Forces: An Overview

> Despite a large literature, uncertainty remains about exactly what transformation is. A transformed military thinks differently about the art of war and about preparation for battle than the one which is not transformed... Financing the Armed Forces is presumably also affected: transformation might make militaries more or less expensive, either per unit of effect or relative to other components of state budgets.
>
> — Stephen J. Cimbala, *Joint Forces Quarterly*, Issue no. 38, June 2005.

> We witness transformation when we see airmen traveling by horseback with tools of trade (GPS and laser range inders) hanging from a saddle. With secure satellite and radio links, they pass target coordinates to bombers, or fighters from the Air Force, Navy or Marines flying miles overhead. We see a venerable 40-year-old B-52 precisely place a JDAM just 800 meters from our friendly positions. No single piece of this equation is transformational but together it yields a transformational asymmetrical advantage over any enemy.
>
> — Gen John P. Jumper, Chief of Staff, US Force, in an interview, *Military Aerospace Technology,* Online Edition vol. 1, issue 2, May 2001.

Transformation as a Process

As the first quotation shows, that there is a degree of ambiguity about what transformation of the military is, what kind of investments are required to bring it about and in what time-frame. Accordingly, there is bound to be uncertainty about how much is required to finance it.

The second quotation, which underlines the point that transformation is not just about new technology and acquisition, is also very relevant in this context. Even existing technology and platforms used innovatively can be transformational. It is the dramatic effect on operations that is the hallmark of transformation.

As per the dominant view, the cultural aspects are more important in bringing about transformation of the armed forces than the technologies. The emphasis is on cultural change where "innovation and informed risk taking are encouraged and rewarded—a culture that is characterized by the information age." This calls for an "increased emphasis on concept development and experimentation, a change in personnel system and information structure."[1] A cultural change is also required to make the armed Services work together. This requires joint doctrine, joint training and interoperability of equipment and systems.

Viewed in this way, the issue of how much to spend on transformation becomes a secondary issue, if not somewhat irrelevant. The financing aspects get more importance when modernisation gets linked to transformation. To provide the link, modernisation is to be viewed as capability building in the context of transformational requirements. Here the most important strategy that has emerged is that of reallocation of resources rather than augmentation of resources.

Defence transformation has preoccupied the US Department of Defence (DoD) for more than a decade. In US defence, two competing views about "transformation" have emerged. Some have defined transformation as a discontinuous or leap-ahead change. This view supports those who believe it is necessary to move money, manpower, and doctrine away from current manpower systems and methods to entirely new technologies and procedures. This is the radical approach. Others tend to define transformation as incremental change using current and modernising technologies in new ways, with the end result of radical improvement.

A conference was held by the Asia-Pacific Centre for Security Studies in February-March 2004, to discuss defence transformation. No strong consensus emerged during the conference as to what "defence, transformation" exactly entailed. Some saw defence transformation as a process, others as an objective. Most definitions of defence transformation, however, see it largely fed by current breakthroughs in Information Technology (IT), creating new synergistic capabilities, and involving significant and fundamental changes in military doctrine, organisations, and institutions.[2]

Vice Admiral Arthur Cebrowski (Retd) the first Director of the Office of Force Transformation in US defence, stated, "Transformation is foremost a continuing process. It does not have an end point. Transformation is meant to create or anticipate the future. Transformation is meant to deal with co-evolution of concepts, processes, organisations and technology. Change in any one of these areas necessitates change in all."[3]

Cebrowski's argument that military transformation is a process not a destination, means that it cannot be achieved through sequential planning. If transformation comprised linear sequential planning, the issue of financing it could be addressed methodically. Nor can "co-evolution of concepts, processes, organisations and technology" be given a financial content.

Even for the US, which is supposed to be in the process of defence transformation for more than a decade, it is difficult to answer the question of how much they are spending on transformation. To quote the Assistant Director of the Office of Force Transformation, Walter Fairbanks, *"A frequent question is how much DoD spends on transformation. That is hard to say, because transformation is far more than a list of programs. The concepts, capabilities, and organizations developed through innovative ideas, experimentation, major training exercises, and assessment of lessons learned on the battlefields of Afghanistan and Iraq cannot be categorized under a transformation line item in the defense budget."*[4]

Issues pertaining to processes have come increasingly into prominence under transformation initiatives in US defence since 2001. It has been recognised that transformation of the armed forces really involves a revolution in management technology and business practices. The attempt is to reform with the aim of capability enhancement, focussed on three primary processes: requirements assessment; programming and budgeting; and system acquisition.

For the assessment of requirements, the most important change was the formation of the Joint Capabilities Integration and Development System (JCIDS) in 2003. The JCIDS process was aimed to achieve two objectives. The first was greater jointness in requirements analysis, taking opportunities to bring about closer links among related Service missions. The second objective of the JCIDS process was to develop requirements using a broad "capabilities-based" approach, rather than the platform-based or system-based approach. "JCIDS would force the DoD to consider whether a new airplane was the best alternative to fulfilling the capability requirement at all; perhaps, there was a more effective or efficient means of creating a given effect on the battlefield."[5]

To bring about this shift in thinking, six Functional Capabilities Boards (FCBs) were set up to look into the requirements for generically defined military capabilities, intended to cover the full range of battlefield needs.

In the area of programming and budgeting, instead of the Planning, Programming and Budgeting System (PPBS), where the 'planning' aspect did not get adequate attention, a revised process called the PPBE process ("E" standing for execution) was installed in 2003. In the revised process, the Office of the Secretary of Defence (OSD) began the process by setting firm goals in the Secretary of Defence's Strategic Planning Guidance (SPG). "The SPG was followed by a period of intense analysis, aimed at providing specific programmatic guidance to the Services, rather than leaving them to develop their program objectives memoranda (POM) in isolation."[6]

As regards the DoD acquisition system, past reform efforts tended to focus narrowly on the acquisition procedures and rules, rather than on the whole system of requirements assessment, programming and budgeting. Now the acquisition system is composed of three overlapping processes, including the JCIDS process for requirements assessment, processes of programming and budgeting and the acquisition process.

The concept of transformation as a process also draws attention to modernisation, which is always considered an ongoing process. But would this ongoing process of modernisation bring about transformation of the armed forces? Or can the process of modernisation be so designed as to bring about transformation? We shall attend to this aspect subsequently.

Transformation and Culture of Innovation

In implementing the transformation process in US defence, the major emphasis now is on bringing about change in human behaviour and creating a *culture of innovation* within the DoD. Another major emphasis is on development of new concepts in meeting asymmetric challenges. That is why they view transformation as a process.

The challenge for us is of a slightly different kind. We are yet to induct Revolution in Military Affairs (RMA) technologies in a significant manner in our military. There are gaps in our technological base. For sophisticated weapons, we are overwhelmingly dependent on imports. In our procurement policy, there is a predilection for imports. While this may be necessary to some extent where there are a lot of technological gaps, it is to be realised that large scale imports are inimical to innovative thinking and would not allow domestic research and development activities to grow. This will prove to be a great hurdle in bringing about transformation of the armed forces. It will baffle many analysts that a country, which could be self-reliant in development of strategic weapons and innovative in its approach, has to depend so much on imports for weapon systems in non-strategic areas.

Therefore, our strategy for transformation in the military would be through adopting a strategy for RMA, based on development of indigenous capabilities. This may involve selective imports of sub-systems, incorporating cutting edge technology to be integrated within the country.

Regardless of how transformation may be defined, Cebrowski has identified some criteria by which military modernisation programmes may be judged for their transformational qualities. *His top criterion is that the weapon system or operating procedure be interoperable.* Interoperability means that the system can function with a variety of other systems, including from other Services. Other criteria Cebrowski has named are judgements as to whether the system helps users to change war-fighting methods as opposed to merely improving existing methods; and whether the system can deal with a wide range of threats.

There is general agreement on these criteria. It is felt that these criteria should be kept uppermost in mind in acquisition of systems in the modernisation process, so that the modernisation effort itself leads to transformation of military forces.

To ensure interoperability of weapon systems, it is important to go through the indigenous route of technological development as the criterion of interoperability can be kept in view in all cases of weapon development, and a system once developed, can be used by more than one Service by some adaptations which would be comparatively easy if the indigenous route of development of the system was taken. Ensuring interoperability of systems leads to cutting down on the duplication of systems.

Barriers to Transformation

It is important to recognise that there are important organisational barriers to bringing in transformation of the armed forces. This can be illustrated with reference to the US armed forces where the top leadership was enthusiastic about transformation. President George Bush, speaking at the US Naval Academy in May 2001, called "for a future force that is defined less by size and more by mobility and swiftness, one that is easier to deploy and sustain, one that relies more heavily on stealth, precision weaponry, and information technologies." He also committed himself "to fostering a military culture where intelligent risk-taking and forward thinking are rewarded, not dreaded, and to ensuring that visionary leaders who take risks are recognized and promoted."[7]

The US armed forces have also accepted the need to transform so as to meet the demands of information-age warfare and have fielded new capabilities such as stealth and precision strikes, new approaches like network-centric warfare and effects-based operations. "Nevertheless," as pointed out by Thomas G. Mahnken, "significant organizational barriers to the adoption of new technology, doctrine and organizations exist. The Services have been particularly reluctant to take measures that are disruptive of Service culture, such as shifting away from traditional platforms and toward new weapon systems, concepts, and organizations. The Army's efforts to field a medium-weight ground force, the Navy's development of network-centric warfare, and the Air Force's experience with unmanned air vehicles illustrate such difficulties. In each case, efforts at transformation have faced opposition from Service traditionalists who perceive threats in new ways of war. For the Defence

Department to succeed in transforming the US armed forces, it must both reallocate resources and nurture new constituencies."[8]

The budget data on acquisition programmes suggest that the US military Services continue to have strongly platform-centric approaches to procurement.

This may be true for the militaries of most countries. Therefore, funds for introducing systems which can transform would be "insufficient." This poses more problems for those who feel enthused about bringing about transformation. Mahnken suggests, "The Defence Department should begin redistributing resources away from legacy systems of declining utility and toward new ways of war. The Pentagon should scale back or cancel weapons that are heavy or have limited mobility, highly detectable signatures, and limited range; it should increase funding for long range precision strike, stealth, and C4ISR systems. The department should increase substantially the funds it devotes to research and development."[9]

This prescription would not be easy to follow because of organisational resistance. All the same, a few important points come out about financing transformation:

(i) There has to be reallocation of resources from legacy systems to resources to transformational systems. Because of constraints of resources, one cannot fund legacy systems with the same vigour as before and, at the same time, fund the new systems which are to bring about transformation.

(ii) The Defence Department should increase substantially the funds it devotes to Research and Development (R&D) as more and more experimentation is required to pursue potentially important technologies through basic research.

Mahnken makes the third point which is more specific:

(iii) In order to meet new challenges, "*the Secretary of Defense should set aside a significant portion of the military's procurement budget for innovative programs*."[10]

As transformation of the armed forces would depend heavily on innovation and experimentation, it would call for more resources being invested in carrying out basic research on science and technology, leading to development of mature technologies which can be exploited militarily. This would also call for a new procurement procedure.

A New Strategy of Investment

In the transformation process, one has to look for investments which are most critical to its success. One cannot proceed on an incremental basis. In the strategy for investment for bringing about transformation, one has to concentrate on a few critical areas for investment. To quote Stuart Johnson, "While there is not one-to-one correspondence between investment spending and force transformation, the process is supported by targeted investment in those technologies that enable force transformation: command, control, and communications: reconnaissance; surveillance; and precision strike, to name four."[11]

The first and most important step could, therefore, be to develop an integrated joint programme through indigenous research and development, for all the three Services in the area of Command, Control, Communication, Computers, Intelligence, Surveillance, Reconnaissance (C4ISR). "An interoperable C4ISR suite is critical to seamless operation of forces that will depend on strong information dominance over the enemy, a shared operational picture and targeting data."[12] It is not easy but will have a very high pay-off.

For obvious security reasons, as also for developing the right operational capability suited to our requirements and cost-effectiveness, one cannot but follow the indigenous route for developing such a major integrated system. The experience of Plan ASCON and Plan AREN of the Indian Army, though two decades old, clearly points to this direction. Following the indigenous route of technological development, with the leadership and management role adopted by the army, was the key to their success. Innovativeness is present in our Service culture which requires the right incentive to flourish.

In recent years, project Samyukta, though it took more time than originally envisaged, indicates the ability of indigenous R&D to take on challenges in the difficult technology of electronic warfare and its ability in system integration. The advantage of undertaking the domestic (R&D)

route is that these systems can be constantly upgraded in the light of new operational challenges, which cannot be done for imported systems, even when domestic production is undertaken through the Transfer of Technology (ToT) route.

To develop the C4ISR suite would provide much many challenges to technology development than ever before. Several agencies can collaborate in this endeavour, with a team of Service officers taking a leadership role.

All the three Services have to undertake transformation in a coordinated manner, as *jointness and interoperability is the key to transformation.*

Capabilities-Based Planning (CBP) Approach for Transformation

The CBP has been recognised as the most important transformational initiative in defence.

Capability is the ability to achieve desired operational effects under specified standards and conditions through a combination of means and ways to perform a set of tasks. As Ryan Henry puts it, "A capability is not a platform or an asset. It's the ability to achieve desired effect in the battle space…Our first task is to determine conceptually what capabilities we need: what we need to be able to do. We will then apply the normal decision-making process."[13]

Defence strategy has to visualise the kind of war the country has to be prepared for, in deciding about the capabilities it needs to develop. That is why the periodic comprehensive defence reviews are so very essential from the strategic point of view. It is necessary to visualise the kind of war or security challenges that the country would be faced with, or is currently engaged in, what should be the "objectives" in meeting these challenges, and consider the "ways" of meeting those challenges, and the means available.

Many organisations will say that they are transforming when they are not considering their purpose. In the transformation process, one has to be clear about the "ends" to be met, the "means" that are available and the "ways" of meeting them. To introduce capability-based planning and to bring about transformation of the armed forces, we need a framework where the "ends," "ways," and "means" are tied together in a strategic framework. "A transforming organization concentrates on ends and, in turn, must emphasize the ways and means of accomplishing those ends."[14]

Warfare has become infinitely more complex since Clausewitz's time. Despite this increased complexity and greater friction in warfare, military organisations tend to maintain a similar structure and organisational mindset towards fighting. In many cases, the means have changed but the mindset has not.

It is significant to note that in formally adopting capability-based planning and the transformational agenda in defence, both came about in the Quadrennial Defence Review (QDR) of 2001 in the USA. In the course of QDR 2001, the US Department of Defence came to the conclusion that even with limited resources, it had to have effective capabilities across a very broad spectrum. This, in turn, led to a totally different force planning construct which is called the "One-Four-Two-One" strategy. This was different from the two Major Regional Conflicts (MRC) visualised in QDR 1997 for force planning and capability building purposes.

In conducting QDR 2006, the Department of Defence recognised that it is engaged in a war that is irregular in nature and that the war would be a long one. The enemies in this war are not traditional conventional forces but rather dispersed terrorist networks. This kind of war requires the US military to adopt an unconventional and indirect approach.

Recognising that this is an era of surprise, and uncertainty, with a wide range of asymmetric threats, the QDR 2006 defines two fundamental imperatives for the US Department of Defence:

- Continuing to reorient the Department's capabilities and forces to be more agile in the time of war, to prepare for wider asymmetric challenges and hedge against uncertainty over the next 20 years.
- Implementing enterprise-wide changes to ensure that organisational structures, processes and procedures effectively support its strategic direction.[15]

As would be seen, the emphasis is no longer on achieving some particular technological capabilities, but reorientation of capabilities towards greater agility in meeting the asymmetric challenges. Further, making organisational structures and procedures more responsive to strategic challenges is the biggest transformational challenge.

QDR 2006 accepts that the Department of Defence must adapt a model of continuous change and reassessment if it has to defeat highly adaptive adversaries. It provides new direction for accelerating the transformation of the Department to focus more on the needs of combatant commanders and to develop portfolios of joint capabilities rather than what is termed as "individual stove-piped programmes." The focus of capability-based planning is invariably on operational needs.

That is why the perceived needs of commanders come first and have highest priority in procurement planning.

Thus, capability-based planning and transformation of the armed forces go together, and both get the right direction through periodic defence reviews which help in developing a framework tying together "ends," "means" and "ways." It is the strategy which would determine the capabilities that are needed to be developed. Therefore, we need a well articulated defence strategy, specifying the kinds of contingencies we should be prepared for, which can be used for capability-based planning.

Transformation and Modernisation

In some writings, a distinction is made between modernisation and transformation. While discussing funding of modernisation, this is treated as what are called "legacy systems" and funding of transformation involves investment in innovative systems. This distinction is not valid, as modernisation can also incorporate transformational technologies. Both modernisation and transformation comprise an ongoing process. But the emphasis in modernisation is on procurement of technologically advanced equipment, while transformation is an all-embracing concept involving, among others, changes in doctrines, operational concepts, and institutional and organisational changes with the focus on strategic requirements.

Cebrowski, in trying to bring harmonisation between modernisation and transformation stated, "One lens that might prove helpful in understanding transformation is that of a commercial corporate strategy of innovation... Any good corporate innovation strategy. .... has three distinct parts."[16] These are: (i) Focus on Core Missions; (ii) A Series of Small Exploratory Jumps; and (iii) Placing a Few Big Bets.

Regarding the focus on "Core Missions," taking the analogy of a corporate strategy, Cebrowski clarified, "This is the bread and butter of any organization and the main point of any corporate effort. This is where modernization, recapitalization, and taking care of capital plant occur. This is basic stuff. This the realm of evolutionary changes where an organization simply tries to get better at what it is already doing. It should be emphasized that transformation and modernization are not in competition. They are different things and any organization must undertake both processes to be successful."

"Small Exploratory Jumps," take place when an organisation pushes out of the boundaries of a core competency and tries to create something new. Changes in this category are within the existing paradigm. Cebrowski gives the example of the US Navy pursuing unmanned underwater vehicles for shallow mine-hunting and anti-submarine warfare. Those missions are already core competencies for the navy. But in so far as using this technology in new ways that makes it possible to do something that the navy could not do before, it is transformational.

Placing a "Few Big Bets" involves big jumps. These are the things which will change a military Service, change the Department of Defence. The global positioning system satellites are a prime example. Their advent changed the military, changed the Department and changed civil society. Yet another example is putting nuclear ballistic missiles to sea in submarines.

In our approach to modernisation also, distinction needs to be made among "core missions," "small jumps" and "big strides." For "core missions" as per normal business practice, the modernisation process should go on by replacement of equipment and systems which have outlived their utility, and the capital budget of a Service should take care of it. For "small jumps," experimentation would be required to be undertaken and the Services should make a separate allocation for research, development and other measures, and the Services can be stakeholders in Defence Research and Development Organisation (DRDO) projects.

For "big strides," there have to be inter-agency and inter-departmental efforts. These would require long-term plans for developing each of these capabilities, which should be funded separately by the government as these cannot be fitted in any Service's budget. C4ISR is such a capability. It is such an important capability that by itself it can transform the entire war-fighting capability. One can have an independent ten-year plan for developing this capability. There should be assured funding for developing this capability, with an inter-agency independent steering committee.

By conceding, however, that transformation and modernisation are different things and both are to be carried out, Cebrowski left the debate inconclusive. Can it happen, for example, that the modernisation process and the transformation process are working at cross-purposes? Is it possible that the modernisation process, by emphasising the need for procurement of "legacy systems" (though of higher capability) in terms of platforms, etc. reinforces the mindset which the transformational process was supposed to change? Can we conceive of a modernisation process, which by its design, brings about transformation of the armed forces? These are basic questions which need to be debated. Particularly, as in our case, defence planning aims at modernisation basically through procurement of equipment and systems.

New Approach to Defence Modernisation and Procurement Required

Transformation of the armed forces cannot come about without adopting a new procurement procedure with renewed emphasis on *research and development,* as also *concept development* and *experimentation*, as the key elements in the procurement procedure. This is because innovation and experimentation are the key requirements of the transformation process.

Modernisation should, first of all, be redefined as modernisation of military capability not just procurement of modern equipment. And it should be that capability which is dictated by strategic needs, as determined by a well-articulated defence policy. This will have its impact on the defence planning itself which needs to be streamlined for determining procurement needs. A streamlined framework has been developed by Glenn A. Kent, and David E. Thaler, which focusses on streamlining the part of the process often referred to as "up-front" planning.[17]

Referring to the procurement procedure in US defence, "up-front' planning is akin to Phase 0, which begins at Milestone 0, when an authority mandates a particular military mission which deserves increased emphasis. It ends at Milestone I when a decision is made to develop and procure new systems that will equip force elements to enhance military capability. The existing process, apart from being time-consuming, suffers from various "disruptive instabilities" because of lack of communication between disparate elements of the Department of Defence.

To correct the problems, the proposed framework emphasises the need to recognise *concept development* as a separate and distinct phase. The following are the main deficiencies in the existing procedure of up-front planning:

I. Concept development is not defined as an explicit and separable activity.
II. The distinctions between concept demonstrations and technological demonstrations are blurred.
III. The current process does not promote purposeful interaction among scientists, development planners, acquisition personnel and others.

In the proposed system, the forum for concept development is called the "Concept Action Group" (CAG) that would be run by senior officers from appropriate major commands. "The CAG would be the forum for causing purposeful interaction among disparate disciplines. It would serve as the engine for accomplishing the daunting task of matching mission needs to technology opportunities."[18] Concept development efforts should involve (i) formulating, defining and testing alternative operational concepts; (ii) defining and pursuing concept demonstrations for promising concepts; and (iii) defining the functional characteristics of new and existing systems, for implementing selected concepts. These efforts are required to be funded, for which a separate budget should be earmarked from the procurement budget.

The purpose of Science and Technology (S&T) efforts should be to forge a path from basic scientific research to mature technology aggregates. The Defence Advanced Research Project Agency (DARPA) and the national, Service and industrial laboratories should conduct these efforts. S&T efforts should begin with basic research; the results of basic research help identify opportunities for new technologies. The most promising new technologies are matured as technology aggregates.[19] The following points from the proposed framework are emphasised:

Concept development (phase 0) is separable from science and technology, on the one hand, and system development and acquisition, on the other.

Concept demonstrations are different in nature and output from technology demonstrations, on the one hand, and engineering/ manufacturing demonstrations, on the other. Concept Action Groups (CAGs) should serve as vehicles for purposeful interaction between disparate communities.

Fig. 4.1 portrays the activities and inter-relationships of S&T, the concept development and acquisition.[20]

Fig 4.1

These ideas were taken further in a later work(2003) prepared by Glenn

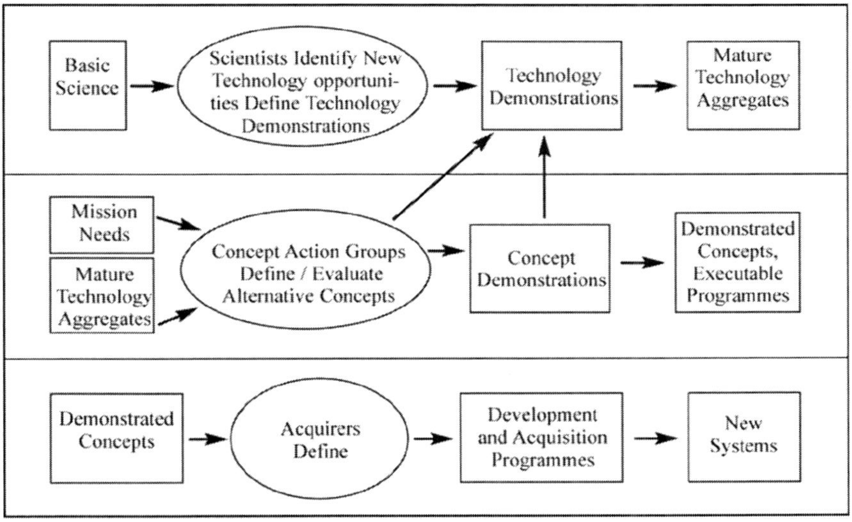

A. Kent and David A. Ochmanek for the US Air Force, which can directly be placed in the context of transformation of the armed forces. It also helps in bringing together the concept of transformation and modernisation of the armed forces through capability building.

First and foremost, modernisation should be conceived as "modernizing operational capabilities." Explaining this, the authors state, "The words 'modernizing operational capabilities' were chosen with care. We could have used the words 'modernizing forces'— but that would suggest that the 'forces' (types of units) remain the same, that we are simply modernizing existing types of platforms or units. More often than not, quantum jumps in operational capabilities have been achieved in the past when new types of forces were conceived."[21]

The authors, therefore, chose to talk in terms of development of the capabilities of the air force when developing a framework for the modernisation of the US Air Force. In this context, they make two more points, right at the beginning, which are important, as they help to put the whole issue in proper perspective. To quote, "Modernizing the operational capabilities provided by the Air Force is a journey, not a one-time event. Modernizing yields 'transformation' and a revolution in military affairs (RMA) when the capabilities of the force are dramatically superior to (or different from) those that have come before."[22] That means that so long as we conceive of modernisation, as *modernising the operational capabilities,* it would automatically lead to transformation and no special purpose is served, at least conceptually, by using the term "transformation" of the armed forces.

In this context, the other point made is equally significant from the Service point of view. The authors state, "Discussions of whether the Air Force is (is not) transforming are of little purpose. The Air Force modernizes (as in the past) as opportunities appear. The Air Force has been on the journey, seizing opportunities to meet the challenges, for many years, and it shows."[23]

That is, opportunities as they arise, are required to be seized by the Service concerned to modernise the operational capabilities, which will not come about just because the policy-makers have decided to bring in "transformation" of the armed forces. But the emphasis should be on modernising the operational capabilities, and not simply modernisation of existing platforms. There is a reason for repeating the point. They state, "There is another reason to talk in terms of capabilities. The Air Force provides capabilities to combat commanders and achieves these capabilities according to a concept of employment (CONEMP) defined by the Air

Force. *If a Service thinks of itself as simply 'providing forces' to combatant commanders, it diminishes its role in the development of operational art within its medium."*[24] (Italics added).

So the journey of modernisation can serve the purpose of transforming the forces if it is properly conceived, and an institutional framework is provided "that promotes innovation and timely progress."

Modernisation and Promoting Innovation

This calls for a look into the procurement procedure. Kent and Ochmanek criticised the procedure incorporated in this regard in the US Department of Defence Directive No. 5000.1 in the Defence Acquisition System (October 2000), particularly the activity called "concept and technology development," for which a formal procedure is laid down. This step incorporates two major efforts, namely, concept exploration and technology development. They make a very significant point, "This effort to systematize and centralize control over thinking about innovation runs counter to experience and common sense, both of which suggest that good ideas must bubble up from people engaged in trying to solve concrete problems."[25] They also criticise the "requirements generation system." The Initial Capabilities Document (ICD) in practice has become a definition of characteristics of the system which is to provide some operational capability.

Constructions such as "there is an operational requirement for this system" or worse, "there is a requirement that a particular system attain this level of performance" are specifically rejected by the authors. "The term 'operational requirement' should refer to the need for an operational *capability*. The term should not be used to refer to a specific system or type of system."[26]

- The model that is recommended is to promote timely innovation in modernising operational capabilities. The following characteristics of the model are worth mentioning:
- The model is "actor oriented" as against "document oriented." It defines the role of various actors in fostering and promoting modernisation. The model's actors address matters that are focussed at the operational and tactical levels, as distinct from a focus at the campaign level (a level higher).

- The model promotes enduring activities associated with exploration and development of new concepts at three levels: (1) new concepts of systems and platforms; (2) new concepts for accomplishing military tasks; and (3) new concepts for acquiring operational objectives.
- By deriving operational challenges, objectives and tasks from potential joint-Service campaigns, the model promotes a joint perspective. At the campaign level, the combatant commander defines the campaign operation plan or campaign strategy to achieve the desired effects. At the operation level, the subordinate commanders define the "*concept of employment*" (CONEMP) to achieve each of the operational objectives.

At the tactical level, the combatants define the *concept of execution* (CONEX) to accomplish each of the stated military tasks.

The top half of the model of Kent and Ochmanek indicating the process, is depicted in Fig 4.2 to give an idea of the actors in the concept development stage in the process of modernisation.

Fig 4.2: A Framework for Modernisation

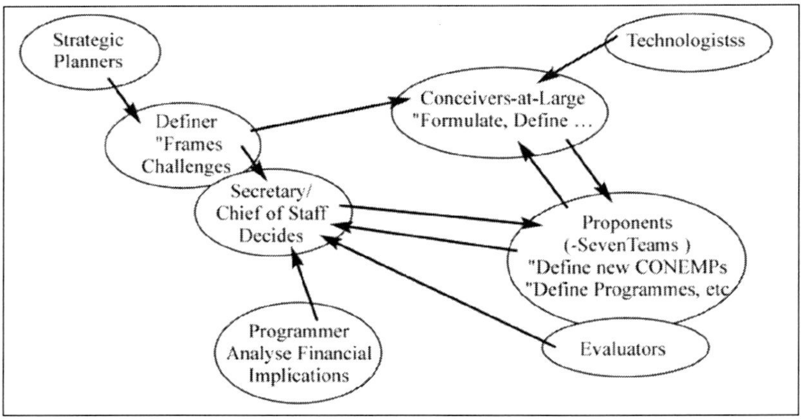

(The top half of the model of Kent and Ochmanek is retained in its entirety as it is the main focus of attention; the bottom half is truncated a bit compared to the original, with some players being left out, as it is not an area of concern for transformation purposes—author.)

The statements of strategic planners, being framed at the strategic level of generality, are not always directly useful in defining the types of operational capability the air force intends to provide. For that reason, the model features a "definer" within the air force who defines what these statements mean in terms of operational capabilities to be provided by the air force. The output of the definer is a set of challenges, which, when approved by the Chief of Staff of the Service, task the air force to develop operational capabilities appropriate to meet each challenge.

The next principal actors in the process are the "proponents." Their primary function is to develop in response to the operational challenges, new concepts of employment that will enable the USAF forces operating in conjunction with the forces of the other Services, to achieve important operational objectives in the face of enemy resistance. The primary input to each team of proponents is one of the chief challenges. Each team is challenged to promote new CONEX and define new CONEMPS so that the air force can provide improved capabilities to fulfill this operational requirement, especially in the future.

Another input to the proponents, generally in the form of new CONEX, stems from conceivers-at-large. The conceivers, in turn , have two primary inputs: (1) a knowledge of existing and emerging technologies; and (2) statement of proponents as to the military tasks that merit the greatest emphasis. With these two inputs, the conceivers define the concept for accomplishing stated military tasks.

The output of conceivers is an evolving portfolio of CONEX from which each proponent can pick and choose. Episodically, the proponents then propose to the chief that they approve the proposed concept and they seek authority and resources to implement it. The Chief of Staff and Secretary of the Air Force are then to decide whether to approve the concept as proposed or amended. If they elect to proceed, they propose to the Secretary of Defence and his principal advisers that the concept be implemented and that resources be allocated to develop the hardware, facilities, and other assets required to make the concept a reality

Among the advisers to the Defence Secretary and evaluators are the financial manager and the programmer who "will determine the financial implications after estimating the full costs of adapting a new CONEMP and the resources required on a year to year basis. They determine if the concept would fit into the overall Air Force budget—again, year-by-year."[27] They have to be proactive in attaining resources for implementation of new concepts. As the authors put it, "They should also act as entrepreneurs and attempt to be creative in financing the proposed concept. They can, for example, suggest possible areas for reduction in other items in the Air Force program."[28]

The important point to note is that most of these processes are at a conceptual plane. Unless there is conceptual clarity about the operational capabilities to be achieved through modernisation, it cannot be the vehicle for bringing about transformation of the armed forces. To reiterate, it is not just modernisation that we need, it is modernising the operational capabilities that we need. Exploration and development of new concepts are required as part of the modernisation process, not only for systems and platforms, but also for accomplishing military tasks and achieving operational objectives and these have to be made part of the decision-making process for new procurements. Only then will the modernisation process yield both RMA and "transformation" of the armed forces.

A Budgeting Process to Advance Transformation

The key tool available to the Defence Minister in giving guidance to the Services on the priorities to be reflected in their programmes under PPBS is the Defence Planning Guidance (DPG) — in our system, it is called the *Raksha Mantri's* (RM's) guidance. In the US system, in response to the DPG, statements of proposed programmes and activities of the Services are submitted in the form of the Programme Objective Memorandum (POM). It has seldom worked in a proper way. As Stuart E. Johnson puts it, "The DPG is usually too late and mostly too broad to provide a framework for service programmers or a metric against which service POM can be evaluated."[29]

Another problem is that the attention of the senior leaders does not focus on the front end of the PPBS process, that is, in the planning phase. More attention get focussed on the back end of the process concerned with submission of the budget to the Office of Management and Budget (OMB).

As Johnson suggests, "One way to shift leadership attention toward the front end of the process is for a few small teams of half a dozen of decision-makers to meet early in the planning phase to enrich their input to the planning of the PPBS. Each group could develop one or two transformational issues that could become an integral part of the DPG. Groups should meet for a limited time, which encourages focus on high-impact transformational initiatives and avoids entanglements with details better handled by staff."[29A] The key would be to ensure that each issue is high leverage and expressed in output terms.

The Five-Year Defence Programme (FYDP) was originally conceived in the 1960s in US defence to give the Secretary of Defence an insight into how money was allocated in major programme areas across military departments. Ten Major Force Programmes (MFPs) were defined that expressed the principal missions the military needed to perform. This allowed the Secretary to see how the objectives of each mission area were being funded, to identify duplication in effort among the Services and enable the Secretary to make strategic choices. But the structure of the FYDP has not kept pace with the change in the security environment. In 1986, MFP11 — special operations forces — was added at the direction of Congress as part of the Goldwater-Nichols Act. Other than that, the structure has changed little. Changes in the categories can be made to make the FYDP more amenable to focussing Service programmes on transformational initiatives. The obvious candidate for an MFP would be C4ISR programmes. Joint expeditionary forces, special operations forces, missile defence could be others. War-fighting functions could be segregated from general support functions to provide insight into the cost of support functions which have a tendency to grow disproportionately.[30]

Some programming must be done jointly. The obvious first step would be have an integrated, joint programme submission in the area of C4ISR programmes. An interoperable C4ISR suite is critical to seamless operation of forces for information dominance over the enemy.

We have not adopted PPBS. But the above brings out how resource allocation decisions and processes are required to be structured to bring in transformation, which remains valid whether we adopt PPBS or programme budgeting or continue with our present system. For this is the rational method of resource allocation in defence. The decision-making process has to undergo a basic change, as indicated above, if we want to bring in transformation.

Essential Elements in Transformation Strategy

As per the Office of Force Transformation of US Defence (set up in 2001, whose first head was Admiral Cebrowski): "The overall strategy of transformation consists of three parts: transforming culture; transforming processes; and transforming capabilities through force or military transformation."[31] It identified four Military Transformation Pillars:

- Strengthening joint operations.
- Exploiting intelligence advantages.
- Concept development and experimentation.
- Developing transformational capabilities.

As would be seen, only one of the four pillars calls for funding. Additional funding is not the most important requirement for embarking on a transformation process. What would be essentially required is reallocation of resources.

This would also be evident from the effect of transformational culture on force structure. In the transformation process, as in the US Army, the emphasis has gone from divisions as viable units in the force structure to independent brigades, for better manoeuvrability. The same feature is seen in the modernisation of the Chinese defence forces (PLA — People's Liberation Army). The other is the emphasis on the role of special operations forces. By the time of Operation Iraqi Freedom, the special operations forces had emerged as pillars of strategy in the US armed forces. As Stephen Cimbala says, "Their performance there was followed by the DoD announcement that US Special Operations Command (SOCOM) would have its own planning structure like other unified and special commands. It would no longer be a mere supplier of forces but now could plan its own missions."[32]

The emphasis on special forces is also observed in the modernisation of the PLA of China. For attaining specific objectives as also meeting asymmetric challenges, more and more attention has to be given to the raising of special forces.

Joint operational concepts, joint capability-building and joint training are the most important ingredients of the transformation process. Since this is the biggest challenge for ushering in a transformation culture, we have to deliberate upon, and bring about, the necessary institutional changes. This underlines the need for a Chief of Defence Staff (CDS) with the mandate of the kind as given to the Chairman, Joint Chiefs of Staff in the Goldwater-Nichols Act, 1986, of the US, without which the transformation process would have never taken off there. This was the most significant contribution of the US Congress to the defence transformation process. Our law-makers should also pay attention to this very important aspect of defence management.

Transformation and Revolution in Military Affairs (RMA)

Since 1997, the US DoD has placed a great deal of emphasis on transforming the force. The emphasis first appeared in the Quadrennial Defence Review (QDR) of 1997. It committed the DoD to "harnessing new technologies to give US forces greater capabilities through advanced concepts, doctrine, and organizations" and linked the RMA to the ongoing transformation of US military capabilities. The QDR of 2001 also linked exploiting the RMA to transforming the country's military forces. It stated that "transforming defence" is at the heart of America's strategic approach to achieving its defence policy goals.

The conceptual basis for the US force transformation is found in Joint Vision 2010, which was released in 1996. It was a landmark document. Without mentioning the term "revolution in military affairs," Joint Vision 2010 discussed technological advances in sensor, command and control, precision force, and stealth capabilities as also doctrinal changes towards increased jointness, littoral warfare and rapidly mobile lethal ground forces.

It discussed organisational changes towards smaller units, decentralised command and control, etc. Joint Vision 2020, released in May 2000, carried forward the ideas expressed in Joint Vision 2010. *In contrast to the more technological focus of Joint Vision 2010, however, Joint Vision 2020 emphasised the need to broaden the focus beyond technology and capture the importance of conceptual innovation as well.* The document stressed that for achieving full-spectrum dominance, even more important than technology is the development of doctrine, organisations, training and education, and the need for leaders to take advantage of the technology. This is a significant shift in emphasis. The new vision offered a second look at the RMA. Joint Vision 2010 states that new sensor technology will make the battlespace more transparent. By contrast, Joint Vision 2020 emphasises the opposite nuance. "We must remember that information superiority neither equates to perfect information nor does it mean the elimination of the fog of war. Information systems, processes, and operations add their own sources of friction and fog to the operational environment."[33]

Whereas Joint Vision 2010 stressed the merits of information superiority during a military operation, Joint Vision 2020 notes that such superiority is only useful when it is translated into superior knowledge and superior decision-making. So the role of leadership is actually enhanced under a transformed military which can be provided by the CDS.

Vision documents are necessary for developing the required strategy. A vision document which provides a basis for defence policy can emanate when there is a CDS.

US Air Force Transformation

The philosophy of transformation of the US Air Force is contained in the following statement "What we require is a capability mix consistent with pre-defined operational concepts and effects-driven methodology. Future programs must be conceived with this mix in mind. Systems or capabilities based on arguments that do not consider the emerging joint character or asymmetric nature of warfare will find themselves obsolete, irrelevant, and candidates for elimination."[34]

They have defined transformation as follows: "A process by which the military achieves and maintains advantage through changes in operational concepts, organization, and/or technologies that significantly improve its war-fighting capabilities or ability to meet the demands of a changing security environment."[35]

The major emphasis is on organisational and operational concepts. It states, "Transformation is more than new hardware. Equally important, if less glamorous, are the organizational concepts that capitalize on the technological advances and allow the US military to truly transform. In addition, the process of transformation begins and ends with people."[36] It also indicates that the Air Force Council has embraced a new vision and construct to *transform human capital management*.

It was announced that all air force operational, programming, and budget decisions would be driven by predefined capability. To make this essential shift, the air force has developed six new concepts (CONOPS) of warfare. It is stated, "The Air Force is transforming around these CONOPS. In addition to serving as the roadmap for operators, the CONOPS construct will form the basis for resource allocation, future system acquisitions, and POM submissions in order to find capabilities-based solutions to war-fighting requirements."[37]

It is apparent that since the main emphasis is on developing operational concepts dictated by change in the security environment and in setting up the required organisation, it would be rather premature to discuss about the financial implications of transformation, before the operational concepts are developed. As the US Air Force Transformation Flight Plan stresses, "Transformation demands innovative thinking and a process that can identify, examine, and turn bright ideas into reality—whether the idea is a new technology, concept, or a novel way to organize."[38]

It mentions that the key components of the innovation in the US Air Force include: *innovation panel, S&T development, air force battle labs, advance technology demonstrations, advanced concept technology demonstrations, agile acquisition, experimentation, war-gaming, modelling and simulation, and training transformation.*

No wonder, as one eminent defence analyst had observed, under the Bush Administration, "The Pentagon's research, development, testing, and evaluation (RDT&E) has actually increased faster than the procurement account in recent years."[39] As per this approach, military transformation basically requires innovative thinking, evolving of relevant war-fighting concepts, technological experimentation, war-gaming, etc, and the issue of "financing the transformation process" would certainly not be in the priority list. Just pumping in more and more money in defence will not bring about transformation, for it basically calls for a cultural change.

Though not in the priority list, finance would pose a problem for acquiring high performance weapon systems and other systems which are expected to play a key role in bringing about transformation. These include high performance stealthy aircraft, unmanned combat aerial vehicles, advanced C4I, miniaturised munitions, etc. For example, because of the budgetary constraints, critics of the plans of the US Air Force to acquire F-22s and JSFs argue that these aircraft are modernisation programmes, and that the air force's requirement for new fighters would be adequately satisfied in the near term by upgrading and procuring F-15s and F-16s. "They argue that the effectiveness of today's fighter and attack aircraft can be maintained through upgrades to their radars, command and control systems, and weapons. Future adversaries, they argue, will increasingly employ mobile cruise, ballistic and surface-to-air missiles... this will jeopardize the forward operating bases... By cancelling or truncating the F-22 and JSF, critics argue, the Air Force can free substantial funds that can be used to more aggressively pursue programs such as space-based assets, directed energy weapons, UCAVs, long range bombers. Such programs are more likely to overcome tomorrow's anti-access threats, and offer more transformation potential."[40]

The point is, there is always competition for resources between one programme and another which are funded by a Service's share of the capital budget. The Service has to decide what its allocation should be to maximise the transformation potential. Upgrades of existing platforms is today a cost-effective option to free resources for other priority programmes which may give a better push towards the transformation process.

How Much of the Forces Needs to be Transformed —and How Quickly?

While considering the financial implications of transformation of the forces, apart from deciding upon the package that will go into transformation, one of the important issues would be to decide how much of the forces needs transforming and how quickly. "Most of the discussion deals with what to transform, but one must also consider how much of the force needs transforming and how quickly."[41] Thus, the basic questions about how much of the force needs to transform, in what way, and how fast, depend on the strategy we want to adopt in fighting our potential enemies and the capabilities we want to have. Without having answers to these strategic questions, transformation cannot be planned nor can the financial implications be discussed.

Financing the RMA and Transformation: The Quadrennial Defence Review (QDR), 1997 Approach

Before going further, let us take a look at how the QDR 1997 wanted to implement the RMA. While it adopted the rhetoric of the RMA movement espousing information superiority, dominant manoeuvre, precision engagement and focussed logistics, it also indicated its explicit decision not to pursue these goals too fast. It adopted a cautious approach. It did not increase the total amount of resources devoted to the acquisition accounts—the sum total of procurement with research, development, testing and evaluation.

For purposes of fiscal planning, the QDR projected a stable annual defence budget of roughly $250 billion per year in constant Financial Year (FY) 1997 dollars. It was felt that if there was no marked deterioration in world events, "the nation is unlikely to support significantly more resources for national defence."[42] It noted that funding for modernisation has been insufficient in the past, with the procurement budget stalled near the $40 billion level. Even though QDR 1997 planned an increase in the procurement budget to $60 billion by 2001, on the basis of assessment of existing trends and assumptions, it estimated that the procurement plan was likely to stall in the range of $45- $50 billion.[43]

The broad direction of the path adopted by the QDR was to focus on balancing near-term and longer-term risks. Following this path required reducing active military personnel, reserve component personnel and civilian personnel by significant numbers. These force reductions were expected to allow increases in the level of investment, with about $60 billion per year applied to procurement which would help in the defence transformation process.

The need for transformation was further encouraged by the National Defence Panel (NDP) which was commissioned by the US Congress to review the new strategy indicated in the QDR 1997.

It is necessary to appreciate the fact that basic changes like "RMA" and "transformation," which have many dimensions and may involve restructuring of forces, cannot be initiated without such a comprehensive defence review based on periodic in-depth deliberations, as in the QDR. Such reviews should be made mandatory and should be an integral part of defence planning and budgeting — in fact, should provide the basis for these as also for defence acquisition.

Further, the operation and maintenance expenditure as also increase in personnel cost, impinge on the procurement budget. Unless specific and determined steps are taken to contain and bring down the personnel cost and maintenance expenditure, as a percentage of each Service's budget, it would be impossible to increase the procurement budget to a level which would be conducive to bring in RMA and transformation of the military.

Funding the Transformation and RMA: The NDP Approach

Both the QDR 1997 and NDP advised caution in the process of transformation. Accordingly, the investment requirement for carrying out the transformation process in the short and medium term was comparatively modest. The report was entitled, significantly, "Transforming Defence, National Security in the 21st Century."

The issue of funding the transformation was addressed by the NDP. The procurement goal could not be met in the past, because increases in Operations and Maintenance (O&M) expenses, coupled with inability to increase the defence budget had "crowded out" procurement spending. This trend, as per the NDP assessment, was likely to continue.

The panel estimated that an annual budget wedge of $5 to 10 billion would be required to support the transformation strategy. This money will fund such initiatives as intelligence, space, urban warfare, joint experimentation, and information operations, the report stated. *Prima facie*, this is not a lot of funds, as it represents about 3-4 per cent of the annual defence budget.[44]

In the absence of additional funding, the panel contended that the transformation could be funded by the infrastructure and acquisition reform, reducing the operational tempo associated with non-fighting activities, cancelling acquisition programmes, or reducing force structure and end strength. There will be no easy answers, and difficult choices must be made, the report stated.[45]

One of the reasons for a comparatively modest assessment of funding for transformation in the medium term was that the NDP was placing much greater emphasis than the QDR on the need to prepare for the putative challenges of the post-2015 world.[46] It laid great stress on diplomacy and cooperation as a part of the security dialogue. It was not very supportive of the existing two-war strategy, and felt that it was a device for preserving the existing force structure. It is worthwhile to look at what the NDP says about better resource management in support activities, where generally the money is. It states: "The Department should shift its strategy for reforming the defence support infrastructure to a bottom-up approach that empowers managers at all levels with greater capability and authority to make common sense decisions for the benefit of the Department." [47]

Points for Us

The following are the five basic principles, which were identified as the key elements in the report, which are applicable in our case also if transformation is the goal:

- **Cost Visibility/Accuracy.** Accurate cost information is a prerequisite for improved resource allocation decisions. The Department should develop financial systems that help managers to identify inefficient practices and target areas for process improvement.
- **Positive Incentives.** The DoD must establish credible mechanisms to ensure that at least a portion of the savings achieved through streamlining efforts is retained by the local organisation for its own use.
- **Choice and Competition.** Choice and competition motivate individuals and organisations to seek innovative approaches to meeting customer needs. Increasing the role of competitive forces in the delivery of support services should be essential to achieving lower costs and improved service quality.

- **Resource Flexibility.** Under the current budget rules, defence managers have little flexibility to shift resources to common sense trade-offs or respond to unanticipated requirements. Greater flexibility in resource management would encourage innovation and process improvement throughout the Department.
- **Civil/Military Integration.** Defence personnel should be integrated into their local communities, using commercial services to the maximum.

For generating funds for transformation, we have to seriously look into streamlining the support infrastructure, where generally the money is. In this regard, the approach of QDR 1997 and the NDP Report 1997 were similar. As per the written statement of Dr. Warner, Assistant Secretary of Defence, in his testimony to the US Congress (House National Security Committee), "The path ultimately chosen in the QDR required modest reductions in today's force structure — concentrated on the 'tail'rather than the 'teeth'of forces — along with a commitment to fundamentally reengineer the Department's infrastructure and support activities to fund badly needed increases in a focused, executable modernization program and in broader transformation efforts."[48]

Comments by the Chairman of the Joint Chiefs of Staff contained in his independent assessment of the QDR 1997 as mandated by law, to the Secretary of Defence also endorsed the above "strategy" to bring in transformation. To quote, "We need to get every dollar we can by reducing our infrastructure... Ultimately, we must commit ourselves to a major reengineering of our infrastructure. Without that reengineering, the patterns of the last four years are likely to continue — investment programs will be cut and the force of the future will be sold to pay current operations and support bills. In short, *we will not be able to realize the promise inherent in the Revolution in Military Affairs unless we embrace the revolution in business affairs*."[49]

The revolution in business affairs would also call for accurate costing of activities. To quote the NDP, "The Panel recommends that the Department accelerate the deployment of financial management systems in defence support organizations with strong activity-based costing capabilities. Such systems enable managers to understand true costs, identify inefficient practices, target areas of process improvement."[50]

In other words, transforming the financial management system, with an accent on activity-based costing should be an integral part of the defence transformation process to bring in economy and efficiency in resource management.

Reallocation of Resources

This is a recurring theme, with the defence analysts looking for funds for transforming the defence in an information age. For example, Jacques Gansler, the eminent defence analyst, writing about the new challenges in 2003, claimed that future adversaries will use the asymmetrical approaches, focussed on areas the nation is potentially weak in, which cannot be contained by conventional forces. In response, the military will need to shift resources, training, organisations, and equipment to non-traditional areas. These areas include special operations forces, urban warfare, cyber warfare defence, ballistic missile defence and 'brilliant' systems for carrying out intelligence, surveillance, reconnaissance, communications, and control activities, as well as precision strikes on adversary activities. In view of the scarcity of resources, what is required is a shift in resources from traditional areas to non-traditional areas or reallocation of resources. "Needless to say, such shifts, particularly of resources and organizations, tend to be countercultural and fiercely resisted by the entrenched institutions in the military, the defence industry, and Congress. Perhaps most difficult, advancing the revolution in military affairs will require reallocating resources and modernizing traditional military organizations. The commanders who have come of age with the 'platform-centric' model in which ships, planes and tanks are critical elements; the industry that builds this equipment; the members of Congress who support business as usual — none of these elements is likely to enthusiastically support the necessary shift to the new and increasingly information-based weaponry needed to deter or defeat future adversaries." This is the negative side of the story. But there is another side. "The good news is that sufficient resources to pay for such changes can be generated out of current defence budgets."[51]

The most important way of finding funds for transforming by following the RMA route is cutting duplication of the support function among the armed Services. These include logistics, communications, medical services, and intelligence currently provided within each military Service and various defence agencies.

RMA in Asia

Systems integration skills are the most demanding aspect of RMA. The qualities of creativity, innovation, and independence of thinking require a lot of encouragement, and these will provide the basic challenge.

Paul Dibb, in a seminal article on RMA in the Asian region, has indicated the challenges posed by RMA for this region. They are:

- The development of a joint force doctrine is required for the organisational changes associated with RMA "By and large, most countries in the region have given insufficient attention to the changes in military culture and organization that are required to maximize the use of RMA." [52] Separate single-Service cultures are the norm in the region. "No appropriate set of joint Service operational concepts exists or is practised in most countries."[53]
- Integrated logistic support and maintenance is part of the overall infrastructure required for joint force operations.
- The systems integration challenge is a formidable one. This is the most crucial skill for ushering in RMA.[54]

What is significant to note in the above list is that financing the RMA for undertaking the transformation process has not been indicated as one of the problem areas. In fact, from what we have described above, financing the transformation process, if a proper phased programme is developed, may not be a problem.

By the late Nineties, analysts noted three variants of a regional RMA within Asia:[55]

- The Australian model, primarily focussed upon building wide area surveillance, information and command links to become a regional military integrator within the region, able to work with the United States and with Australia's adjacent allies

- The Japanese model drew upon its technological relationship with the United States and its military relationship with the US Navy to put in place a naval RMA to adjacent military technology areas.
- The South Korean model had been based on the effort of large industrial combines to work with the United States and Europe to forge global partnerships that would allow Korean firms to become partners in the development of their own military platforms.

Chinese military and civilian officials have affirmed the importance of a "revolution in military affairs" to China's modernisation. The December 2004 White Paper for Defence describes the process of modernisation of defence in China in the context of global trends in military transformation. The general assessment in the West is that "China's indigenous military and civilian technology sectors are insufficiently advanced to spur a dramatic reappraisal of People's Liberation Army doctrine and organization."[56] RMA advocates within China commonly observe that Chinese military technology is flagging relative to cutting edge technology. That China must import most of its technologically advanced military equipment demonstrates that its indigenous technology lags behind. Recent acquisitions made by China have enabled it to develop some "pockets of excellence" which do not necessarily lead to RMA. All the same, there is no doubt that major steps towards force modernisation and RMA have been taken.

From the Chinese experience, one learns that for a developing country, RMA should come through the efforts at modernisation of the armed forces. And for generating funds for modernisation, apart from increase in defence budgets, it is necessary to streamline the force structure. The PLA has undergone two large reductions in force in the past decade, starting with three million people in 1995, and losing 500,000 people from 1997 to 2000 and another 200,000 from 2003 to 2005. Chinese sources noted that by the end of 2005, the PLA was likely to have 2.3 million people on its active duty roster.[57] The PLA has adopted the term "revolution in military affairs (RMA) with Chinese characteristics" to describe how it will build a smaller, more technologically advanced force through "mechanization and informationization."[58] The conduct of joint operations is an important element of all levels of professional education. The Chinese have also the streamlined the logistic system.

These lessons are important. If India has to transform its forces, it has to be part of the modernisation efforts, with focus on RMA technologies. The forces have to be streamlined, particularly in the support areas, to generate funds for modernisation. Periodic comprehensive defence reviews would be the key tool to bring in transformation in defence. The results of the reviews should be published in a White Paper on Defence.

The Chinese experience also underlines the point that advance in military science and technology is the key to RMA, as experimentation and innovation provide it the needed impetus. As indigenous abilities in critical technologies having military application may be limited, collaborative efforts would be required.

The recently promulgated policy of "offsets" in defence procurement should be directed towards obtaining critical technologies which would help in ushering in RMA.

In this way, the defence procurement process itself can help in financing the transformation, by getting the critical technologies and also generating collaborative research and development in cutting-edge technology. An Indian strategy and a model for ushering in RMA is urgently called for.

This also brings in the issue of adequacy of India's industrial base for ushering in RMA technology. It would be a moot point to decide as to what extent overseas companies with relevant technologies could be allowed to play a role in this regard and what incentives e.g. in the shape of ownership percentages, orders, etc can be offered to them to get interested in the matter. The indigenous route would be difficult to follow, given the level of technology we have imbibed.

RMA technologies cannot be obtained only by spending money. National governments will continue to control diffusion of RMA related technologies. Therefore, government-to-government understanding would be required to obtain these technologies. What would be the nature of strategic partnership that would be required if high technology items are to be obtained, is a matter of major policy . The USA which has the RMA technologies, will see to what extent its national interest is served in relaxing the export laws and licensing norms to India for the high technology items. This is an area of diplomacy where constructive and sustained efforts are required to be made through strategic dialogues to get the necessary cooperative attitude in the matter.

India has also to make its own efforts to develop the technologies. If the government decides to set up a Defence Technology Commission (as recommended by the DRDO Review Committee), one of its first tasks would be to develop a strategy of how to go forward in RMA technologies, what kind of investments are required and where; and how public-private partnership can be used to achieve the necessary breakthroughs.

Some words of caution, however, are in order. It is well to remember that setting in military operations will determine the advantage provided by access to new technology. There is also the question of opportunities provided by the prevailing political conditions to use these technologies. The Gulf War (1991) which dramatically demonstrated the possibilities of RMA, could take place because of the end of the Cold War. It appeared to validate a particular line of technological and doctrinal development. As Lawrence Freedman almost prophetically put it, "Whether or not this presaged a revolution in military affairs, depended on whether future patterns of conflict offer similar opportunities."[59] He observed that the apparent Western advantages in conventional military strength must be "qualified by reference to opportunities available to a determined and intelligent opponent to take advantage of local conditions," and it may be difficult for an "expeditionary force" to succeed.[60] Even with RMA, it is not easy to obtain "dominant situational awareness" which will enable one to make an attack with confidence.[61]

Secondly, the impression should not be carried that emerging technologies have made the conventional force structure and legacy systems obsolete. Drawing defence planning lessons from the war in Iraq, the eminent strategic analyst Macubin T. Owens, comments, "A transformed military is a valid objective, but the war in Iraq illustrates the limits of transformation."[62] He further observes, "There is no question that the effectiveness and efficacy of US forces have been enhanced by precision strike weapons and networking, but the idea that technology can banish friction, chance, and uncertainty from war has been shown to be overly optimistic."[63]

That means that for defence planning purposes, financing for conventional forces and the legacy system cannot be curtailed. There can be streamlining by economising on support infrastructure to generate some funds for transformation.

In this context, it is necessary to determine what outputs of RMA technology would receive the main funding support. Probably, RMA in India will be concentrating on developing Network-Centric Warfare (NCW) capabilities, as that has the largest pay-off.

The basic output of such networking is to generate enhanced situational awareness, better collaborative effort and improved offensive potential. Achieving this output can only be through a long-term project that will require the concurrent development of both the human and networking dimensions of NCW.

The change in the networking dimension would have a profound effect on the human dimension of NCW. Realising the human dimension would require high standards of training, education, suitable doctrine and leadership. The investment in human resources and ushering in proper manpower planning is a must if we have to use RMA technologies. The NCW has, therefore, to necessarily follow an evolutionary path which will call for a long-term capability plan to be approved by the government and funding at a steady rate for defence modernisation.

This would also call for linking planning with budgeting through the programming route. The reform in the budgeting process should be treated, as far as we are concerned, as part of the defence transformation process.

In today's world, where potential adversaries are adopting RMA with enthusiasm, adoption of RMA and transformation of the armed forces as a process is necessary. Modernisation of the armed forces has to adopt the transformational route. There is no alternative to it.

The defence budget for the year 2012-13 has been hiked by 17.6 percent. Does it make us any wiser about its impact on modernisation and preparedness, without knowing its impact programme-wise, as to which is getting a boost and which is not?

From the Revised Estimates provision of 2011-12, it was seen that the Ministry of Defence failed to spend Rs.3,055 crore allocated to it under the capital budget. Which programme could not spend and why , is a matter of speculation. No informed comments can be made about them.

The allocation for the capital budget for the year 2012-13 has gone up by 15 per cent. The capital budget represents 41 percent of the defence budget , which totals Rs 1,93 lakh crore . In the absence of programme–wise allocation, we would not know how much of it is for capability in the near-term and how much for future capability building and what are these capabilities. In the absence of an approved five-year defence plan, one cannot link these very significant allocations to the 'objectives' of the plan. In other words, there is a total lack of linkage between 'input' and 'output' , so one would not know how efficiently the defence budget is being spent.

There is an announcement in the Finance Minister's budget speech of a "Medium Term Expenditure Framework", that would set forth a three-year rolling target for expenditure budgets. This is with the basic objective of achieving "fiscal consolidation", which is to be attained through budgetary management from now on.

The government has indicated its commitment to achieving fiscal consolidation by bringing amendments to the Fiscal Responsibility and Budget Management Act along with the Finance Bill 2012.

To quote the Finance Minister from the budget speech, "The government had to deviate from targets(for fiscal and revenue deficits) due to injection of fiscal stimulus at that time. Following my announcement in the last Budget speech, I am now introducing amendments to the FRBM Act as part of the Finance Bill."[64]

As part of the amendments, the government has fixed new targets for fiscal and revenue deficits with a deadline of March,1915.

The revenue deficit would be capped at 2 per cent of the GDP by 2014-15 from the budgeted 3.4 percent for the next financial year, while the fiscal deficit would be reduced to 3.9 percent by March 31, 2015, from the estimated 5.1 percent in 2012-13.

These are indeed very ambitious targets, but are being brought about by legislative amendments. The deviations from targets are stated to be subject to audit. So the seriousness of purpose in achieving fiscal consolidation cannot be doubted.

Laying down yearly fiscal and revenue deficit targets would imply targets for likely budgetary provisions for the next three years, for both expenditure and revenue. The major spending Ministries like the Ministry of Defence, should, therefore, get to know their likely budgetary allocations for the next three years. This can be the basis for a proper expenditure plan for three years for the Ministry of Defence and would be the 'input' side of the plan. The 'output' side of the plan should now be put together in terms of a capability plan , to link input to output, as multi-year planning should now be possible.

Uncertainty remains as to what the 'transformation' is. But the end result should be that a transformed military thinks differently about the art of war and preparation for battle than an untransformed one. There is still no model to emulate in bringing about *transformation,* which can even be viewed as a cultural change rather than about acquisitions requiring a lot of investment. It happens over time if enabling conditions are made available and decision-makers are clear about the objectives .Since conceptual issues dominate the scene, financing of *transformation* has not been an important theme.

But network-enabled warfare has been a central concept in both transformation philosophy and the RMA. To bring this about calls for substantial investment and over a period of time, which would call for long-term planning.

What about financing the RMA? It is sometimes assumed that that it would be brought about through the modernisation process, involving acquisition of sophisticated weapons, which have been designed, keeping in view the challeges and potentialities of the information age. In one sense it does; in another, it does not. A basic tenet of RMA philosophy is joint planning and joint operation. This need not be ushered in by acquisitions by the individual Services. It calls for organisational changes which are to be treated as part of transformation and RMA. The fact that the Goldwater-Nichols Act came in 1986, before RMA and transformation became familiar concepts, should not blind us to the fact that the Act provided the basic impetus as also the framework within which these concepts could be given operational meaning. The success of the first Gulf War could be attributed to a large extent to the process of 'jointness' and the importance given to theatre commanders in resource planning and strategy formulation. Transformation also calls for transformational organisational changes. But even then, the 'joint' concept, as seen from the US experience, has not taken firm root, and analysts are thinking of a new architecture to bring it about.

And how does RMA merge into the transformation process? The QDR of 2001 made a mention about exploiting RMA to transform US military forces. RMA cannot all be about technology, nor can 'transformation' be just about doctrine, organisation and training. Both have to merge, for which there has to be innovative thinking and exploratory analysis. The innovative thinking process has to be both top-down and bottom-up.

Does RMA only mean going in for high-performace equipment?

As Martin Libicki points out, "This raises the question of platforms—a question that is an unintended but logical result of the information revolution. Today, platforms rule… Platforms have become more capable, but only by also growing more complex and costly. As they become more costly, fewer are bought; with fewer in the inventory, owners want them better protected. Self-defense systems are, thus, needed, raising the costs further."[65] In this route, fewer and fewer platforms would be affordable in the future.

The current RMA is based on what comes from commercial sources as well as what comes from defence labs. Distributed sensors and weapons can be built on civilian specifications which benefit from economies of scale. Computer power can be used to covert the small pictures into big ones. Information technology is the heart of RMA.

Libicki adds, " Information technology suggests *that it may be logical to convert from a platform-based to a knowledge-based military.* In the former, operators, local sensors, weapons, self-protection are all bundled as *platforms that work together but each essentially as an autonomous fighting unit.* They are given intelligence, but once in combat, they usually work with data they collect themselves.

"In a knowledge- based military , fused data from networked sensors go into creating a shared knowledge base of the battlefield."[66] (Italics mine.)

Information systems need to generate 'situational awareness' to operators and soldiers to enable them to take initiative in action. This creates complexity but complexity has to be mastered at the operating level. Speed is necessary because it permits action before the adversary can react. It may not be possible to wait for commands from the higher levels.

So RMA or transformation is not about acquiring more complex and high-performance weapon systems. One has to *transform from a platform-based to a knowledge-based military*. That would be real transformation.

How to go about it? One way we have already mentioned:

"For technology to find its way into military transformation, it must impact on doctrine, organization, and training related to combat."[67]

Soldiers are the ultimate determinant of combat effectiveness. Validation of technology effectiveness in terms of tasks to be performed, has to be done by "*smart soldiers*".

As earlier indicated, the emphasis on special operation forces for ensuring success in a mission, is a pointer to this direction. In both the Afghanistan and Iraq Wars, they played significant roles. This underlines the message that the transformed forces must be smaller, faster and smarter, as also thinkers. But in land warfare, numbers also matter. Therefore, there has to be a proper combination of both.

The basic point remains : it is the smarter and motivated military that can take maximum advantage of technological innovation. If competence regarding proper use of information technology at the operation level is lacking, then the transformation process would get delayed.

The next point for transformation to a knowledge-based military is more significant.

To quote Stephen Cimbala regarding the US experience, in this regard, "The most important transformation in the armed forces since World War II was the change from a draft to an all-volunteer force (AVF)."[68]

Creating an all-volunteer force in the 1970s led to an improvement in the quality of personnel joining the army and paved the way for RMA and transformation initiatives. "Those who fail to see this have put the cart before the horse, crediting technology with accomplishments that rightly belong to an empowered military with smarter and motivated people."[69]

By the Eighties, the US military forces started getting shaped by the volunteer force and by the mid-Nineties, the force was exclusively the product of the volunteer era. The enlisted force is today more highly educated than ever before and *grading in terms of aptitudes* of the military personnel has gone up significantly since the 1970s.

As an analyst who has worked on the changing manpower profile in the US military and given figures to prove his point, observes, "The figure shows that, generally, the higher the grade, the higher the educational achievement. The figure and earlier ones show that the proportion of college graduates grew over time as well as across all grades and occupations."[70]

Officers have always been mostly college graduates. But Non-Commissioned Officers (NCOs) and Petty Officers (POs) are now becoming more educated as well. " In recent years, officer duties have devolved to NCOs and POs. Many types of work, from administration and paper work to missile launching, have become sergeant and PO work—largely because of technology and a faster operational tempo."[71]

Officers 'lead' in the broad sense of leadership; they set direction and align forces. This differentiates the officer corps from the NCOs and POs. But as more educated enlisted forces supplant the earlier corps who were less educated, they would look for more status. "As the edge in human capital enjoyed by junior officers over the senior enlisted shrinks, many issues related to the scope of the latter's responsibility, job design, status, and compensation become salient."[72]

How to enrich the human capital, so that it is endowed with the necessary skill and aptitude to usher in the transformation process, should now be the central concern for us. Cognitive skill and motivation at the ground level are absolutely essential to bring about transformation. Innovative as also adaptive capability is essential for success when the future is uncertain, and long-term planning to meet all kinds of situations is not possible.

In this context, it is worth mentioning that the Indian Army has long drawn attention to a significant shortage at the junior officer level. This has become an endemic feature. A figure of 20 per cent shortage has sometimes been mentioned. This shows that there is a lack of attraction to the Army as a career, when there are better opportunities for the educated and smart young people.

This kind of shortage at the ground level leadership would make it difficult to bring about transformational changes.

On the other side, the educational level prescribed for the recruitment of Other Ranks (ORs) is not adequate to endow them with cognitive skill to make effective use of information technology or the cutting edge technologies that are being made available on the basis of the RMA concept. There is, however, no shortage of trained personnel at this level, because of poor employment opportunities in the civil sector for persons with such education and skill. However, it is difficult to conceive of them taking any kind of leadership role even after a lot of training and experience.

Thus, on one side, we have a shortage of junior officers to provide leadership at the ground level, and on the other, we are not insisting on the necessary educational and aptitude requirements for recruitment of ORs, so that in the course of time, through the necessary training, they become the most important participants in RMA as also after gaining the required experience, provide leadership at the ground level.

If transformation is the goal of the Army, which it should be, then there is no alternative but to prescribe higher educational standards for ORs and examinations for judging their cognitive skills. If not for the bulk, as numbers are also important, but for a significant number, higher educational standards should be laid down. Persons at the higher educational level cannot be recruited at the level of sepoys. They have to be inducted at the higher level of NCOs. The aim should be to get the kind of recruits who, after ten to twelve years of experience, if found fit, can be promoted to the junior officer level.

To attract college educated persons to join the military, the salary package should be attractive enough.

This is where finance should not be a problem. Financing towards investing in the human capital to enhance their skill and aptitude would be immensely helpful in bringing about transformation in the military. This would be the most important enabling step to convert from a platform-based to a knowledge-based military.

To get focussed attention, enhancing the knowledge base of ORs should be treated as a programme, and the required funds allocated for the purpose.

Financing of transformation of the military, whether through additional allocation or reallocation or both has to be through planning, programming and budgeting viewed as a system .This provides the framework for transformation within the resource constraints. But to be meaningful in real world conditions, it has to provide a decision-making framework within the annual budgeting process.

Programming is the key concept, which has to be widened to include planning. The objective setting exercise cannot be segregated from the programming exercise. General strategic guidelines can hardly provide a basis for programming. One need not conceive of 'planning' to precede 'programming' just because logically it is more elegant.

Planning has to merge with programming.

Similarly, the budgeting exercise need not come after the programming exercise is complete. Programming and budgeting should not only be *simultaneous processes*, there should be frequent *feedback* between the two processes. This to ensure that budgeting is *informed* by the programming aspects, and programmes are, in turn, *informed* by the budgetary constraints. In this way, we can have resource informed planning and programming.

The whole process should be conceived in a multi-year budgeting framework, as a rolling concept, so that the cost implications of programmes are not seen only in the context of the coming year's budget, but in the context of a multi-year budget, and decisions taken accordingly.

What is being emphasised is that planning, programming and budgeting should not be treated as *sequential* processes. This is to distinguish it from the PPBS introduced by McNamara in the early Sixties and followed for decades thereafter in the US defence planning process. This became a time consuming process and by the time the budgeting stage came, the cost implications worked out in the programming phase became outdated. Many decisions were taken in the budgeting phase to be within the resource constraints, thus, negating the logic of the whole system. Nor was multi-year budgeting instituted, leading to mismatches between strategy and resources. This malady continues to this day.

This luxury is not available to us. Therefore, programming and budgeting should be simultaneous processes to be completed within the annual budget cycle. This should not be difficult as most of the programmes are ongoing programmes and only changes , if any , should be considered.

By following this process, financing of transformation can take place in a smooth manner, without discontinuous jumps. Transformation of the military demands a steady state of activity, well thought out and well executed over a period of time.

Notes

1. Department of Defence, "Elements of Defense Transformation," http://www/oft.osd.mil/library_files/document_383-Elements of Transformation_LR.pdf. 2004.
2. Executive Summary, "Defence Transformation in Asia-Pacific Region: Meeting the Challenge," March 30-April 1, 2004 http://www.apcss.org/core')/ Confèrenee/CR-ES/Defènse Trans. doc.
3. Vice Admiral Arthur K. Cebrowski (Retd), "What is Transformation ?" http://www.oft.osd.mil/what is _transformation.cfm.
4. Walter P. Fairbanks, "Implementing the Transformation Vision," September 30, 2006, http:// www.trackpads.com/magazine/publish/printer_1738.shtml).
5. Douglas Berenson and Kerala T. Cowart, "QDR 2006: Transformation Via Process Reform," *DFI Quarterly International*, Spring 2006, p. 12.
6. Ibid., p. 13.
7. Quoted by Thomas G. Mahnken, "Transforming the US Armed Forces, Rhetoric or Reality?" *Naval War College Review*, vol. 54, no. 3, Summer 2001.
8. Ibid., p. 216.
9. Ibid., p. 225.
10. Ibid.
11. Stuart E. Johnson, "A New PPBS Process to Advance Transformation," *Defence Horizons*, no. 32, September 2003, a publication of the Centre for Technology and National Security Policy, National Defence University of the USA.
12. Ibid.
13. Ryan Henry, "Defence Transformation and the Quadrennial Defense Review," *Parameters*, Winter 2005-06.
14. Col Jack D. Kem (Retd.) "Military Transformation: Ends, Ways and Means," *Air and Space Power Journal*, Fall 2006, p. 88.
15. Quadrennial Defence Review Report, US Department of Defence http://www.global security. org/military/ library/policy/dod/qdr-2006-report.htm)
16. Cebrowski, n. 3.
17. Glenn A. Kent and David E. Thaler, *A New Concept for Streamlining Up-Front Planning* (RAND, 1992).
18. Ibid., p. 11.
19. Ibid., p. 7.

20. Ibid., p. 7.
21. Glenn A. Kent and David A. Ochmanek, *A Framework for Modernization Within the United States Air Force* (RAND, 2003), p.1.
22. Ibid.
23. Ibid., p. 13.
24. Ibid.
25. Ibid., p. 2.
26. Ibid., p. 10.
27. Ibid., p. 16.
28. Ibid., p. 17.
29. Johnson, n. 11.
29A. Ibid.
30. Ibid.
31. n. 1, p. 6.
32. Stephen Cimbala, "Transformation in Concept and Policy", *Joint Forces Quarterly,* June 27, 2005.
33. Quoted by Elinor C. Sloan, *The Revolution in Military Affairs, Implications for Canada and NATO* (McGill-Queen's University Press, 2002).
34. The US Air Force Transformation Flight Plan, November 2003, http.// www.dtie. mil?jointvision/af _trans flight plan.pdf
35. Ibid.
36. Ibid.
37. n. 34.
38. Ibid.
39. Michael 0'Hanlon, *Defence Strategy (For the Post-Saddam Era)* (Manas Publications in collaboration with Brookings Institution Press), p.75.
40. "Air Force Transformation," CRS Report for Congress, updated January 18, 2006, http://www.Fas.org/spg/crs/natssec/RS 20859 pdf.
41. Thomas 1. Searle, "The Air Force of the Future," *Air-Space Power Journal*, Summer 2004.
42. QDR 1997, Section iv, http: /www.defenselink.mil/puhs/qdr/sec4.html
43. Ibid., http://www.defenselink.mail/pubs/qdr/sec4.html
44. Report of the NDP, December 1997, section on "A Transformation Strategy," http:// www.fas.org/man/docs/ndp
45. Ibid.
46. Carl Conetta, "Future Tense: An Assessment of the Report of the National Defence Pane," http://www.comw.org/qdr/ndppda 1.htm.
47. NDP Report, hitp: www.fas.org/man/docs/ndp/front.him
48. Written statement of Dr. Edward L. Warner, Assistant Secretary of Defence for strategy and requirements, testimony to the House National Security Committee,

Military Personnel Subcommittee, January 29, 1998, on the QDR 1997. http : / / www.globalsecurity.org /military /library /congress / 1 9 9 8 _hr / 0 1 - 2 9 -98warner. htm.

49. Comments by the Chairman of the Joint Chiefs of Staff on the QDR 1997, http:// www.fas.org/man/docs/qdr/sec10.hmtl.
50. The NDP Report, http://www.fas.org/man/doc.sindp/part 05.htm
51. Jacques S. Gansler, "Next Steps in Defence Restructuring," *Issues in Science and Technology*, Summer 2003, http://www.issues.org/19.4/gansler.html.
52. Paul Dibb, "The Revolution in Military Affairs and Asian Security," paper presented at the Annual Conference on Security Challenges in the Rising Asia-Pacific, Singapore, September 1997.
53. Ibid.
54. Ibid.
55. Source: Robbin F. Laird and Hogler H. Mey, "The Revolution in Military Affairs: Allied Perspectives," *McNair Paper*, 60, April 1999.
56. Jason Kelly, "A Chinese Revolution in Military Affairs?," *Yale Journal of International Affairs*, Winter-Spring 2006.
57. Ibid., p. 60.
58. Lt. Col. Dennis J. Blasko (Retd), "China's National Defence in 2004," *Military Review*, September-October 2005. "Revolution in Military Affairs," quoted by Lt. Col. Blasco mentioned above.
59. Lawrence Freedman, "The Revolution in Strategic Affairs," *Adelphi Paper* 318, p. 32.
60. Ibid., p. 45.
61. Ibid., p. 47.
62. Macubin T. Owens, "Transforming Transformation: Defence-Planning Lessons from Iraq," Editorial, National Review Online, Ashbrook Centre, April 2003, http:// www.ashbrook.org/publicat/oped/owens/03/transform.html
63. Ibid.
64. FM Pranab Mukherjee, while tabling the Union Budget, 2012-13, in the Lok Sabha.
65. Martin Libicki, "Incorporating Information Technology in Defense Planning", in Stuart E. Johnson, et. al., ed.,, *New Challenges New Tools for Defense Decisionmaking* (RAND, 2003), p.113.
66. Ibid., p. 114.
67. Stephen. J. Cimbala, "Transformation in Concept and Policy", *Joint Forces Quarterly (JFQ)*, June, 2005 issue thirty-eight,p-30.
68. Ibid.
69. Ibid.

70. Harry J. Thie, “Planning The Future Military Workforce”, in Johnson, et. al., ed., n.65, p.168.
71. Ibid.
72. Ibid., p.170.

5

Internal Audit and Internal Control: Of Greater Relevance Today

Introduction

As per tradition, it is held that internal auditing should be confined to ensuring that accounting and allied records are properly maintained, the procedure to safeguard assets is in place, and, in a limited sense, to see that policies relating to resource management are complied with.

With changing times and with new challenges, the concept of internal audit has undergone a sea-change the world over, with regard to both its definition and scope, with international bodies dealing with audit laying down new standards of internal audit.

In today's world, internal audit, is defined as an independent appraisal within an organisation to evaluate activities and as a service to the organisation to improve economy and efficiency.

The basic objective of an internal audit is to assist the members of an organisation in an effective discharge of responsibilities relating to resource management. The objective of auditing includes promoting effective control over resource management at a reasonable cost. That is why internal auditing is regarded as an integral part of management activity and any lacunae in this regard would adversely affect resource management in both the private and public sectors.

The reason for this is that the scope of internal auditing has today been expanded to include examination and evaluation of the adequacy and effectiveness of an organisation's internal control system. In fact, today, in view of the challenges in maintaining a proper standard of management of resources, internal auditing is required to be viewed as the most important component of the internal control system.

Internal control systems in public sector expenditure management are basically management control systems with a view to ensuring not only compliance with rules and regulations and reliability of financial data and reports, but also to facilitate efficiency of operations in the delivery of the service in which it is engaged. As far as the activities of the government are concerned, a sound internal control framework, of which internal audit is to be regarded as an important element, apart from ensuring maintenance of satisfactory accounting records, is required to assure:

(i) that government operations attain some basic fiduciary standards in guarding against misuse and inefficient use of resources;
(ii) for safeguarding government assets from misuse;
(iii) for countering fraud and error;
(iv) for checking whether budgetary objectives set out in the government policies are being achieved.

Thus, "Internal controls can be regarded as one of the foundations of good governance and the first line of defense against improprieties. They also provide the public with 'reasonable assurances' that if improprieties do occur, they will be made transparent and appropriately addressed."[1]

Though internal audit is also a part of the internal control system, it has a distinct role in that it is one of the tools for evaluating and improving the internal control system. Internal audit in government also involves audit on the basis of standards of financial propriety (as does the external audit) and, therefore, is required to observe upon cases of impropriety in financial operations.

A robust internal control system and an effective internal audit system are the foundations for sound financial management. However, these systems, unless updated continuously, have a tendency to become obsolete over time, because of the inability to cope with new challenges.

One of the main weaknesses of the financial management in the Government of India emanates from the fact that the system of internal audit and internal control in the financial management of the government have not been updated over several decades, nor has the government given due importance to it in securing 'value for money' and accountability.

It is still carried out in a routine and traditional manner, quite unaffected by all the changes that have been brought about in various countries in increasing the scope of internal audit to enable management in securing economy and efficiency in resource management and to prevent fraud.

We may briefly review what kind of changes have been brought about in reviewing the scope of internal audit and control in other parts of the world to make it an effective tool of management for establishing accountability in public expenditure management and for preventing fraud.

Internal Audit as a Management Tool

In the face of the demand for improved accountability and greater transparency within the government, the mandate given to internal audit has increased significantly all over the world.

This has led to improved internal audit procedures so that public sector managers get 'reasonable assurance' about the functioning of various control systems to achieve the desired objectives. These procedures have got incorporated in the international standards for government auditing.

The modern concept of internal auditing goes far beyond its traditional limits. Internal audit is no longer considered as a mere routine review of financial and other records by specially assigned staff. The Institute of Internal Auditors, Florida, USA, defines the scope of internal auditing as "the examination and evaluation of the adequacy and effectiveness of the organization's system of internal control and the quality of performance in carrying out assigned responsibilities."[2] Thus, internal auditing in the corporate world is concerned with an evaluation of both internal controls as well as the quality of the actual performance.

International standards for government accounting and auditing emphasise that internal audit is a central component of internal financial control aimed at protecting the government's financial interests.

Both the International Organisation of Supreme Audit Institutions (INTOSAI) as well as the Institute of Internal Auditors (IIA) have issued auditing standards to guide the auditing and accounting professions. These standards are regarded as reflecting "best practices" which the countries are expected to keep in view while setting up internal auditing standards.

The standards adopt a broad view of the role of internal audit, placing it as a more central element of Public Expenditure Management (PEM). It goes beyond the narrow function of compliance or financial regularity. "The emphasis is on internal audit as a management tool. It is treated as an integral part of both management controls and communication processes."[3]

In this changed perspective, the purpose of the internal audit is to review, and appraise on, the soundness and adequacy of internal controls. We are yet to assign internal audit this role. This has adversely affected our financial management system as the traditional control systems are unable to cope with the prevalence of mismanagement and fraud in the government sector.

Standards of Internal Audit

It is now accepted that internal control is an essential prerequisite for efficient and effective management of any organisation. Before undertaking a detailed verification of transactions, a modern-day auditor, whether in the government or the private sector, is supposed to carry out a review of relevant internal control systems in the organisation, in order to determine the degree of reliance he can place on various systems and procedures.

In the statement on Standard Auditing Practices (SAP), the Institute of Chartered Accountants of India defines the system of internal control as, "All the methods and procedures adopted by the management of an entity in achieving management's objective of ensuring, as far as practicable, the orderly and efficient conduct of business, while following the policies of management, the safeguarding of assets, prevention and detection of fraud and error, the accuracy and completeness of records and timely preparation of reliable financial information. The system of internal control extends beyond those matters which relate directly to the functions of the accounting system."[4]

The scope of internal control, according to this definition, extends much beyond accounting controls. One of the basic reasons for the neglect of internal audit in India is due to not giving much importance to evaluation of internal control systems in an organisation under audit. While external audit can do the evaluation of an internal control system, it is the internal audit, given the mandate, that is best placed to conduct these assessments.

This is because, being part of the organisation, it gives the internal auditor the opportunity to know the areas of weaknesses in the financial operations of the organisation. Further, assessment of internal control should be a continuous process. It cannot be performed well by occasional visits by an external auditor because of the constraint on resources. In India, external audit has tried to evaluate internal control system in states, as internal audit has failed to do it; but the impact of such audit is not much.

Internal control has been a matter of constant interest to INTOSAI. In 1992, they offered general standards for an internal control structure. The control processes of an organisation ensure proper planning, resource allocation and coordination of an organisation's activities. It also includes feedback of these activities for prioritisation and planning. This emphasises the need for relevant and timely information. It is now regarded that internal audit can make a substantial contribution in this direction.

Because of these challenges, internal auditing standards for the government have been laid down in many countries. In India, on the other hand, the internal auditing standards in government, after it was inherited from the colonial era, have not evolved at all.

Function of Internal Audit in Government of India

Internal audit in the Government of India is conducted on the basis of departmental codes and manuals, which are a legacy of the past. Internal audit, for example in the Defence Accounts Department—where it is fairly well organised — is done with reference to rules laid down in the Defence Audit Code, Financial and other Regulations for Defence Services and other orders issued by the government and other competent financial authorities. Similarly, in the civil departments, internal audit is conducted with reference to relevant departmental codes and manuals.

These codes mainly emphasise regularity of audit and do not encompass management audit and operational audit. These codes and manuals also do not contemplate evaluation of the internal control system of the units under audit.

Internal audit units have been set up in the accounts organisations in the Ministries. The respective (Chief) Controllers of Accounts oversee the functioning of each unit. As mentioned above, the main objectives of an internal audit are to check the accuracy of accounts and to point out the irregularities in accounting. The work relating to the internal audit is conducted by local audit staff by on-the-spot verification of accounting records. An Inspection Wing is a part of the Controller General of Accounts and Controller General of Defence Accounts for inspection of audit work. The reports of internal audit are issued to audited units. Important audit observations are brought to the attention of the Secretary of the Department concerned.

The Revenue Departments have their own internal Audit Departments. The focus of audit is on post assessment reviews. The reports of such audit are not sent to the Secretaries of the Departments.

Standards of Financial Propriety

The Audit Codes relating to internal audit also refer to "Standards of the Financial Propriety". Internal audit involving principles of financial propriety comprises going beyond the observance of rules or orders of the competent authorities to see whether the principles of orthodox finance are being observed or not. "It is an essential function of audit to bring to light not only cases of clear irregularity but also every matter which, in its judgement, appears to involve improper expenditure or waste of public money or stores, even though the accounts themselves may be in order and no obvious irregularity has occurred. It is, thus, not sufficient to see that sundry rules or orders of the competent authority have been observed. It is of equal importance to see that the broad principles of orthodox finance are borne in mind not only by disbursing officers but also by sanctioning authorities."[5]

The internal audit code also states that no precise rules can be laid down for regulating the course of audit against propriety. Audit officers, in the performance of their duties, are supposed to ensure application of the principles of financial propriety.[6]

Two of the principles given below are very well known:

- The expenditure does not seem *prima facie* more than the occasion demands, and every government servant exercises the same vigilance in respect of expenditure of government money as he would for his own money.

- The public moneys are not utilised for the benefit of a particular person or section of the community, unless the expenditure is in pursuance of a recognised policy or custom.

Two very important points come out from the above. First, the same principles of financial propriety mentioned above are supposed to govern the financial adviser and his officers in the performance of their duties in the scrutiny of proposals involving expenditure of public money, as laid down in the financial regulations.

This brings out the point that the objective of the financial advice system and audit is the same, i.e., securing economy, efficiency and effectiveness.

But, at the same time, it is necessary to recognise that for effective financial management, it is essential to distinguish the role of audit, including internal audit, from the financial advice role. The financial advice role involves functioning closely with the executive in giving concurrence to the proposals put up for approval. These sanctions are also to be looked at by internal audit from the point of view of propriety principles, if the audit is play its proper role as a part of checks and balances. The basic role of audit is to check whether there is waste and misuse of public money. This role cannot be combined with the finance role.

Second, in the application of principles of financial propriety, the auditors cannot be left to apply only their judgements in highlighting cases of financial improprieties. In this endeavour, internal auditors should be able to refer to universally acceptable norms relating to financial propriety and not just to general principles. Our codes and manuals have not gone into these aspects and, therefore, these general principles of financial propriety cannot be operationalised.

Internal Audit Today is Just Compliance Audit

The problem is that no hard and fast rules can be laid down for enforcement of the principles contained in the standards of financial propriety. No auditing standard can evolve out of these principles. And the application of the first principle, that the expenditure is not more than the occasion demands, involves going into a host of questions and in-depth examination of issues, which the internal audit, with its present mandate, can hardly attempt. It involves full-fledged performance auditing. So they remain as ethical principles, but having little impact on the internal auditing techniques. Internal audit is, thus, basically confined to a compliance audit or a regularity audit, notwithstanding the fact that standards of financial propriety are enshrined in internal audit codes and manuals to guide internal audit.

As the internal audit is conducted on the basis of departmental codes and manuals, which are issued by accounting departments (therefore, limited in scope), it does not necessarily bind the audited entity to take action on the basis of the observations and recommendations of the internal audit.

Further, the audit is undertaken at the clerical level, which enables them to bring out only routine observations and minor objections pertaining to not following a particular rule or instruction. Internal audit today in India has neither the mandate nor the capacity to look into the internal control systems. Sanctions issued by the government are not subjected to internal audit.

Internal audit in the central government, thus, is basically a regularity audit, conducted in a routine manner, and the result of this audit in improving financial management is insignificant. Thus, the large number of mandays devoted to internal audit in India is not cost-effective and involves a waste of resources.

The present position of internal audit in the central government is so much in disharmony with international standards and practice (as brought out in the opening paragraphs) that unless urgent steps are taken to rectify the situation, the financial management of the government will remain much below the desired international standards.

In defence, where internal audit is comparatively well organised, the (Chief) Controller of Defence Accounts is required to prepare — on the basis of audit conducted at the field level—quarterly reports on major financial and accounting irregularities, dealing with matters relating to units and formations within his audit jurisdiction. The following types of irregularities are required to be highlighted in the report:

(a) Cases involving irregular or non-maintenance of accounts.
(b) Cases in which the value of financial irregularities or loss involved crosses a particular financial limit, and cases that disclose loopholes or fraud.

As regards (b) above, since the audit is basically a compliance audit and conducted at low levels (with no mandate for an investigative audit), the chances of finding 'loopholes' or 'fraud' are rare. So it remains confined to mentioning of cases of loss due to various reasons. Since no in-depth investigations in the alleged cases of loopholes/fraud get carried out, the lacunae in the system do not get refined. General audit observations do not help in rectification of any internal control system.

Then there is the system of rendition of Annual Appropriation Accounts. The object of the Appropriation Accounts for all the Departments is to present the audited accounts of expenditure from the appropriation for the year, with explanation of variations between final appropriation and actual expenditure. It includes statement of losses of cash, arrear payments, etc., dealt with during the year; statement of various kinds of store losses dealt with; and finally statement of infrastructure expenditure exceeding a particular amount, etc. Very important audit points concerning serious irregularities can also be brought out while rendering the appropriation accounts and these need to be brought to the attention of the Public Accounts Committee. But such occasions rarely occur, as the internal audit is not structured to detect serious cases of irregularity.

Since the internal audit conducted at the field level is very limited in scope, the rendition of Annual Appropriation Accounts takes the form of a routinised activity, with an elaborate form but not much in content.

Financial Advice and Audit

One of the features of expenditure management in the government is the assumption that financial advice and audit are closely linked, and the one emanates from the other. This is underlined by the fact that both the activities are performed by the same authority. For example, in defence, the regional controllers of defence are ex-officio financial advisers to various military authorities in the field, exercising financial powers in the discharge of their duties. The regional controllers are also accounting and auditing authorities, and the two activities get linked. To substantiate the point, we shall quote a para from the Defence Audit Code:

> Financial advice tendered to the above authorities can be divided into two portions namely:
> Responding financial advice which consists of: *(a) advice on definite points referred to controllers by unit authorities; and (b) advice on the results of investigation into fact and original financial advice, which consists of any method by which equal efficiency can be obtained with less expenditure.* Audit will not only see that authority for expenditure is quoted but on legitimate occasions investigate the necessity for it. It will examine whether the individual items were in furtherance of schemes for which the budget provided; whether the same results could have been obtained otherwise with greater economy; whether the rate and scale were justified in the circumstances; in fact, they ask every question that might be expected from an intelligent taxpayer bent upon getting best value for money. (Emphasis added).[7]

As would be seen from the italicised portion, the critical scrutiny while rendering financial advice is designated as auditing activity and no distinction is made between auditing and offering financial advice.

The similarity of the roles envisaged of the Financial Adviser, at the Ministry level and that of (Chief) Controller of Defence Accounts in the field, is quite evident. It is becoming difficult for the Defence Accounts Department to raise these points relating to economy and efficiency, after assuming the role of Integrated Financial Advisers.

Such points are also difficult to raise on the basis of the compliance audit that is conducted now. To quote from the Defence Audit Code about the restricted scope of internal audit, "The primary function of audit is to verify the accuracy and completeness of accounts to secure that receipts are brought to account under the proper head and that expenditure and disbursements are authorised, vouched and correctly classified and that the final accounts represent a complete and true state of financial transactions".[8]

It is relevant to quote from practice in defence, not only because defence represents the largest single item of expenditure, after interest payments, and, therefore, expenditure management in defence has a lot of significance for the overall expenditure management of the central government, but also because internal audit in defence has a long tradition and is fairly well organised, and, therefore, the codes and manuals can be cited to indicate the way the internal audit is carried out in the government sector in general.

To underline the point that there is indeed a very limited mandate for internal audit, we shall quote from another paragraph of the Defence Audit Code, which says that a clear distinction between auditorial and administrative functions should always be borne in mind. "It is the function of Government to make Financial Rules and Orders for the Defence Services and for the Defence Accounts Department responsible for making payments to apply these rules and orders. It is the function of audit to verify that these rules and orders are properly applied. It is not the function of audit to prescribe what such rules and orders shall be or interfere with their administrative application".[9]

The principles can be treated as a general philosophy underlying the conduct of internal audit in the government sector, limited in scope and mandate, not effective at all in the prevention and detection of fraud.

Important points in an audit, when the question of application of standards of financial propriety arises, as stated above, can only be raised when a particular case or transaction is seen from the administrator's point of view. If the audit is to get involved in assessment of the internal control system, this kind of distinction between auditorial and administrative functions would not be helpful at all. Nothing should, however, be done in the internal audit which can be treated as interference with the administrative function. But that should not prevent it from looking at the adequacy of the internal control system to prevent fraud and mismanagement.

A lot of mental reservations about the role of internal audit have to be overcome if it is to play an effective role in the improvement of the financial management system in India and prevention of fraud.

Internal Audit in Private Sector

Models for functioning of the internal audit in the government sector in countries that have tried to reform the internal audit system have, to a great extent, been derived from the evolution of internal audit in the private sector. We have already indicated the role of audit in the evaluation of the internal control system in the achievement of management objectives as laid down by SAP6 of the Institute of Chartered Accountants of India, in 1988. The standard clearly states that this kind of evaluation of the internal control system would take audit much beyond the function of the accounting system.

The scope of internal audit has expanded because of challenges faced in corporate governance in the 1980 and 1990s. In 1985, following a series of high profile business failures in the USA, the Treadway Commission was formed by private sector initiative. The Treadway Report, published in 1987, highlighted the need for a proper control environment, independent audit committees and an objective internal audit function. It called for published reports on the effectiveness of internal control. It also requested the sponsoring organisations to develop an integrated set of internal control criteria to enable companies to improve their controls.

As a result of this initial report, the Committee of Sponsoring Organisations (COSO) was formed, involving a major CPA firm to study issues and author a report regarding an integrated framework of internal control. COSO is sponsored and funded by five main professional accounting associations and institutes.

COSO has established a common definition of internal control standards and criteria against which companies and organisations can assess their control systems.

The Treadway Commission, among other items, recommended that the organisations sponsoring the Commission work together to develop integrated guidance on internal control.

A report entitled "Internal Control—Integrated Framework" came out in 1992. This report is the standard that US companies use to evaluate their compliance with relevant laws.

COSO Framework

The COSO Framework defines internal control as a process, effected by an entity's board of directors, management and other personnel, designed to provide reasonable assurance regarding the achievement of objectives in the following categories:

- Effectiveness and efficiency of operations.
- Reliability of financial reporting.
- Compliance with applicable laws and regulations.

According to the COSO Framework[10], internal control consists of interrelated components. These components provide an effective framework for describing and analysing the internal control system implemented in an organisation. These five components are: control environment, risk assessment, control activities, information and communication.

The control environment is by far the most important component, as it sets the tone of an organisation, influencing the control consciousness of its people. It is the foundation for all other components of internal control, providing discipline and structure. The control environment encompasses integrity and ethical values, management's operating style, as well as processes.

Risk Assessment: Every entity faces a variety of risks from external and internal sources that must be assessed. A precondition to risk assessment is establishment of objectives. Therefore, risk assessment is the identification and analysis of relevant risks to achievement of assigned objectives. Risk assessment is a prerequisite for determining how the risks should be managed.

Control Activities: Control activities are the policies and procedures that help to ensure management directives are carried out. They help to ensure that necessary actions are taken to address risks to achievement of the entity's objectives. They include a range of activities like approvals, authorisations, verifications, reconciliations, reviews of operating performance, security of assets and segregation of duties.

Information and Communications: Information systems plays a key role in internal control systems as they produce reports, including operational, financial and compliance related information. Communication involves communicating the audit report in an effective manner.

As stated above, though these components are interrelated, the most important component is the control environment. It should, therefore, be the first endeavour of any management, be it in the private or public sector, to foster an adequate control environment through pronouncements about the importance of these controls. In the public sector, the control environment can be created by the enactment of laws, making it mandatory to institute a proper internal control system and get it continuously assessed for efficacy. The role of internal audit should be defined in this background.

The following points are to be kept in view in this regard. First, internal auditors have to play a valuable role in evaluating the effectiveness of the control system. It should be, therefore, an independent function, which should be able to report to the top management. Only then can internal audit assess the internal control system objectively, and contribute to the organisation's effectiveness. It can also play a significant monitoring role. The support of the top management of the Ministry/Department in the independent functioning of internal audit is absolutely essential.

On the basis of the above background, two points need to be stressed at the outset. As mentioned above, the scope of internal audit described in the International Standards is based on the broader view of internal audit as a tool of management. The internal audit function is supposed to close the loop in the pubic expenditure management cycle to ensure efficient and effective use of resources. Therefore, internal audit should get involved in broader management issues pertaining to management of resources.

The second point that needs to be stressed is that in order to preserve its independence of judgement, internal audit should not take any direct responsibility in designing, establishing or maintaining the controls it is supposed to evaluate. From this principle another important point follows. The accounting and payment system is also one of the important control systems. Internal audit should be able to evaluate it also. Therefore, on the basis of the above principles, internal audit, if it is to get involved in assessment of the accounting and control system, should not be part of the accounting system. If we have to maintain the independence of internal audit, then it should not be part of accounting activity, and organisationally it should function independently from the accounting activity.

In the UK, the report of the Cadbury Committee (Sir Adrian Cadbury) in 1992 provided the framework for corporate governance which has become the basis for the arrangements whereby UK companies govern themselves.

It contained a recommendation that the Boards of listed companies should report on the effectiveness of their systems of internal control. It also recommended that auditors should report on the statement, which became controversial as responsibility for expressing an opinion on the internal control system was not easy. It was resolved in 1999 by the Turnbull Report which required the companies to report whether the Board has reviewed the system of "internal control and risk management". The close coupling of internal control and risk management in the Turnbull Report echoed similar developments in the USA and Canada where other important reports had emphasised the importance of risk management as well as internal control. Both the Cadbury Committee and Turnbull Report expanded the role of internal audit in the business community in the UK.[11]

The corporate world in India could not remain indifferent to developments that were taking place in the UK. This led to laying down our ground rules on corporate governance.

The stress in the Cadbury Report is on the crucial role of the board and the need for it to observe a Code of Best Practices. Its important recommendations include the setting up of an Audit Committee with independent members.

In India, the emphasis in the past few years, as far as the private sector is concerned, has been mainly limited to only some of the recommendations of the Cadbury Committee—such as the role and composition of Audit Committees and the importance of making all the necessary disclosures with annual statements of accounts, which are considered important for investors' protection.[12]

From these developments in the corporate world, it would be seen that risk assessment and risk management did not become a major theme of corporate governance till the late Nineties. In the Indian corporate world, the importance of evaluating the internal control system and the need for independent Audit Committees is being felt. Risk assessment and risk management do not seem to have made a major impact in the corporate sector.

In many respects, entity risk management may be regarded as a natural evolution of the internal control model. Most organisations will seek to fully apply the internal control model before implementing the concepts inherent within entity risk management. Therefore, one need not, before a securing a proper internal control model, seek to focus on risk management as a primary objective of internal control and internal audit.

These points need to be kept in view while determining the scope of internal audit in the public sector in India.

Steps Towards Effective Internal Audit (IA) in Government Sector

However, this is yet to happen in many parts of the world, including India. As Jack Diamond observes, "For many parts of the world, the IA has often been, and continues to be, defined rather narrowly—focusing on financial compliance and regularity, rather than broader management issues. Moreover, governance problems and lack of professional competence also constrain the IA to this role and hinder its ability to generate timely and relevant reports."[13]

To approach international standards, the first point to be noted is that internal audit should be treated as a tool of management. Lack of professional competence often restrains the internal audit from playing its rightful role in implementing the international standards. This poses a basic problem in implementing international standards.

In many countries, audit skills are in short supply, and professional proficiency can be very low, or the government's pay scale cannot attract or maintain suitable staff. These factors often represent important constraint on attempts to strengthen internal audit.[14]

The problem of professional proficiency is not just confined to technical competence. Professional proficiency assumes an appropriate audit methodology, technical competence, and sufficient level of resources for the internal audit function. If the government wants to have a proper internal audit system, then adequate resources should be allocated for its development, as a part of deliberate policy to promote better internal control and better financial management.

To strengthen internal audit as a tool of management, apart from increasing its scope, and securing it an independent functioning, the problem of professional proficiency has to be tackled. But, at the same time, it must be remembered that internal audit is not a substitute for good financial management. Also, it cannot substitute for weak external audit. The two systems, internal and external audit, must go hand in hand and complement each other.

Internal audit, rightly designed, can play a very important role in improving the public expenditure management. Though practices vary, in recent years, a number of countries have reoriented internal audit away from compliance audit towards performance issues.[15]

The Task Force on Internal Audit

That the present role and function of internal audit has been a cause of concern to the Government of India is brought out by the fact that at the request of the Ministry of Finance, the Department of Expenditure and the Comptroller and Auditor General of India, constituted a Task Force on July 17, 2006, for benchmarking the status of internal audit in the central government and determination of a roadmap for its improvement.

The Task Force, it is understood, after detailed deliberation, came to the conclusion that due to a severely restricted mandate and lack of interest of the management, the internal audit has not been able to systematically evaluate the risks associated with various activities of the Ministries/Departments for determining their audit strategies and thrust areas. Public Sector Undertakings (PSUs) and autonomous bodies have been kept outside the purview of internal audit, thus, diluting its usefulness and effectiveness. Internal audit is also not conducting evaluation of the adequacy of the internal control mechanisms in various Ministries/Departments. Inadequate inspection of each section/desk in the Department by internal audit has resulted in continued non-observance of prescribed procedures and systems, the Task Force has observed.

The Task Force has noted that countries like the USA, Canada, UK, etc. have formally prescribed internal audit standards for their government departments. Canada has outlined its policy on internal audit of the government departments in a detailed document. It observes that there are international audit standards, which have been laid down by the Institute of Internal Auditors (IIA), which are basically applicable to the private sector and International Organisation of Supreme Audit Institutions (INTOSAI) for the government. The UK issued the Government Internal Audit Standards in October 2001.

We are yet to evolve such standards for internal audit, confining it to a fairly insignificant role. The government does not pay much attention to the findings of internal audit, which, as indicated above, contain basically routine observations.

Independence is a major issue in internal audit. The Task Force felt that independence was the "cornerstone" of effective functioning of internal audit which is accepted internationally.[16]

The Task Force noted that the Government of India had redefined the charter of Financial Advisers by the Ministry of Finance, Department of Expenditure OM No. F.No.5(6)/L&C/2006 dated June 1, 2006. The redefined charter *inter alia* has made the Financial Adviser (FA) responsible for regularly reviewing the progress of internal audit and action taken thereon, so as to make it an important tool for financial management.[17]

As the Task Force observes, there was no segregation of duties, especially at the supervisory levels, between those who are responsible for internal audit and those responsible for pre-audit, disbursement and accounting functions. The internal audit set-up also did not report directly to the chief executive in any of the organisations. In the Department of Telecommunications, internal audit functions and accounting functions were not segregated at the supervisory levels.

In defence, sanctions issued by the Ministry of Defence, were not subject to internal audit. While there was segregation of duties in respect of personnel engaged in internal audit in defence up to the supervisory level, they reported to the Controllers of Defence Accounts, who were responsible for other functions also. The inspection wing of the Railways, both on the revenue as well as expenditure side, functioned under the concerned FA&CAO, who was also responsible for accounting and pre-audit functions.

The Task Force observed that both the Secretary (Defence Finance) and FC (Railways) were of the view that realigning the existing structure and ensuring greater independence for internal audit would increase its effectiveness.

The Task Force particularly noted that in the civil Ministries, the oversight of internal audit vested with the Chief Controllers of Accounts, who were also responsible for accounting and payment functions. In defence, the Chief Controller/Controller of Defence Accounts, is responsible for both payment functions and internal audit. This means that internal audit did not have the required independence for effective functioning. An independent internal audit should be able to look into payments made after the approval of the Controller of Accounts, at least from the propriety angle.

The Task Force did not support the present approach of internal audit that it should be confined only to ensuring that accounting and allied records have been properly maintained, asset management is in place, and policy and procedures are being adhered to. It subscribed to the modern view that internal auditing should not be restricted to financial issues alone, but should also extend to issues like cost-benefit analysis, utilisation and deployment of resources, matters of propriety, effectiveness of management, etc. and the focus should be on risk, control and governance issues.

In view of the required change in mandate for internal audit, the Task Force considered it necessary that in the interest of independence and more effective functioning of internal audit, there is need for segregation of duties relating to internal audit from those relating to financial advice and accounting functions. All the reports of the internal audit, the Task Force felt, must be submitted directly to the Secretary of the Department.

The Task Force noted that although instructions had been issued earlier by the Department of Expenditure that the internal audit should report directly to the Secretary, in actual practice this does not happen. This is because the (Chief) Controllers of Accounts have other responsibilities for which they report to the Financial Adviser.

At the same time, Ministry of Finance OM F.No.5(6)/L&C/2006 dated June 1, 2006, enjoins upon the Financial Advisers to "review the progress of internal audit." This has resulted in the (Chief) Controller of Accounts who is in-charge of internal audit, being put under the administrative control of the FA (para 8.1.4). The Task Force came to the conclusions that this has resulted in compromising the intended independence of internal auditing functions. Therefore, they felt the need for an effective alternative model.

An Alternative Model

After considering various models that are available internationally, the Task Force felt that the Inspector General model of the USA, with appropriate modifications, was the one most suited for effective internal audit. But it felt that it might not be possible for us to implement that model immediately. It did not, however, specify any reasons. Noting that the work of internal audit was now totally decentralised, at both policy and operational levels, and there was no single authority for either prescribing standards or supervising internal audit, whether administratively or through technical guidance, the Task Force felt that there was a strong case for the setting up of an Apex Board to prescribe internal audit standards and processes across jurisdictions. There was need for legislated internal audit standards and policies.

In the interim period, it recommended that to facilitate moving towards legislated internal audit, a Board of Internal Audit (BIA) comprising the Controller General of Accounts, Controller General of Defence Accounts, Financial Commissioner, Railways and Member (Finance) Telecommunications, might be constituted for the oversight of internal audit in the Government of India. Eventually, under a proper mandate through a specific statute or Cabinet resolution, the internal audit in each Ministry/Department should be established as an entity directly reporting to the Secretary of the Department/Ministry, and becoming exclusively responsible for internal audit activities. The internal auditor will act strictly in accordance with the prescribed standards and processes.

The Task Force recommended that in the interest of independence of internal audit and its more effective functioning, the ultimate objective of the government should be to appoint a Chief Internal Auditor (CIA), professionally trained in auditing. The CIA should function in accordance with standards and procedures prescribed by BIA. This kind of interim solution recommended is no solution at all, given the present weakness of internal audit.

The Task Force is right in its conclusions that if internal audit has to function independently, it should not be combined with financial advice. Accordingly, the Financial Adviser, while drawing upon the findings of internal audit to the extent these helps in financial advice, should not be controlling the internal audit work.

Similarly, the Accounts Departments should confine itself to maintenance of accounts, disbursement of payments, and local financial advice to field level officers. It need not control the internal audit work, which has a distinct function to perform. In its envisaged expanded role in the management of expenditure, internal audit has to go much beyond the scrutiny of accounts of transactions (the role envisaged in the departmental codes and manuals issued by the Accounts Departments), and get into issues which would have earlier been regarded as 'encroachment' on the functions of administrative authorities.

The concept of Chief Internal Auditors (CIA) for each Department/ Ministry as envisaged by the Task Force, who are professionally trained in auditing, reporting to the Secretary, is the right concept. *But to be effective, they must have a proper mandate for which there has to be legislation to grant them sufficient independence as also an adequate charter of duties.*

But the Task Force recommends that this should happen "eventually" and appointment of the CIA should be "the ultimate objective of the government". In view of the lacunae pointed out in the existing system, the time for bringing out the basic reform is now, and not some time later. Since reform in internal audit is urgently required for better financial management in the government, let us look at a suitable model.

Since internal audit has to function independently of both finance and accounts, the concept of Board of Internal Audit (BIA) consisting of the Controller General of Accounts, Controller General of Defence Accounts, Financial Commissioner (Railways), Member Finance Telecommunication for "oversight of internal audit in Government of India" even for an interim period, is not the correct solution.

What is urgently required is to enact provisions of internal audit with the required institutional support and with clear policies regarding its role and method of functioning.

The Inspector General Model as an Alternative

The Task Force referred to the Inspector General model of the United States which, with appropriate modifications, might be the one most suited to effective functioning of the internal audit, though it was hesitant to recommend its adoption immediately.

Let us look into the basic features of the Inspector General (IG) model to appreciate why this was felt by the Task Force to be an appropriate model.

The Inspectors General are appointed by the President of the USA with the advice and consent of the Senate. The most important feature of the Inspector General Act of 1978 in the USA was to combine internal audit and investigations into programmes and activities under one authority—that of the IG.

The basic purpose of the Act was "to create independent and objective units to conduct and supervise audits and investigations relating to programs and operations of the establishments listed."[18] The IGs were also to provide leadership and coordination and recommend policies for activities designed, to promote economy, efficiency and effectiveness in the administration of, and to prevent and detect fraud and abuse in such, programme and operations.

The IGs were also to keep the head of the establishment and Congress fully and currently informed about the problems and deficiencies relating to administration of such programmes and operations.[19]

The point to note from the above provisions is that, unless some authority provides leadership and coordination as well as takes a proactive role in audit and allied activities, it is not possible to achieve economy, efficiency and effectiveness in the administration of programmes.

The other important point is that in internal audit, prevention and detection of fraud is as important as promoting economy and efficiency. Unless frauds get detected in time, the steps taken towards economy and efficiency would be nullified. Therefore, prevention and detection of fraud is as important a part of financial management for getting best value for money as other steps like adopting proper criteria for selection of projects, evaluation and monitoring of programmes and setting up internal audit standards.

The Inspectors General in the US federal government have four major responsibilities:

- Providing an independent set of "eyes and ears" on the efficiency and effectiveness of departmental operations.
- Serving as objective fact finders in controversial, high profile matters of agency concern.
- Bringing to justice those attempting to defraud the US government
- Finally, most importantly, the Inspector General community works to

ensure that the interests of citizens are represented when governmental decisions are made.

As per the Act, each Inspector General is to appoint an Assistant Inspector General for Audit, who shall have the responsibility for supervising the performance of auditing activities relating to programmes and operations of the establishment; and an Assistant Inspector General for Investigations with the responsibility for supervising the investigation activities relating to programmes and activities.[20] Thus, auditing and investigation are given equal highlight importance to enforce accountability.

The IG Act has ,therefore, features which lead to the strengthening of internal auditing and internal control which are relevant to Indian conditions today in public expenditure management, as corruption has become fairly widespread. It is not only adversely affecting the normal activities of the government but very badly affecting the expenditure undertaken as part of the inclusive development model where much of the amounts does not reach the intended beneficiaries or does not get spent for the purpose it is meant. Many of the challenges in internal security, particularly in backward regions, as per the analysts, are arising out of this factor.

Corruption is increasing because persons indulging in it know that the existing machinery for the checks and balances is feeble and inadequate to apprehend them. There are collusions at all levels of government, making the existing checks totally ineffective. Lack of auditing infrastructure and its limited mandate make it all the more difficult to ensure accountability in public spending.

There is a basic challenge to governance today by this factor alone, which makes much of theorising about public expenditure management to attain economy and efficiency quite irrelevant in the present context.

Strengthening internal audit by providing it an adequate mandate and infrastructure to do in-depth audit at required intervals and to go into details of the cases detected in audit with a view to fix responsibility, should be done though legislation. Financial irregularities involving public money should be treated as a criminal offence and punishable as such. Such a step is essential for strengthening the governance of the country.

To substantiate the necessity of combining audit with investigation, one can quote from a Sub-Committee of the Central Public Accounts Committee (PAC) headed by E. Ayyapu Reddy, who observed that the delayed response on the part of Departments to audit findings was responsible for the constant and repeated failures to enforce accountability, and observed: "It is very depressing to find that in spite of audit reports revealing loss of public funds or misuse and misapplication of public funds, there is no investigating agency charged with the duty to probe into these aspects and identify the culprits responsible for these. Recommendations of the Public Accounts Committee (PAC) for investigation to enforce accountability for undisputed misuse of public funds are not yielding any tangible results for the simple reason that the long lapse of time between transaction and recommendations normally results in disappearance of incriminating evidence."[21]

In this context, it is also worthwhile to note the summary of recommendations relating to audit made by the Second Administrative Reforms Commission (ARC), Fourth Report, "Ethics in Governance".

Audit

(a) It should be prescribed that as soon as any major irregularity is detected or suspected by the audit team, it should be immediately taken note of by the government. A suitable mechanism for this may be put in place. It shall be the responsibility of the head of the office to enquire into any such irregularity and initiate action; and

(b) Audit teams should be imparted training in forensic audit.[22]

Elaborating the point at (a) above, the ARC stated: "The audit authorities often do not convey information which has come to their knowledge in respect of serious irregularities in which criminal misconduct is involved, to the anti-corruption bodies. The information becomes available to the anti-corruption bodies only when the audit report of the CAG is laid before the Parliament or the State Legislature as the case may be. By the time a serious irregularity (which is detected in audit and reported to the Department for response as an audit query and incorporated as a part of the annual audit report laid before the House), comes to the knowledge of the anti-corruption bodies, a lot of time is lost. Such delays not only alert the culprits in the organisation but also give them enough time to cover their tracks and destroy the evidence and material records, thus, making it extremely difficult for the investigating agencies to successfully complete their investigations."[23]

The ARC felt that it would be desirable to make a standing arrangement with the CAG and AG to report such instances as soon as they are unearthed in the audit.

As external audit takes place on a test check basis and at long intervals, it may be much better to follow the IG model of the USA to revamp the internal audit system, and entrust a single authority with both internal audit and investigation, so that the audit can be focussed on high risk areas, and as soon the audit indicates a likely fraud or serious irregularity, investigation may follow immediately. Otherwise, incriminating evidence may disappear, as pointed out by the sub-committee of the PAC in 1987.

The advantage of internal audit is that it can be done on a continuous basis and soon after the transactions take place. It is in a much better position to do the risk analysis, because of its familiarity with the systems and procedures in a particular Department.

Therefore, internal audit should be empowered to investigate the cases of irregularity unearthed during their audit. This would reduce the chances of disappearance of incriminating evidence. Empowerment of internal audit in this regard itself will have a salutary effect in creating a suitable 'control environment', which is essential for effective functioning of internal audit. Being located in the Departments concerned, internal auditors have a much better opportunity to identify weak areas of control and concentrate their attention on those areas where cases of irregularity and misuse of authorities are most likely to occur. They can also monitor the corrective action taken and make it part of the periodic audit report furnished to the top management.

Falling ethical standards make it necessary that audit authorities, both internal and external, are empowered with power of investigation in cases of financial irregularities detected by them to fix responsibility.

Recommendations

On the basis of the above analysis, the following recommendations are made to strengthen the function of internal audit and control in the central government:

- There should be a specific legislation for strengthening internal audit and internal control. Suitable provisions should be incorporated in the legislation for appointment of a Chief Internal Auditor (CIA) in each Ministry/Department in the rank of Additional Secretary. He should be entrusted with the responsibilities of both audit and investigation.
- Auditing standards should be laid down by the government in consultation with the CAG which should lead to the modification of departmental codes and manuals for conducting internal audit.
- There should be Audit Committees in each Ministry/Department. These should be headed by the Secretary of the Ministry/Department. This Committee should also consist of the Chief Internal Auditor, Financial Adviser, CGA/CGDA/Financial Controller (Railways), as the case may be and the head of the concerned unit or division of the Ministry. Subject experts may be associated wherever necessary.
- The Audit Committee should give concurrence to the audit plan covering various activities of the Ministry/Department on a quarterly basis, as also for reviewing the actions taken on the earlier recommendations of the internal audit report. The Audit Committee should be a sub-committee of the Financial Management Board. The Board should also decide on the action to be taken on the internal audit reports, as also those of the external audit.
- The Audit Committee of the Department should also be empowered to appoint professional audit firms for carrying out audit in specialised fields on a temporary basis, in conjunction with internal auditors of the Department to fill up the capacity gaps and impart the required professionalism.
- A strategic decision to be taken by the Audit Committee is where best to deploy the scarce audit skills. There are ways to economise on the use of audit resources. One of them would be to move away from routine audit to focus on priority areas and key weaknesses. One important function, as mentioned above, in internal audit, is to examine and evaluate the adequacy and effectiveness of internal controls in existing systems. Another would

be to empower them to conduct special audit in specific areas, which are vulnerable from the risk assessment point of view. The Audit Committees should mandate the internal audit teams to go into them.

The report of internal audit should be considered by the Audit Committees for further action.

Need for Forensic Audit

To detect fraud and misuse of public money, there would be a need for a forensic audit. This will be in keeping with the recommendations of the ARC relating to this kind of audit, which they term as "innovation". To quote: "A second innovation in this regard would be to equip the agency concerned in the mechanics of forensic audit so that aspects crucial for criminal investigation could be taken due care of. It would be in the fitness of things if the anti-corruption bodies are equipped to undertake such forensic audit of such government Departments where such irregularities come to their notice. The idea is to have an in-house forensic team in these offices. Similar capability could be built in the local fund audit departments."[24] In keeping with the spirit of this recommendation, instead of placing anti-corruption bodies in the Departments, it would be better to place internal audit teams within Departments which should be suitably empowered to investigate and reach appropriate conclusions before deciding to hand over cases to prosecution agencies.

Shri M. Veerappa Moily, Chairman, Second Administrative Reforms Commission, in a speech commenting on the internal control systems in India, stated: "The internal control system has not worked in India. This is for several reasons. First, there is collusion at work at all levels of government and a sharing of the gains from corruption. As a result, there have been very few cases in which corruption is reported, and even in those few cases, there are the usual delays and soft actions, which characterise the process of investigation in India."[25]

It is considered that adopting a model like that of the IG of the USA of 1978 provides a most suitable option where unearthing of irregularities and timely investigations into them would strengthen the financial management system in a big way by detection and prevention of fraud.

The staff functioning as internal auditors in various Departments should be brought under the Chief Internal Auditor of the Ministry/Department, forming a separate cadre. To impart professionalism, these auditors should be trained in the modern concepts of auditing. Some of the internal auditors in the Ministries/Department should be trained in forensic audit, i.e., auditing practices carried out to detect possible criminal activity concealed in financial accounts.

Relationship Between Internal and External Audit

The relationship between internal and external audit functions should be recognised as symbiotic. It is important for internal audit that there is strong external audit, and vice versa. External audit should use the work of internal audit.[26]

The external auditor should review the performance of internal auditors to determine whether they are performing according to their objectives and plans. An assessment of the quality of internal audit work should be part of audit reports relating to the Departments concerned. This should be made part of the CAG Act by suitable amendments.

There should be access to each other's audit plans and programmes. Periodic meetings should be organised to ensure common understanding and sharing of audit techniques and methods. With these interactions, internal audit would get further strengthened.

The Way Forward

As presented above, internal audit, though it has a distinct role, is a part of, what in management literature is described as the 'Internal Control System'. In fact, internal audit has an evaluating role in improving the internal control system, by pointing out its lacunae in preventing fraud and mismanagement of resources.

Internal controls are regarded as the foundation of good governance. A robust internal control system, supported by an effective internal audit system comprises the foundation for a sound financial management system. A sound internal control system is required to assure that government operations attain some basic fiduciary standards in guarding against misuse and inefficient use of resources, for safeguarding government assets, and, above all, for *countering fraud.*

We have not been able to visualise internal controls as a system, which has to improve its functioning as challenges grow, through a feedback mechanism. An internal audit, properly designed, apart from its basic role in audit, can become the most important feedback mechanism, for developing a sound internal control framework to prevent fraud and mismanagement.

Unfortunately, we have failed to give adequate importance to internal controls as a management tool to support administration in its aim to prevent corruption, mismanagement and fraud. This is basically because administrative reform has not been a serious agenda in our governance; what has been attempted is piecemeal reforms without an overall objective.

We have, since the colonial era, given importance only to the financial advice system as an internal control mechanism to prevent excess expenditure and wasteful management of resources. As long it was part of the Finance Ministry (till 1983 in the Department of Defence and till 1976 in other Departments), it had a certain degree of independence in its functioning to prevent wasteful expenditure. After becoming an integral part of the Ministries and Departments concerned, its role in this regard has diminished.

The financial advice system, however, was never designed to prevent fraud. This role ostensibly was given to the Accounts Departments, which, apart from its payment and accounting, works also to conducts the internal audit. This internal audit, as can be visualised from the organisational set-up, has an extremely limited mandate, which has been described above. It works at the field level, carrying out the compliance audit. Even at the field level, it cannot go into the fraud and mismanagement aspects, because of the lack of an investigative role, though there has been large delegation of financial powers in the field level. It is not in a position to even point out likely cases of fraud and mismanagement, because of the low level of its functional efficiency and total lack of attention at all levels to its findings, whatever they are worth.

We have put a financial adviser in overall charge of the internal audit, without recognising that the finance and audit roles are distinct; they have different objectives. Whatever justification it had in the past, when the financial advice role was under the Finance Ministry, after integration with the administrative Ministries, putting overseeing of internal audit under financial advisers lacks all justification from the internal control point of view.

The overall effect has been that internal audit has become the most neglected aspect of governance in India.

While the world over, be it in the private sector or in the public sector, the role of internal audit as a control mechanism, has been given more and more importance and international standards have been set up for the functioning of the internal audit, we are confronted with just the opposite phenomenon of deterioration of internal audit in its functional aspects. It hardly performs any worthwhile role in the establishment of internal control . This is adversely affecting governance in preventing fraud and mismanagement of resources.

While the external audit under CAG functions on the basis of international standards of audit and is an important member of INTOSAI , the internal audit which has a complementary role in prevention of fraud and mismanagement as an aid to management, hardly performs any meaningful role when compared with international standards.

The result is there for all of us to see. Serious irregularities, having very high financial implications, have been detected through the CAG's audit findings in recent years, to the embarrassment of the government and with serious repercussions.

These is sufficient evidence that the internal control mechanism of the government is in disarray. The financial advice system, which has lost its teeth, is unable to prevent cases of mismanagement and fraud and may even be just an onlooker.

If there was a strong and effective internal audit system as in the Inspector General (IG) model of the USA, these irregularities could have been prevented. The most important feature of the IG Act of 1978 was to combine internal audit and investigations under one authority of the IG. It is also to recommend activities to promote economy, efficiency and effectiveness in administration to detect and prevent fraud and abuse in various programmes.

Here also, the IG takes a programme-based approach, a concept which is still to be introduced by us in our resource management. The IGs are to keep heads of establishment and the US Congress fully informed about the problems and deficiencies relating to administration of such programmes and operations.

The important point that comes out of the IG model is that steps toward improving economy and efficiency in administration of resources, cannot be segregated from those of prevention and detection of fraud.

Prevention and detection of fraud is as important a part of management for getting best value for money, as other steps like approval of programmes after due analysis, adopting proper criteria for selection of projects for implementation, and evaluation and monitoring of programmes.

Adopting an IG model would be of great help in this regard. The most important feature of this model, to reiterate, is that *auditing* and *investigation* are given equal importance to enforce *accountability*. There are two important functionaries under the IG: one for supervising the audit from the performance angle and another for investigation with the responsibility of supervising the investigation activities. Both activities are coordinated by the IG.

This model has been very effective for strengthening the internal control mechanism of the US government for achieving economy and efficiency and for prevention of fraud and mismanagement.

Is there any problem in adopting this model in India?

As stated above , the Task Force (2006) set up to look into the effectiveness of internal audit, felt that internal audit did not have the required independence to be effective and that its mandate needed to be extended. It also felt that the IG model of the United States, with appropriate modifications, might be most suited for effective functioning of internal audit. But it was hesitant to recommend its adoption immediately. Instead, it came up with very weak recommendations and an interim measure which could be accommodated within the existing system. But it could hardly meet the present challenges, which call for systemic change.

The hesitance regarding the IG model, no doubt, emanated from the basic change from the existing system of control and management that would be required, with diminution in the role of financial advisers, who guided the task force. It would also call for suitable legislation to invest the internal audit authorities with suitable power and responsibility, which it probably felt was beyond its mandate.

As developments during the last two years have shown, as in the case of 2G scam, there is no scope for further hesitance in the matter. The time to implement the IG model is now.

The Second Administration Reforms Commission was perturbed about the trends which were already evident, which they reflected in their Fourth Report, "Ethics in Governance". They also came to the conclusion that the internal control system has not worked in India as there is collusion at all levels of government and a sharing of gains from corruption. Therefore, few cases of corruption are reported and even when reported, there are delays and only soft action.

Detection of fraud and misuse of public money cannot be done through a normal audit. It would require what is called a 'forensic audit.' This would involve immediate reporting of cases of serious irregularity by CAG to the anti-corruption bodies and a standing arrangement with the audit authorities in this regard. The anti-corruption bodies should be equipped to carry out the forensic audit, which should be an in-house facility in various Departments of the government.

The 'forensic audit' concept in controlling corruption is logically flawed. It can probably pinpoint the culprits once the fraud in detected. But this is after the event has taken place. Secondly, CAG basically conducts a post audit, which means, that normally they would look at transactions a year or two after their completion. By then, the culprits can destroy the evidence and the trail gets cold.

Placing an anti-corruption body within a Department would hardly serve the purpose, as CAG does not carry out a concurrent audit. It is also not desirable as a Department should be able to take decisions exercising its own judgment, unhindered by the fact that it may immediately be questioned or have to take recourse to getting audit advice before taking decisions. This would be against the basic principles of governance, as one is supposed to take those decisions which one's position dictates and for which one is accountable.

CAG's role is relevant in the context of parliamentary control and not for administrative control. It is the Parliamentary Accounts Committee (PAC) that should go through the audit reports.

How then, can one control the corruption which has become quite widespread? The IG model for strengthening the internal audit is the answer to the problem. Instead of placing anti-corruption bodies within the Departments, it would be much better to place an internal audit team within the Departments, which should be suitably empowered by legislation to investigate suspected cases of irregularities, and reach appropriate conclusions before deciding to hand over the cases to prosecuting agencies.

The internal control system, as reported by ARC, has failed. But the only alternative, as seen from experience the world over, is to strengthen it by taking bold and efficacious measures to improve internal audit, segregating it from both the accounting function and financial advice. An internal audit has to be an independent function to do the performance audit, and for detection of fraud and corruption by integrating the auditing and investigating functions under one head. *The IG model provides the only way forward to ensure good governance in controlling corruption and preventing fraud, by not only timely detection of such cases, but in creating a control environment where there are greater chances of such detection, than through any external check which comes on the scene ex-post facto.*

This point would get further strengthened when we look at the provisions of the Jan Lokpal Bill, 2011, brought in the wake of the 2G scam, after a lot of deliberation. Section 6 (a) of the Bill says that the Lokpal will exercise superintendence over investigation of acts of corruption. Section(c) empowers the Lokpal to punish acts of corruption. There is a provision in the Bill authorising him to receive complaints and another to enable him to initiate prosecution .

There are about 5.5 million government employees, including those in the railways. There can be any number of complaints, some genuine and others not so genuine. It will require creating a huge 'parallel bureaucracy' to handle these complaints and supervise the investigation process.[27]

But the problem may be that the complaints may not be specific and detailed enough (which calls for intimate knowledge of the facts of the case), to ensure thorough investigation, leading to prosecution. Then, as the ARC noted in the context of failure of the internal control system, very few cases of corruption are reported today as there is collusion at work at all levels of government, and sharing of the gains of corruption.

There is hardly any reason to feel , therefore, that real complaints would get generated. The reason why the internal control system has not worked in India may also make the Lokpal not so effective in controlling corruption. To make a system work on the basis of complaints, given the state of things, may not be the correct way to go about it. False complaints also cannot be ruled out. If they proliferate, that may make administration difficult.

The right step, therefore, would be, first, to strengthen the internal control system by suitable legislation with a view to give functional independence to internal audit and empower it with investigative power. Then, when the Lokpal comes into existence, it can supervise its functioning, apart from other activities, including receiving of complaints, the veracity of which can be judged on the basis of inputs from the internal audit and other internal control mechanisms.

This would have the advantage of keeping the infrastructure of the Lokpal comparatively small, as also make use of the existing infrastructure in internal audit which would be suitably strengthened by bringing professionalism into its functioning, and investing it with power and responsibility.

This model can also work in the states, with suitable strengthening of the internal audit, where it is almost non-functional.

This could be the most important piece of administrative reform, which is long pending.

Notes

1. Jack Diamond, *Budget System Reform in Emerging Economies* (IMF Publication, 2006), p. 44.
2. The Institute of Internal Auditors, *Standards for Professional Practice of Internal Auditing*, (Florida, USA, 1978), p. 1.
3. Diamond, n. 1, p. 45.
4. Institute of Chartered Accountants of India, "Study and Evaluation of the Accounting System and Related Internal Controls in Connection with Audit, Statement on Standards Auditing Practices (SAP)", 1988.

5. Defence Audit Code, Vol. 1, 1992 edition, "Audit Against Propriety", Clause 38.
6. Ibid., Clause 39.
7. Ibid., Clause 74.
8. Ibid., Clause 15.
9. Ibid., Clause 16.
10. http://en.wikipedia.org/wiki/coso
11. Michael Page and Laura F. Spira, "The Turnbull Report, Internal Control and Risk Management: Developing Role of Internal Audit", Executive Summary—http://www.icas.org.uk/site/cms/countriesarticle.asp
12. Address by Vepa Kamesam, Deputy Governor, Reserve Bank of India, at Administrative Staff College of India, Hyderabad, on November 22, 2001, http://www.geocities.com/kstability/inbank/corpgovrn/index.html
13. Jack Diamond, "The Role of Internal Audit in Government Financial Management: An International Perspective", IMF Working Paper, 2002.
14. Ibid.
15. Ibid.
16. Government of India (2007), "Report of the Task Force for Benchmarking the Status of Internal Audit in the Central Government", para 5.1.1.
17. Ministry of Finance, Government of India, Office Memorandum, F.No. 5(6) L&C/2006 dated 1 June, 2006, para 9 (XIII).
18. Inspector General Act of 1978, USA, Section 2.
19. Ibid., Section 2 of the Act, Provisions (1), (2) and (3).
20. Ibid., Section 3 of the Act.
21. India: Accountability of Administration, Lok Sabha Secretariat, February 1987, quoted by B. P. Mathur, *Government Accountability and Public Audit* (Uppal Publishing House, 2007), p. 206.
22. Second Administrative Reforms Commission (2007), "Ethics in Governance", para 6.13.2, p. 153.
23. Ibid., para 6.13.1, pp. 152-153.
24. Ibid., para 6.13.1.
25. Speech on the occasion of the National Colloquium on Ethics in Governance on September 1, 2006, incorporated as Annexure 1 (2) in the Fourth Report of Administrative Reforms Commission (ARC), p. 219.
26. Diamond, n. 13.
27. Justice Markandey Katju, "The 90%", *The Indian Express*, April 9, 2012.

6

Budgeting for Desired Defence Capability

The defence procurement policy and procedure as brought out as early as in DPP-2006 (Defence Procurement Policy, 2006) indicated that for policy decisions relating to acquisition of weapons and systems, we are basing them on capability planning in the context of operational requirements. It talked in terms of existing 'capability gaps', and examination of alternative means of overcoming them, while processing a case for policy decisions. Capability planning has various implications from the resource allocation angle, and particularly for defence budgeting, which are yet to be addressed in a systematic manner. An attempt has been made below to highlight some of the issues and the possible ways to tackle them.

Budgeting as a means for obtaining optimum defence capability would call for reform in the defence budgeting process in three important aspects. First, the budgetary process has to be changed so as to treat defence budgeting as a part of the decision-making process for optimum resource allocation for achieving specific defence capabilities. The process should be so designed that choice could be exercised in allocating limited means for achieving identified 'objectives' with a view to achieving maximum effectiveness in defence spending. To develop optimum defence capability, the objective should be clear.

Second, the budgeting process should be closely linked with the defence planning process. Budgeting should be treated as the execution portion of the defence planning cycle, so that there is close coordination between capability planning and budgeting. This will call for an extended time horizon for defence budgeting as also change in the format of the defence budget.

Third, attention should be focussed on the end products of defence budgeting through the concept of programmes for capability building, making it an output-oriented budget.

In this context, it is good to remember that for optimum capability building through objective-based defence planning, a relationship is required to be established between the identified objectives and the various activities to enhance military capabilities.

Military capabilities are capabilities to perform specified tasks. Therefore, the basis for resource allocation decisions in the capability-based defence plans should be military tasks that are required to be performed. It is the military tasks conceived in the framework of an objective- based approach that would provide the basis for development of programmes for those tasks. Programmes by themselves have no sanctity, unless they are linked to the performance of military tasks that have been identified as necessary for carrying out national security policy. There should be an explicit link between the aims of policy and the military forces required to achieve the aims. Programmes should be considered as providing that link.

In the capability-based approach, the defence forces must be manned, equipped, and trained to carry out the identified military tasks for which they are assigned. So the programmes should be developed on a composite basis, taking into account all the elements required to develop capabilities to carry out specific tasks. Clearly, in the capability-based approach, programmes cannot merely be conceived as equipment acquisition programmes, as we often tend to do, and make our defence plans equipment acquisition plans. Defence plans have to be much more than that.

So, what we are following today is a truncated approach to defence planning, which may not be the right approach to developing optimum defence capability. Because of the basic importance of military tasks to provide the building blocks for defence programmes, there should be an adequate planning and resource allocation mechanism in Service Headquarters. We have not adequately emphasised upon it, as our planners have mostly concentrated on acquisitions of equipment and systems.

Programme planning and budgeting for capability building to achieve identified objectives have to take place at the level of Service Headquarters, within the overall guidance provided by the formulation of military policy and strategy at the Ministry and higher level. The policy objectives, however, cannot be set at the Service Headquarters level.

Planning and Programming

When Arthur Smithies, in his seminal work in the 1950s, first conceived of budgeting as a part of the decision-making process, he conceived a process consisting of six stages: determination of policy objectives, planning, programming, budget formulation, budget or programme execution, budget or programme review. What was the role of planning in the decision-making process, as conceived by Smithies? In his words: "Planning, as the term is used here, means the preparation of alternative plans that will further particular policy objectives in varying measure and are within the reasonable bounds of feasibility."[1] His definition of programming was, "Programming denotes a further step in the direction of finality and feasibility, and may involve selection among alternative plans or a combination of elements from a number of plans."[2]

Basic decisions that greatly influence the size of the budget are required to be taken at the programming stage. To quote him once again, "The distribution of the defense program among the three Services are budgetary questions, since the national objective is to obtain the most efficient use of resources devoted to defense. While these questions are largely settled before a budget is prepared, the programming decisions should be based on the relative costs of the various defense alternatives."[3] Costing of programmes again assumes central importance, both for decision-making and budgeting. That is why for budgeting for defence capability, the programming stage should be properly designed and should precede budgeting.

Arthur Smithies has been quoted for two reasons. First, to indicate that in the quest for rational allocation of resources for capability building, setting of policy objectives followed by planning and programming are essential steps, before budgeting is attempted. Secondly, these steps have their validity in any rational system of decision-making in resource allocation, and were visualised much before the Programming, Planning, and Budgeting System (PPBS) was introduced in US defence in the Sixties. One may criticise PPBS for various reasons, but that does not make the concept of planning and programming invalid. The validity is derived from need for rational allocation of resources for achieving optimum defence capability.

Force Structure and Capability Building

The main determinant of defence capability is the force structure. So force planning becomes the key element in capability planning. When programme budgeting or its variant PPBS was introduced in the Sixties in US defence, the Five-Year Defence Programme (FYDS), and ten Major Force Programmes (MFPs), were its central foci. Defence budgets were allocated among these MFPs to achieve optimal allocation of resources. The ten MFPs were so defined that they expressed the principal missions the military needed to perform.

Without defining the missions and tasks, and allocating resources for carrying the military tasks, capability planning cannot be attempted. The most important ingredient of capability planning is force structure planning. In India, we are yet to attempt force structure planning through our Five-Year Plans. The main drivers of cost in defence are the strength and composition of forces. If we want to use budgeting for building up desired defence capabilities, then an affordable force planning should be its main focus for all the three Services.

In determining an appropriate force structure, there has to be a well conceived and well debated defence strategy. National security strategy would have to relate 'means' to 'ends'. There is no strategy in the absence of choice about 'means' and 'ends', or their relationship. In a democratic society, difficulties are often faced in coming to grips with the 'ends' rather than the 'means' of strategy. This is why there is absolute necessity of periodic comprehensive defence reviews, in defining the 'ends' and establishing the relationship between 'ends' and 'means' towards formulating a defence strategy and broad allocation of resources in a multi-year perspective. We are yet to undertake such a review. It may be worthwhile in this context to quote from the report of the Estimates Committee of the Parliament (1992-93) on defence force levels: "The Committee is apprised that the force level under the Ministry of Defence is determined by the dynamic perspective of the security scenario coupled with the annual availability of resources within the plan period, competing demands of other priority sectors, the technological developments and other systemic inputs. They are shocked to find that the question of force level which is inherently linked with perspectives on national security should be dealt with on such vague and unpredictable considerations."[4] The issue is still unresolved.

Policy decisions regarding broad military tasks and missions to be aimed at are to be taken to provide a basis for approving a force level and a force structure which can be addressed though a defence review — which is long overdue. Nothing is more urgent than having a defence review from the point of view of public interest and policy, if the government wants to address the unresolved issues as brought out in the Report of the Estimates Committee of 1993 on defence force levels, manpower, etc. Without it, defence capability building may take an ad hoc character and may not meet the desired objectives. Naturally, defence budgeting would also take an ad hoc character, as is very much evident.

Budgeting for Defence Capability and Budgeting for Modernisation

Budgeting for defence capability has to have a close link with the strategic planning process for national security. Resource allocation under capability-based planning would look for capability gaps on the basis of objectives to be attained. Budgeting should aim at allocating funds on a priority basis for meeting the capability gaps, based on strategic considerations. There should be a close link between defence strategy and defence budgeting. In a sense, defence budgeting for capability is defence strategy. This is because defence capability building is not done for its own sake. Capabilities are developed to achieve national military objectives and operational objectives, and budgeting is the means to do so. Defence budgeting has to be viewed as a resource allocation process for building up required military capability for carrying out military tasks based on operational objectives. Important elements of defence capability building viz. manpower, training, ammunition and various other stores meant for operation and maintenance purposes, are in the revenue side of the defence budget. When capability building is the objective, the entire defence budget has to be considered for allocation to develop specific defence capabilities. In capability planning, major emphasis is given to operational concepts and operational challenges, and resource allocation has to be done on that basis.

Capability Planning and Programme Budgeting

PPBS, introduced in the 1960s, in the USA laid the foundation for capability-based planning. While it has undergone a number of changes over the past four decades, the core element and the basic process still provide the basis for allocation of resources for capability building. After the operation of PPBS for nearly two decades, many analysts pointed out that the first 'P', which stood for strategic planning, was missing. Some of the reforms brought about in the mid-Eighties, were really concerned with the front end of planning — meaning strategic planning.

The Group of Ministers (GoM), in their report on Reforming the National Security System (2001) stated, "A need has been felt for a review of the form and content of the Defence Services Estimates and the expansion of the budgetary classification to promote programme-based budgeting, while ensuring compliance with security requirements (Para 6.52)." They also stated that "optimal allocation of resources cannot be achieved unless greater emphasis and attention is given to the process of budget formulation and implementation, including forecasting, monitoring and control (Para 6.51)." But they did not emphasise the need for strategic planning and the need for linking the budgeting process to it. In fact, without it, the budgeting process cannot be improved.

Unfortunately, the GoM did not go into the implications of adopting programme budgeting nor did they emphasise that the programming process should precede budget making to bring about optimal allocation of resources. As David Novick has pointed out, "Planning and programming are aspects of the same process; they differ only in the emphasis."[5]

Planning here does not mean the Five-Year Plans, as we formulate them — a list of schemes. It is an activity concerned with selection of the best course of action among various alternatives, given the limitation of resources. To quote Novick again, "Planning is the production of the range of meaningful potentials for selection of a course of action through systematic consideration of alternatives. Programming is the specific determination of the manpower, material, and facilities necessary for accomplishing a programme. In addition, except in the very short term where dollars are in effect 'given', programming entails interest in dollar requirements for meeting the manpower, material, and facility needs."[6]

By adopting the programme budgeting concept in this sense, budgeting for desired defence capability became possible. The GoM did not get into these aspects of programme budgeting. Thus, a great opportunity of reforming the defence budgetary process in India to develop defence capability was lost. They got more concerned with the defence procurement process, with a view to expedite it, and recommended organisational changes, which were promptly adopted. Procurement planning cannot substitute for defence planning which calls for consideration of alternatives to achieve defence objectives. Without strategic planning to back it up, defence procurement takes on an ad hoc character.

Defence Capability Plan and Defence Budgeting

Budgeting for desired defence capability would very much be dependent on a well-conceived Defence Capability Plan. Till the 10th Defence Plan, we had not specifically adopted capability-based planning in defence. The aim of the Five-Year Plans has been to modernise the defence forces. The projections of the Ministry of the Defence for the 10th Plan were reviewed thrice between March 2003 and July 2004 bearing in mind the needs of defence modernisation. As per the 11th Report of the Standing Committee on Defence on Demands and Grants (2006-07), the Ministry of Finance had finally agreed in principle to the projections made by the Ministry of Defence of Rs. 4,18,101 crore for the 10th Defence Plan 2002-07. "However, the total allocation for the 10th Plan on the basis of annual plan allocation comes to Rs. 3,64,000 crore. Hence, there has been a gap of Rs. 5,41,000 crore between the indicative figure given and the total allocation made by the Ministry of Finance for the 10th Plan.[7]" This, in fact, with reference to original projection, was around Rs. 1,29,000 crore.

It is clear that the projections made by Ministry for the plan are not taken very seriously. In capability-based planning, there has to be a close link between planning and budgeting as the desired capabilities are required to be achieved within a given time-frame, to meet specific challenges. So the most important lesson for budgeting for capability building is that the projected five-year budget should have in-principle approval from the government, say of the Cabinet Committee on Security (CSS). It cannot be left to be a debate between the Ministry of Defence and Ministry of Finance. The capability plan should be based on it.

It has been reported keeping in view the experience of the 10th Defence Plan, that the 11th Defence Plan (2007-12) has been drawn up keeping in view the financial constraints, with the aim of filling up defence capability gaps.

The aim and objectives to be achieved in the 11th Defence Plan by the three Services, as intimated by the Ministry of Defence to the Standing Committee on Defence while discussing the Demands for Grants 2006-07, were briefly as under:[8]

- Army: Development of capability to attain military objectives in a short, high intensity war against a nuclear backdrop. Continued upgradation of capability for countering proxy war/ insurgencies and other emerging internal security challenges.
- Navy: Impetus on improving the capability in the area of airborne maritime surveillance, anti-submarine warfare, air defence capability through induction of aircraft, integral helos and UAVs (Unmanned Aerial Vehicles). Arresting the force level decline of submarines and networking platforms for more effective maritime operations.
- Air Force: The formulation of the 11th IAF Plan (2007-12) has been driven by the imperative of keeping an equal focus on several vital issues: strategic reach, enhancement of firepower of combat forces, enhancement of airlift capability and operating infrastructure with due regard to the perceived security concerns and technological environment. The broad thrust of the plan has been on containing the adverse effect of force depletion to the extent possible.

What confuses a layman is that the goal of capability planning for each Service is different. The element of 'jointness' in capability planning is missing. While the army would be developing capability to attain military objectives "in a short, high intensity war", the air force in its capability plan does not mention anything of this "high intensity" war or how it would support the army to attain military objectives in such a war. The thrust of the plan is containing the adverse impact of "force depletion". The navy in its capability plan aims at all round improvement in capability and arresting force level decline but does not mention about developing specific capability based on operational concepts. Budgeting for each Service based on this kind of planning would have a different thrust and would not lead to optimal allocation of resources for attaining strategic objectives.

Defence Strategy and Capability Building

Defence strategy, force planning and capability building are closely interrelated. Deliberations and methodology adopted for capability planning in the USA in the context of the Quadrennial Defence Review, 1997 (QDR '97) as also subsequent QDRs, clearly indicate the interrelationship. The QDR took a "capabilities analysis" perspective by emphasising the need to have operational capabilities for a highly diverse set of military contingencies. It drew on the ideas in Joint Vision 2010 and the revolution in military affairs.

But equally important, the capability planning in QDR'97 was based on the assumption that the defence budget was likely to remain constant in real terms during the plan period. For capability planning, the assumption about the likely availability of budgets for the next five years or more is absolutely essential.

If it is expected to grow, then the assumption about the rate it is likely to grow at annually is very important for capability planning. Assumption might relate to real terms growth in the defence budget and if that was not possible, growth may be assumed in numerical terms. For defence planning in India, it will require decisions at the level of the Cabinet Committee on Security (CCS). The Finance Ministry on its own cannot give this kind of commitment. So the most important point relating to budgeting for defence capability is that it calls for long-term budgeting.

In Australia, for example, the 2000 Defence White Paper committed the government to increase defence spending by an average of 3 percent real growth a year from 2000-01 to 2010-11. In 2006, the Australian government decided to increase defence spending by 3 percent in real terms per year until 2015-16. Because of the long-term commitment of funding, it became possible to earmark $2.2 billion to acquire heavy airlift capability enabling rapid deployment of combat vehicles, helicopters and supplies, as also to earmark $1.5 billion for a ten-year period for a networked army and to increase in its size.[9]

Long-Term View of Funding is Necessary for Determining Affordability

When considering phasing out of any type of aircraft, the analyst may have to look 20 years or more into the future to have some assurance that he is recommending an affordable acquisition plan since, "In the long view of fighter modernisation, long-term averages of budgets and expenditures assume more importance than what happens in the next year or two."[10] Affordability is assuming increasing importance as a design consideration for new fighter aircraft, even in US defence.

One cannot confidently predict the size of future defence budgets. But it is not impossible to make projections about allocation for defence and the likely share of the air force, army and navy keeping in view past trends of allocation for the defence budget and the share of the respective Services in the defence budget. Any projection for the defence budget for the next ten years, assuming more than 9 percent annual growth on the present level, given the operation of the FRBM Act, would appear optimistic. In making projections for the long-term, one has to make conservative estimates.

It may not be possible to maintain the present high level of allocation for capital expenditure which has now touched almost 43 percent of the defence budget, as no rationalisation of expenditure on support services has taken place. Keeping in view past trends, the percentage of allocation for the revenue budget would have to increase from the present levels, particularly with implementation of the recommendations of the Sixth Pay Commission. Without change in force levels in terms of manpower, it may be difficult to sustain a capital budget of more than 35 percent on the average during the next ten years. One can even consider the possibility of sustaining a capital budget at 37-38 percent with changes in force level and other reforms during the next ten years.

On the basis of such possibilities, one can attempt to calculate likely availability of funds for various segments of defence capabilities. For this, each Service has to work out the competing needs for capital expenditure out of its share of the capital budget and the affordability of various aspects of modernisation. For the air force, for example, in the current context for capability building, one has to assess the broad possibility of affordability of fighter aircraft modernisation, keeping in view the amounts required for other segments of modernisation of the air force.

Assessing Affordability of Force Structure

We have avoided issues relating to force structure as we did not have a long-term consideration of affordability. For example, in the air force, there is a concept of high-low mix. High-low mix refers to buying some aircraft that are highly capable and highly expensive (the high side of the mix) and some that have less capability and are of low cost (low end of the mix). It is recognised that not all aircraft in a total fighter force posture need to have comparable capabilities. Because of reasons of total cost, it is expected that a majority of the force will consist of "low-end" aircraft; these aircraft are designed to be "general purpose" in character.

Buying a force consisting only of specialised "high-end" aircraft will reduce the total force size significantly unless allocation for the air force is increased significantly. Though our air force evolved into having a 'highlow' in recent debates, this aspect has been ignored. The SU-30MKI is a high, end aircraft which is also being 'produced' in the country. The Mirage 2000, MiG-29, Jaguars are all high end aircraft. From the Request for Proposal (RfP) for 126 aircraft, it is obvious that these would fulfill the role of the 'high-end' aircraft. Then which one would be in the 'low-end' of the mix? Certainly not the Light Combat Aircraft (LCA) whose cost will be four to five times that of the updated MiG-21, though much more capable. Are we planning to have a smaller size air force structure? But there has been no debate on this in India.

No country, however rich, can do without this kind of debate as the question of affordability in capability planning is a must. For example, in the mid-Nineties when the US Air Force was considering various options about the force mix in fighter aircraft, in the context of future induction of the F-22 fighter which was under development, one point that came up repeatedly into consideration was the high cost of the aircraft and its likely impact on the US Air Force structure. As one analyst, bringing out the nature of choice that has to be made, put it, "For a given level of modernization funding, each $10 million increase in the flyaway cost of the multi-role aircraft subtracts three to four wings of force structure. As it buys more expensive aircraft, the air force must weigh the capability of each individual aircraft against the desirability of having a larger force. Acquisition of a $45 million multi-role fighter does not appear consistent with maintaining a force of 20 wings or more, particularly since even typical procurement growth in the F-22 program would subtract about two additional wings from each force structure that could be envisaged on the basis possible range of future funding of the US Air Force." [11]

Each Service has to consider this kind of trade-off while modernising its forces because resources are limited. We do not seem to be making any deliberate choice in this regard, and are leaving the force structure to evolve out of the normal process of induction of new equipment as part of the modernisation effort and de induction of equipment on completion of its service life. This is particularly true in the case of the air force, as would be evident from the following two excerpts from the Report of the Standing Committee on Defence of the Parliament on the Demands for Grants (2006-2007). In reply to questions raised while examining the Demands for Grants for 2005-06 regarding air force squadron strength, the Ministry of Defence in their action taken note, said, "The present squadron strength of the Air Force is 37 against the authorised strength of 39.5 squadrons. With the planned inductions of SU-30, Jaguar, Multi-Role Combat Aircraft, Light Combat Aircraft and phasing out of certain aircraft during 2005-2017, the combat squadron strength at the end of the X, XI and XII Plan periods is expected to be 29, 34 and 36 squadrons, respectively."[12]

One is left to wonder why a squadron strength of 29 that is considered adequate at the end of 10th Plan, is allowed to go up to 36 at the end of the 12th Plan when more advanced combat aircraft would be in the inventory. Or, if the desired squadron strength of the air force is 36, then why is it allowed to fall below that level in the 10th and 11th Plan periods? The calculations undergo change when a reply is given on this very issue when the Demand for Grants for 2006-07 is discussed, as the following evidence given by the Ministry of Defence would show: "By the end of the Eleventh Plan, we will be reaching 31.5 squadrons, and by the end of the Twelfth Plan, we will be reaching 26.5 squadrons. However, by the addition of the MMRCA, these 126 aircraft will go to make six squadrons. Starting from the Eleventh Plan onwards, progressive increase in squadrons would take place. We expect that at the end of the Eleventh Plan, we would have approximately two squadrons, therefore, rising by about 33.5 and at the end of the Twelfth Plan, rising by six squadrons, that means, making it 32.5 squadrons with the MMRCA."[13]

From the affordability point of view, for the Air Force to maintain 36 squadrons or more of fighter aircraft, a general purpose aircraft like the MiG-21 on a new platform, though more capable, with cost not more than 20 to 25 percent over the updated MiG -21s, may have to be there in the inventory. If this option is not feasible, then from the affordability point of view, squadron strength has to fall. One has to decide about the optimum squadron strength of the Air Force from the affordability point of view, keeping in view not only the acquisition cost, but more importantly the maintenance and operation costs which are often ignored. This would not help in defence capability planning.

The most important thing in budgeting for desired capability would be to examine what are the options available within a budgetary allocation, which in real terms may not grow by more than 3 or 4 percent per year. There has to an integrated approach for evaluation of options for capability building to get best value for money. The options would be to acquire new capabilities such as advanced aircraft incorporating advanced technology, tactical missile defence, UAVs, and C4ISR, which would come under the option of modernisation. The costs of these elements of modernisation have to be balanced against reduction of air force squadrons, reduction of army divisions by x number as against modernisation options, for more firepower, greater mobility, more attack helicopters, UAVs, C4ISR for the navy, reduction of the number of surface ships as against increase in submarine strength or vice versa. These options are to be examined on the basis of criteria of costs and effectiveness. It should be annualised costs of each option. This could be obtained by amortising acquisition costs over the expected life of the system, adding operating costs and support costs and discounting future costs.

For effectiveness estimates for capabilities, expert judgements are to be the basis. These could be on the basis of score cards for assessing their efficiency against various contingencies. The options are to be arranged in a descending order of cost-effectiveness—top options buy more for the money spent. The composite assessment, of course, depends on the relative emphasis given to different components of the defence strategy. Each evaluation would depend on many assumptions, such as planning scenarios to test the capabilities and perceived worth of different hedges against strategic uncertainty. Capability assessment and evaluation should be made against each component of defence strategy. So formulating a well articulated defence strategy is a most essential step for deciding about the capabilities that need to be acquired.

Rational allocation of resources—which defence budgeting should aim at—is to be done on the basis of military tasks to be performed based on national military objectives and operational objectives. If the aim is to achieve optimum defence capability within the given resources, then planning and programming should precede defence budgeting. In other words, it should be programme-based budgeting whose key points are: (i) expenditure plans for a sequence of future years; (ii) expenditures are related to 'outputs' or capabilities to be acquired; (iii) the concept of 'affordability' in the medium and long terms, both in terms of revenue and capital expenditure, is always explicitly considered; (iv) the concept of rolling budgeting is to be introduced as priorities may change because of the change in environment.[14]

Multi-year expenditure plans and multi-year budgeting on a roll-on basis are the main aspects of programme-based budgeting. Both force planning and cost projection should be done on a multi-year basis if building of optimum defence capability is to be the goal of defence budgeting.

The Concept of 'Capability Gap'

We started by stating that our procurement policy as indicated by the procurement procedure (all the versions) is aimed at establishing priority for meeting the 'capability gaps' as derived from envisaged operational requirements.

The concept of 'capability gap' is derived from the methodology of Capability-Based Planning (CBP) , which is distinct from threat-based planning.

In adopting this concept of procurement, the influence of the QDR 2001 was obvious. To quote from the QDR 2001 Report issued by the US Department of Defence on September 30, 2001, "The new defense strategy is built around the concept of shifting to a 'capability-based' approach to defense. That concept reflects the fact that the United States cannot know with confidence what nations, combination of nations, or nation-state actors are threat to vital US interests..."[15] It is, however, possible " to anticipate the capabilities that an adversary might employ". This thought led to the adoption of the capability-based approach in QDR 2001, which was continued in QDR 2006.

It meant for US defence the broadening of the strategic perspective compared to threat-based planning in focussing on emerging threats from adversaries relying on asymmetric warfare to attain their objectives. It also meant exploiting opportunities provided by the information-led technological revolution .

"Moving to a capabilities-based force also requires the United States to focus on emerging opportunities that certain capabilities , including advanced remote sensing, long-range precision strike, transformed maneuver and expeditionary forces and systems, to overcome anti-access and area denial threats, *can confer on the US military over time*."[16] (Italics mine.) Some of these capabilities were being developed. So, basically, this approach meant adopting a long-term plan to develop these capabilities.

The important point to remember is that CBP is *more of an approach towards planning*, rather *long-term planning* for capability-building, than a total system incorporating costing and resource management aspects, in both the short and long terms. Therefore, in US defence, PPBS (renamed as PPBES) is still operating as the core of the planning and resource management system. CBP has not been able to supplant it.

So at best , it would be a supplementary process to buttress programming, if a long-term view is lacking. The enthusiasm of those outside the USA who thought that CBP could be used as an alternative approach to defence planning has not been corroborated by events.

CBP is no doubt the correct approach to defence planning if the country feels, as the USA did in the beginning of this century, that it is difficult for it to anticipate "what nations, combination of nations or nation-state actors" would threaten its vital interests, so it has to plan for a wide range of capabilities.

One obvious point for countries like ours would be, that it is not very uncertain to visualise where threats may emanate from and the kind of adversary capabilities that one would be confronted with. The problem of on 'what' grounds, 'when' and 'where', however, remains. To that extent, the uncertainty factors remain.

Therefore, it would be wrong to pose the issue as 'threat-based' vs 'capability-based' planning. CBP, to be meaningful, has to incorporate 'threats' but the scenarios have to be drawn up in more detail so that uncertainty factors can be squarely faced, and modern tools of analysis employed to find out probable capability solutions.

Paul Davis, explaining the idea behind the CBP concept, which is widely quoted as the most acceptable definition, said it involves , "planning under uncertainty, to provide capabilities suitable for a wide range of modern-day challenges and circumstances while working *within an economic framework that necessitates choice."*[17] (Italics mine.)

The important condition highlighted above is that the planning has to be within the economic framework *necessitating choice*. That means CBP has to be within strict budgetary constraints; a choice has to be made between on-going programmes and new programmes; and funds have to be made available through short closing of, or economising on, existing programmes. That means no additional financing can be asked for implementing it , apart from whatever is made available as part of the budgetary exercise.

The important aspect of CBP as per the QDR Report was to arrive at capability needs on the basis of a joint force. Keeping this in mind , in March 2003, the US Secretary of Defence chartered the Joint Capabilities Study to examine how to develop, and find resources to provide joint capabilities. The recommendations of that study were reflected in the Strategic Planning Guidance (SPG) for Fiscal Years 2006-2011.[18]

Under CBP, defence acquisition has to widen its perspective , among other things , to:

- Infuse technological reality to planning and decisions.
- Shape, engineer, and validate solutions to the capability needs.

- Take decisions on the basis of systems perspective, in other words, take decisions in the capabilities context.
- Take decisions on the basis of joint capabilities needs.
- Provide a coherent logistics transformation strategy supporting distributed adaptive operations.

In the CBP acquisition process relating to weapon development, concept refinement and concept decisions play a major part. Technological development takes place only after a decision on the concept has been taken which is followed by systems development and demonstration.

What the adoption of CBP in the QDR 2001 meant was summed up by United States General Accounting Office (GAO) report on the subject on November 2002: "The review shifted the basis of defense planning from the long-standing 'threat-based' model, which focuses on specific adversaries and geographical locations (e.g. two-major- theater – war scenario), to a 'capabilities-based' construct that emphasizes the need to prepare for a range of potential military operations against unknown enemies."[19]

It also underscored the need to transform the Services' military capabilities and business processes to meet future threats and to use defense resources more efficiently. To support the transformation effort, the senior leadership decided to establish a new transformation office reporting directly to the Secretary of Defence and to develop transformation roadmaps for the Services and defence agencies.

QDR 2001 also contained the vision for making the Department more efficient by reforming the financial systems, reducing the size of headquarters staff, consolidating DoD's facilities and supply chains. These aspects are not often given importance in our literature while discussing capability-based planning.

The GAO report *inter alia* observes, "The quadrennial legislation also requires DoD to identify a budget plan to successfully execute the full range of missions called for in the defense strategy at a low to moderate level of operational risk…Although some study teams were tasked with addressing the budget issues in their limited area of research, we did not find any requirement for a team to address this issue from a departmentwide perspective."[20]

QDR was supposed to usher in long-term planning with focus on long-term threats and force planning.

But the GAO Report found limitations in the QDR on the force structure issues and observed, "The force analysis had a near-term focus that provided few insights into future threats and planned technological advances in US capabilities that may affect future force structure requirements."[21] In assessing force requirements "it relied primarily on existing military war plans and military judgment; *it used analytical tools such as computer modeling and simulation only to a limited extent. Such tools can provide a significant amount of additional data and insights to help decision-makers assess operational risk and evaluate force structure requirements for a range of scenarios and timeframes.*"[22]

In other words, these analytical tools, computer modelling and simulation can help in locating the 'capability gaps' in the context of relevant operational plans. To reemphasise the point, the GAO Report subsequently stated , "*We believe that more extensive use of analytical tools such as modeling and simulation, along with analysis of a broad range of longer-term scenarios and threats, would have enhanced the QDR's usefulness in fundamentally reassessing force structure requirements.*"[23]

Though we are supposed to have adopted CBP, we have not made any attempt to introduce in any such tools or felt its necessity to identify the capability needs and existing capability gaps. It is primarily based on judgement.

It is also clear from the GAO observations that capability needs and identification of gaps require detailed analysis of threat and scenario building exercises.

For identifying capability needs (and capability gaps) under the CBP approach as per QDR 2001, the requirements of the joint force were to be the basis. We have a single Service approach to establish the capability needs and capability gaps for each Service.

The basic question to be asked under the CBP approach is, "*What does the joint force need to be prepared to do?*" And not just *what equipment is to be purchased?* We have confined the CBP to answering the second question.

It is also important to note that while the US Secretary of Defence, directed that CBP be used across the Department , his guidance did not provide *implementing instructions.* In the absence of an overarching implementing instruction, the linkages among elements in CBP remain undefined. So many challenges remain in the process. There are independent processes which present separate and distinct views of the future, capability gaps, priorities, and remedies to the senior leadership, without a basis of common assumptions.[24]

But let us remember that CBP is a mainly a methodology for identifying capability needs and capability gaps rather than a resource management system, which has to be separately addressed.

The methodological approach under CBP for assessing the needs of the joint force is as follows.

Based on strategic guidance and war plans, etc, the Department of Defence, using planning horizons, must identify the range of military missions the joint force will be required to accomplish in a given period.

Next, from a variety of intelligence sources, the Department must identify all *plausible threat capabilities* that could challenge the joint force.

The Department then must narrow down the range of plausible *threat capabilities* to the "most likely" and "most dangerous" challenges based on the defence strategy.

There has to be a common understanding of how the joint force will operate. "Without a common understanding, the possibility arises for gaps and seams in our capability development process."[25]

After following the above methodological approach, one can assess the capability gaps in the joint force and prioritise them.

Then, there is an important decision to be made.

The list of prioritised gaps requires that a decision be made whether to accept the risk or solve the gap.

There are several options in CBP to solve the capability gap. For example, one can develop concepts to determine potential options to solve the gap, followed by experimentation to determine the best option. Then, one can identify a material or non-material solution.

The important point to note is that selecting the best option would be *largely based on how much information we have about the gap. Information to consider would include the operational needs, the ability to solve the gap with current capabilities, the cost involved, the technological advancements, and the impact joint interdependence has on the gap.*[26]

Following the above methodology, we can the answer the question as to how to *solve* the capability gap. The key phrase is how *to solve* the capability gap, not just how to *fill it*, which points toward a material solution, without considering all the alternatives.

What about the fiscal aspects?

Cost is a very important factor in determining which solution is chosen to solve a capability gap. As Bankston and Boyd point out, "CBP is fiscally constrained... in most cases, divestures pay for new capabilities...The bottom line is that with a zero-sum resource environment, new capabilities can only be funded by divestitures".[27]

This also indicates that CBP has to work within an economic framework which necessitates choice after considering all the alternatives.

In US defence, in making capability-based assessment of capability needs and arriving at functional solutions, the Chairman of the Joint Chiefs of Staff plays a key role. India has still to establish such a position. There is also a difference in perspective as to what should be regarded as *operating units*. In India, it has to be Service-wise. For the Army, it would be the perspective of the corps, which is the highest level for having an operational perspective, and in the Air Force it would be the Command HQ.

In US defence, operating units of the Department of Defence are the Combatant Commands (COCOMS). This makes it easier for them to develop a joint operation perspective, and assessment of capability needs can be made for each COCOM separately, depending on the strategic requirement of the theatre in question. Resources also can be allocated accordingly. For example, the Central Command (CENTCOM) gained most of the additional resources during the last few years in terms of additional ground units and special training units for carrying out the Global War on Terror (GWOT) and Counter-Insurgency (COIN) strategy. For responding to the rising China strategy, it would be the Pacific Command (PACOM) which may get resources in terms of a significant additional naval force and additional capabilities in terms of Intelligence, Surveillance and Reconnaissance (ISR). Resource costs in terms of dollar implications have to be worked out in terms of increase or decrease of forces in the COCOMS.

This perspective in terms of operating units is very important for developing capability-based planning.

It is also true that we can no longer think of defence modernisation without bringing in the capability-based approach. The aim is to arrive at an optimal force structure within the available resources. The question is how to go about it in a simpler manner. Let us take the model of the Department of National Defence of Canada that has also adopted capability-based planning for their force structure development. They start with likely future operational scenarios as the starting point for defence planning.

CBP provides the institutional framework to identify options to make resource-informed decisions on the capabilities required to meet the commitments as set out in the Defence White Papers. The aim is to arrive at an optimal force structure within the available resources.

What about other countries?

The key intuition behind CBP is correct: *that is, start by defining what needs to be done, then derive from it an affordable force structure that can do that.* This is fundamentally different from starting with the current force and then working out how to improve it.[28] As per the Anglo-Saxon approach as indicated in the Technical Cooperation Programme, a collaborative approach among countries in defence matters(Australia, Canada, New Zealand, the UK and the US), *the scenarios still play a central role within the CBP process.*[29]

The most important trend in the CBP identified by De Spiegeleire, is the trend towards "joint" capabilities. This is distinctly different from the position obtaining a decade ago when defence capabilities were identified, acquired and used by the individual Services. Capabilities were thought of primarily in terms of material and, to a smaller extent, in terms of personnel. "Most countries are now taking a step further by recognising that true defence capabilities consist of more than just material and personnel solutions. They have broadened the definition to include important capability elements such as doctrine, training, leadership, and so on, leading to new acronyms such as

DOTMLPF in the US, TEPID OIL in the UK and PRICIE in Canada."[30]

This trend is most visible in new concrete capability areas such as counter-IEDs (Improvised Explosive Devices). When confronted with this threat, the first reaction of defence organisations was to find material solutions. Ultimately , most adopted different solutions, such as increasing emphasis on training or tactics, techniques and procedure "in order to provide better value for money than instinctive material-only solutions."[31]

The key trend here is that the very term 'capability' is moving away from being equated with military hardware to instead a much broader conception of capability, which would have profound consequences for defence planning.

The emphasis on performance management in government in the Nineties has also influenced how CBP is to be implemented. To this end, having determined the term 'capability', each nation must go about determining what tasks the defence forces must be able to accomplish and what is the desired level of accomplishment in terms of performance.

Tasks must be oriented towards conducting 'activities'. An advantage of an activity-oriented task list is the clarity of roles and responsibilities. One can use the cascading of task delegation through hierarchy towards the goal of efficient activity management. The aim is to link output as efficiently as possible.[32]

One of the concepts that tended to influence CBP in the first decade of this century is what is known as effects-based planning which was reflected in the White Papers of some of the countries attempting capability-based planning. The centrality of effects in planning has declined significantly. The centrality of tasks and activities cannot be taken away either from planning or operations, as 'effects' come thereafter.

We have been concentrating on how capability 'needs' are to be assessed, the methodology to be followed in this regard, with its implications for arriving at 'capability gaps' which require solutions. We have also indicated that in the wider concept of capability needs, the material solution is only one of the solutions and not the most important one.

The capability building processes need more attention than arriving at 'solutions' prematurely. As it is conceived, the process has to start with defence guidance, to the generation of capability needs, assessing the capability gaps and then the performance management and goals.

The important change in the process now in the countries mentioned above is the 'capability gap' being substituted by 'capability audit' indicating that the process is more complicated , as we have tried to bring out, than earlier conceived. The audit process takes stock of the current and planned capability against the goals, and, thus, identifies the *areas to divest or invest in.*[33]

It means institutionalising what is called "balance of investment" studies and incorporating it in the planning process. It means conducting cost-benefit analysis for developing one capability over another, balancing a capability's 'worth' in both functional and financial terms.[34]

Then there is added emphasis on the use of scenarios. Scenarios provide the context for capabilities-based planning. Their robustness will determine the effectiveness of CBP as a process. The UK makes most use of scenarios, followed by Australia.

The richness of scenarios increases the likelihood of generating the right kind of capabilities in the future.

Notes

1. Arthur Smithies, *The Budgetary Process in the United States* (McGraw Hill, 1955), pp. 20-34, excerpts in Golembiewski and Rabin, ed., *Public Budgeting and Finance* (P.E. Peacock Publishers, 1975).
2. Ibid.
3. Ibid.
4. Estimates Committee of the Parliament (1992-93), para 1.65.
5. David Novick, *Program Budgeting* (RAND, 1965), p. 91.
6. Ibid.
7. Standing Committee on Defence Report, para 2.1, p. 29.
8. Standing Committee on Defence, Demands for Grants 2006-07, para 2.8, p. 3132.
9. At http://www.budget.gov.au/2006-06/overview/html/overview_13.htm.
10. William L. Stanley, "Assessing the Affordability of Fighter Aircraft Force Modernization", in Paul K. Davis, ed., *New Challenges of Defense Planning* (RAND 1994)," p. 568.
11. Ibid., p. 583.
12. Standing Committee on Defence, Demands for Grants 2006-07, para 5.4, p. 60.

13. Ibid., para 5.6.
14. Richard J. Hillestad & Paul K. Davis, *Resource Allocation for the New Defense Strategy, The Dyna Rank Decision Support System* (RAND, 1998), pp. 12-15.
15. QDR 2001 Report, p-14.
16. Ibid.
17. Paul Davis, "New Challenges for Defense Planning", RAND, 1994, also Paul Davis, "Analytic Architecture for Capabilities Based Planning, Mission-System Analysis and Transformation", 2002, RAND.
18. Boyd Bankston and Todd Key ,"Draft White Paper on Capabilities Based Planning", March 30, 2006. www.mors.org/userFiles/file/meetings/06cbpIL/ bankston_key.pdf
19. GAO Report, "Quarennial Defense Review", November, 2002 p-1, www.gao.gov/ docdblite/ accno= A05465.
20. Ibid., p.16.
21. Ibid., p.18.
22. Ibid.
23. Ibid., p.31.
24. Bankston and Key, n.18.
25. Ibid.
26. Ibid.
27. Ibid.
28. Stephan De Spiegeleire, " Ten Trends in Capability Planning for Defence and Security", *RUSI Journal*, October/November, 2011.
29. Ibid.
30. Ibid.
31. Ibid.
32. The Hague Centre for Strategic Studies, "Closing the Loop, Towards Strategic Defence Management", April 2009, p-135.
33. Ibid., p.137.
34. Ibid., p.139.

7

Programme Evaluation and Investments for Sustained Modernisation

To make budgeting respond to the challenges posed by the requirements of capability building and modernisation, the programming process in the Service Headquarters has to be revitalised with concepts of detailed evaluation of ongoing programmes, feedback and revision of programmes, looking also for inputs from commanders in the field, all being made in the context of a long-term plan, which would be subject to annual review. This mode of developing programmes on a continuing basis would require a proper institutional set-up.

These programming aspects of the budgeting system, I shall, for convenience of exposition, call "micro aspects" of defence planning and budgeting, in contrast to "macro aspects" of defence planning and budgeting which involve setting strategic objectives, decisions about broad capabilities to be built, and the direction of modernisation efforts and financial commitments on a long-term basis for investment in various aspects of capability building.

"Macro-analysis" of capability building through the programming concept is an essential aspect of decision-making in a Service Headquarters for the following reasons:

- It involves making final recommendations for resource allocation among various programmes out of the resources likely to be allocated to the Service and they have to satisfy themselves about the right balance among the various capabilities to be built.
- Costs of various weapon systems have to be studied along with their effectiveness. Programme budgeting, as Fredrick Mosher stated, "... called for systems analysis, cost-benefit analysis, operational research and related techniques," in the context of attempts being made in the mid-

Sixties to introduce programme budgeting in all Departments of the federal government (because of its success in the US Department of Defence). These were not the weapons with the traditional budgeteer of 1965, who had typically been the product of general administrative training and experience supplemented by work in accounting. This new orientation was basically that of economics, and the Planning, Programming and Budgeting System (PPBS) was in part a culmination of the swing toward economics that had begun with the Kennedy Administration in defence and, from the top down, in the Bureau of Budget.[7]

Traditional budgeteers in India still have a general administrative background with exposure to accounting. They are ill-equipped to usher in programme budgeting. The lead has to come from the Service Headquarters as far as programming aspects are concerned.

- There is a third important reason for attending to the "micro-aspects" of budgeting in the Service Headquarters which has an important bearing on optimum allocation of resources in defence. Robert McNamara summed up the position as follows:

> In addition to the defence budget, as the one we have, we begin to encounter the law of diminishing returns, where each additional increment of resources applied produces a smaller increment of overall defence capability. While benefits cannot be measured with precision, careful cost-effectiveness analysis can greatly assist in the elimination of program proposals, which clearly contribute little military worth in relation to resource expenditure involved. We have applied the principle throughout our program and budget reviews.[8]

Application of these principles requires a lot of judgement and intuitive understanding of the core values of a Service, which need to be preserved. Hence, such studies are best done by each Service Headquarters, because precise measurement is not possible. The above also underlines the vital necessity of constant reviews of programmes and budget allocations, with a zero-based approach, as a part of the annual exercise towards budget formulation.

This brings out the central importance of evaluation studies which have to be institutionalised in each Service Headquarters and made an integral part of programming and budgeting.

The recommendations of the Group of Ministers (GoM) relating to reforms in budgeting emphasised this point when they recommended, in the context of formulation of the 10th Defence Plan, "...introduction of zero-based budgeting approach for all ongoing schemes may be undertaken in a time-bound manner."[9]

There is no mechanism instituted to make such studies nor have criteria or parameters been laid down for assessing the worth of ongoing programmes. While we are quite vocal about non-approval of the Plans, we do not say anything about the zero-based approach which was to precede the formulation of the proposals.

The GoM stated very clearly: "Optimal utilisation of resources cannot be achieved unless greater emphasis and attention is given to the process of budget formulation and implementation, including forecasting, monitoring and control. There is also a need for rigorous prioritisation and the order of the charge on the budget being established with reference to Plan objectives." [10]

Our budgeting continues to be in the same incremental mode, without any prioritisation exercise taking place; it is more of a statistical exercise than a reflection of the decision-making process for national resource allocation for defence.

Being aware of the limitations of the existing system of budgeting, the GoM, recommended "budgetary classification to promote programme-based budgeting."[11]

Unfortunately, they confined themselves only to the format of programme budgeting, ignoring other essential elements of programme budgeting, as mentioned above. Nor did they recommend anything about rationalising the budgeting process, in order to use it as a management tool. In this, their approach has been in the traditional mode that programme budgeting only relates to budgeting and can be introduced without bringing in basic changes in the management attitudes and techniques.

Programme budgeting has many elements apart from the budget classification aspects. Most important of them is establishing a process of laying down objectives through the planning process, that is, the 'ends' aspect of policy-making and a mechanism of relating them to the 'means' i.e. the resources, so that budgeting becomes a means of translating the policy into resource allocation.

The other elements are:

- A budget organised in terms of categories that are closer to 'outputs' than traditional categories. But this will mean that close attention has to be given to defining the nature of outputs or the capabilities desired to be achieved. Broad programme categories which were brought in when PPBS, for example, was introduced in US defence, would hardly be useful.
- A programme budget implies a budget that employs a longer time horizon than is found in traditional budgeting with a horizon of one year. The reason is that with a longer time horizon, the full cost implications of alternation levies are less likely to be neglected.

  This brings into focus the necessity of meticulous costing of programmes, including both the cost of acquisition and the operating cost. The cost of the entire capability package has to be assessed as well as its impact on annual budgets spreading over to several years in the future. From the technique point of view, proper costing is the most essential element of programme budgeting. We have still to institute any costing device in the Service Headquarters to make such calculations, without which national decisions cannot be taken.
- Extensive use of cost utility analysis of relating input to output. Utility analysis has necessarily to be done in the context of the objectives to be achieved and on the basis of establishment of criteria of effectiveness in achieving the objectives, keeping in view the law of diminishing returns, as mentioned above.
- Institutional reorganisation to bring relevant administration functions under the jurisdiction of the authority making the final programme decisions.

All the above are essential elements of programme budgeting. It is a package. Only attending to the budget classification will bring about a cosmetic change, but not programme budgeting in the real sense.

The main ingredient of a programme is the programming function. Under the PPBS model as adopted in US defence, the programming function allocates resources to requirements that achieve national security objectives established in the planning phase of PPBS. The programming function and related decision-making take place in the Service Headquarters.

It has been realised that evaluation of existing programmes by establishing a proper institutional mechanism in the Service Headquarters, which would review the programme, provides the most important inputs to the programming process. A specific study relating to the army by RAND recommends that there should be proper resource guidance from the top across the army, which "is integral to the total resource programming and process." The same applies to the navy and air force. There must be "strategic planning guidance that provides army goals and objectives for the near -, mid-, and far term."[12]

The need has also been felt for a Vision Document to provide a Service Headquarters what its leadership wants, for example, the army, to look like in the next 15 to 20 years. These are the inputs from the top required for proper resource allocation in the Service Headquarters for budgeting purposes. So budgeting becomes both a top-down as also a bottom-up process.

In India, the budget formulation process in the Service Headquarters follows a bottom-up approach. Explaining the process in the Indian Army, an expert says: "Budget follows a bottom-up approach. Units/ Establishments project their requirement of funds to Estimating Authorities who compile and forward the same to the Financial Planning (FP) Directorate. FP Directorate vets the demands, discusses these with representatives of the Estimating Authorities where necessary and forwards the same to MoD (Finance). The consolidated estimates of the Services are sent to the MoF."[13]

In order to introduce the features of programme budgeting in a Service Headquarters, the budgeting process has to be both top-down and bottom-up; top-down in the shape of programming and financial guidance, emanating from the top leadership; bottom-up in the shape of evaluation studies of ongoing programmes, examination of alternatives, cost utility analyses and budget formulation on the basis of review of programmes.

In our existing process of budgeting, there is no stage of programming or programme reviews. There is no time for it as the budget gets formulated and finalised in a span of two and a half months. Hence, the best one can do is to take the existing base as given and follow an incremental mode of budgeting to provide for increase in costs. Budgeting does not, and cannot, function in these circumstances as a decision-making device for exercising choice in resource allocation decisions, whether it is for capability building or modernisation. Our budget is a control-oriented budget. The information and decision flow is from the bottom.

The process has to be reversed if the objective is to lay emphasis on modernisation and capability building as an important goal of budgeting. It has to be plan-oriented budgeting, a resource-constrained, long-term capability plan approved at the top decision-making level, which would be the main driving force for budgeting. The 'planning' function has to predominate in this budgeting system, as opposed to the 'control' function, which is the basic feature of our input budgeting today. Control would flow from planning, monitoring and evaluation of results.

In the process of formulating the plan objectives into budget allocations, the programming function in each Service Headquarters would play the most crucial role. This point has not been adequately appreciated in our discussions on budgeting reforms.

Programming decisions have to go through an iterative process and have to take place on a continuous basis. Therefore, there has to be a proper institutional arrangement in each Service Headquarters for both planning and programming. This has to be designed properly. The recent RAND study on programming in Army Headquarters of the United States quoted earlier brings out the organisation aspects and the programming with suggestions for improvement. Service organisational elements are involved in the process in Army Headquarters.

A key role is played by groups called Programme Evaluation Groups

(PEGs), which evaluate ongoing programmes. The principal function of these groups is to allocate resources to areas and activities assigned to each of them. These include among others, manpower, general purpose forces, supply and maintenance, modernisation, military construction, housing, information management, base operations, intelligence, etc. There are 14 such PEGs. PEGs are organised by staff function, responsibility and major programmes. As would be seen, "modernisation" is one such function, for which there is a PEG. Whatever priorities are given to this function compared to other functions, from the resources allocation point of view, can only come from the top. This cannot be left to the bottom-up exercise. Establishing *inter-se* priority is always a top level function.

Each PEG resource allocation iteration is reviewed by overseeing organisations such as the Programme Budget Committee (PBC), where membership is at the general officer and senior executive level. The PBC adjusts resource allocations to balance the broader programmes.

Between the PEG and PBC, there is the Council of Colonels (COC), which is an ad-hoc body representing all major headquarters staff functions that assist in preparation, execution, and review of programming functions.

The process identifies key resource issues in the context of resource requirements, which progresses through hierarchy. Only a few issues remain for decisions by the army leadership.

The Director of Programme and Evaluation (DPA&E) guides the PEG and Director of the Army Budget (DAB).

Inputs from Major Commands (MACOMS) are essential inputs for resource allocation decisions.

The organisation set-up is depicted to bring home the point that the programming process requires proper institutional arrangements which function in an interactive mode (refer Fig 7.1).

Fig 7.1

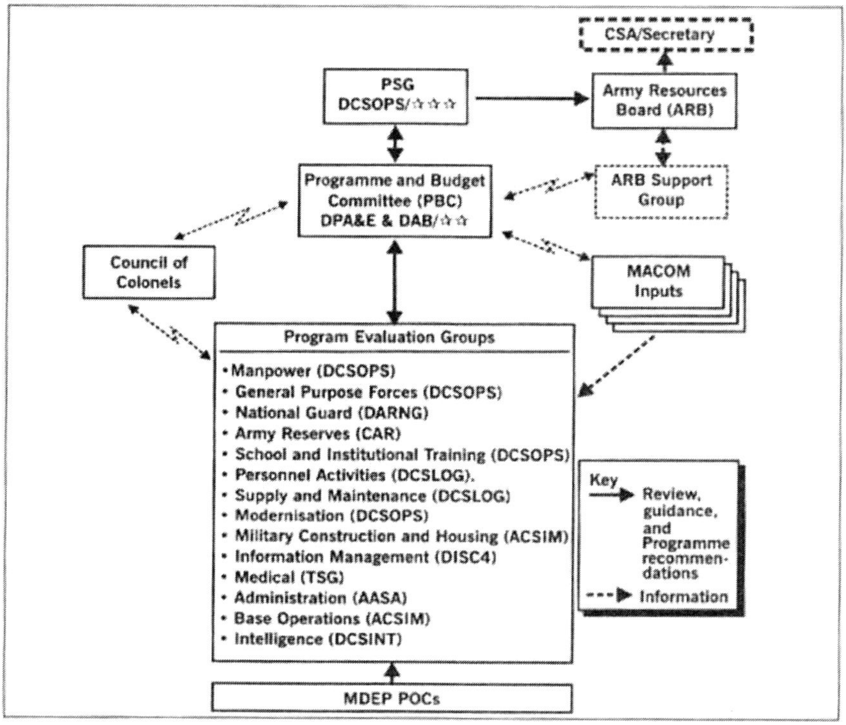

The planning process in the Army Headquarters starts with the senior army leadership approving The Army Plan (TAP) which provides specific objectives, programme priorities and guidance for programmes. "TAP emphasises an iterative method of establishing requirements and providing guidance and priorities to PEG... for interpreting TAP guidance against requirements within their areas of responsibility.[14]

The RAND team was also asked to look into the programming phase and suggest a framework to make programming decisions more balanced and effective towards capabilities development. The team developed certain essential criteria for the proposed framework, which, I believe, is of utmost importance, to make the programming function in a Service Headquarters more effective towards capability building.

- *The framework has* to be both *top-down and bottom-up.*

The generation of a hierarchical set of options is inherent in the process. The options could be within each particular function, e.g. manning, training, recruiting, equipping, outfitting and repairing military equipment, constructing, maintaining, etc. "The leadership should also be presented with options that cut across resource areas: greater equipping versus reduction in manning; reductions in equipping versus greater technology investment, long-term research and development, etc."

- *All the army's resources have to be considered* within the *capability packages.*

  "For instance, the identification of the Patriot missile system as a defence against incoming Scud missiles has to include all the associated resources, including those needed for deployment and sustainment of the system...... Such an approach eliminates the practice of resourcing within stovepipes (a single functional area) because all the resources associated with providing a capability have to be accounted for within a single package."[15]
- *The framework also has* to *ensure that trade-off analyses are performed in a disciplined and consistent manner. Inter-temporal issues are to be addressed within the trade-off.*
- *The framework has to accommodate the army's culture and enhance the army's case capability.*

These parameters for programming are of universal application as they are derived from the philosophy of programme budgeting.

I have gone into details relating to establishing a framework for resource allocations decisions within a Service Headquarters, as in our discussion of budgetary reform in defence, we pay hardly any attention to the programming aspect in a Service Headquarters, its required institutional framework for decision-making and the laying down of basic criteria for rational resource allocation decisions for capability-building.

Fig 7.2

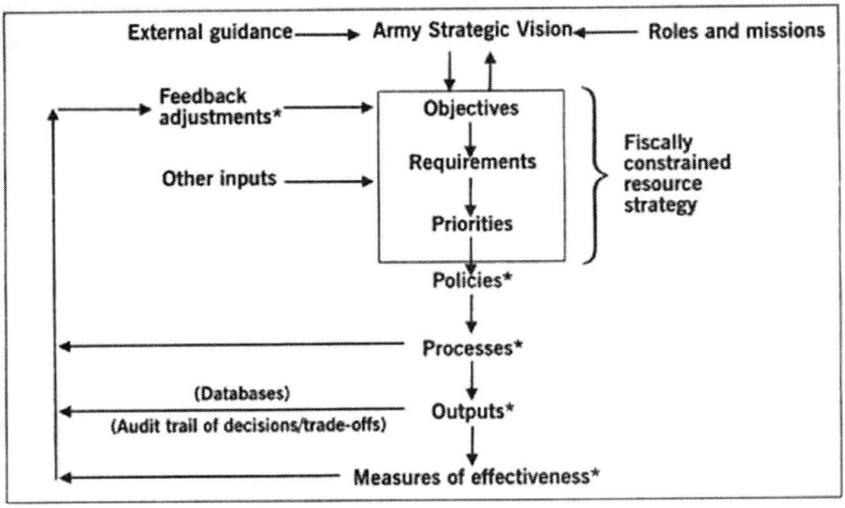

There is another aspect to the proposed framework for decision-making which cannot be ignored, that is, the planning and programming strategy has to be resource-constrained. This had been ignored in the earlier models of PPBS. The RAND study suggests a framework for conceptual overview, which I have adapted for presentation purposes (refer Fig 7.2).

The army's strategic vision is the basis from which the army defines its objectives, requirements, and priorities (the central box), all of which are essential for a resource strategy for capability building and modernisation. Each Service Headquarters has to develop its own Vision Document.

When capability building and modernisation become the main goals of the resource allocation process, the decision-making process requires inputs from various sources and levels and, as explained above, it has to be an iterative process. The hierarchical model of decision-making has to be suitably modified to accommodate these challenges and innovative ideas. As already explained, the programming process has to be both top-down and bottom-up.

Modernisation and Investments for RMA

A few years ago, it would have been difficult to initiate a discussion about modernisation of the military without referring to the contemporary Revolution in Military Affairs (RMA) brought about by the information revolution; it still is, but the debate is not as vigorous as before. This is partly because RMA is no longer regarded in the West as a 'hypothesis' to be proved. It is operational.

The other and more important reason is that the term has been replaced by military transformation, the meaning being almost the same, but transformation covering more aspects than RMA . Both term refers to a radical change in the character and conduct of war. It is also helpful to think that RMA leads to transformation.[16]

From the 1991 Gulf War, until the time the terrorist attacks of September 11, 2001, when attention shifted to irregular forms of warfare, the defence profession was dominated by the RMA hypothesis. "Even with increased emphasis on counterterrorism and counterinsurgency, the RMA has not disappeared. Rather, it has matured into the concept of transformation."[17]

The RMA concept emanated from the technical revolution in conventional warfare. In the early 1980s, Soviet observers led by Marshal Nikolai Ogarkov, chief of the Soviet General Staff, advanced the notion of imminent *technical revolution* that would give conventional weapons a level of effectiveness in the field comparable to *that of small tactical weapons*. Armour on the march, the way Soviets visualised warfare, might be detected and attacked by conventional missiles showering self-guided anti-tank weapons in an operation conducted from a distance of several hundred miles. They realised that they could not possibly keep up in an arms race driven by the information age technologies.

"Soviet conceptions of a military-technical revolution seeped into the West, chiefly through the US Department of Defense and its Office of Net Assessment."[18] The idea got currency in the USA because of the efforts of the Pentagon's long-time Director of Net Assessment, Andrew Marshal.

The origin of contemporary RMA explains why many analysts initially felt that it was the technical side of RMA that needed major attention. Benjamin Lambeth, who revisited the Soviet classic writings to go back to the origin of this thought of military revolution, finds that fifteen years before Marshal Orgarkov, that is in the mid-1960s, Soviet Air Force Lt Gen

N.A. Sbitov, captured the *essence* of the 'revolution in military affairs.' The essence lay, according to his Soviet forebears, in the capacity of what in the mid-Sixties were called 'new in principle' weapons, that led to *"radically change the nature of modern war."*

This change in the nature of war, as per Sbitov, was due the ability of modern weapons to achieve strategic military and military-political goals *at the very beginning of the war without going through the classic sequence of methodical plodding from tactical through operational level to strategic goals.*[19]

This, as Lambeth observed, "comes close to capturing the essence of the concept of 'revolution in military affairs' as articulated by its leading Western proponents today."[20]

What is, however, to be remembered is that this was the characterisation, by the Soviets of *the impact of nuclear weapons and ballistic missile delivery systems* on warfare. That was the RMA which preceded the present information age RMA. The nuclear age RMA cannot be compared with the contemporary RMA, referring to conventional warfare, which was the context in which Orgarkov expressed concern at the growing sophistication of NATO conventional forces, particularly about the coming together of a number of developing technologies: the ability to hit from a distance with precision weapons, reconnaissance assets, and command, control and communication technologies. Nuclear war could not be fought but information age war has been fought and would be fought.

It, however, gradually became clear that the Soviets had portrayed the revolution too narrowly. They had focussed on technology and weapons rather than the organisational dimension of warfare. The "1991 war with Iraq crystallized awareness among military planners in the United Stated on this momentous issue."[21]

Andrew Marshall defined the contemporary RMA "as a major change in the nature of warfare". He added that it was not brought about only by advancement of technology but "by the innovative application of new technologies which, combined with dramatic changes in military doctrine and operational and organizational concepts, fundamentally alter the character and conduct of military revolutions."[22]

He makes no distinction between change in the *nature* of war and *character* of war.Many analysts do not accept this point and hold that present and past RMAs changed the character of warfare but not its basis nature.

Anyway, technology cannot alone explain the new revolution—it has to be accompanied by, as Marshal put it, "dramatic" changes in doctrine, operational concepts and organisational concepts. And these do not easily change as the military has its conservatism and for good reasons. As Lambeth himself adds, "A 'revolution in military affairs' cannot be spawned merely by platforms, munitions and other hardware equities. These necessary but insufficient preconditions must be supported by an important set of intangibles that have determined war results since the days of Alexander the Great—namely, clarity of goals backed by proficiency and boldness in execution."[23]

It was earlier felt on the basis of Operation Desert Storm that air power would play the pivotal role in the new RMA. The 'pivotal' role of air power in Operation Desert Storm was, however, by no means self-evident. It widened the divide among analysts. "Land warfare specialists continue to insist that it takes 'boots on the ground' to consummate a win and that air operations can at best, produce only transitory effects on an able opponent. Air power proponents, in contrast, have grown more and more inclined to argue that the ability of modern air power to affect land warfare has crossed a threshold in which its effects are fundamentally greater than ever before."[24] There is also another development. By the 1990s, the Western societies appeared unwilling to tolerate large scale casualties as in the past wars. This also led to emphasis on RMA and the pivotal role to be played by air power.

In technology, ideas, and organisations, the United States is in a class of its own and it is not expected to face peer competition in the near future. It is advancing the frontier of regular military capability. The military revolution currently underway in the United States is keyed technologically *to the exploitation of the computer*, and is designed to succeed against both regular and irregular enemies.[25]

The question arises: is this RMA only about exploitation of the computer or rather of emerging technology?

In an oft -quoted article(1994) on RMA titled, "Cavalry to Computer: The Pattern of Military Revolution", Andrew F. Krepinevich begins by saying: "Over the next several decades, the world is destined to experience a revolution in the *character* of warfare. Indeed, the way in which the United States and its allies won a quick and overwhelming victory in the Gulf War suggests to many that we are already in the early stages of a military revolution. But if so, there is much more to come."[26]

Thus, Krepinevich puts the present information-led revolution as a continuum to earlier RMAs, as also in the context of future warfare. This was done with a view to draw lessons from them, and indicate important elements and conditions necessary for the success of an RMA. It also stated that it is the *character* of war that would undergo change and, by implication, not the *nature* of war.

There have been several RMAs in the past and there would be future RMAs.

The record of past RMAs is spread over seven centuries, beginning in the 14th century with the Infantry Revolution which saw infantry displacing the dominant role of cavalry on the battlefield. This was succeeded by the Artillery Revolution in the 15th century which was made possible by several technological improvements, namely, lengthening of the gun barrel, metallurgical breakthroughs and improvements in gunpowder. The Artillery Revolution was expensive to exploit.

Napoleon's genius was to integrate the advances in technology, military systems, military organisations, including his staff system, to realise a dramatic leap in military effectiveness over military formations that existed only a short time before.

The Naval Revolution was led by the French. In 1846, they pioneered the adoption of steam propulsion and screw propellers on auxiliary ships. In the late 1850s, France began constructing the first sea-going iron-clad fleet. The British responded quickly to the French innovation.

Between the Napoleonic Wars and the American Civil War, the introduction of railroads and telegraph again dramatically transformed the character of war. In the Civil War, the railway nets greatly enhanced strategic mobility and the ability to sustain large armies in the field. The telegraph dramatically enhanced the ability of military leaders to mass their forces quickly at the point of decision and coordinate widely dispersed operations.

Finally, in the mid-20th century, the Nuclear Revolution, especially after the coupling of nuclear warheads to ballistic missiles, brought the prospect of near instantaneous and complete destruction of a state's economic and political fabric and convinced all observers that a fundamental change in the *character of warfare* was at hand. In the eyes of some important analysts, once nuclear weapons were stockpiled in significant numbers, they could not be employed effectively and *their only utility was in deterring war*. But the important point is that this did not prevent the emergence of very different war-fighting doctrines and military organisations among nuclear states. That meant that the nature of warfare does not change.

RMA refers to radical change in the *character* of war, not in its *nature.* Engines of such change include, but are by no means limited to, technological innovations. It was expected to have profound consequences for global and regional military balances, and, thus, for US defence planning.[27]

The military revolutions changed "the rules of the game" and in so doing, they often "devalued formerly dominant elements of military power, including weaponry, weapons platforms and doctrines. *Military organizations that did not adapt in a rapidly changing, highly competitive environment, have declined, often quite quickly."*[28] (Italics mine.)

From this kind of historical survey of previous revolutions in military affairs, the most important observation that comes out and is relevant for us is: emerging technologies only make military revolutions possible but to exploit their full potential, these technologies must be incorporated within new processes and executed by new organisational structures. "*Failure to realize a great increase in military effectiveness typically resulted not so much from technological change as from a failure to create new operational concepts and build new organizations."*[29]

This bring to the fore the organisational dimension of RMA and innovative operational concepts, the neglected aspects in our modernisation effort. The most important example of organisational innovation occurred in early 1940 when Germany defeated the Allied forces and conquered France in six weeks, though at that time British and French armoured forces were equal to Germany in size and quality; both the Allies and the Germans had modern aircraft and radios. In the inter-war years, however, it was the German military that identified both the operational concept to integrate these new military systems and the organisation needed to activate this concept. It was the operational concepts and organisational flexibility that allowed the Germans to exploit these concepts and the *blitzkrieg* concept became a reality.

Another important point that emerges is the importance of *perception of future contingencies* and *likely enemies* that would determine whether and when there is full exploitation of the advantages offered by the military revolution. This should be a very important aspect of modernisation, not for example, preparing for a "spectrum of conflict" which is appearing in our strategic literature. In the name of the 'uncertainty' factor, one need not ignore who would be the likely adversary and the capabilities that are likely to employed against us by the enemy, to gain strategic advantage.

Despite the experience of War World I, the world's major naval powers tended to discount the effectiveness of strategic warfare conducted by submarines.

In strategic matters involving modernisation, *focus* on the most likely contingency and the enemy is important, not preparing for various contingencies. In the inter-war period, while Britain prepared for various naval contingencies, the United States and Japan saw each other as by far the most prominent challenger, and organised their naval forces around a single contingency, that is, a Pacific War. As a result, " The Americans and the Japanese exploited the revolution in naval aviation far more proficiently than the British, *in part because of their ability to focus more precisely.*"[30]

The Gulf War of 1991showed us only glimpse of a potential influence of this revolution in military effectiveness. It is also clear that there is not only one path for unfolding of this revolution but several. As long as there are several competitors exploiting the potential of the emerging military revolution, the revolution will take several paths. This is because of the competitors' different strategic goals, access to relevant resources and *strategic culture*.

Strategic culture will no doubt play a big part in how the potentiality of revolution exploited. But the overwhelming importance of strategic goals in defining the path cannot be denied.

After analysing the contemporary military revolution and the past revolutions, Krepinevich distinguishes four elements (widely accepted) which are essential to comprise a revolution. These elements are: technological change, systems development, operational innovation, and organisational adaptation. "Each of these elements is in itself a necessary, but not a sufficient condition for realizing the large gains in military effectiveness that characterize military revolutions. In particular, while advances in technology typically underwrite a military revolution, they do not alone constitute a revolution. The phenomena is much broader in scope and consequence than technological innovation, however dramatic."[31]

Most analysts define RMA as a discontinuous increase in military capability and effectiveness arising from simultaneous and mutually supportive change in technology, systems, operational methods, and military organisations.

The current RMA is characterised by four types of change:

- extremely precise, stand-off strikes;
- dramatically improved command, control, and intelligence;
- information warfare; and
- non-lethality.

Some analysts draw attention to another important point: the current revolution in military affairs seems to have at least two stages. The drive to limit military casualties, stand-off platforms, stealth, precision, information dominance, and missile defence is the first stage.

The second would be robotics, non-lethality, and elaborate cyber defence. Non-lethality because there would increasingly be security challenges where using lethal equipment may be counter-productive.

Steps are now required to be taken for ushering in the second stage, by reinvesting in robotics, nano-technology and micro-electrics, that is, more attention in R&D to these technologies, by making adequate investments. The scope and possibilities are enormous.

It was contended by analysts that the RMA may see a transition from concern with *centres of gravity to a* less mechanistic and more sophisticated notion of interlinked systems.

Some important observations are contained in an insightful paper by Stephen Metz and James Keivit in June 1995, prepared for the Strategic Studies Institute of the US Army, analysing the experience of earlier RMAs:

- In every RMA, there is a point of critical mass where concepts, organisations, and technologies meld to bring about the revolution. For a military revolution to reach critical mass, and get a breakthrough, there has to some protection from the higher level management while it changes concepts,and reorganises.[32]
- Revolutionary breakthroughs eventually generate responses from other states.
- Responses can be symmetric, asymmetric, or, most often, a combination of the two.
- Revolutions in military affairs appear to follow a cyclical pattern with initial stasis followed by initiation, critical mass, consolidation, response, and return to stasis.
- In the 21st century, the quantum increase in the pace of organisational adaptation and the extent of global communication will make the advantages flowing from a revolutionary breakthrough, *fleeting*. The revolutionary cycle,in other words, will be compressed. Future RMAs will occur in such rapid sequence that military affairs will appear to be in "permanent revolution."
- One risk is that the current RMA, if it continues in its present trajectory, will not generate increased combat effectiveness against the most likely or most dangerous future opponents. The "perfect" opponent for a military structured around the current RMA is a "middle level" enemy with rigid, centralised decision-making, relying on limited range, easy-to detect weapon platforms such as tanks, conventional artillery, and manned aircraft. But the utility of the current RMA, with its stress on precision, stand-off strikes, falls dramatically toward the poles of the military/technology spectrum. Opponents at the low end of the spectrum tend to operate in a widely dispersed fashion and emit a limited electronic signature, thus, complicating targeting. Their organisation is often cellular, making decapitation difficult. If they are insurgents, they intermingle with the population.

- Another risk is that the greater the intensity with which the United States pursues the current RMA, the greater the intensity with which opponents or potential opponents will seek counter-measures.

Why then, should the USA actively pursue the current RMA? The authors answer it in the following way:

First, it should bring significant increases in combat effectiveness against some mid-level opponents.

Second,as many analysts have pointed out, a force built around stand-off, precision weapons and disruptive information warfare capabilities would, because of decreased friendly casualties and reduced collateral damage, be more politically usable than traditional force projection military.

Third, by removing some of the fetters on the use of American military power, the RMA could augment deterrence.

Technological development is the easy part of RMA; reshaping attitudes and adapting organisations, doctrine, education, and training is extraordinarily hard.

The three points made above indicate why RMA became such an important concept in US strategic thinking during the last two decades.

There was some disagreement among analysts as to whether the 1991 Gulf War was the harbinger of a revolution involving long-range high-precision efficient warfare or more of a culmination of trends that had been underway for decades . Many exponents of air power declared that the Gulf War was in realisation of the 50-year quest for the decisive application of air power in war.

But something more fundamental was happening, that is the increasing, importance of a new medium. It is the importance of cyberspace, which may be understood as the sum of the globe's communication links and computational nodes. Because of this medium, any piece of data can show up anywhere almost instantly which, as Martin Libicki, in an important article points out ,can transform the geography of national security. With each new medium comes a new geographical logic. When ballistic missiles made space a medium of conflict, that permitted the United States and the Soviet Union to hold each other directly at risk.[33]

Cyberspace is a medium which is largely in the future, Libicki wrote in 1996, when computer application was in the early stages. "It is virtually certain that electronics will be ten times more cost-effective in five years, and , probably, hundred times more cost-effective in ten years. It is this more pervasive cyberspace of tomorrow that is the proper realm of consideration."[34]

In the contemporary revolution of military affairs, there are new instruments of national power that erase geography, "culminating in new instruments for the international security arrangement.." This is an extremely important point to which we shall come later.

The point that needs emphasis now, is consideration of a "vast set of devices—sensing, emitting, communicating, redirecting, cuing, filtering, pinpointing, classifying, and creating target determinations—and then picturing the artificial lines among them, segregating them into air force, navy, marine, and army assets, each reporting up their separate chains of command. Silly, no doubt–yet all that today's jointness aspires to be able to do, is to define, after years of wrangling, the various ways in which these devices may be allowed to talk to each other if given permission."[35] A system of systems can only then emerge.

How might a potential adversary counter such a system of system? Weapons of mass destruction comprise one such method. However, in an era of proliferating information technology and burgeoning arms market, an adversary can keep the United States at bay without such weapons as a "relatively low cost system of systems can be cobbled together using third –party satellite imagery, UAVs, digital cameras, cellular communications , and detailed terrain imagery on Cd-ROMs."[36]

In the UK, *The Economist* in March 1997, noting this as an "embryonic revolution," observed that unlike the development of nuclear warfare, this has not emerged in response to a specific threat to the United States or its allies, but would be useful in the future if a threat emerges. "In that, it may resemble *blitzkrieg* , which was based on the technologies of the 1920s, when defence budgets were declining and there seemed little prospect of another war."[37] It quoted Andrew Marshall of the Pentagon, who stated that the revolution was just beginning , it was "in the phase of thinking, analysis and war-games" and in the future, more money would need to be spent "on getting the forces to experiment with new sorts of operation."

This made it clear that RMA was not just about technology or air power, but about how future warfare would be conducted, for which a lot more experiments and exploratory analyses would be involved.

The article in *The Economist* also raised some basic questions:

- How will it affect the way armies fight and are organised?
- Will it make much difference to "low-intensity" conflicts such as guerrilla warfare?
- How easily can the new techniques be countered?
- Will this revolution make America unchallengeable?

The continued validity of these questions can be seen from subsequent developments.

There were also some serious strategic implications of this revolution which was unfolding which properly interpreted very important implications for modernisation and force planning.

Since defences against missiles will not be foolproof, ports and air bases would be increasingly vulnerable and logistical chains will be harder to sustain. That means forces will need to carry more supplies with them. Further, "Warriors and their machines will find stealth and mobility more useful than armour."[38]

But there were two more important points emanating from the RMA which may change the character of future war. The new warfare will be 'multi-dimensional' in that not only air, sea and land operations will get integrated, but also that *information* and *outer space* will be other dimensions of modern war which would gain more and more importance.

"Information warfare" could mean disabling an enemy by wrecking his computing, financial, telecom or air traffic control systems. In this context, the potent weapons would be computer viruses, eletro-magnetic pulses, microwave beams, etc.

On the battlefield, the information warrior will aim to create an 'information gap' between his side and the foe. He will target the enemy's information gathering capacity and try to mislead it.

Chronologically speaking, by 1998, there was rough consensus among strategic analysts that "the pace at which information and communications technologies have been evolving, coupled with other late twentieth century technical innovations, could make current times the most *discontinuous period of warfare* since modern armored forces, *blitzkrieg* tactics, combat aircraft, aircraft carriers, and radar were developed in the period from roughly 1915 to 1945. *There is also agreement that RMAs do not simply happen; they are created by a combination of technological breakthrough, institutional adaptation, and warfighting innovation."* (Italics mine.)[39]

As the RMA is to be created by war-fighting innovations and institutional adaptation backed up by technological breakthroughs, there is no predetermined path for an RMA.

We have also to take note of the point that the perceived importance of air power changed irreversibly in the popular imagination after the first Gulf War, where it played a pivotal role. As Benjamin Lambeth , a great supporter of this point of view, put it in an important article in 1997, "This change was the product of long-sought convergence of modern technology, intensive and realistic training, astute planning, leadership quality, bold concepts of operation and focused strategy."[40] He listed new air and space technologies that will shape future warfare. "These technologies are mainly in the areas of projecting power, imposing lethal effects from a safe distance, and enhancing situational awareness."[41]

These new technology options for the US Air Force were divided into four categories:

- Combat and Combat Support Platforms.
- Munitions and Other Disabling Mechanisms.
- Sensors and Other Awareness Enhancements.
- Information-Processing and Communications Systems.

Operation Desert Storm showed glimpses of what this RMA could do in the last century, and in this century, it was more decisively shown in Operation Iraqi Freedom (as part of the global war on terror) which was launched on March 19, 2003, by the USA and Coalition forces under the strategy of 'preemption' with a view to change the regime which posed, as per their assessment , a threat to peace with weapons of mass murder.

After about seven weeks of war ,President Bush declared on May 1, 2003, that major combat operations in Iraq had ended and the United States and its allies had prevailed. It was supposed to be a crucial advance in the campaign against terror and as President Bush stated, "No terrorist network will gain weapons of mass destruction from the Iraqi regime, because that regime is no more."[42] From the way the US President described the war in his speech, there was no doubt that in his view and that of his close advisers, it exhibited the most efficient application of the principles of the contemporary RMA. To quote, "Operation Iraqi Freedom was carried out with the combination of precision and speed and boldness the enemy did not expect, and the world had not seen before. From distant bases or ships at sea, we sent planes and missiles that could destroy an enemy division, or strike a single bunker."[43] He added, "With new tactics and precision weapons, we can achieve military objectives without directing violence against civilians."

If any aspect has influenced our thoughts in our modernisation effort, one can probably say it is that of realising the importance of air power in having a decisive influence on warfare , though there has not been in-depth analysis of this aspect in the context of RMA. Interpretation of RMA has also varied depending on the Service perspective. Air power, in most of the discussions in the air force has been referred to as aerospace power , which means synergy between air and space in the operational context ,leading to enormous increase in the capabilities of air power.

Noting that the information revolution is primarily based on satellite-based capabilities which also enhances the capability for surveillance, reconnaissance, communication, global positioning and timing, one eminent air force office states that these "vital space capabilities are translated into a 'revolution in military affairs' by leading to a *fundamental change in the nature of warfare.*."[44] (Italics mine.)

This fundamental change in the nature of warfare is supposed to occur due to enhanced situational awareness , simultaneous prosecution of war from the periphery to the deep centre, transformation from linear to non-linear prosecution of war and classical division levels of war, that, is strategic, operational and tactical.

This is, no doubt, a highly ambitious version of the RMA. As mentioned above, this was the characteristic of the nuclear era RMA. Nuclear weapons in the mid-Sixties were supposed to *"radically change the nature of modern war."* This change in the nature of war brought about by nuclear weapons was due to their ability to achieve strategic military and military political goals at the very beginning of the war without going through the classic sequence of methodical plodding from tactical through operational-level to strategic goals.[45]

Aerospace capability makes it possible to target the leadership command and control from the very beginning and it is possible to achieve "paralysis of the leadership" which can lead to "strategic paralysis" of the enemy. "This singular transformation of the nature of war from the age-old pattern of 'destruction-based warfare' is almost entirely due to aerospace power." This transformation, it is contended, has ensured that future wars would be dominated by the aerospace paradigm.[46]

This point of view is not shared by most of the analysts of RMA. For many of them, it is still a hypothesis. The claim of most analysts is that RMA changes the *character of war*, but its *nature,* as defined by Clausewitz, remains the same. The grammar of war is always evolving, but it would be subordinated to political purposes. Therefore, the distinction between strategy and tactics will always remain.

From aerospace power, attention gets drawn to India's space capabilities and modernisation of the military gets linked to it. It is stressed, that in spite of limited budgetary resources, "there is inescapable need to give due cognisance to the development of a credible, if modest, capability in space" and, therefore, "the Services need to finance and direct a infrastructure dedicated to the development and manufacture of space vehicles and related hardware."[47] The emphasis here is on a common space programme to be used by all the three Services. In the same context, it is stated that that we have today a number of sensors providing a variety of information, all of which is being analysed more or less in isolation. The quality of the data output would be enhanced manifold were all types of data to be integrated and fused under the same roof.

Recommendation is also made for setting up a dedicated Space Command, the need for which has been expressed in several forums.

Space systems have already become vitally important to the performance of greater military powers and especially to the USA. This importance will grow. The information dominance, that is the core of the US approach to future warfare, and the capability for distant precision strike are critically dependent on C4ISTAR benefits. The extensive use of space gives unequal advantages in favour of the USA.

As Colin Gray points out, on the basis of evidence of history, "It is a rule in strategy...that anything of great strategic importance to one belligerent, for that reason, has to be worth attacking by others. And the greater that importance, the greater has to be the incentive to damage, disable, capture or destroy it."[48] Therefore, space war is a certainty in the future. In this context, one has to make a distinction between space control and space denial. The enemies of the USA, for example, may be more interested in space denial than space control.

An anti-satellite can be anything ground-based. Signal transmitters on the ground direct ascent rockets which are deployed on the ground and many more. Then there is also the concept of dual use. "Ballistic Missile Defence (BMD), save of the most modest kind, can hardly avoid providing anti-satellite capability against spacecraft in LEO. Satellites are far more fragile than are reentry vehicles with warheads."[49]

War from space has to be seen in the context of war as a whole. Therefore, space warfare will have both political and strategic contexts. Warfare inherently is a joint undertaking.

Eliot Cohen, who was not an enthusiast of RMA, noted, "The Gulf War showed air power off to great advantage but in extremely favorable circumstances : the United States brought to bear a force sized and trained to fight the Soviet Union...chose the time and place at which combat would begin in a theater ideally suited to air operations. Knowledgeable observers remained skeptical that a revolution had taken place."[50] Cohen also points out that despite the attention lavished on "smart" bombs during the1991 Persian Gulf War, for example, most of the ordnance in that conflict consisted of 1950s technology unguided bombs dropped by aircraft developed in the 1960s and, in some cases, in the 1970s. But he also stated, "A revolution in military affairs is underway. It will require change of a magnitude that military people still do not completely grasp and political leaders do not fully imagine."[51] For the moment, it appeared that RMA had offered the United States, the prospect of military power which could not be imagined earlier.

What implications it has it for India's modernisation effort may be the most important question to be tackled by the Ministry of Defence and Government of India.

Network-Centric Warfare (NCW) has become the most important concept under transformation. The goal is to exploit information technologies to shift from platform-centric to network-centric operations. In the current platform-centric model of operation, individual military assets (e.g. ships, aircraft, etc) engage enemy targets head-to-head; in the future, a decentralised network of forces will be used in order to engage targets efficiently, precisely and quickly, from greater distance and from all directions. A network of sensors will provide unmatched awareness of the battle space. Smaller, lighter, faster and less complex nodes linked by networks will present adversaries with fewer high-value targets. NCW promises to achieve greater effects using smaller and dispersed groups of forces. This is the most important implication of NCW, that is, military transformation requires major changes not only in doctrine and organisation but also in the equipment that the Services buy. For example, most classes of warships for the US Navy have been multi-role, and, thus, require complex integrated sub-systems within relatively large hulls. Network-centric ships would introduce new metrics which are intended to be deployed in large numbers to facilitate 'self-synchronisation' and they will serve as nodes for the network. This will call for new ship designs with different qualities and capabilities.[52]

NCW is likely to rely on unmanned vehicles, particularly UAVs. Whether it would have the required support of operational users, who have a platform-centric approach, is the big question. But UAVs require intense human operator participation, where the 'capability gap' may arise.

Absence of analysis in India of issues pertaining to RMA could mean that either we are not overwhelmed by the RMA thesis or we may still be treating it as a 'hypothesis' to be proved, or kept away from discussions, as we are content to treat 'modernisation as an on-going process' and implementation of RMA would call for discontinuity in our investment efforts. But this is surprising, especially after China, having analysed the way the second Gulf War was conducted, issued a White Paper on National Defence in 2004. It cannot be anybody's case that RMA debates are the concern only of the USA as the information revolution has affected all the countries and there is fast diffusion of technology.

Absence of debate may also to lead to inadvertently following the path in which a lot of scepticism is present, and we may be investing in a way which may have only limited returns.

The current RMA gains its potency from the integration of various technologies to form systems and networks. So there is no easy route to it. It is a creative endeavour, and, therefore, a challenge for innovative thinking. Not accepting the challenge means we are happy with the conservative view. That may be necessary to some extent, but not adequate in an era of fast changes. Analyses of trends in the RMA debate should help us to be selective in our modernisation efforts and also help in putting in place institutions within Service Headquarters for creative endeavours which RMA demands. It is creative thinking which RMA can foster, which is of importance, as also healthy scepticism of extravagant claims made by proponents of RMA which detailed analyses of its various aspects can bring about.

The QDR of the USA of 1997 became the basis for modernisation of the US military which was influenced by the RMA analysis. Joint Vision 2010 prepared at the same time by the Chairman, Joint Chiefs of Staff, was about achieving information superiority, dominant manoeuvre, precision engagement, full dimensional protection, and focussed logistics within a decade.

Gaining information superiority over the enemy became the key concept under RMA. The Chairman, Joint Chiefs of Staff, in 1999 noted, "Information operations and information superiority are the core of military innovation and our vision for the future of joint warfare... The capability to penetrate, manipulate, and deny an adversary's battle space awareness is of utmost importance."[53]

The Kosovo operation (1999) exposed the problems with this concept of information superiority, though it was claimed as a great success in terms of showing the efficacy of RMA capabilities and these of air power.

Even with complete information superiority, one cannot destroy the target if the enemy knows that an attack is coming and simply moves it or replaces it with a dummy target.

Though bigger claims were made by the Pentagon about battlefield damage caused by precision bombing in the Kosovo operation, in July 1999, The *Aviation Week and Space Technology* reported that NATO had dropped 3,000 precision-guided weapons that resulted in 500 hits on decoys, but destroyed only 50 Yugoslav tanks. One report citing the British Ministry of Defence sources stated that damage done to tanks was perhaps even less than the lowest quoted figure of 13 tank kills.[54] Damage to artillery pieces was also not much. There were informed comments to the effect that it was not air power but Russia's withdrawal of support for Serbia that probably brought an end to the war.

If the analysis is inadequate, then information superiority is not enough. There can be miscalculation because of the inability of information technology systems and analysts to properly assess and interpret what the 'information superiority picture' really showed. The Commander-in-Chief of NATO's Allied Forces, Southern Europe, noted in an interview in September 1999, that too much information has the potential to reduce a military leader's awareness of an unfolding situation. "Information saturation is additive to the 'fog of war'... uncontrolled, it will control you and your staffs and lengthen your decision-cycle times."[55] The most important lesson learnt from the Kosovo War was that information superiority overload can actually hurt mission performance.

In the 2001 QDR, the emphasis was on *transformation* though the route was through RMA. The concept of CBP was introduced . CBP covered more dimensions than technology and the order for its implementation was issued by the US Secretary of Defence in 2003.

But by 2004, it was realised that the challenges of asymmetric warfare called for change in priorities in the modernisation effort. The Strategic Planning Guidance (SPG) 2006-11, issued in March 2004 reflected the

Pentagon's thinking that traditional warfare capability must go hand in hand with a broader set of capabilities to deal with new security challenges presented by the global war on terrorism.

In this context, the lessons of the Lebanon War of 2006 where Israeli Defence Force–IDF faced unexpected challenges from Hezbollah are important. The Israeli leadership put their faith in air power as a low-casualty answer for modern warfare. They assumed that strategic bombing could win the war without the commitment of land forces. The successful NATO aerial operation of 1999 in Kosovo was referred to by Israeli leaders for basing their strategy on air power. They were influenced by the doctrine of 'effect-based' operations.

But the adversary in Lebanon was significantly different from the adversary in Kosovo. Whereas the Serbians used more conventional tactics, Hezbollah relied on guerrilla style tactics against which air power had less impact. Hezbollah hid the rocket launchers among the civilian population. "Not only were the targets difficult to hit using air power, Hezbollah's tactic of hiding targets among civilians meant that the inevitable casualties fanned the flames of support for Hezbollah."[56] Hezbollah's advantage was that it lacked high–value targets. Therefore, Isarel's main targets became the Hezbollah leadership, fielded forces, and weapons hidden among civilians, and difficult to target. The collateral damage had the opposite effect.

The centres of gravity against asymmetric adversaries may become the political will of the citizens.[57] Again , probably one basic lesson learnt was that the very nature of war makes bloodshed likely, and the leadership should be prepared for it.

What would be the possible directions that an RMA can take? Kane and Lonsdale try to answer the question by directing attention to elements of the *nature of war* as brought out by Clausewitz. "Core elements of the nature of war influence the possible direction RMAs can take. Purported RMAs come and go, but the nature of war is constant. There are four elements of the Clausewitzian nature of war that most heavily influence how changes to the character may develop: policy(which itself develops from geo-strategic conditions), interaction with the enemy, the climate of war, and war's polymorphous character. Individually, these four elements are not so dominant, but taken together, they produce an inescapable reality."[58]

A developing RMA will be shaped by policy requirements. For example, during the inter-war years, various European powers perceived armoured forces differently, which can be partially explained by differences in policy objectives. "Military innovation is rarely contained in one actor. Thus, different variants of an RMA may develop from the same technological base."[59]

For the United States, the current RMA is about digitisation of forces and an increased reliance on stand-off unmanned capabilities. Those facing the conventional superiority of the United States may adopt a different approach. They may adopt a more primitive form of irregular warfare, using the technology of the information age where it enhances their operations like making good use of modern communication and encryption to better co-ordinate their operations. War is an interactive pursuit. Clausewitz described it as a duel on a larger scale where each side has the objective of throwing the other off balance. The enemy has various options to circumvent or offset RMA-based capabilities. Also the security environment changes and policy objectives may change, leading to change in missions. Such a change was clearly evident after 9/11 and at the end of regular hostilities in Iraq. Counter-insurgency operations in Iraq and Afghanistan called for an approach based on dismounted operations.

The other relates to space. Military satellites would play a crucial role in it. America, which has made maximum use of space and has undisputed superiority, has not apparently deployed space-based weapons. But if, at some point, a power such as China sought to challenge American superiority by launching sophisticated military satellites, America might be tempted to militarise space.

Perhaps, a tacit understanding on non-militarising space would emerge among the major powers.

America is quite concerned in its strategic thinking about the implications of a "rising China" and the Chinese capability in launching satellites and other space-based capabilities is no longer in doubt.

We may briefly look at the PLA's approach to RMA in the context of modernisation, as depicted by Western analysts. An official 1998 US

Department of Defence report noted, “In recent years, the PLA has shown an exceptional interest in information warfare and has begun programs to develop IW capabilities at strategic, operational, and tactical levels. The PLA’s interest in IW is reflected particularly in the number of articles which appear frequently in military publications and in the use of IW-related scenarios in exercises and war-games.”[60]

The NATO attacks on the former Yugoslavia in 1999 produced a major debate in the PLA. They were particularly impressed by the success of the aerial bombardment campaign in Yugoslavia. As the PLA was primarily a ground force, analysts argued that it had to adjust its force structure, command and control system, training and education as well as weapons acquisition. More importantly, the PLA had to change its air defence concepts. The extensive use of cruise missiles and other PGMs from a distance in the Kosovo campaign meant that war could be prosecuted from great distances and prompted the PLA to undertake a review of strategic air defences and offensive counter-weapons capable of destroying enemy targets from a distance. “As a result of the Yugoslav War, and particularly as a result of the lessons derived from the PLA’s study of the air war, a new program known as the ‘three attacks and three defenses’ was initiated throughout the military beginning in late 1999. The ‘three attacks’ are attacking stealth aircraft, cruise missiles, and armed helicopters. The ‘three defenses’ are defending against enemy reconnaissance and surveillance, precision strikes, and electronic interference. Since 2000, units in various military regions have reported that they have integrated the new strategy into their training regimen.”[61]

But, as Shambaugh points out, PLA analysts took consolation in the Serbian fortitude against NATO’s firepower and were heartened to realise that it would be much easier for China to absorb such punishment as the expanse of China would definitely play to China’s advantage.[62] On the other hand, with regard to China’s potential coercion of Taiwan, the Yugoslav conflict was not encouraging either. Throughout the 1990s, the PLA doctrine evolved a great deal as a result of study of foreign conflicts. ‘Jointness’, mobility, surprise and preemptive attacks were now seen as important ingredients of modern war. If ground forces had to be committed to combat, the enemy's command , control , and logistics should be destroyed first.

By 1999, the PLA completed a new version of 'military doctrine' or the principles that guide military operations, which include both operational doctrine and operational practice. China's primary operational strategy guideline is called "active defense". While in explanation of this strategy they maintain that it is oriented towards self-defence and they would attack only after the enemy has struck, this is not what the PLA officers are taught where they are told that under high-tech conditions, for the defensive side, the strategy of striking only after the enemy has struck does not mean to wait passively until the enemy has struck.[63]

At the same time, Shambaugh felt that despite progress and the importance attached to information warfare and related technologies, there are impediments to the PLA developing and assimilating RMA era technologies into the force structure. "Some are cultural, some political, some organizational, some technological, and some generational. To begin with, information is a controlled commodity in China….Generally speaking, technical information, particularly in the scientific and military sectors, is disseminated on the 'need to know basis'. The general bifurcation of civilian and military information in China is a further impediment. For the PLA to join the RMA requires a more fundamental loosening of information flow within Chinese society and between civilian and military sectors."[64] Rigid social and professional hierarchies discourage flexibility.

The Chinese doctrine has evolved in this century. In this decade, the major evolution in strategy and operations involves shifting from "Joint Operations"(JO) to "Integrated Joint Operations" (IJO) It shows that the PLA is beginning to incorporate lessons learnt from the American campaigns in the last two decades and has realised the benefits of organisational change and widespread use of information technologies. IJO begins to accept that Service divisions do not matter when command chains can be flat. The move toward IJO was reflected in the 2004 decision by the PLA to make commanders of the navy, air force, and Second Artillery members of the Central Military Commission's high command.[65]

PLA scholars at the Academy of Military Science in Beijing tried to learn what they could from the American think-tanks about RMA. As per a recent article, Gen Chen Zhou, the main author of four most recent defence White Papers , in a meeting with *The Economist* said, "We studied RMA exhaustively. Our great hero was Andy Marshall in the Pentagon [the powerful head of the Office of Net Assessment who was known as the Pentagon's futurist-in-chief]. We translated every word he wrote."[66]

Gen Chen described the period upto 2010 as "laying the foundations of modernized forces." The next decade could see the roll-out of what is called *mechanisation*, which means deployment of advanced military platforms and *informatisation*, which means bringing them together as a network. As per the Chinese assessment, the two processes should be completed in terms of equipment, integration and training by 2020. In other words, the steps toward RMA as far as the Chinese are concerned, though challenging, are well thought out and well planned out. As they candidly say, the biggest challenge is in the technology. "We do not always know how to make our investments when technology is both overlapping and leapfrogging."[67] According to reports by RAND and CSBA, China is well on it way to having the means to deter American aircraft carriers and aircraft from operating within what is known as the 'first island chain'.[68]

It does not come as a surprise that along with doctrinal and structural reforms in the PLA to bring in RMA, the last fifteen years have seen enormous progress in the modernisation of China's military-industrial sector. This has been the key to their modernisation efforts and would take them to a more advanced level of RMA than has been witnessed so far. For example, China is developing military lasers for a range of applications. Revelations in 2006 that China had used high-power lasers against US satellites again focussed attention to this threat. "In the next decade, it is possible that the PLA will field new laser weapons for anti-air and ground attack missions. Lasers could arm unmanned aerial vehicles (UAVs) and satellites as well."[69] The PLA is also developing a family of radio frequency weapons, including Electromagnetic Pulse (EMP) warheads and High-Power Microwave (HPM) on short range ballistic missiles as key future weapons for information warfare. EMP weapons could be used to disable an aircraft carrier by degrading all important integrated circuits and chips and, thus, paralysing the radar and telecommunication system of the aircraft carrier and vessels around it. The PLA is developing a range of airborne unmanned aircraft (UAV, UCAV), as also unmanned ship and underwater vehicles.

"The PLA is investing heavily in nanotechnology and appears to understand that this is a key transformational military technology."[70]

Widespread use of foreign advanced modelling and design software and all-round absorption of foreign-made military components have played a key role in the growing success of China's defence industries. There is also lot of competition among firms. In 2002, there were about 10,000 firms in the PRC in direct relationships with the PLA. There are efforts to promote competition among consortia of industries. The PLA has allowed this sector to have access to sources of funding other than state funds. In June 2007, the Commission of Science, Technology and Industry for National Defence (COSTIND), National Development and Resource Commission, issued new guidelines to allow domestic and foreign investment in defence firms which enabled state-owned weapons development and production concerns to invest in riskier technologies.[71]

This indicates that the RMA is moving into the second and more radical phase. The way war is fought may be transformed. New breakthrough technologies can bring this about. Till now, technology has been the enabler of the RMA. But technology, as Stephen Metz points out, "can also be *an independent variable, forcing uncomfortable changes* and sometimes, eroding stability and order. New technologies or new combinations of technology have the potential to alter not only tactics and operational methods, but military strategy itself."[72] (Italics mine.) For example, " Coming decades are likely to see the proliferation of robots around the world and in many walks of life...However fast the evolution of robotics proceeds, it will invariably affect armed conflict. Initially, the prime function of military robotics will be to replace humans in particularly dangerous or tedious functions...The real breakthrough and decision point will come when robots advance to the point that they have potential for combat use."[73] The other arena is miniaturisation. True revolution will come from maturation of micro-electro-mechanical systems or "MEMS". This technology will entail the construction of very tiny mechanical devices coupled to electrical sensors and actuators. To quote, the Defence Advanced Research Project Agency (DARPA) of USA, MEMS "will merge the functions of compute, communicate, and power together with sense, actuate, and control to change completely the way people and machines interact with the physical world."[74] Important analysts of RAND like Martin Libicki have speculated on modes of warfare to make maximum use of MEMS-based technology.

Are we taking steps toward the next round of RMA or steps to deter adversaries from going into the second phase of RMA? This is how our modernisation effort has to be given direction. Achieving technological breakthroughs, keeping pace with leapfrogging technology would be our main challenges toward modernisation, not acquiring more modern platforms. But our DRDO is moving at a sluggish pace. The attempt to set up the Defence Technology Mission is yet to succeed because of the bureaucratic sluggishness. The Services' linkages with industry are at a rudimentary stage. Guidelines for foreign investments in high technology areas are lacking. The example of China shows what need to be done to modernise our forces.

Modernisation also has a strategy depending on the likely adversary and the area of attack and its geography.

China's strategy is to deter America from intervening in a future crisis over Taiwan. As per the report in *The Economist*, China is investing heavily in "asymmetric capabilities" designed to blunt America's 'once- overwhelming' capacity to project power in this region. "This 'anti-access/ area denial' approach includes thousands of accurate land-based ballistic and cruise missiles, modern jets with anti-ship missiles, a fleet of submarines (both conventionally and nuclear-powered), long range radars and surveillance satellites, cyber and space weapons intended to 'blind' American forces."[75] The Pentagon's planners also think, as brought out by *The Economist*, that China is intent on acquiring what is "called in the jargon A2/ AD or 'anti-access/anti-satellite weapons to destroy or disable another nation's military assets from afar."[76]

America has also taken measures to counter these 'anti-access' capabilities by its transforming force structure, particularly for the navy. Here 'transformation' means transformation of the programmes. The decision taken to "transform the program to develop the next generation of destroyer, formerly known as DD-

21, into the Future Surface Combatant Program, now designated as DD(X) may provide an interesting example of this analysis. Two industrial teams ('Blue' and 'Gold') are competing in this high stakes game to 'produce a family of advanced technology surface combatants, not a single ship class'. The program will encompass everything from small littoral combatants to the next-generation cruiser."[77] Packing many complex technologies into a single hull is no longer the strategically right thing to do. These need to be dispersed to circumvent enemy capabilities. Military transformation requires not only major changes in doctrine and organisation but new kinds of equipment for the Services, incorporating innovations that support NCW.

In our modernisation effort towards transforming our forces, the biggest challenge is how to make the industry a partner of the military Services in inducting innovating technologies . Investments have to be made by them where risks are involved.

The Defence Ministry can help in this process by mitigating risks, allowing foreign investments, issuing the necessary guidelines and establishing partnerships with industry, which are the main challenges for getting into the RMA process which will be determined by technological breakthroughs achieved by the industry , both private and public. Modernisation can come only through this route not just by procurement from abroad.

Notes

1. Report of *The Hindu*, October 21, 2006.
2. Air Cmde Jasjit Singh "The Budget and the Blind Men," *The Indian Express,* March 3, 2005.
3. Lawrence Freedman, "Strategic Defence in the Nuclear Age," *Adephi Paper*, No. 221 (International Institute of Strategic Studies), Autumn 1987, pp. 14-15.
4. Arthur Smithies "Conceptual Framework of Program Budget" in David Novkked, ed., *Program Budgeting* (Harvard University Press).
5. Ibid., p. 45.
6. Ibid.
7. Frederick C. Mosher and John E. Harr, *Programming Systems and Foreign Affairs Leadership; An Attempted Innovation* (Oxford University Press, 1970), pp. 93-94.
8. Quoted by W. W. Kamufman in *The McNamara Revolution* (1964), p. 188.
9. Report of the Group of Ministers on National Security, February 1991, para 6.50 & 6.51.

10. Ibid., para 6.51.
11. Ibid., para 6.22.
12. RAND Arroyo Centre, "Improving the Army, Planning, Programming, Budgeting, and Execution System (PPBES), in Lesle Lewise et., al. *The Programming Plane* (1999), p. XVII.
13. Maj Gen Bains, ADGEP, Army HQ: "Budgeting and Financial Management in the Army," paper presented in a joint seminar on financial management at ASC Centre & College, Bangalore, August 2004.
14. RAND study, n. 12, pp. 6-7.
15. Ibid.
16. Colin S. Gray, *Another Bloody Century, Future Warfare* (Phoenix, 2005), p.118.
17. Thomas J. Kane and David J. Lonsdale, *Understanding Contemporary Strategy* (Routledge, 2012), p. 67.
18. Eliot A. Cohen, "A Revolution in Warfare", *Foreign Affairs*, March-April, 1996, p. 39.
19. Quoted by Benjamin S. Lambeth, "The Technology Revolution in Air Warfare", *Survival*, Spring 1997, pp.74-75.
20. Ibid.
21. Cohen., n.18.
22. Lambeth, n.19, pp. 74-75.
23. Ibid.
24. Ibid.
25. Gray, n.16, p. 51.
26. Andrew F. Krepinevich, "Cavalry to Computer: the Pattern of Military Revolution", *The National Interest*, Fall 1994, n. 37.
27. Ibid.
28. Ibid.
29. Ibid.
30. Ibid.
31. Ibid.
32. Stephen Metz and James Keivit, "Strategy and Revolution in Military Affairs: From Theory to Policy", paper prepared for Strategic Studies Institute of the US Army, June 27, 1995, in pdf.
33. Martin Libicki, "The Emerging Primacy of Information", *Orbis*, Spring 1996, p. 261.
34. Ibid.
35. Ibid., p. 264.
36. Ibid.
37. "The Future of Warfare", *The Economist*, March 8, 1997.
38. Ibid.

39. Michael E. O'Hanlon, "Beware the "RMA'nia", paper presented at the National Defence University, September 9, 1998. www.brooking.edu/views/ohanlon1998ndu.html.
40. Lambeth, n.19, pp. 65-83.
41. Ibid.
42. From excepts of the speech of President Bush to the crew of the USS *Abraham Lincoln* on May 1, 2003, in John Ehrenberg, et al., eds., *The Iraqi Papers* (Oxford University Press, 2010), p.175.
43. Ibid.
44. Air Cmde (nowAir Vice Mshl) M. Matheswaran, "Air Power to Aerospace Power", in Air Cmde Jasjit Singh (Retd), ed., *Aerospace Power and India's Defence* (Knowledge World and Centre for Air Power Studies, 2007), p.280.
45. Lambeth, n.19, pp. 74-75.
46. Matheswaran, n.44.
47. Air Vice Mshl D. N. Ganesh, "Military Objectives in Space Today", in Singh, ed., n.44, p. 258.
48. Colin S. Gray, "Another Bloody Century", Widenfield and Nicolson, 2005, 306-307.
49. Ibid., p.311.
50. Cohen, n.16, p. 41.
51. Ibid., p. 54.
52. Dombrowski, Gholz and Ross, "Buying Military Transformation: Defense Industry and Innovation", *Orbis*, 2002.
53. Quoted by Timothy L. Thomas, "Kosovo and the Current Myth of Information Superiority", *Parameters*, Spring 2000, p. 13.
54. Ibid.
55. Ibid.
56. Sarah E. Kreps, 'The 2006 Lebanon War: Lessons Learnt", *Parameters*, Spring 2007, p.78.
57. Ibid.
58. Kane and Lonsdale, n.17, p.79.
59. Ibid.
60. *Future Military Capabilities and Strategy of the People's Republic of China*, Report to Congress submitted by Secretary of Defence in 1998, quoted by David Shambaugh, Modernizing China's Military (University of California Press, 2002), p. 80.
61. Shambaugh, Ibid., pp. 86-87.
62. Fisher.
63. Richard D. Fisher Jr, *China's Military Modernization* (Stanford Security Studies,

2010), p. 69.

64. Shambuagh, n. 60, p. 80.
65. Fisher, n. 63, p. 70.
66. "The Dragon's New Teeth", *The Economist*, April 7, 2012.
67. Gen Chen, quoted by *The Economist*, April 7, 2012.
68. Ibid.
69. Ibid., p. 83.
70. Ibid., p. 86.
71. Ibid., pp. 97-99.
72. Steven Metz, "The Next Twist of the RMA", *Parameters*, Autumn, 2000, p. 46.
73. Ibid.
74. Ibid.
75. "China's Military Rise", *The Economist*, June 7, 2012.
76. n.66.
77. Dombrowski, et. al., n.52.

8

Challenges in Defence Planning

Defence Policy, Planning and Management

When the Standing Committee on Defence (1995-96) of the Tenth Lok Sabha presented its report on Defence Policy, Planning and Management in February 1996, it seemed that in the Committee's view, defence policy, planning and management were interconnected. The Committee made important recommendations regarding all the three aspects; but the issues were discussed independently of each other in three separate chapters. The close linkage between management and planning was not emphasised nor did it discuss how defence planning and budgeting could be given an 'output' orientation. It was more concerned with the delay in approving the defence plans already submitted.

The report of the Standing Committee, emphasising the need for defence planning, stated, "The Defence Planning is the formulation of policies and strategies that will govern the allocation of funds and acquisition, use and disposition of resources to achieve these objectives."[1]

Keeping in view the importance of an approved plan for preparing the annual budget on that basis and for achieving rational allocation of resources during the plan period, the Ninth Five-Year Defence Plan was approved on January 1, 1998. After that, no other, Five-Year Plan has been approved. Explaining the inability to finalise the Eleventh Plan, the Defence Secretary, deposing before the Standing Committee 2005-06, stated that in the absence of an "indicative figure" or an "outer limit" of the amount that could be made available by the Ministry of Finance for the plan, it was not possible to do so.[2]

Two points, however, should be clear at the outset. In our system, absence of an approved five-year defence plan, does not mean that the projects in the priority list do not get approved nor does the fact that a project/scheme is included in the plan, give it a special sanctity. All the schemes and projects have to go through the normal process of sanctioning, keeping in view budgetary provisions. The costs of the scheme will determine at what level the scheme will be sanctioned. So the process of modernisation can go on irrespective of whether a defence plan has been sanctioned or not.

Secondly, most of the amounts provided under the defence budget go towards meeting the obligatory expenditure and committed expenditure on account of schemes which have been earlier approved, leaving a comparatively a small amount for new modernisation schemes. Since our planning process does not involve looking into the committed expenditure and obligatory expenditure, the attention of planners gets confined to provisions for new modernisation schemes, which form a small portion of the defence budget.

One can as well ask the question: what purpose is served by approving a defence plan? The question gets further relevance from the fact that most of the time during the last two decades, defence has carried on its process of modernisation without approved five-year plans.

The Standing Committee Report (1995-96) mentioned above, referred to the "ad hocism" in defence planning which was "evident from the fact that in a period of about 20 years, 6 Defence Five-Year Plans were prepared but none could be completed for one reason or another and had to be either deferred or reframed midway. The Committee expressed its concern that the 7th Five-Year Plan could be finalised only in the last year of the plan and the 8th Five-Year Plan for the period 1992-1997 was not yet finalised."[3]

The Standing Committee Report (1995-96) recognised that the national defence policy was an integral part of the national security policy, which by its very nature was multi-disciplinary in character. It unambiguously stated, "Defence Policy has to evolve from the identification and acceptance of national interests and their relative importance."[4] It also held the view that the strategic policy of the nation "should be discussed publicly" (para 1.11) and referred to the conclusion contained in the Ninth Report of the Estimates Committee (1992-93) wherein it was recommended that the country should have a formal National Security Doctrine (para 1.12). It was not convinced by the argument that there was a defence policy but there was no policy document.

Stressing the need for a formal defence policy document, the Committee stated, "In the absence of any document explaining articulated policy with stated national objectives and national interests, it is not possible for the policy to be analysed and modified. The Committee, therefore, desired the Government to examine the feasibility of preparing a formal National Defence Policy Document for being placed before the Parliament."[5]

Though ten years have passed since the Standing Committee on Defence submitted its reports, on the subject of defence policy and planning we still do not have a clearly enunciated National Security Policy document, nor do we have a defence policy document. In the meantime, the Group of Ministers (GoM) formed to review the national security system, in its report in 2001, commented about the handicap that the defence planning process suffered from, due to the absence of a National Security Doctrine.

Plans and Budgets

Let us look at the budgetary provisions in the context of plan provisions. Issues in regard to shortfall in the budgetary allocations compared to planned allocations (as per the approved five-year plans) or absence of 'commitment' to make the required funds available, were repeatedly brought before the Standing Committee. The feasibility of formulating five-year plans in the context of the annual budgetary allocation was specifically raised. To quote from the report, "Regarding the feasibility of formulation of the Five-Year Defence Plan, the Ministry have stated that giving assurance about five yearly allocations will not be feasible under the present system. The budget, being a yearly allocation, has to take note of the latest assessment of the availability of resources, change in requirements and change imposed by external factors."[6] The obvious conclusion, that it called for a systemic look at both the planning process and budgeting process so as to bring a closer linkage between the two with a view to aim at optimal allocation of resources, was not drawn.

In fact, in the debates about defence planning in India, the basic issue of optimal resource allocation and utilisation in defence, choosing doctrines and techniques to get the most out of available resources, does not get the attention it deserves. Force planning is not the central concern of defence planners. Most analysts focus on the need for long-term commitment of budgetary resources for modernisation, meaning acquisition of new equipment in replacement of the old. So attention gets concentrated on the capital portion of the defence budget. Since attention gets concentrated on capital expenditure for planning purposes, the need for establishing a linkage between the overall defence budget and defence planning is not felt.

In fact, the programme concept in formulating the defence plan is totally missing. No wonder that defence planning and budgeting activities in India continue to remain in two separate compartments. One of the most important challenges in defence planning in India is to bring these two activities closer together and become a major aid to management. That requires a closer look at the present process and roles of both these activities.

Formulation of Defence Plans

This raises the question: how should the defence plan be formulated and what should be its conceptual basis, so that not only does it gets approved in time but also plays a more meaningful role in defence resource management than in the past? K. Subrahmanyam, the noted defence analyst, commenting on the role of defence planning in India in the early Seventies, stated, "There is a widespread impression that planning is only a compilation of schemes for the next five years, as proposed by each of the three Services and which have been vetted by the Ministry of Defence and Ministry of Finance (Defence) with reference to the necessity for the schemes, the scope of the schemes and their costs."[7] He also mentioned about the absence of a perspective view.

Among the shortcomings of defence planning in India, Subrahmanyam mentioned about the absence of the perspective view. All the three Services were concerned with short-term planning rather than with long-term planning. "There are not even facilities available at the present moment in the three Services to acquire, collate and compile the necessary data on developing technology, strategic doctrines and international developments which should form the basis for such long-term planning."[8] Further, there was no organisation available to deal with inter-Service plans and to deal with inter-scheme priorities.

The position has not changed much since then except that the need for an integrated 15-year perspective planning system, as a basis for drawing up five-year plans, is stressed more and more. The perspective plan cannot just be an acquisition plan, as is thought in some quarters, without an in-depth analysis of the threat scenario, challenges likely to be faced in future, and evaluation of options and alternatives. It needs to be an integrated plan covering also R&D and defence production to meet the defence needs. As two eminent defence analysts put it, "Perspective planning needs to be done in Integrated Defence Headquarters, where military, technical and R&D experts take an integrated view of future threats, and challenges. These have to be based on future battlefield scenarios, and an array of forecasts, evaluation of strategic options and force mixes, analysis of potential technical and industrial capabilities."[9] But then, the problem gets shifted to approval of the Long-Term Integrated Perspective Plan (LTIPP).

Drawing up an integrated perspective plan, becomes a challenging task involving decisions and judgement, about which scenarios are to be accepted as relevant for force planning purposes, and what force mixes would best serve the purpose. This also brings out the point that defence planning is more about force planning and capability building than just about acquisitions.

Scenarios have to be built on the basis of analysis and judgement. The role of military operational analysis and systems analysis to identify the most cost-effective programme of expenditure from future defence budgets, has to be given due importance. Referring to these planning tools, Gen Malik and Brig Kanwal say, "Systems analysis can assist in developing rational procedures for procurement of new weapon systems...Planners all over the world are using computerised war-gaming techniques and structure analysis. Prospects exist for a more enlightened approach that can bring together military officers, historians, technologists and quantitative analysts."[10]

All these ingredients are required for arriving at an optimum force-mix. This calls for looking at the operation, maintenance and capital budgets for defence planning purposes. Since the Task Force on Defence Management appointed by the Group of Ministers (GoM) submitted its recommendations in 2001, it is defence procurement which has received focussed attention from the organisational point of view and for streamlining of the procedure. A major restructuring of the procurement organisational set-up has taken place. Procurement procedures have been streamlined. As per the procurement procedure, the planning process covers the long-term, medium-term and short-term perspectives as follows:

- 15-Year Long-Term Perspective Plan (LTPP).
- 5-Year Services Capital Acquisition Plan (SCAP).
- Annual Acquisition Plan.

From this, one gets the impression that the main concern of perspective plans and five-year plans is acquisition of weapons and equipment.

The importance of formulating the 15-year perspective plan as the basis of both the five-year plans and annual plan of acquisition indicates that all these plans basically are investment plans. The aim of defence planning should to achieve a cost-effective force mix to meet the operational requirements, now and in the future.

Defence Plans and Operational Analysis

No defence capability plan will attain its objective if it does not keep the enemy and the kind of tactics he is likely to employ in view. Challenges, both in the short-term and long-term, have to be met. Even the long-term investment plan which the perspective plan is concerned with must keep in view the potentiality of the enemy's capabilities and how he is likely to use them.

That is why operational analysis as also studies on life-cycle cost of alternative equipment options are so very important in making appropriate investment decisions. A dedicated set-up is required in the MoD to carry out operational studies. In this context, mention may be made that a review of UK equipment procedures (Report of the EPC Efficiency Scrutiny, May17, 1991, the Buckley Report) called for substantial changes to the decision-making machinery. "In particular, it specified that future proposals, for equipment procurement should be accompanied, *inter alia*, by a cost-effectiveness report based on the results of operational analysis and on forecasts of the life-cycle cost of the alternative equipment options."[11] There is already an established procedure in the United States of requiring a Cost and Operational Effectiveness Analysis (COEA) to support key decisions by the Defence Acquisitions Board. The new procurement process in the UK is now based on, along with the requirement definition justifying the operational requirement and alternative ways of meeting it, a procurement strategy and Combined Operational Effectiveness and Investment Appraisal (COEIA). In the UK, incidentally, operational analysis is undertaken by the Centre for Defence Analysis (CDA) on behalf of the MoD.

For proper operation analysis, it must be based on an approved operational scenario as also concepts of operation. Both these inputs are essential for making cost-effectiveness studies. And without such studies, we cannot arrive at what would be the optimum force mix for a country.

In this regard, we can refer to the present practice in the UK, as described by Kirkpatrick. "To identify the most-effective future force mix, hence, the most effective programme of expenditure from the UK's future defence budgets, military operational analyses at the Centre for Defence Analysis (CDA) use MoD-approved scenarios and concepts of operation to consider different increments to force cost and effectiveness which would result from procurement and operation in service of various numbers of different classes of equipment to supplement or replace the existing national inventory" (ref. 10, p. 13). The results of any such needs and number studies depend on military tasks envisaged for military forces, the level of effectiveness to be achieved and the limits of defence budgets.

Capability-Based Planning

Experts on defence planning in India are advocating a shift to the capability-based planning model. To quote Gen Malik and Brig Kanwal, "In the prevailing era of strategic uncertainty, the changing nature of warfare demands a judicious mix of threat and capabilities-based forces that can operate efficiently as combined arms, joint Services teams."[12]

One need not mix these two models of planning as Capability-Based Planning (CBP) takes account of the potentiality of different kind of threats through scenario-building exercises. It is not based on standard scenarios for force planning purposes. As is well known, the concept of capability-based defence planning was introduced in the United States through the Quadrennial Defence Review (QDR) 2001.

In the course of the 2001 QDR—even before 9/11—the Defence Department came to the conclusion that even with limited resources, it had to have capabilities across a very broad spectrum. A new set of transformational programmes and conceptual tools was developed and built into the analytical process. These programmes and concepts revolve around what is called "capabilities-based planning", as opposed to threat-based planning, which is based on specific threats. Since we are talking of the capability-based planning model and in the context of what has been stated above, it is necessary to go into the concept of 'capability'.

There is a tendency to equate it with acquiring more capable equipment than that in the inventory. It was conceived in a different way in the QDR, 2001. According to its working definition, "capability" is the ability to achieve "desired operational effects under specified standards and conditions through means and ways to perform a set of tasks." For the purposes of the QDR, "A capability is not a platform or asset. It's the ability to achieve a desired effect affecting the battlespace."[13] It is necessary to understand the operational environment in which the armed forces have to operate, to decide on what would be the needed capability. Thus, it is a much more demanding planning framework than the threat-based planning.

The CBP method involves a functional analysis of operational requirements. Capabilities are identified based on tasks required. Capabilities, or the ability to perform a particular task, provide the common framework used for relating disparate elements of the defence organisation. CBP relies on scenarios to provide the context against which to measure the level of capability. The concept of CBP recognises the interdependence of systems (including material and people), doctrine, organisation and support in delivering defence capability. It emphasises the need to examine options and trade-offs among the capability elements in terms of performance, risk and cost, so as to identify optimum force development investments. " It focuses on goals and end-states and encourages innovation. It starts by asking questions regarding what we need to do rather than what equipment we are replacing."[14]

Viewed in this way, the CBP method of defence planning is applicable to all countries attempting to achieve optimisation of resource allocation. This is applicable even when the resources are a given. Therefore, the stress is on innovative concepts in the use of emerging technology. That is why it is a challenging task which has to be accepted. What should be remembered is that CBP is "concept-led", and use of personnel experiences in concepts and operations is critical to its successful implementation.

The outcome of CBP should be an effective investment strategy that develops and sustains the capability priorities identified through the planning process. As would be evident, a CBP model would be difficult to adopt without operation analysis based on approved scenarios for force planning and detailed costing. What is visualised is jointness of operation, which calls for joint organisations for structuring and war planning. This leads to cost-effective planning. Without introducing jointness in force structure and joint doctrine, it is not possible to introduce the capability-based planning model.

Integrated Perspective Plan and Force Planning

There is a need for an integrated perspective plan based on operational plans. This is the basic challenge for defence planning in India. Recognising its need, the Group of Ministers in their report on "Reforming the National Security System" submitted in May 2001, stressed on the need for an integrated perspective plan for defence. They stated, "In the past, individual Services have prepared their long-term perspective plans. However, with the induction of the CDS and other related structures, there would be a need to prepare a holistic and integrated defence perspective plan for the 15-20 years through a rigorous process of inter-Service and intra-Service priorities. The Five-Year Defence Plans by the Services should be prepared on the basis of LTIPP."[15]

What the GoM report did not stress was that preparation of an integrated perspective plan was necessary for cost-effective defence planning and was not contingent on the appointment of a CDS. Consequent to the GoM report, an Integrated Defence Staff (IDS) structure was put in place by merging the erstwhile Directorate General of Defence Planning Staff and the Military Wing. It began functioning in October 2001. IDS has evolved a Long-Term Integrated Perspective Plan (LTIPP) (2002-17) after obtaining the perspective plans of the three Services. It was subsequently asked to work on a new LTIPP (2007-22). Commenting on the result, one analyst puts it, "There has been no serious effort towards inter-Service prioritisation in the LTIPP. It continues to be largely a sum of the perspective plans of individual Services. This compels one to remark that the more things change, the more they remain the same."[16]

The military force structure that is existing today has evolved out of the perspective plans of each Service, prepared on the basis of their organisational interests. The perspective plans of the Services have not been sanctioned by the government and have remained an in-house exercise of the respective Service. The Five-Year Plans have not addressed the issue of rationalisation of force structures. In the Indian Army, Navy and Air Force, force levels have always been sanctioned as additions to existing levels.[17] The government has imposed ceilings on manpower, but ceilings have been revised upwards from time to time on the basis of requirements indicated by the Service Headquarters.[18] It was maintained by the MoD in its evidence before the Estimates Committee in 1992-93 that ceiling on manpower did not mean the ceiling on the force levels.[19] Clearly, the possibility of rationalisation of the force structure has not been one of the aims of the Ministry of Defence or of the Services.

The Estimates Committee 1992-93, observed, "With the growth in absolute numbers of personnel and the fact that personnel costs today constitute a large part of the Services' budget, the share of resources available for modernisation schemes gets affected."[20]

The five-year plans have not addressed the issue of rationalisation of force structure as these are basically acquisition oriented plans based on the perspective plans of individual Services. Planning for an optimal force structure within the resources available has not been the major objective of the plans.

Improving the "tooth-to-tail ratio" which should be a major concern of defence management has not been given the importance it deserves. That is why it is so very important to establish a linkage between defence management and defence planning. In the business world, planning itself is a tool of management for achieving its goals. Defence has to be perceived as a giant business. In the capability-based planning model for defence, which has now been ushered in by many Western countries, the concept of the business model of planning is given prime importance. Military capabilities are generated when plans, people and equipment are combined to achieve government goals. Capability-based planning would provide the process to bring about the right blend of plans, people, equipment and activity to optimise the capacity of our military forces to perform their assigned roles. It is the best tool for identifying what capabilities are necessary for carrying out their mandates. Corporate priorities regarding capability have to be fixed to carry out defence business. In the UK, it is fixed by the Defence Management Board, and in Canada, it is done by the Defence Management Committee. It is the corporate priorities that govern planning and resource prioritisation and allocation of budgets. In India, we are still to regard defence as a business, as a corporate activity.

Evolving Optimal Force Structure

Evolving an optimal force structure for defence in the light of challenges faced by it should be one of the central aims of the business approach to defence management. For this, an integrated perspective plan based on long-term costing of force structure, clearly keeping in view the likely availability of budgets, is essential. Preparation of an open-ended long-term plan, without reference to cost and likely availability of budgets, would hardly be of any use. One should be realistic about the availability of funds on a long-term basis. As Air Cmde Jasjit Singh stated, "Financial resources would be a major factor in determining the capabilities we can actually possess (as compared to what we may wish for). The level of funding available during the next 5-10 years, therefore, would be the determining factor of the capabilities that our Army would actually possess in 2020. In turn, this raises the importance of long-term planning, especially the perspective plans and the more definitive Five-Year Defence Plan." He goes on to add, "Based on the record of the past decade and a half of the fiscal resources for defence... spending would go anything above a figure of around 2.3-2.4 percent of the GDP for the next 15 years..The core conclusion that can be drawn is that capabilities for 2020 would have to be tailored to the broad level of resources available, regardless of perceived necessities." This may well be around an average of 2.4 percent of the GDP, equivalent to around 13.5-14.0 percent of the CGE (Central Government Expenditure).[21]

If such a direction about assumption to be made about likely availability of budgets on a long-term basis came from the government, preparation of the perspective plan on a realistic basis would be very much helped and the chance of getting the plan approved would brighten. One way would be to make alternative assumptions about long-term availability of funds, for example, one on the basis of 2.4 percent of the GDP, another on the basis of 2.45 percent and yet another on 2.5 percent. This would give the government a choice after considering what capabilities get added at a higher level of allocation. The government can also indicate for what planning purposes the growth of GDP may be assumed.

This still leaves out the costing aspect. Costing for planning purposes can be only on the basis of programmes. Assessing the cost of alternatives is essential to find out whether these are feasible alternatives. If there is no institutionalised system of costing of various elements of a proposed programme, then a vital input for strategic decision-making, which involves choice among alternatives, would be missing.

The concept of perspective planning on an integrated basis cannot be introduced without introducing programme planning on a mission-oriented basis and programme budgeting. The choice between alternative force structures can be part of the planning process only when the programming technique is introduced.

Unfortunately, we are yet to introduce the concept of programme in defence planning, which automatically introduces costing of various programme elements. That is why the link between planning and budgeting is totally missing.

Introducing Programme-Based Budgeting

It may be mentioned that the problem which PPBS was intended to solve in the US defence was not the lack of systems analysis in defence, but the inadequate link between planning and budgeting. A purpose of the introduction of PPBS in defence was to increase the impact of relevant analyses on high-level decisions by connecting them to budgeting via the programme concept. Before the introduction of PPBS in the Department of Defence in the US, there was a clear separation between planning and budgeting. As Enthoven and Smith put it, "Perhaps the key reason for the limited usefulness of the defence budget was the fact that defence budgeting was, in effect, conceived as being largely unrelated to military strategy. They were treated as almost independent activities. They were carried out by different people, at different times, with different terms of reference, and without a method of integrating their activities. This gap between strategy and forces, on the one hand, and budgets, on the other, poses a serious obstacle to rational defence planning."[23]

The problem was more in the way financial planning was done. As the authors stated, "The fact that financial planning for the Defense Department looked only a year ahead also led to a number of serious consequences. Because total system costs (operations as well as procurement, support as well as direct costs) were not known and, therefore, not used in procurement decisions, program decisions in effect were made in ignorance of their future cost implications. This one-year-at-a time financial planning in the context of separate financial and force planning laid undue emphasis on this year's costs to the neglect of effectiveness and future costs."[24] The other consequence of this approach, with which we are quite familiar, is the overcommitment of expenditure, leading to less and less flexibility in the future years' budgets for carrying out new modernisation schemes.

If the business approach to defence management and planning is adopted, then financial planning and force planning cannot follow separate models. One need not be looking for long-term financial commitments for planning, for that can never be made and can become an excuse for not planning. This planning has to be on the basis of programmes for capability building and it should be a continuous activity.

The overall approach to defence planning should be to create a common framework in which methods of strategic, programmatic and operations planning could be integrated. This is the basic challenge of defence planning. An important challenge in defence planning, as Paul K. Davis puts it, is establishing a "common intellectual framework", which needs to reflect an operational perspective. "That is, all types of planners should have the objective of producing effective capabilities for real-world operations."[25]

In the endeavour to establish a common intellectual framework, bringing in planning for capability (which includes force planning) and financial planning into the same framework would be a major step. What one should look for is a financial plan which helps capability planning and force planning. One need not look for financial commitment.

Need For a Dynamic Planning Model

What is required today is a dynamic model of planning instead of a static model of planning at periodic intervals. It should be planning for adaptiveness and for retaining adequate flexibility to face various challenges. So the programmes become the most important focus of attention and the plan should emerge out of the programmes which are under execution and under active consideration. Explaining the PPBS, K. Subrahmanyam said, "It was recognised from the beginning that the defence programme is extremely dynamic and that changes would be required at various times during a financial year. Accordingly, a formal programme change control system was established....Hundreds of programme change proposals (PCP) are submitted each year, requesting changes involving billions of dollars."[26] The crucial link in the PPBS is programming. This involves preparation of documents, the most important of which are: force structure plan in terms of equipment and units and forces for the next 8 years; financial plan, which gave the cost of these forces over the next 8 years; operating expenses, which gave the details of the maintenance costs of the forces in the next 8 years; manpower plan which showed the manpower requirement for the next 8 years; fiscal plan which gave the appropriation which is likely to be asked for year by year for the next 8 years. It also included the logistic plan. There were nine such documents. "These nine documents link the planning process with the budgeting process and give all the data in terms of programme elements and programme packages to enable as many of the objectives underlying an ideal budget to be realised."[27]

McNamara, with his business background, introduced a dynamic planning model to accommodate the changes in defence programmes during the financial year and the concept of a rolling plan was brought in. The Five-

Year Defence Plan itself was visualised as a huge programme. The basic directive governing the defence programme clearly and forcefully brought this out and how programming was designed to introduce management control. The "Five-Year Force Structure and Financial Programme" is the official programme for the Department of Defence. The programming system, outlined herein, will provide the means for submission, review, record keeping, and decision-making on the DoD programme. The planning, programming, resource, material, and financial management systems of all DoD components will be correlated with the programming system set forth herein.[28]

So programming was the most important innovation as a tool of management, to correlate all the other activities in the Department concerned with resource allocation with the basic objective of bringing output orientation to defence planning and to bring control. As far as the legislative control is concerned, it is through the budgetary allocation, while for the Department of Defence, it is through programming.

McNamara not only thought it necessary to introduce the programming technique but also introduced a dynamic planning model to accommodate the changes in defence programmes during the financial year and the concept of rolling plan was brought in. Explaining the process, Subrahmanyam says, "Every year, as the plan for a particular year is implemented, an additional year is added and once again a Five-Year Force Structure and Financial Programme is presented on a continuous rolling basis."[29] The force structure plan as well as the financial programme were formally presented for five years, though estimates were given for a longer period. But designating the Five-Year Defence Plan (FYDP) as a "Five-Year Force Structure and Financial Programme" properly captured the philosophy behind the new planning technique.

We should also introduce the rolling plan model as we did in the Seventies, not because of financial stringency and inability to commit funds for a longer period, but as a management tool to take care of the change in priorities and to accommodate changes in programmes. In this context, the role of the Five-Year Defence Plan (FYDP) under programme budgeting, needs to be appreciated. To put it in the words of Enthoven and Smith, "What did the FYDP do? Most importantly, it tied together force and financial planning. As we have argued, sound decisions on forces cannot be made without carefully reviewing their total cost and manpower implications. For example, when deciding how many tactical aircraft to buy and operate, defence planners should consider not only the costs of aircraft but the costs of personnel required to operate and maintain them, the costs of training the pilots, and the costs of the housing, runways, depot stocks, hospitals, equipment, and other resources needed to support the force. With the aid of such tools as the FYDP, for example, defence planners found that every dollar spent directly to buy and operate a tactical aircraft leads to at least another dollar in support cost."[30] By clearly relating forces to their costs and to the defence budget, the FYDP gave financial planning the same output orientation as force planning.

In our planning process, we would be basically concerned with the cost of buying the tactical aircraft, ignoring most of the costs which are catered for by the revenue portion of the budget. Therefore, the link between force planning and budgeting cannot be established and the budget remains input oriented. Many defence analysts in India have criticised the defence budget as 'input' oriented, but few have indicated the reasons for it. It is mainly because of the absence of programming, which can provide a bridge between defence planning and budgeting, which can make both output oriented. To say the obvious, unless the defence plan is output oriented, the defence budget cannot be output oriented and unless the costs of programmes are worked out in all their dimensions, the link between planning and budgeting would be very weak.

Need For A Medium-Term Expenditure Framework

There is also the question of determining the feasibility of schemes to be undertaken as part of the plan. Feasibility would be determined by whether the programmes (which have been costed) are affordable on the basis of defence budgets likely to be available and the amounts likely to be available after meeting the competing needs. The consequences of today's decisions on future budgets are required to be worked out. So a medium-term framework for defence budgeting is absolutely essential. Not just to know what further commitments can be made, but more, importantly, to know what would be the consequences in resource terms on future defence budgets of present decisions. Therefore, for countries that have not yet attempted to put together a medium-term expenditure framework, in which allocation for defence is specifically indicated, this is a major challenge. It is this medium-term expenditure framework which will provide the basis for a financial plan or a budget plan. Commitment is required to establish such a 'budget plan' but the task is not easy as it involves skill in determining the growth of GDP, revenue generation and providing for other demands, for which various inputs are required. One can go wrong in making such estimates either because of optimistic projections made or because of unforeseen events. But if defence planning is to be placed on a proper footing, such a framework has to be developed. It should be on the basis of conservative estimates relating to GDP growth and revenue generation and realistic estimates of expenditure growth. It should be reviewed every year to make whatever corrections are required and moved forward by one more year. This will provide the basis for the medium-term budget plan for defence which can also be on a rolling basis along with the programme plan.

If programming techniques are introduced in planning and budgeting and a medium-term expenditure framework can be put in place, it would be possible to put defence planning on a sound footing. Ideas which were developed in the US Department of Defence in the 1960s remain valid for any country aspiring for optimal utilisation of resources in defence.

Basic Principles of Sound Defence Planning

Some of these ideas were described by Alain C. Enthoven and K. Wayne Smith in their book *How Much is Enough* (Harper and Row, 1971) which is of enduring value and great relevance. We would like to mention four of them:

- Decisions should be based on explicit criteria of national interest, "as opposed to decision-making by compromise among institutional, parochial, or other vested interests in the Defence Department."[31]
- Needs and costs should be considered simultaneously. "Put another way, decisions on forces and budgets should be made together...Ends and means interact. What is worth trying to do depends in large part on how much it costs."[32]

- Major decisions should be made by choices among explicit, balanced, feasible alternatives.[33]
- A multi-year force and financial plan should project the consequences of present decisions into the future. It is not to be an inflexible blueprint for the future, rather "a projection of the implications of past decisions, a set of official planning assumptions, and a point of departure in the continuing search for improvements."[34]

These four ideas can almost be treated as the basic principles of defence planning. We have already mentioned about the necessity of national security policy based upon explicit criteria of national interest.

Essentiality of 'First Order' Decisions

Policies are not general statements; policies involve decisions. The hallmark of a policy document is decisions which indicate a choice has been made after weighing the alternatives. The policy decisions are about what to do and about how to do it. That means there are two kinds of decisions. Defence management is not the same thing as defence policy-making. As John Garnett states, "There are a good many 'first order' decisions to be taken in the defence field, and it is doubtful whether the various techniques of the programmatic approach have much to offer by way of improving them." The first order decisions pertain to *what to do* and are policy issues. Defence management is concerned with *how to do it* which deals with procurement, allocation and organisation of men, money and material. The economic constraints on defence policy are all pervasive but as Garnett points out, "It is worth saying here that fundamentally, defence expenditure is determined not by economic but by political constraints."[35]

Strategic planning has to cover these "first order decisions." Often, the need for such "first order decisions" in the defence planning and resource allocation process is overlooked in the hustle and bustle of weapon acquisition and in the quest for 'modernisation' for developing various capabilities. This failure is fairly pervasive. Even where an elaborate system of planning, programming and budgeting was introduced, as in the Department of Defence of the USA, with a view to linking the processes mentioned above in a methodical manner, this failure persisted. PPBS which was introduced in 1962, is the formal process for planning and allocating resources in US defence. Its central purpose was to design a military strategy and force posture that can achieve the nation's strategic objectives at the least cost. The first "P" stands for planning, which is to translate the overall defence priorities established by the President and his senior advisers into guidance for force development. Programming develops and evaluates specific multi-year force structure alternatives on a mission oriented basis. When a review was made in the mid-Eighties in US defence, it was found that the model of PPBS, as a series of interlocking functions, the output of one forming the input of the next, had not been realised. There was broad agreement that the first "P" in PPBS was silent. More precisely, the planning that took place in the Department of Defence was not linked adequately to subsequent programming and budgeting decisions.[36]

As William Kaufmann put it, the PPBS as a system "*is both a process and, what participants in it frequently forget, a method. Each can endure with the other,* but it was McNamara's intent that they should be combined so as to link resources with objectives and the forces to reach them *But the system can also serve as a facade behind which each Service can go its own way. The facade is easy to maintain*" (italics mine). Kaufmann commented, as far as US defence was concerned, in the mid-Eighties, the PPBS remained in place "as a process" but "despite all the machinery, despite all the bloated committees, it is the objectives of the individual Services that still dominates the force planning."[37] He put the issue succinctly, when he said that the Secretary of Defence could choose to exercise his authority in different ways, but "whatever the tactics, *the basic choice is between central planning and direction, on the one hand, and the free enterprise of the services, valuable in a market economy but out of place in the Defence Department.*"[38]

This choice has to be exerised, and the centralised planning process has to be adopted in the interest of proper defence planning. Institutional reforms would be required by way of strengthening institutions like the Defence Council and Defence Management Board, as in the UK, in order to provide guidance to the Department on key strategic issues, for closer alignment of strategic objectives and resource allocation and for sharper focus on performance. It cannot be confined to acquisition issues.

In the USA, the President's Blue Ribbon Commission on Defence Management, known as the Packard Commission and the Goldwater Nichols Department of Defence Reorganisation Act of 1986 addressed, among other issues, those relating to PPBS. The Packard Commission highlighted the key problem in national security when it said in the summary that there was no rational system to reach a coherent and enduring agreement between the Executive Branch and the Congress on national military strategy, the forces to carry it out, and the funding that would be provided in the light of competing claims on national resources. The Commission stressed the need for long-range planning. Most of the Commission's recommendations about the PPBS had to do with the front end of the planning process in an attempt to rectify the absence of a longer view. More specifically, the first part of the Commission's recommendations was that "defence planning would start with a comprehensive statement on national security objectives and priorities, based on the recommendation of the National Security Council."[39]

The basic problem with this formulation is to do with the word priorities. It is usually expressed in an imprecise manner. As an analyst put it, "What is important is not some ordinal list, but a specific, quantitative allocation of resources among national security objectives.. So many important factors directly affect force requirements that an NSC ordinal list of priorities is ultimately of little use to military planners."[40]

That is why it is necessary to have defence reviews for force planning and capability development, as was done by the Base Force Review (1990), Bottom-Up Review (1993) and now through the Quadrennial Defence Reviews since 1997, in order to make specific allocation of resources among various programmes. It is to be noted that the defence budget in the USA had already begun to decline in real terms by 1986 because of the pressures of fiscal deficit and specific limitations imposed by the Gramm-Rudman-Hollings law. So a five-year budget plan was very necessary for defence planning purposes.

In the Goldwater-Nichols Act 1986, the Chairman of the Joint Chiefs of Staff was given the responsibility for submitting to the Secretary alternative programme recommendations and budget proposals, within the projected resource levels and guidance provided by the Secretary, in order to achieve greater conformance with strategic plans and the requirements of the unified and specified combatant commanders. The era of budget-driven strategic plans started. Even the Quadrennial Defence Review (QDR) 1997, was a budget-driven exercise.

Goal for Defence Planning: Affordable and Effective Defence

The basic challenge for defence planners is to develop an affordable and effective defence.This calls for introducing greater realism in national security planning.

A brief exercise made in the late Eighties towards budgetary projections for US defence on the basis of some options, including the one that matched the Gramm-Rudman-Rollings Act of "balanced budget requirement" showed enormous differences among the results of four options, in terms of equipment and force structure. By the end of the five-year period, among the four options, there was an annual difference of $150 billion.[41] Though the US defence budget base is enormous compared to other countries, the lesson is relevant in terms of percentage of uncertainty: "Such a large annual uncertainty precludes an efficient or effective weapons-acquisition program and credible national-security posture. It is not the number of dollars that causes the problem; it is the large annual uncertainty. *Once we pick a multi-year budget plan and stick to it, efficiency and credibility may follow.*"[42] (Italics mine).

We should also make projections about the availability of funds on the basis of some realistic assumptions: to project on the basis of the budgetary trend of the last five years; to project a "constant rupee" budget for the next five years, providing only for the effects of inflation; to provide for the defence budget to keep up with the requirements of the Fiscal Responsibility and Budget Management Act 2003, which now seeks to reduce the fiscal deficit and eliminate the revenue deficit by March 31, 2015; to project allocation to the defence budget in terms of a constant percentage of GDP, keeping the percentage at the realistic level, making a conservative estimate of the growth of GDP in the next five years. Whatever option or combination of options we choose, for projection of likely defence budgets in the next five years, the aim should be to arrive at a multi-year defence budget plan and stick to it. The cost of the existing force structure should also be projected on a realistic basis for the next 10 years. The mismatch between the two should be resolved through taking appropriate decisions regarding savings to be made and rationalisation of force structure, giving particular attention to the tooth-to-tail ratio. These issues cannot be addressed sequentially.

As explained above, most of the issues are interlinked and cannot be dealt with in a sequential manner. There has to be feedback from each stage of decision-making and from different aspects of national policy-making, so as to bring coherence in the whole process. As Liotta and Lloyd put it, "Strategy and force planning are not a rigid, sequential process; feedback and iteration must exist at all levels...Military, political, economic, technological, and even basic value assessments may suggest a need to revise the initial choice to better meet strategic objectives. It may also be necessary to review the national objectives to ensure more has not been attempted than the strategy can accomplish with the available resources and technology."[43]

In the absence of strategy, there is no clear direction for the future. Without a clear set of objectives and a focussed national security strategy, one can only react to, rather than shape, events affecting a country's interest.

That is why it is so very important to develop a national security and strategy document and a defence policy which will emerge out of a defence review of the defence force structure and what it should be in the light of national priorities and affordability, and lay down clear guidelines for capability building, including that of research in critical areas of technology to help in the capability building exercise.

For developing a joint vision and strategic look at the country's security interests and defence needs in the light of new and emerging strategic realities, to develop an integrated capability plan and optimal force structure keeping in view the financial constraints, a comprehensive defence review is very necessary on the basis of realistic planning assumptions regarding the wars to be fought and their nature. Since making realistic assumptions for force planning is crucial, such reviews have to be made periodically. Such defence reviews should be the basis for planning, programming as also for decisions on defence acquisitions. Only then can one aim at optimal allocation and utilisation of defence resources.

Thinking systematically and coherently about national strategy in the absence of a tradition requires what may be called a 'strategic community' which emerges slowly. Strategy as it deals with national policy requires an inter-disciplinary perspective. Today, there is a strategic community in the country and the inter-disciplinary perspective is also emerging. So it should be possible to develop a formal national security strategy document and on that basis, undertake a comprehensive defence policy review, which will form the basis for force planning and capability building. This is the basic challenge for defence planning.

Notes

1. Report of the Standing Committee on Defence,1995-96, on Defence Policy, Planning and Management. Sixth Report, March 1996, Lok Sabha Secretariat, New Delhi, para 2.1.
2. Report of the Standing Committee on Defence, Demands for Grants 2005-06, para 2.6, p. 21.
3. Ibid., p.21, para 2.33.
4. Ibid., para 1.3.
5. Ibid., para 1.18.
6. Report of the Standing Committee on Defence, 1995-96, Sixth Report, Lok Sabha Secretariat, March, 1996, para 2.14.
7. K. Subrahmanyam, *Perspectives in Defence Planning* (Abhinav Publications, 1972).
8. Ibid., p. 135.
9. Gen V. P. Malik P. and Brig Gurmeet Kanwal, *Defence Planning in India*, p. 6, www.observerindia.com/pulications/PolicyBrief/ Pyo50120pdf.
10. Ibid.
11. David Kirkpatrick, *Choose your Weapon: Combined Operational Effectiveness and Investment Appraisal* (COEIA), RUSI Whitehall Paper Series 1996, p. 7.
12. Malik and Kanwal, n.9, p.10.
13. Ryan Henry, "Defence Transformation and the 2005 Quadrennial Defence Review", *Parameters*, US Army War College Quaterly, vol xxxv, (4) 2005-06.
14. Technical Cooperation Program, TTCP Technical Report. Guide to capability-based planning, Tr-JSA-TP3-2-2004, 1 Oct 2004. http//www.mors.org/meetings/cbp/read/ TP -3_ CBP.pdf.
15. Para 6.46 of the GoM report.
16. Brig Vinod Anand, "Of Integration and Jointness: A Review of Defence Reforms. *Pinnacle,* ARTRAC Journal, October 2005.
17. Report of the Estimates Committee 1992-93,19th Report, Defence Force Levels, Manpower, Management and Policy, para 1.49, p. 19.

18. Report of Estimates Committee, 1992-93, para 2.24, p. 44.
19. Ibid., para 2.99, p. 64.
20. Ibid., para 2.96, p. 62.
21. Air Cmde Singh Jasjit, "Army 2020: Synchronising Military Power With National Aspirations", in Lt Gen Vijay Oberoi, ed., *ARMY 2020* (New Delhi: Knowledge World & Centre for Land Warfare Studies, 2005), p. 97.
22. GOM Report, para 6.51.
23. Alain C. Enthoven and K.Wayne Smith, *How Much Is Enough?* (Harper &Row, 1971), p. 13.
24. Ibid., p. 19.
25. Paul K. Davis, ed., *New Challenges for Defence Planning, Rethinking How Much is Enough* (RAND, 1994), p. 91.
26. Subrahmanyam, n.7 p. 110.
27. Ibid., p. 112.
28. US Department of Defence Directive Number 7045.1, October 30, 1964, Subject: DoD Programming System Section I.C.
29. Subrahmanyam, n.7.
30. Enthoven and Smith, n. 23, p. 49.
31. Ibid., p. 33.
32. Ibid., p. 35.
33. Ibid., p. 39.
34. Ibid., p. 45.
35. John C. Garnett, "Some Constraints on Defence Policy Makers", in Lawrence Martin, ed., *The Management of Defence* (National Defence College Publication, 1976, Macmillan Press Ltd), pp. 30-35.
36. Report of the "Defense Organization Project" of the Center for Strategic and International Studies, 1985, edited by Blechman and Lynn (Ballinger Publishing Co.), p. 26.
37. William W. Kaufmann, *A Reasonable Defense* (The Brookings Institute, 1986), pp. 95-96.
38. Ibid., p. 99 (italics mine).
39. Report of the Blue Ribbon Commission on Defense Management, 1985, "Quest for Excellence", p. xix.
40. Murray Russell, ed., "Force Planning, Programming and Budgeting", in *Making Defense Reform Work* (Brasseys, 1990), p. 203.
41. Jacques S. Gansler, *Affording Defense* (The MIT Press, 1989), pp. 67-68.
42. Ibid., p. 69.
43. P.H. Liotta and Richmond M. Lloyd, "The Strategy and Force Planning Framework", *Naval War College Review*, Spring 2005, 58 (2), 135.

9

Arguments for Introducing Long-Term Budgeting for Defence in India: Need and Pre-Conditions

The feasibility of instituting long-term budgeting in defence is a very important point for consideration to make budgeting help in the implementation of the long-term plan for defence for capability building. This presupposes that an approved long-term plan in defence exits, which needs to be implemented. Unfortunately, it is not so. In fact, one process (long-term budgeting) can reinforce the other process (long-term planning).

Not that long-term defence plans are not in existence. Long-term defence plans in India are called perspective plans which are prepared by individual Services for their planning purposes. These are not put up for approval by the government nor has the government shown any keenness to approve them.

From their perspective plans, the Services are supposed to draw up their respective five-year plans. These get consolidated (earlier by the DG, Defence Planning Staff and now by the Intergrated Defence Staff), and after getting inputs from defence R&D and defence production, the Ministry of Defence (MoD) projects the Defence Five-Year Plan to the Ministry of Finance (MoF). Since perspective plans are not approved, the MoF is under no obligation to approve the five-year plans as they are projected, and tries to confine them to the kind of financial commitments it is in a position to make in the medium-term, keeping in view macro-economic considerations. If there is a consensus in this regard, then the five-year plans get approved. On this basis, the 6th, 7th, and 9th Plan (1998-2002), were approved. Since the 9th Plan, no other five-year plan got approval as no consensus could be reached about the extent of financial commitment that could be made for the plans.

Perspective plans, however, continue to be drawn up by the individual Services containing their own assumptions about the future battlefield scenario, operational contingencies and challenges, to serve as their internal guide for planning purposes as also as a plan of action for 15-year period for the development of force structure, capital acquisition and capability building.

With the advent of the RMA technologies, with network-centric warfare as the most important outcome, the need for a strategy based on adapting information age technologies to specific needs, such as surveillance, intelligence and interoperability, and likely fundamental changes in the conduct of military operations, from innovative use of technologies and concepts of joint warfare, made it imperative to have an integrated approach to long-term plans for defence. In the past, there was no institutional mechanism for integrating the perspective plans into a cohesive and integrated plan.

The need for a Long-Term Integrated Perspective Plan (LTIPP) was first emphasised by the GoM in their report on the National Security System, in May 2001. After setting up of the Integrated Defence Staff (IDS), this lacuna has been met, but an integrated perspective plan which was stated to be towards finalisation, is yet to be approved.

A draft Long-Term Integrated Perspective Plan (LTIPP) covering the 15-year period from the Tenth to the Twelfth Plan (2002-2017) was formulated in June 2004. As the Tenth Five-Year Plan did not get approved, a revised LTIPP covering the period 2007-22 was drawn up. But the Eleventh Five-Year Plan did not get approved. So the revised LTIPP also remained unapproved. It is learnt that the LTIPP for 2012-27 has been approved in April 2012, as also the Five-Year Defence Plan 2012-17.

Because of the advent of RMA, which among other things, involves a judicious mixture of enabling technologies, C4ISR, upgraded platforms, and appropriate organisational changes, which would require time-bound action, drawing up, and approving, a long-term plan (incorporating these features) is absolutely necessary if we want to modernise our armed forces to meet the future challenges.

The most critical military assets in the future would lie increasingly in the integration of systems and skills to produce combat effects. The ability to undertake effective and joint combined operations would be the main challenge.

Therefore, a new and integrated approach to the perspective plan would be required, involving greater reliance on the information technology system. It has to recognise that the most critical capability and investment challenge in the future is in the realm of aerospace combat power and has also to take into consideration the high replacement costs of modern aircraft which may inevitably lead to shrinkage in force structure. Therefore, the plan has to look for innovative capability solutions by adopting an RMA-type approach. One has to think of preparatory steps for drawing up such a plan as it would not emerge automatically, though the Services are fully aware of future potentialities of the RMA-type approach in capability-building.

In October 2004, a formal Indian Army Doctrine was promulgated, which highlights the influence of RMA. It indicates the need to evolve a new force structure, induct new weapon systems and formulation of new operational level doctrines. In the Foreword to the Indian Army Doctrine, the then Army Chief wrote, " Like all other modern armed forces, the Indian Army has been considerably influenced by the Revolution in Military Affairs and the great strides made in technology development. *This has necessitated a transformation in strategic thinking along with a paradigm shift in organisation and conduct of operations. As a consequence, military doctrines, weapon systems and force structures need to undergo a review.*"

The need for a comprehensive review has been underlined. Fund scarcity should not be an obstacle, rather it should be treated as a challenge. As Gen Vij put it, "Funds scarcity or shortfall is a challenge faced by all armies of the world and, hence, there is need for improved operating culture and optimisation of resources. The winning armies of the future will not necessarily be the ones with greater combat power but ones that can visualise and comprehend battles more clearly."[1]

The Air Force and Naval Doctrines emphasise strategic reach in their respective Services and need to operate in a joint Service environment. A Joint Military Doctrine was formulated in 2006.

The doctrines are important inputs for long-term planning. But there remains the challenge of integrating them.

From 1972 to date, the approach to force structuring, and acquisition of weapons and systems for the Services has been based on medium/ long-term perspective plans drawn up by each Service.

There was not enough clarity as to what the perspective plan was supposed to be. It was often equated it with the long-term plan for acquisition, which it is not supposed to be. Sometimes, it was regarded as composed of three five-year plans: the first one being in concrete terms, the second as continuation of the projects and schemes started in the first plan and some new ones complementing the ongoing projects, and the third plan being more in conceptual form.

As per deposition before the Estimates Committee of Parliament in 1992, the following are the factors to be taken into account in drawing up the perspective plan by the Services:

- The plan has to encompass the scientific, technological and environmental assessment that is likely to prevail over a 15-year period. It has to particularly take into account the impact of technical changes that are to take place on the effectiveness of weapons and plan acquisition on that basis.
- The environmental assessment is to take into account: (a) the geo-political situation, and likely stresses that may develop in future; and (b) the capability which is being acquired by the country's likely adversaries or those with whom India's national policy is likely to come under conflict.
- Assessment regarding likely availability of resources during the perspective plan period, keeping in view the socio-economic situation; perspective regarding the concept of warfare (which is three-dimensional in the case of the navy), therefore, developing the correct mix of capabilities
- The maritime interests, which may undergo change with the change in geo-political situation.
- For the air force, the force level spelt out is in terms of aircraft, helicopters, radars and other equipment and systems required with a view to have a versatile air force capable of defending the country's air space on the basis of the perceived air threat and force deployment objectives.[2]

As indicated above, a perspective plan has to have a vision regarding the nature of future warfare, futuristic technologies, how the international relations would take shape, what would be the nature of power equations and the nature of future challenges and conflict, all of which cannot be put in militaristic terms but are extremely important in the context of a long-term defence plan. Quite clearly, all the required inputs are not available with the Service Headquarters. Therefore, the perspective plan often reduced itself to acquisition plans.

In a proper perspective planning model, one should normally start with a nation's vital interests and how to protect them. This is easier said than done. Merely listing the interests would not do. For helping in the perspective planning exercise, the interests are required to be weighed and evaluated. This evaluation has to be done in terms of a specific region and time period and also to comprehend how these different interests complement and contradict each other.

Then there has to be strategic and policy assessment which would involve evaluation of current national security objectives and military objectives. Who would be doing that? Can it be done by each Service?

This is to be followed by a scenario building exercise for developing alternative futures. One has to be careful that the scenario building does not become predictive in nature nor a speculative exercise.

Essentially, a scenario is a description of a hypothetical chain of events, commencing with the development of circumstances that serve to generate the external aggressor's intentions and terminating with the final features of the plan of attack or pressures. In view of its force planning implications, it is important to understand who would develop them and who would take final decisions regarding the relevant scenario out of the alternatives developed?

The GoM which was assisted by a multi-disciplinary Task Force which viewed the entire issue of defence management in their report "Reforming the National Security System" (February 2001), stressed the need for preparing "a holistic and integrated defence perspective plan through a rigorous process of inter-Service and intra-Service priorities. The Five-Year Defence Plans by the Services should be prepared on the basis of LDTPP.... The defence planning process incorporating the long-term defence plan, 5-year plan and annual budget should be revised at the earliest."[3] They followed it up by another recommendation relating to financing of the plan: "The MoF should give firm indication of the availability of financial resources, at least six months before the commencement of the ensuing Five-Year Plan."[4]

The basic point to be noted is that before inter-Service prioritisation takes place, there has to be a strategic plan for defence which needs to be articulated. It has to take account of the contingencies that the defence forces may have to face in the future. Then only, inter-Service prioritisation of investment decisions can take place which should be reflected in the capability plan. Then the question arises: what would be the mechanism to do it?

The GoM report stressed the need for the appointment of a Chief of Defence Staff (CDS) and Vice Chief of Defence Staff (VCDS).

One should distinguish between the perspective plan which is vision-oriented and the long-term defence plan which has to be action oriented. A perspective plan cannot be both. For example, one cannot logically maintain that first two plans of the perspective plan (first ten years) should be a plan of action, with the third one more in the nature of vision because the programmes and schemes undertaken in the first two plans may mostly be completed only in the third plan, rendering the vision element irrelevant.

One may, therefore, conclude that the perspective plan should be visionary in nature, providing the philosophy and direction to the five-year plans which are to be drawn up by further studies, rather than serve as a plan of action .

In other words, a perpective plan need not be equated with the long-term plan.

A long-term defence plan has to be conceived in more concrete terms, laying down milestones in achievement of various defence capabilities and objectives and allocation of resources for achievement of these objectives. While the need for approving a perspective plan can be debated, there can be no debate about the need for approving a long-term action plan. It has to be approved.

In defence, achievement of capabilities invariably requires long-term planning and defence projects normally are all of long-term duration.

Therefore, a defence capability plan has to be a long-term plan. In fact, a short-term defence capability plan is a contradiction in terms.

For example, a long-term plan for acquisition has its own validity as it has maximum impact on force structuring, particularly for the navy and air force which are capital intensive Services. The army's force structure is manpower oriented and the army's budget has a high portion of expenditure on the revenue account. Therefore, a long-term defence plan has to be approved as it should provide the basis for action. Such a long-term plan has to be supported with a long-term budget in an indicative way, but in clear terms.

Long-term planning for defence in a comprehensive sense should include expenditure on both the revenue account and capital account, particularly expenditure related to human resources and upgrading them commensurate with the challenges of new technologies and warfare. In this plan, one has to consider providing attractive packages to them to attract and retain them

Linking budgeting with medium-term and long-term planning is essential for achieving optimal allocation of resources for capability-building. It is difficult to conceive of optimal allocation of resources through yearly budgeting in defence if the time horizon for decision-making is only one year, as is the present practice. The present system of annual budgeting, mainly caters for existing liabilities and obligational expenditure, leaving a minimum amount for future investments. Existing liabilities, of course, include capital expenditure arising out of past decisions. To a great extent, the present is a prisoner of the past, not in a metaphorical sense, but underlining the fact that after catering for requirements of 'ongoing' modernisation schemes, not much is left for new schemes for new capabilities to meet new challenges, nor is one induced to relook at priorities because the time horizon for resource allocation decision is only one year.

Not unexpectedly, the present budgeting process is confined to two and half months, as no significant decision needs to be taken in framing it.

Under the present procedure, there can be no commitment to the financing of an LTIPP. In fact, by delaying the approval of the five-year plans, the LTIPP, which should precede five-year plans, gets automatically derailed. So the huge defence expenditure takes place without either an approved five-year plan or a long-term perspective plan. Is it fair from the point of view of Indian taxpayers?

Instead of a perspective plan as a basis for long-term budgeting, we should talk of financing a long-term capability plan, which should be for ten years and an action plan, which is to be reviewed every year.

Need for a Long-Term Capability Plan

The defence long-term capability plan cannot just be an acquisition plan for 10 years or 15 years. Since defence planning and expenditure should be output-oriented in terms of various capabilities, many countries are designating their long-term plans as defence capability plans.In formulation of such a capability plan, a lot of analytical and visionary inputs go in. Thus, it combines the benefit of a perspective plan and a plan of action with a clear aim of achieving value for money in defence expenditure.

"Capability" in the context of defence is the combined effect of multiple inputs. As per the Defence Capability Development Manual (2006) of the Australian government, in defence "Fundamental Inputs to Capability" (FIC) are categorised as follows:

- Personnel: this input incorporates recruiting, training and all conditions of service and employment.
- Organisation: flexible functional groupings with appropriate balance of competency, structure and command and control to accomplish their tasks.
- Collective training: a defined training regime keeping in view operational requirements.
- Major systems: systems that have significant policy and joint Service implications.
- Supplies: supplies needed for defence to operate, including stock holdings, provisioning lead times, etc.
- Facilities: buildings, structures, plant, equipment, training areas, civil engineering works, etc.
- Infrastructure and services from the wider national support base which are integral to the maintenance of defence effort.
- Command and management: written guidance such as regulations, directions, doctrine, tactical level procedures and preparedness documents

required for defence to support decision-making, administration and operation.

"This comprehensive approach to capability not only focuses attention on the combination and integration of the FIC, rather than on individual inputs seperately, but also enables defence to better understand the whole of life funding implications of the new capability. Capability is thus viewed as a 'system' of interlocking and interdependent FIC." (Defence Capability Development Manual, 2006, http://www.defence.god.au?capability/outputs/-pubs/dcdm.pdf).

Thus, the entire gamut of defence activity is to be kept in view in capability planning. The management of relevant portions of the defence budget under various heads—under both revenue and capital heads—can be considered as a fundamental input for a specific capability that has to be developed. It would be wrong to confine attention only to the acquisition aspect under the capital outlay head for determining capability, as has often been done in India while analysing the defence budget, for that would be a truncated view of capability development. Having said that, it is also to be recognised that equipment and systems as required in the present-day warfare would be the most crucial aspect of capability planning.

Determination of Defence Capabilities: The South African Model

The establishment, development, preparation and maintenance of defence capabilities constitute the main cost elements of defence. The determination of force design and force structure is the prime area of deliberation.

Capabilities are required to meet possible future threats or contingencies. The first step, therefore, in deciding about capabilities to be aimed at is determination of defence contingencies. This entails describing in some detail the possible future events that defence forces might have to counter.

Explaining the South African defence planning model for determination of optimum defence capability , Maj Gen L. N. Le Roux (Retd) indicates, on the "need" side, various possible defence contingencies in which the South African defence forces may need to be deployed, were determined and described. Next, they were subjected to probability and impact studies to evaluate the relative risks associated with these contingencies.

For each of the defined contingencies, the best operational concept and corresponding defence capabilities (mini-force design) requirement had to be determined. War-gaming and simulation processes were found to be best tools for doing this.

The full life-cycle sustainable cost for each of these force designs was determined as accurately as possible. This cost consists of annual personnel cost, annual operating cost and annualised capital cost. (Annualised capital cost is calculated by adding the full acquisition cost and the mid-life upgrade cost of capital equipment and dividing it through the operational life of such equipment. This shows the effect that the inclusion of such equipment in the force design will have on the annual budget.)

On the 'cost constrained' side, various defence budget scenarios were determined within what was considered to be the affordable range of the national economy.

"Various amalgamated force design options were then determined within various budget scenarios and these were used as the basis for exhaustive consultation between the DoD and the Parliamentary Defence Committee and to some extent with the civil society. The discussions could focus on evaluating options with a clear indication of cost and risk implications."[5] In this context, along with the concept of 'cost', the concept of 'defence value' can also be brought in, in determining allocation of resources towards optimum capability development. As Le Roux points out, "During the South African process, it was argued that as defence is concerned with possible future events or threats (defence contingencies), each of which carries an implied risk to the state, defence value should be equated to risk reduction." Each defence contingency carries with it an associated risk, each having a different impact, including that on civil society. If, therefore, the relative risk value of such contingencies can be determined, this would help in the development of a system of determining relative defence values.

This is not an easy process, but it must be attempted if we want to achieve optimum defence capability within the given resources. This is a step by step approach, with each having its own importance.

Summarising the South African defence capability development approach, Le Roux says: "Once the list of contingencies, defence value calculations (relative risk reduction values) and the cost of the elements of the force design were available, calculations of best value for money were done. *The whole process was supported by a strong computer-based system due to its complexity and size. The South African Department of Defence used the services of a decision-making support consultancy service for computer support to the process.... the project was known as Project Optimum.*[6] (Italics mine.)

This was an inclusive process in decision-making where political decision-makers, and other government departments, academics, civil society and defence experts participated. This process ultimately led to, and culminated in, the approval by the South African government of the force design of the armed forces.

This was essential at that time (1998), le Roux points out, as the defence forces needed a clear commitment by the Government of South Africa for development, preparation and maintenance of such a force. "Without it, no meaningful long-term planning or medium-term programming and budgeting could be done."[7]

The force design, which was arrived at on the above basis, together with required support structures, formed the basis for other long-term plans such as the capital acquisition plan, the facilities or infrastructure plan and the personnel plan. But, as mentioned, the basic step is approval of the force design arrived at on a scientific basis, as outlined above. The involvement of political decision-makers, other government agencies and civil society is necessary for developing the force design, so that long-term commitment in terms of budgetary resources can be made for capability development.

The Australian Model of Capability-Building

We can now look at the Australian capability development model. The Australian government concentrated on the procurement procedure as apart from continuing delays in delivery of major equipment and cost overruns, they were not sure that the right mix of capabilities was being developed to match the capability to defence strategy. They came to the conclusion that the procurement procedure required fundamental reforms and towards that end, appointed a Review Committee for Defence Procurement under the chairmanship of Macolm Kinnaird, which submitted its report in 2003.

The report pointed out that determination of strategic priorities for defence and security of the nation has obvious implications for capability development.

In capability planning, most importantly, judgements need to be made concerning what mix of capability and what trade-offs between new and existing equipment are in the nation's interest. The Committee was unambiguous on the point that these *judgements are clearly the prerogative of the elected government.*[8] "**But for the government to remain confident that it is controlling the decision-making process, the Australian Defence Organisation (Defence) must provide greater clarity in setting out options available to develop and sustain ADF capabilities within a defence budget**."[9]

To ensure this, they made the following recommendations:

Defence should present to the government, the following information in a succinct form on an annual basis:

- An assessment of the types of contingencies Australia might face in carrying out the strategic tasks endorsed by the government in the Defence White Papers.
- Advice on the military force required in each contingency and the capacity of the Australian Defence Force (ADF) to apply this force now and in the future; and advice on the capability to be sustained, acquired or retired to ensure that this can be achieved at an acceptable cost.

In this regard, similarity with the South African model is to be noticed. This indicates that assessment of the contingencies to be faced and the capacity of the defence forces to face them and make judgement about the capability gaps that are there and are to be made up, is the basic step in the capability planning and that is where the government has to be actively involved in the process.

Capability Definition and Assessment

For proper capability planning, it is essential to define it properly and make a proper assessment of the 'need' aspect. For achieving this, institution of a proper institutional mechanism and accountability are very important factors. This issue was squarely faced by the Kinnaird Committee in its deliberations. Referring to the Australian situation , the Committee observed that the government had, in the past, often been asked to approve acquisition proposals at a stage "where there has not been sufficient analysis within defence to give the confidence that financially and technically robust decisions are being made. Too often, poorly defined and inaccurately costed projects had been put to the government and passed." They observed that accountability for the process of defining and assessing capability and management of outcome was diffused. The position of the Vice Chief of Defence Force, they observed, was intended to bring focus to the management of development of defence capabilities, which, however, did not happen because of his numerous functions.

But capability definition and assessment was a vital task which required close and sustained attention. Therefore, they recommended, "A single point of accountability is needed to provide better integration of the capability definition and assessment process and it maintains a joint warfare focus."[10] They recommended that a three-star officer, military or civilian, should be responsible and accountable for managing capability definition and assessment. This appointment should be on a full-time basis, with a defined tenure.

The Australian government agreed that the organisation charged with developing capability proposals for government consideration needed to be strengthened, and appointed a three-star military officer as the Chief Capability Development Executive, who bears the responsibility for translating strategic directions expressed through the government's Defence White Papers and subsequent defence strategic updates and rigorous capability requirements analysis, into comprehensive business cases for new capabilities for government consideration.

The Australian government has also implemented a rigorous 'two-pass' approval system for its capability proposals. (The Kinnaird Committee also recommended that the 'two-pass' system should be incorporated in the Cabinet Handbook to ensure that all proposals are considered using the same disciplined approach.)

Under the two-pass approval system, the government is presented at 'first pass' with an initial business case which seeks the government's agreement to the level of capability required by the ADF and agreement on a range of options that might meet the schedule and capability requirements.

At its second consideration, the government is presented with very detailed acquisition business cases for each valid option containing tender quality data resulting from engagement with potential contractors.

At this stage, the government is exposed to the full cost of acquiring the capability and operating for the life of the capability across what is termed as Fundamental Inputs to Capability (which we have earlier brought out): organisation, collective training, supplies, support, personnel, facilities, etc. "The costs involved in these 'hidden' aspects of a capability had previously been either glossed over or ignored during the decision-making process, often quite unintentionally. The relationship of the fundamental inputs to capability with platforms and other hardware being acquired was not sufficienly understood or costed, leading to unpleasant surprises for the government and disappoinment to ADO after contract signature had occurred."[11]

A Defence Procurement Advisory Board (DPAB) was established (as recommended by the Review Committee) consisting of external business and public sector advisers to operate independently of operational processes, and free to provide advice and support to the Chief Executive Officer of the Defence Material Organisation.

It was realised that the organisational and process changes that occurred as a result of the Kinnaird Review and subsequent refinement were not sufficient to ensure that defence capabilities were properly structured. It was necessary to provide sufficient guidance that links capability planning to defence strategy and strategic circumstances.

The classified Australia's Military Strategy (AMS) describes how the military power of the nation might be applied to achieve national security policy objectives. AMS considers alternative approaches to potential contingencies and evaluates the types of operation the Australian Defence Forces might be involved in. Then there is the Defence Planning Guidance (DPG) which is a classified strategic planning document. The DPG articulates the strategic priorities. It includes an analysis of the strategic environment, identifying the contingencies that Australia might face in the time-frames of 0 to 5, 10 to 15 and 20 or more years.[12]

The description of the future strategic environment within DPG is intended to directly guide capability planning. Contingencies judged as high priority are developed further into the Australian Illustrative Planning Scenarios (AIPS) which are used to test the concepts and capabilities. The DPG identifies the objectives and relative priority for a defence capability to respond to, or shape, the future strategic environment. Then, there is Future Joint Operating Concept which assists in articulating future roles, missions and methods of the ADF. This shared understanding guides operational planning and capability planning.

The Defence Capability Strategy sets the vision and capability goals, and it specifically explains how capability requirements are linked to strategic guidance. It provides comprehensive guidance to capability managers regarding priorities for, and balance between, various capabilities. Capability managers, the most prominent being the Service Chiefs, are made responsible and accountable, as recommended by the Kinnaird Committee, for monitoring and reporting to the government on all aspects of approved defence capabilities.

On the above basis, the Defence Capability Plan (DCP) is prepared which articulates the government's ten-year programme of new capital investment "The plan is reviewed annually to take account of changing strategic circumstances, new technologies and changed priorities, in the context of the overall defence budget."[13]

The White Paper and other guidance provided by the government, together with the 'strategic trail' laid by planning documents, as mentioned above, inform about development of more detailed capability, workforce, preparedness and financial guidance.

One thing is clear from the above: the government has to be closely involved in the development of the capability plan.

The adoption of capability-based planning is not as an in-fashion thing—it is to achieve a 'transformation' of defence with four basic aims:

- It should seek to align defence with the real requirement of the nation through a clear role definition.

- It should help in meeting the contingencies.
- It should make defence efficient and effective i.e the defence force should be able to achieve its task in a professional and mission oriented manner.
- It should make defence cost-effective.

Since we have announced the shift to capability-based planning, it is necessary to know how others are doing it and what are the steps involved in framing it. The South African and Australian models of capability planning are very relevant in this regard.

Linking Budgeting with Capability Planning

While discussing the Australian model, it is important to note that in the year 2000, the Australian Department of Defence moved away from the old Five-Year Defence Programme system which they had borrowed from the US defence to a ten-year budgeting system. It is not just a coincidence that the introduction of the ten-year budgeting system coincided with the Australian government announcing a White Paper which provided a ten-year capability plan and a ten-year funding commitment.

The Defence White Paper 2000 set out the government's long-term strategic direction and capability enhancement for the next decade. In the White Paper, the Australian government committed to increase defence funding by an average of about 3 per cent in real terms in the next decade. While committing this funding for the next ten years, the Australian government assessed the strategic environment, Australia's interest and objectives, as also costed the capabilities required by the Australian Defence Forces to protect the country's strategic interests. In practice, the government met or exceeded its White Paper funding commitment. In the 2006-07 budget, the government also decided to continue to increase defence spending by 3 percent per annum until 2015-16. This meant a 15-year commitment to 3 per cent real growth in defence funding.

The Ten-Year Defence Management and Financial Plan (DMFP) in Australia

The annual DMFP sets out ten-year financial plan. It is unique in defence as it is to finance the long-term defence capability plan. "DMFP enables Ministers to make informed budgetary and strategic decisions on defence by bringing in one document the expected financial position of the portfolio taking into account existing commitments and new investments."[14]

The logic in the above contention is important. In defence, it is the long-term financial plan which enables proper decision-making regarding investments and prioritisation rather than the other way round as there are competing demands. Therefore, the drawing up of a long-term financing plan is equally important, if not more, for putting in position an affordable capability plan. Sequentially, the decision to move to the ten-year budgeting system and provide for an annual increase of the defence budget by 3 percent in real terms was made in the year 2000, even before prioritisation under the capability plan took shape.

The DMFP is a rolling plan from which the annual plan is derived. Each year, Year 1 becomes the budget and a new Year 10 is added.[15] It is to finance the defence capability plan which is reviewed regularly to take account of changing strategic circumstances, new technologies and changed priorities derived from the Defence Planning Guidance and Defence Capability Strategy.

RMA and Capability Plan

RMA can be taken as shorthand for the integration of the full spectrum of advances in military technology. One has to conceive of a future battlespace scenario in which network-enabled synchronised operations, tailored effects, cyber-manoeuvre and joint war-fighting would predominate.

Any capability planning today has to take note of RMA on the future battlespace scenario to develop RMA-related capabilities within a given time-frame.

By the beginning of 2000, Australia's response to RMA had the following characteristics.

Australian planners tended to use a 2020 time-frame for assessing the value of RMA technologies.

Secondly, Australian strategists tended to view information networking, involving the rapid dissemination of real-time surveillance and targeting data as the most important outcome likely to emerge from RMA technologies during the next two decades. This was termed as the knowledge edge philosophy.

Thirdly, Australian policy-makers concentrated on trying to refine a set of indigenous concepts while relying on technological experimentation.

In adopting the RMA philosophy, the Australian policy-makers took note of the challenge of a huge financial burden to reequip the ADF for 21st century operations because of obsolescence of existing capabilities. According to one calculation, the sum required for new investment was estimated as between $80 and 100 billion for the period 2000-20, which exceeded the likely level of investment by a big sum. It was felt that application of RMA technologies may present innovative capability solutions that could yield financial savings. The most critical ADF assets in the future would lie, according to influential writings on RMA , not simply in the power of platforms and weapons, but increasingly in the integration of systems and skills to produce combat effects.[16]

The White Paper 2000 acknowledged the overriding importance of RMA, which it thought, was based on the global information technology revolution, and it felt that effective use of information was at the heart of Australia's defence capability. The main characteristics of the RMA were identified in the White Paper as follows:

- Trend towards the integration of military forces for joint operations.
- The networking of individual systems and capabilities to achieve whole-of-force effects and multiplied combat power.
- Changes to military organisation and doctrine.

Spaced-based technologies such as Unmanned Aerial Vehicles (UAVs) and Unmanned Combat Aerial Vehicles (UCAVs) were identified in Defence 2000 as emergent systems that offered a great deal of potential for surveillance, reconnaissance, information gathering and, eventually, delivery of combat power. "To facilitate the drive towards cutting edge RMA-Knowledge Edge research, the White Paper designated Information

Capabilities to be an integral part of a $16 billion, ten-year Defence Capability Plan (DCP) unveiled in the document." [17] In fact, in terms of capital expenditure, information technologies ranked third in Australia's defence-spending hierarchy.

The long-term funding commitment made in the White Paper was based on these considerations.

Combined Operational Effectiveness and Investment Appraisal: Its Role in the UK's Defence Procurement.

The aim of capability planning is basically to identify the most cost-effective future force mix and, hence, the most effective programme of expenditure from future defence budgets. In this sense, what capability planning is trying to achieve is not very different from what systems analysis or operational analysis in a broader sense was trying to achieve in the past. Instead of going through the route of identifying the contingencies and developing capabilities to meet them, one can go through the route of identifying the military tasks which the armed forces must be organised, trained and equipped to undertake successfully and, on that basis, determine what equipment would be needed. Concepts of operation are required to be developed to see how the tasks may best be performed; force-mix studies are required to be made to identify the most cost-effective mix of equipment to provide the necessary capabilities in future years. For this scenario, analysis is also required.

This is basically the approach which has been adopted by the UK MoD during the last two decades. "To identify the most cost-effective future force mix…, the military operational analyses at the Centre for Defence Analysis use MoD-approved scenarios and concepts of operation to consider the different increments to force cost and effectiveness which would result from the procurement and operation in service of various numbers of different classes of equipment to supplement or replace the existing national inventory."[18] An extensive programme of operational analysis studies can suggest an optimal balance of investment in various classes of equipment to maximise effectiveness of military forces in a given scenario, and the same process, on a larger scale, can suggest the optimal force-mix in alternative scenarios.

Though theoretically possible, this kind of optimisation procedure is not always justifiable because of the uncertainties inherent in military operation analysis at the campaign level and because of the uncertainty in postulated cost and effectiveness of future equipment. "In practice, analysts select, with military advice, a set of candidate force mixes, each containing different numbers of different classes of equipment chosen so that numbers are operationally plausible so that the total cost of the force mix is close to a target budget."[19]

The results of such studies would depend on future military tasks envisaged for the UK forces, on the level of effectiveness to be achieved by the UK forces and on the limits of the UK defence budget.

Organisational and Procedural Reforms in the UK for Better Procurement Planning

It was recognised by the beginning of the Eighties, that in all major future operations by the UK forces, the sea, land and air elements of these forces will be interdependent.

In 1985, the Ministry of Defence (MoD) was reorganised to create a tri-Service Defence Staff responsible for all future planning for defence policy, operations and procurement.

The Defence Staff now directs operational analysis of the future military operations which help in determining the future defence roles of the UK forces.

It also helps in directing scientific research in key areas of defence technology to explore their potentialities and identify problems.

The operational analysis and scientific research studies are generally undertaken on behalf of the MoD by the Centre for Defence Analysis (CDA) and Defence Research Agency (DRA) respectively. Both these organisations are divisions of the Defence Research and Evaluation Agency (DERA) which was formed in 1995 to be the MoD's principal adviser on defence technology and equipment.

The Defence Staff uses the results of operational analysis studies to establish future needs for a particular military capability. It uses the results of scientific research to formulate a Staff Target. Subsequently, after getting further inputs, the Staff Requirement is also formulated which defines the qualities of new defence equipment which is needed to provide a particular defence capability.[20]

In the past, the UK procedure for selection and procurement of military equipment on the basis of specification and justification of military operational requirements by the Defence Staff was followed by identification and procurement by the Procurement Executive of the most economical equipment to meet the requirement. There was hardly any debate on Staff Requirements which the customer service had already formulated nor were the Defence Staff receptive to any questioning of what was considered as an essential requirement.

A review of the UK equipment procedures in 1991, contained in what is known as the Buckley Report, called for substantial change in procurement decision-making.

In particular, it specified that future proposals for equipment procurement should be accompanied by a cost-effectiveness report. The report should be based on results of operational analysis and forecasts of life-cycle cost of alternative equipment options.

The UK MoD's implementation of the Buckley Committee Report led to the establishment of a high level Equipment Approvals Committee (EAC) with only four members: Chief Scientific Adviser (CSA), who is the Chairman and Vice Chief of Defence Staff(VCDS), Chief of Defence Procurement (CDP) and 2nd Permanent Under Secretary (2nd PUS). It also prepared a set of Internal Guidelines contained in 7 Dossier Papers which contribute to the EAC's decision.

Among the Dossier Papers are:

- Covering Paper which should present to the EAC their staff's conclusion and recommendations, noting particularly the trade-offs between alternatives and any uncertainties which could influence decision-making.
- Requirement Definition, presenting and justifying the operational requirement, and alternative ways of meeting it; this paper may refer to the Staff Target.
- Combined Operational Effectiveness and Investment Appraisal (COEIA): this is the heart of the matter, which presents forecasts of

relative operational effectiveness and life-cycle cost of all practicable alternative equipment options , fully describing the main features of COEIA studies; this paper may refer to detailed information on scenarios, specifications and methodology in other reports, which do not accompany the dossier.

- Procurement issues and strategy.

The new procurement process became more integrated, with the Defence Staff and Procurement Executive working closely together to identify the most cost-effective option in the procurement of defence equipment to provide the required military capability.[21]

In this new process, a COEIA study was required to be undertaken in support of each EAC decision to allocate substantial funds to the project's procurement.

But problems relating to procurement continued. There were slippages due to technical difficulties, redefinition of requirements, as also budgetary constraints leading to postponement of expenditure. There were serious cost overruns due to programme changes, changes in equipment specification and poor estimating.

Consequently, reform of the defence procurement policy was identified as one of main objectives of the MoD's Strategic Defence Review (SDR) when it was announced in May 1997.

Smart Procurement Initiative

The key reform to come out of the SDR was the Smart Procurement Initiative (SPI), which aimed to establish a new customer/supplier relationship between the MoD and industry and to deliver equipment "faster, cheaper and better."[22]

The key elements of the SPI were as follows:

- The introduction of a "through-life system approach" covering both initial acquisition and in-service management of equipment. This approach led to the establishment of Integrated Project Teams (IPTs) bringing together the main stakeholders for the life of the project. Industry would be part of the IPT except for the competitive evaluation phase.

- More comprehensive project planning earlier in the procurement cycle with appropriate trade-offs between military requirements, time and costs to avoid later time and cost overruns and delays.
- Partnering arrangements with industry, where open competition was unviable.
- Incremental acquisition whereby equipment would be initially accepted into service with less ambitious capability and subsequently upgraded in lower-risks steps.

Organisational Changes

The SDR concluded that the Procurement Executive (PE) should be more commercially focussed and have a more closely defined relationship with its customer. *The review recommended that this could best be achieved by turning the PE into an Agency and establishment of a new central customer in the MoD Headquarters called Equipment Capability Customer (ECC).*

The role of the ECC would be to determine equipment capability requirements. Directors of Equipment Capability would act as the primary customer and liaison point for Integrated Project Teams within the Defence Procurement Agency (DPA) and Defence Logistic Organisation (DLO).

The DPA was launched in April 1999. The Agency slimmed down the top management structure and placed IPTs at the centre of its work.

The IPT concept of bringing together the main stakeholders in a programme, including the MoD, armed forces and industry, was a major reform. It was considered to be the most efficient method for delivering the 'through life approach' envisaged under SPI.

The IPT would be responsible for delivering equipment solutions to meet the requirements of the ECC. A leader would be appointed to each IPT and would have authority over the programme.

The DLO which was also launched in April 1999 was a change of huge significance for defence. It was felt by the SDR that single Service logistic structures, given the present context, have outlived their utility. *The objective of DLO was to bring together the three single Service logistics organisations and to establish a consolidated approach to the in-service management of defence stores and equipment. DLO was tasked with streamlining logistic management, promoting best practices and rationalising stock holdings within each of the Services.*

The other major change related to the Defence Evaluation and Research Agency (DERA), including the UK government's research establishment which has been split into two separate organisations. One is QinetiQ which is to enter into Public Private Partnership (having both government and private stakeholders) and will seek to win business from commercial organisations as also from the MoD. The other is the Defence Science and Technology Laboratory (DSTL) which would be an integral part of the MoD and was to undertake those sensitive areas of research which need to remain under government control. These areas include operational analysis to plan the future UK force structure required for potential military operations.

An important element of smart acquisition continues to be the MoD's Combined Operational Effectiveness and Investment Appraisal (COEIA) procedure mentioned above. COEIA uses both military operational analysis and discounted cash flow methodologies to provide a structured and traceable comparison of the military and financial aspects of alternative equipment proposals being considered for procurement.

A key issue in any new project is the selection of the best equipment strategy. The UK MoD has in the past years used a mix of strategies, suited to the class of equipment being procured. Sometimes it has funded development of new equipment and sometimes it has bought existing equipment off-the-shelf. "National development of major projects is now extremely rare, since fixed costs of design and development of many classes of equipment... have escalated to unaffordable levels."[23]

Financial management of the acquisition budget is extremely important. It must be ensured that funding profiles of various MoD branches are consistent and synchronised so that funding profiles of all current projects combine to give the total budget profile, without large fluctuations.

The budget planning horizon should be neither too short or too long. As a compromise, the UK MoD now uses a 10-year horizon.[24]

Need For A Budget Plan

When there are several competing demands, and systems are costly, one cannot be sure that the available funds would be adequate or not to meet the requirements, unless there is indication of likely budgets in future years. Since items to be inducted are to be planned for several years in advance, uncertainty about the budgetary provisions, say, five or six years from now, would be inimical for any long-term planning for acquisition programmes. In many cases, commitments are to be made now as also down payments are required to be made, which can be done with confidence that there will be adequate money to induct the systems when they are ready.

Costing of programmes is another essential step for proper planning. If indications are available about the likely budgets in future years, it is possible to work out, through undertaking a proper costing exercise for each programme on the anvil, about the adequacy or otherwise of the future years' budgets.

If there is likely to be a deficit between the likely budget and the aggregate cost of programmes , then various cost cutting options can be considered. One approach would be to eliminate one or more major equipment programmes from the list. The other would be to undertake a cost saving exercise by taking a fresh look at the specifications of the items to be procured and confine it to the essentials, without giving up any programme. The remaining options would be either to postpone one or more programmes, to find cheaper alternatives or to impose cuts across the board by reducing the numbers or the capability.

The point is, considering these options in the light of limited resources and arriving at an appropriate decision, is the very heart of defence planning.

The fact that we are not faced with these issues in defence means we are not really in the planning business and indulge in ad hoc decision-making, without bothering about the long-term financial consequences of today's decisions. It is implicitly assumed that there is no resource constraint in the long run.

This approach will not lead to optimal allocation of resources, and is rather tailor-made for wastage and inefficient use of the taxpayer's money. That there is a resource constraint is made very explicit every year by the MoF by imposing a budgetary ceiling on the defence budget, irrespective of the requirements projected. What is true for the yearly budget would also be true for the future years' budgets, though it is not spelt out. Since ceilings on future years' budgets are not spelt out, there is no inhibition in making budgetary commitments for future years by placing orders today for equipment and weapon systems which would mature after several years.

When ceilings are imposed in the course of the budgetary exercise, as it is done today, the total commitments made in terms of orders made in advance may, along with other obligatory payments, make it difficult to make new commitments. It would then lead to stretchouts of programmes, or inability to take up urgently required new programmes.

If, however, a budget plan for defence is announced covering the next ten-years, then these problems can be avoided. Rather, it would lead to better planning by bringing in prioritisation as the total resources available in the next ten years will be known. What is also required is long-term costing of ongoing programmes and those which are about to be implemented.

Drawing up, and sanctioning, a budget plan, accompanied by detailed costing of programmes, therefore, would be the basic steps for evolving a credible and affordable defence plan.

Linking Defence Budget with Defence Strategy

In defence strategy, the most important element is the objective setting exercise; in fact, objective setting can be identified as the most important strategy-making exercise, as it will throw open the alternatives out of which choices have to be made.

So on one side is strategic planning and on the other is defence budgeting. Can these two together be linked? PPBS, introduced in the US defence, attempted this in the 1960s.

PPBS was the formal attempt to link planning in the sense of strategy-making with budgeting through the device of programming, in a single system. In the programming stage, various alternatives to achieve the strategic objectives were evaluated through cost-benefit analyses and decisions taken to pursue a particular course. The link between strategy and budgets was done on the basis of "outputs" rather than "inputs". The outputs were the "mission-oriented building blocks" such as Strategic Retaliatory Forces, (which incidentally was the basic thrust of PPBS in achieving economy, as maximum duplication of programmes was taking place in this), instead of internal structural divisions such as the army, navy and air force. Thus, planning was to be done around strategic thrust areas rather than around Services or Departments.

The portion of the defence budget which can be linked to the strategy-making exercise is the capital outlay budget which in recent years amounted to more than 40 percent of the defence budget.

While theoretically sound, in practice, programme budgeting reduced itself to capital budgeting and the strategy aspects were gradually lost sight of. P (Planning in the sense of objective setting exercise and means of achieving them) did not get linked to PB (Programming and Budgeting). It was no more than proposals for capital investments, and capital budgeting was the crux of the whole business.

The question then arose as to whether capital budgeting could itself be treated as some form of strategy-making. In defence budgeting in India, there is an implicit faith in treating capital budgeting by enabling modernisation of the military as the essence of strategy-making.

Two points, however, came out through analysis of capital budgeting techniques in the private sector:

One, in capital budgeting, the information about the projects rests with the sponsors below. It is not with the reviewers above. It is the former who conceive the projects and carry out the cost-benefit analyses. It is really bottom up planning.

Two, a great deal of subjective judgement goes into the projections of costs and benefits which may defy analytical treatment. It is also the experience in capital budgeting that once a project is sponsored, it is always approved by the top management, for rejection of a proposal is tantamount to lack of trust in the sponsors.

Capital Outlay and Formulation of Strategy

We have already indicated that proposals for capital outlay follow a bottom-up approach. We also know that strategy formulation is the domain of top management. But one cannot help feeling that there must be a close link between strategy formulation and capital budgeting, as in any case, the capital outlay proposals are to be approved at the top.

To quote Henry Mintzberg on the subject, " Our own suspicion , however, is that links are typically informal at best, that, in fact, most capital budgeting takes place in the context of existing strategies that are implied rather than new ones that are explicated. What this means is that most capital budgeting probably takes place in the absence of any fresh strategy formulation activity at all , perhaps even any discussion of strategy *per se*. Strategy is implicitly assumed to be a given."[25]

But what is important to note is that capital projects proposed can decisively influence the strategy pursued. Firstly, by functioning within a given strategic context, if there is one, capital outlay budgeting can reinforce existing strategy. The proposed projects follow the existing pattern. Secondly, what is more important, as Mintzberg points out,a capital project "may break an established pattern and thereby create a precedent that changes the strategy."[26] The strategy formulation gets done inadvertently. It means that an organisation makes its investment decisions on an ad hoc basis, project by project and in this process, patterns form to become strategies. A small opening through capital budgeting can stimulate a large change in strategy.

It is the strategic plan which should determine capital acquisition in defence rather than the other way round. Resource limitation is another reason for strategic planning.

Strategic planning is extremely important in defence as it is a process of deciding on objectives, changes in these objectives and on determining the resources to be used to attain these objectives. It involves also determining the policies that are to govern acquisition and use of these resources. In the private sector, the objective of a firm is clear: to make more and more profit. In the public sector and particularly in defence, objectives are required to be determined in an uncertain environment. That is why system analysis is so very important to help in strategic planning in defence

In the public sector, for strategic planning, there is need to make a clear distinction between the decisions regarding goals and the planning to achieve the goals. Planning is to be done by professional planners. Decisions on goals are a political function. Therefore, strategic planning must involve a scheme for interaction between politicians and planners. Keeping this in mind, one can say that defence planning in India is still to take on the character of strategic planning. Absence of a Defence White Paper is clear indication of the fact that strategic planning is absent in the defence sector in India. The other pointer is the absence of a link between planning and budgeting, as brought out above.

Selection of weapons is an important aspect of strategic planning. Therefore, establishing a linkage between strategic objectives, budgets and selection of weapons is essential. The process should be a closed cycle from strategy to budgets and from budgets to weapon selection and back to potential strategies on the basis of weapons deployed.

To develop a credible strategy, the "affordability" constraint has to be introduced in the planning process. This is the only way to develop a credible strategy and link it with the weapons we buy and the numbers we can buy. Numbers are important. The national security strategy should be resource constrained to make it credible. But linkage is not the only way. "Proper planning requires a defined strategy, a long-term affordability constraint, and the constant reiteration of the two…"[27]

The basic change required is to develop a long-range resource plan which is tied to security objectives. Plans should be drawn up on the basis of fiscal constraints, not in a general sense, but properly specified and made known to the Services while they are drawing up the long-term plans.

As Gansler observed, " Long-range resource plans, in the presence of realistic 5-15 year fiscal constraints, will force the military to set up long-term priorities rather than leave this role to civilians in the Office of the Secretary of Defense or to Congress."[28] The broad objective is to focus the Defence Department's weapon selection process and establishment of funding priorities on a period of 5-15 years, rather than on the next year's budget.

If the total amount to be available on a 15-year basis can be indicated, it will lead to several advantages.

That is why long-term budgeting is important in defence, to get priorities right and make necessary trade-offs in view of indicated ceilings in future budgets. But, as explained above, in the context of the experience of several countries, introduction of system planning is of utmost importance in the MoD, in Service Headquarters, as also in the lower echelons.

For establishing priorities we cannot delay in appointing a CDS, to give a new thrust to the modernisation of forces.

Why A Break From the Past May be Necessary for Modernisation

Let us look into the question of what happens when a five-year plan is not approved. Nothing much, to go by the deposition made by the MoD before the Standing Committee on Defence regarding the objectives of the 10th Plan and how they would be achieved in the absence of an approved plan. To quote from their written note on the subject, "The underlying theme of the 10th Plan is to make up deficiencies and voids, and to maintain sustained thrust towards continuous upgradation and modernisation of the existing assets besides inducting suitable replacements for equipment to be phased out on life expiry." So the implication is that given its limited scope, absence of an approved plan does not really matter. As to what is to be done is well known and availability of resources would determine the pace at which "deficiencies and voids" would be made good. Non-approval of the plan and not making available the indicated amounts for the plan also do not matter as most of the modernisation plan is an ongoing process and, shortfalls if any, would be made up in the subsequent plan periods.

So there is a great deal of complacency in the matter ,as it is business as usual. But should this be so? But how do you identify the gaps? It requires strategic planning with the probable operational situation in view.

Investments for Modernisation

Why a Break From the Past may be Necessary: To regard modernisation as an 'ongoing process' means that a scheme once started has to be finished at whatever cost, even though its relevance can be questioned in view of the changing security scenario and resources being required elsewhere. The effect of treating modernisation as an "ongoing process" is that there is no scope for zero-based review of ongoing schemes.

In fact, one of the best ways to generate funds for new modernisation schemes would be to foreclose those schemes which have lost their utility in view of the changing security scenario.

It is also not in keeping with the current thought that capability is required to be developed to operate effectively in a joint Services environment, in the entire spectrum of conflict, in the regional context.

The joint Services concept should mean a relook at the ongoing schemes to avoid duplication and overlap between the capabilities being acquired by each of the Services, on the basis of their own perspective plans.

Secondly, the concept of 'replacement' of the existing assets as a driving force for modernisation is not such an innocuous proposition, when the new item could be ten times costlier than the item being replaced . This is because in recent years, the Unit Production Cost (UPC) of most classes of equipment has grown between 5 per cent and 10 per cent per year in real (inflation adjusted) terms. For a few classes of equipment with rapidly rising military effectiveness, such as anti-tank and anti-submarine helicopters, the growth has been above 10 per cent. During the Cold War, for example the real UPC of tactical combat aircraft procured for the UK forces increased at about 10 percent per year which is equivalent to a ten-fold increase in real cost between generations 25 years apart.[29]

Therefore, one-to-one replacement of equipment and systems which have outlived their utility is out of the question, and it may call for reduction in force level. This will call for a comprehensive review of force planning, so that overall capabilities increase, even though there is a decrease in the numbers of equipment/ platforms.

Thirdly, developing the 'entire spectrum of capability' is also a new concept in defence planning which calls for the 'portfolio management' approach to investment for defence capability. Under the portfolio management approach, which is a 'mixed strategy' approach to defence investment, investments should address a number of objectives, to a greater or lesser degree, mitigating various kinds of risk. Instead of going in for a one-dimensional priority list and funding item after item in the list until the budget is exhausted, one thinks from the outset about doing something in all categories of challenge. This approach, therefore, calls for a close look at all ongoing schemes. Within a given regional category, one can think in terms of capabilities for different classes of scenarios.

Portfolio analysis in investment analysis can assist "in 'balancing' programmes and in marginal analysis, where to add and where to subtract the marginal dollar. Such actions are essential in capabilities-based planning."[30]

Even for identifying gaps in capability, portfolio analysis is required. It helps decision-makers decide how to adjust the portfolio so as to fill the gaps.

The portfolio analysis tool enables a user to compare and contrast investment options according to a number of quantitative and qualitative criteria. For strategic planning, as Paul Davis explains, such a tool can generate top-down depictions of alternatives and their implications over many years in the future. He calls for strategic judgement amidst uncertainty and conflicting demands. The aim should be to choose an investment programme that is flexible and adaptive. The investment programme is the strategy. We are yet to develop such a tool of analysis.

The portfolio analysis in investment planning leads to a top-down approach

This means a break from the past practice of concentrating on capability building only of an individual Service through a bottom-up approach.

There are other reasons for breaking away from the past such as the advent of RMA which calls for a holistic look at capability building for future investments. The future becomes important, not the commitments on the basis of decisions made several years back in the past but in the light of new technologies and future challenges.

Visualising the future scenario is also essential to develop capabilities and decide about the nature of weapons required. As Y. Dror put it in his inimitable way, "Thus, when two alternative designs for tanks are considered, the correct question is not what benefits and costs of the different tank designs are by themselves. The more correct question is what the different effects of the two tanks' designs on the total defence capacity will be...This is a totally different question, the answer to which depends on interrelations between the tanks and other components of defense systems. For instance, if combined land-air operations are potentially important, a slower tank may add more to the overall fighting capability than a faster tank, which conclusions cannot be reached in terms of the characteristics of each tank by itself."[31]

This again brings to the fore the need for scenario building in terms of the likely political military conflicts the country will be faced with and the objectives the country would pursue when faced with such conflicts.

Only in such a context can meaningful cost-effectiveness studies can be made.

In the hearings on the defence budget for FY 1965, Secretary McNamara was asked about his decision-making techniques and whether he was relying more and more on cost-effectiveness studies for decision-making. McNamara replied that he and his colleagues were relying more on "sophisticated analyses of potential political military conflicts and an appraisal of the advantage to the United States of alternative force sizes in relation to those contingencies. The cost-effectiveness study, as it would be narrowly defined, comes into importance only in choosing between alternative means of satisfying an established force requirement."[32] We need to question whether McNamara was describing an ideal process as it should be or the real process as obtaining, but the importance to be ascribed to the analysis of potential political-military situations, as they might emerge in the future, in long-term resource allocation decisions, comes out clearly.

Without clarification of strategic objectives, considering alternatives and without cost-effectiveness studies of each of the alternatives, no meaningful planning in defence can take place. This is one important lesson to be learnt from the PPBS experience of the Sixties.

When this focus is lost, as happened in subsequent Administrations in the USA when the Secretary of Defence assumed a more passive role in planning and the role of system analysis was downgraded, the 'planning' activity as conceived in the PPBS also lost its importance and by the beginning of Eighties, it was commented by many defence analysts in the USA that the first 'P' of PPBS was silent.

Institutional Changes for Proper Resource Allocation Decisions: The US Experience

The debate, going on for almost four years, resulting in the Goldwater-Nichols Department of Defense Act of 1986 which addressed some of the basic lacunae in the system of resource management in defence, originated at the highest level of the Joint Chiefs of Staffs (JCS) structure[33].

The Goldwater-Nichols Act 1986 gives the Chairman JCS the power to make budgetary recommendations in order to make the Services' budgetary proposals conform to the Secretary of Defence's strategic guidance and to the needs of Commanders-in-Chiefs (CINCs). The Act also empowers the Chairman to make recommendations on cross-Service budgetary trade-offs.

One of the most critical developments in the budgetary area, however, has been the emergence of the Vice Chairman JCS and a joint body called the Joint Requirement Oversight Council (JROC) as major players in resource allocation decisions. As the head of the JROC, the Vice Chairman has a lot of power to give shape to the long-term capability plan by his vision. The Vice Chairman is also Co-Chairman of the Defence Acquisition Board, a DoD body co-chaired by Undersecretary of Defence for Acquisition and Technology. This body is responsible for making the final recommendations to the Secretary of Defence on weapon procurement.

JROC tried to bring in the concept of joint capabilities and interoperability in the equipment procurement planning. JROC was also to authenticate that the proposed capability was required and not duplicative of another Service's programme and the submitted documentation adequately addressed all JCS -level joint-warfare and interoperability concerns.

Studies conducted during the Bush (2nd) Administration, however, concluded that the Service-initiated bottom up system was not conducive to commonality, interoperability and jointness. A decision was taken to direct the JCS to take responsibility for initiating material requirement from top-down to ensure that requirements were "born joint". In June 2003, the Joint Capabilities Integration Development System(JCIDS) was promulgated. This turned the traditional system of requirement generation of equipment, upside-down. "The decades-old threat-driven, bottom-up development process of warfare material requirements was summarily replaced by a revolutionary, capabilities-driven, top-down process."[34]

The JCIDS process encourages interoperability at the earliest stage of programme development. A proposal from one of the Services to build a new weapon system would be judged in large part on how it could contribute to joint war-fighting, as opposed to just the need of the Service. Officials would also guard against unnecessary duplication of effort, thereby promoting efficiency in the expenditure of DoD resources.[35] It also led to the establishment of Functional Capability Boards (FCBs), which have to vet the proposals for fielding new capabilities, which include representatives from the Joint Staff, Office of the Secretary of Defence, and the Services and combatant commandants. The Boards support Pentagon decision-makers, including the JROC and Joint Capabilities Board, in analysing and prioritising proposed war-fighting requirements. They also help in identifying gaps in capabilities.

Thus, deciding on proper investment for defence capabilities calls for many organisational and procedural changes, some of them quite drastic in nature. Capabilities are to be provided for a wide range of modern-day challenges and circumstances while working within an economic framework that necessitates hard choice.

Basic Requirements for Shifting to Capability Planning

The needs of joint operations are to be stressed in planning for capability. The Ministry of Defence has to identify the range of military missions that the joint force of the future will be required to accomplish within a given time-frame.

Defence Planning Scenarios (DPS) are required to be selected, developed and updated by the Ministry of Defence, on the basis of military and intelligence inputs. Each DPS should include a concept of operations which is to be based on the concept of joint operations applied to specific conditions, including geography and enemy force capabilities. The Services are to use DPS as starting points for analyses supporting planning, programming and acquisition efforts.

Threats are also to be conceived in terms of capabilities. What are the possible threat capabilities that are likely to faced by the joint force, and those which are 'most-likely' and with the largest impact would be the starting point for capability-based planning. This should lead to the development of what may be called 'prioritised capability gaps.' A decision is required to be made whether to accept the risk and allow the gap to continue, or solve the gap, after which, identify whether it requires a material or non-material solution. Then only can the optimum solution be found. Selecting the best option would be based largely on how much information is known about the capability gap. Information to be considered includes the operational needs, the ability to solve the gap without current capabilities, and technological advancements.

What would be the institutional mechanism for addressing these issues in a systematic and objective manner and make suitable recommendations to decision-makers? This cannot obviously done by the individual Services with their viewpoint limited by the capability requirement of the Service concerned.

Cost would be a major factor in determining which solution is adopted for solving the capability gap. It is now well recognised even in US defence, that the CPB must be not just fiscally informed, it is to be fiscally constrained, fixing the budget ceilings for several years for future choices in capability-based planning. These choices should include adding new capabilities while, at the same time, divesting the less needed capabilities.

To a significant extent, divestures should pay for the addition of new capabilities. We can no longer treat modernisation of forces just as an on-going activity.

CPB is more than developing capabilities. Metrics are required to assess the readiness and sufficiency of the current force. If the assessment shows unacceptable risks, resources have to be provided, by reducing the requirement of future capability.

Without these changes, as seen from the experience of other countries, it would not be possible to shift to capability-based planning nor can a long-term budgetary commitment be supported.

Why is a Long-Term Finance Plan Essential in Defence?

Let us mention at the outset that the issue of financing of the long-term defence plan is yet to be taken up as an issue for discussion and debate. One of the reasons for this would be that even the five-year plans do not get approved. Another is that no parameter is available for drawing up the long-term financial plan. For example, the long-term defence financial plan of Australia is based on 3 percent growth in real terms for 15 years. This is based on the policy decision of the Australian government as announced in periodic Defence White Papers since 2000. The third reason is that our short-term financial management, as seen from the management of the annual budget, leaves much to be desired (e.g. Budget Estimates getting frequently revised at the Revised Estimates stage), therefore, even thinking of long-term financial planning seems to be too ambitious.

The presumption is that financing of long-term plans on a sound basis would depend on how well financial management is done in the short run. This presumption may not be correct. It is also possible that if there is a clear long-term financial plan which can be the basis for financial commitment and can provide a framework, then short-term financial management would improve. It has often been held in budgetary literature that the existence of a medium-term expenditure plan which is adhered to with a certain degree of strictness, and provides a basis for annual budgeting, is a necessary condition for efficient short-term financial management. For defence, since it is concerned with force structure development and capability planning, a long-term financial plan is necessary.

In fact, short-term and long-term expenditure management is inextricably linked in defence. This point has to be appreciated.

Since our budget is prepared on the cash-outgo basis, and the unobligated amount annually available in the capital budget is quite significant in absolute terms, it permits entering into contracts with large commitments of expenditure in future years because only a limited amount needs to be provided in the budget initially on the cash-outgo basis. With several such contractual obligations bunching together, the 'obligational' expenditure as a percentage of the defence budget would go up considerably in future years. Commitments made for a large number of weapon programmes because of a large increase in the capital budget, would create what is called in the USA a "stern wave" of defence spending in the later part of the decade and will be more pronounced upto the middle of the next decade. There would also be a "bow wave" of defence expenditure, which will raise defence expenditure to a still higher level in the next decade.*

Long-Term Costing and Long-Term Budget Plan

We have not yet introduced the concept of long-term costing in defence. In the UK, a major plank of defence planning has been long-term or ten-year costing. The need for it was felt even before introducing programme budgeting. The process of resource allocation in the UK defence is known as Long-Term Costing (LTC).

LTC provides a framework for assessing the affordability of expenditure proposals. Since much of defence spending involves long-term commitment, the UK MoD undertook annual costing of programmes, looking ten years ahead. These are examined in relation to budgetary planning assumptions. The LTC looks forward four years for operating costs and ten years for equipment. It starts with programmes approved the previous year. So the costing exercise is essentially a recosting. The programme is issued for recosting in April each year in the form of a departmental plan, which is an internal classified document which sets out a range of management and performance objectives which the MoD must meet, and the force levels and readiness levels for the identified military tasks. It goes to the Service Chiefs and the Top-Level Budget(TLB) holders, who have their own management plans which point out in increasing levels of detail, the specific outputs required from each Command and management area. In this way, programme assumptions are passed down the budgetary chain to individual budget holders and to project directors of equipment. The assumptions are then recosted by budget holders and project directors. Each budget holder must show how he can manage his activities within previously-agreed resources. They must show how cost growth in one area can be offset elsewhere.

---

* The term "stern wave", reflects the fact that spending commitments already made push up the level of defence spending from behind. The term "bow wave" refers to increased weapon procurement funding or commitment of expenditure, brought about by the movement of several weapons programmes from the R&D stage to the production stage. It may also refer to future contractual commitments for the purchase of new weapons.

The costings are progressively aggregated up the budgetary hierarchy and closely scrutinised at each level of management.

The central assessment of the full recosting begins in December each year, following the Chancellor's announcement of the new three-year plans for public expenditure The new cash plans are used to calculate a ten-year benchmark against which one can judge the recosted programme. Final decisions on the content of the programme are taken by the Secretary of State.

The result is a long-term plan and costings which set objectives and match policy, commitment and resources. It forms the basis for the defence budget, for the allocation of cash to budget holders and setting of objectives down the management hierarchy. It also provides the programme assumptions on which the Department bases its next Public Expenditure Survey (PES) bid for the budget and LTC cycle.

Within a framework established by the LTC , under the UK system, the procurement of weapon system, proceeds on a step-by-step basis. In fact, it cannot be otherwise, as the LTC makes it resource constrained defence planning . Therefore ,the obsolescence of an existing system is not sufficient reason to buy a replacement The replacement must be justified by showing that a gap in capability exists and demonstrating its military value of filling it in the context of defence policy and the planning assumptions about the sort of operations to which British forces might be committed in future. We have already discussed further steps taken by them under the COEIA procedure.

The approval of the LTC is a very significant step. This means that the Secretary of State has agreed, for internal planning purposes, to a set of key assumptions deriving directly from government policy. This includes the size and shape of the armed forces over the next ten years, the order and delivery schedule of equipment, development programmes that would be undertaken, and many other assumptions about commitments, deployment of major units and exercises. In other words, it covers the entire gamut of defence activities.

If we have to establish a link between long-term planning and budgeting, it can only be through a device like the LTC.[36]

Let us note, however, that the LTC procedure does not usher in a long-term budget plan.

The budget plan under the Public Expenditure Survey (PES) system in the UK provides budget ceilings for three years , as for other Departments. This is not good enough for defence, as brought out above, either for control or for planning purposes. Here there is a contradictory stance. The LTC was introduced to bring in cost consciousness in long-term defence planning and to stay within affordable limits from the budgetary point of view by keeping control over commitments. As the aim is to decide about the size and shape of the armed forces over the next ten years, the order and delivery schedule of equipment, development programmes that would be undertaken, and assumptions about commitments, deployments and exercises, then logically and inevitably, it should lead to a ten-year budget plan, though on a rolling basis. Otherwise, contradiction might arise between planning and budgeting; ultimately, the force structure might suffer and not meet the planned requirement. It seems from recent experiences of defence expenditure management in the UK that this is what has happened. The British Strategic Defence Review was done in 1998 , with a major force review, which was hailed as a rigorous exercise keeping in view the resource constraints. In terms of procurement requirements, the centrepiece was the decision to focus on expeditionary warfare with two new large aircraft carriers as the main capability. The major casualty, however, in order to protect the funding for the Future Aircraft Carrier (CVF) budget during this period has been the surface fleet of the Royal Navy. The 1998 plan was to reduce the surface fleet from 35 to32 ships and 25 to 22 minehunters, but the figures ten years later were 26 surface ships and 16 minehunters, which has major implications for operational capability and manpower planning.[37]

Therefore, this LTC model, even when backed up by a comprehensive strategic review, is not good enough for adoption for force planning purposes, particularly, in an environment of fiscal consolidation. Further, a defence review should take place at periodic intervals to enable mid-course correction.

The costing exercises should take place within a ten-year budgetary plan, with a view to stay within the budgetary ceilings by making necessary adjustments within competing programmes. Costing should not lead to more bargaining for resources. Costing has to be reviewed every year. The cap on resources on a long-term basis has to be accepted for stability of the availability of resources, leading to better long-term planning, which would make defence capability building an affordable exercise.

The sequence in a resource constrained ten-year capability plan should be clear:

- Have a comprehensive defence review at periodic intervals.
- Draw up a ten-year budget plan.
- Formulate programmes and programme elements for various capabilies.
- Undertake costing of programmes and programme elements on the basis of life-cycle costs and subject them to yearly review.
- Adjust programmes to keep within budgetary ceilings not only for this year but also for future years as envisaged for the ten-year budget plan.

It is feasible to have a ten-year budget plan for defence in India, after the projections made for the defence budget upto 2014-15 in the Thirteenth Finance Commission, which took into account inputs from both the Ministry of Defence and Ministry of Finance, while emphasising the need for fiscal consolidation and returning to the goals laid down by the FRBM Act regarding revenue and fiscal deficit, though with an altered time-frame. The point has been accepted in principle by the Finance Minister.

To quote from the report, "For defence expenditure, the Ministry of Finance has projected a growth rate of 7 per cent per annum for defence revenue expenditure. Capital expenditure is projected to grow at 10 percent per annum. The Ministry of Defence has emphasised the need to provide adequately for enhanced force multipliers. We also recognise the need for some real growth in defence revenue expenditure, to allow for adequate depreciation and maintenance. We are of the view that the Finance Ministry's projections address these needs and have, therefore, adopted them. The resultant projection for the overall annual growth rate of defence expenditure works out to 8.33 per cent."

The projected defence budget as per the Thirteenth Finance Commission, 2010-15 (p. 83 of the report, para 6.27 read with Annex 6.3) looks as follows:

This projection is based on overall annual growth of 8.33 percent, comprising annual growth of 10 per cent in the capital budget and 7 percent in the revenue budget.

This projection can be made for the next five years upto 2020-21 on an overall basis and can be made for capability planning purposes, taking full care of maintenance requirements. As mentioned above, we make no distinction between the two categories of expenditure in a programme concept which should be the building block for capability.

It is also to be seen that if we add up the projected allocations under the capital expenditure alone for the ten-year period, on the basis of a rough calculation, it comes to $185 billion, which is a very sizeable amount for any country. Not to have a long-term plan to spend it on the basis of strategic direction would be a major failure in governance, particularly for a developing country which has adopted inclusive growth as a goal.

Table 9.1

Projected Defence Budget (Rs. crore) As Per Finance Commission						
Period	2009-2010 Reassessed	2010-2011	2011-2012	2012-2013	2013-2014	2014-2015
Defence Expenditure	128792	139452	151023	163585	177225	192039

Projected Defence Budget (Rs. crore) as Suggested						
Period	2015-2016	2016-2017	2017-2018	2018-2019	2019-2020	2020-2021
Defence Expenditure	208036	225365	244138	264475	286505	310371

The Thirteenth Finance Commission 2010-15 goes on to observe, “We are of the view that there exists considerable scope to improve the quality and efficiency of defence expenditure through increased private sector engagement, import substitution and indigenisation; improvements in procedures and practices and better project management, within the parameters of the Government of India’s policy. Efforts in this direction will further expand the fiscal space available for defence spending.” (Paras 6.27, p. 83).

That means that a long-term financial plan should be accompanied by a yearly savings plan. Emphasis on performance orientation in the expenditure management is missing.

The Commission was apparently unaware of the concepts of budget holders and budget centres introduced in the Nineties in the logistic sector of defence on the analogy of the Authority and Responsibility Centres in the UK, with the specific purpose of bringing in performance orientation in defence. A lot of delegation of powers in both revenue and capital expenditure was done and continues to be done, to the Service Headquarters and subordinate organisations, precisely to improve the 'quality and efficiency' of defence expenditure. A large number of internal financial advisers have been posted in the field to help the competent authorities to discharge their functions efficiently. Unfortunately, performance goals are still to be laid down for the budget holders, thus, the benefit of introducing the concept of budget holders has not been realised. But the framework exists, as publication of DSE Vol II indicates.

A high level committee needs to be set up under the chairmanship of the Defence Secretary to go into why these concepts were introduced, with what hopes and mandate, why they failed, what needs to be done to rejuvenate them with a view to achieve economy and efficiency in expenditure through decentralised management, and bring in performance orientation. It would be most unfortunate if such a major initiative to improve financial management is allowed to go waste. If more private sector engagements are required to render a service more efficiently, a High Level Budget Holder with the advice of the Internal Financial Adviser posted with him, should be able to do so. Some of the policy level decisions in this regard may require the support of the Top Level Budget Holders (at the level of Service Chiefs), which concept is still missing. Without them, performance objectives cannot be set at the top and cascaded down. Now that the Defence Secretary is designated as the Chief Accounting Authority, with full responsibly for ensuring efficient financial management with performance orientation, it is for him to make the budget holder concept effective.

Performance orientation in defence budgeting, with a view to generating economy and efficiency in defence spending, should be regarded as one of the preconditions for introducing long-term budgeting. One of the reasons would be generation of internal savings for reinvestment in defence capability in the next ten years for which specific goals should be laid down. For example, in the Defence White Paper 2009, of the Government of Australia, from which has emerged "Force 2030", which makes a funding commitment of 3 per cent real growth in defence budgets till 2017-18, it is also stated that the planned force structure depends on the success of the A$20 billion defence strategic reform which is intended to generate internal savings for reinvestment.[38] The observation of the Finance Commission for improving the quality and efficiency of defence expenditure for increasing the fiscal space available is also relevant.

Without an in-depth strategic assessment of the security scenario, it is difficult to take decisions about the force structure to be aimed at . Mere endorsement by the Minister on the strategic guidance will not solve the problem of force planning.

Appointment of a CDS, with a proper mandate for undertaking force planning in an integrated way, is necessary for a long-term capability plan.

For providing a basis for proper long-term planning capabilities based on RMA concepts , for regularly reviewing the strategic context and for laying down force structure priorities, there has to be a comprehensive defence review, as stressed in the context of the Army Doctrine, 2004. There should be an institutional mechanism for doing this which should bring out its findings in one document or closely associated documents. Appointment of a Chief of Defence Staff assumes importance in this regard.

Recommendations accepted by the government as also a ten-year budget plan should be published as a White Paper. The most important component of it will be India's strategic assessment, in the context of the regional security environment, as affected by China's efforts towards rapid modernisation of its armed forces and its increasingly assertive policies. It has also to bring out how important the Indian Ocean is in Indian strategic thinking because of its growing importance as a trade route and energy supplies, and what needs to be done to protect India's national interest in terms of improving its maritime capability. A force structure review should be done on the basis of these strategic assessments and form an integral part of the White Paper. In other words, the implications of India's defence policy have to be articulated in the White Paper. Though no cost assessment need be made for various initiatives , there should be a funding commitment in terms of a ten-year budget plan in the White Paper.

A ten-year capability plan should be prepared on the basis of the White Paper and approved by the government.

Notes

1. Foreword to Indian Army Doctrine , October , 2004
2. Drawn from Appendix 1 of the Estimates Committee 1992-1993, 19th Report, on Ministry of Defence, Defence Force Levels, Manpower, etc. p. 110, regarding. drawing up of perspective plan for the Army, Navy and Air Force.
3. Ibid., para 6.46.
4. Ibid., para 6.48.
5. Maj Gen L.N. Le Roux (Retd), "Optimising Defence Spending- the South African Defence Force Transformation Experience", paper presented at the International Seminar on Defence Economics and Finance, New Delhi, November 13-15, 2006.
6. Ibid.
7. Ibid.
8. Executive Summary, The Kinnaird Report, 2003.
9. Ibid.
10. Ibid., p. iv.
11. Rear Admiral Matt Tripovitch, "Capability Development and Acquisition reforms in Australian Defence Organisation" , paper presented at the International Seminar on Defence Finance and Economics, November 2006, New Delhi
12. Ibid.
13. Ibid.
14. George Veitch, "Defence Planning and Budgeting : An Australian Department of Defence Perspective," paper presented at the International Seminar on Defence Finance and Economics, New Delhi, November 2006.
15. Ibid.
16. Michael Evans, "Australia and the Revolution in Military Affairs," Land Warfare Studies Centre , Working Paper no 115.August 2001.
17. Ibid.
18. David Kirkpatick, "Choose Your Weapon," *RUSI Whitehall Paper Series* 1996, p. 13.
19. Ibid.

20. Ibid., p. 4.
21. Ibid., p. 9.
22. The Strategic Defence Review, Cm 3999, July 1998, para 161.
23. David Kirkpatrick, "A UK Perspective on Defence Equipment Acquisition", paper presented to Institute of Defence and Strategic Studies, Singapore, 2003.
24. Ibid.
25. Henry Mintzberg, *The Rise and Fall of Strategic Planning* (New York: The Free Press, 1994), p. 128.
26. Ibid.
27. Jaques S. Gansler, *Affording Defense* (Massachusetts: The MIT Press, 1989), p. 135.
28. Ibid., p. 137.
29. David Kirkpatrick, "The Affordability of Defence Equipment", *RUSI Journal*, June 1997.
30. Paul K. Davis , "Methods for Portfolio Analysis in Defence Planning", paper presented at the International Seminar on Defence Finance and Economics, November 13-15, 2006, New Delhi.
31. Yehezkel Dror, *Public Policy Making Reexamined* (California: Chandler Publishing Company, 1968), pp. 139-140.
32. Quoted by Seymon Brown, "Scenarios in Systems Analysis" in E.S. Quade and W.I. Boucher, eds., *Systems Analysis and Policy Planning* (American Elsevier Publishing Co.1968), cited by Amiya Kumar Ghosh, *Defence Budgeting and Planning in India: The Way Forward* (New Delhi: Knowledge World 2006), p. 292.
33. Gordon Nathaniel Lederman, *Reorganizing the Joint Chiefs of Staff* (Greenwood Press, 1999), p. 37.
34. David F. Matthews, "The New Joint Capabilities Integration Development System (JCIDS) and its Potential." in Gregory A.Garrett and Rene G. Rendon, eds., *U.S. Military Program Management* (Management Concepts, INC. 2007).
35. Ibid., p. 21.
36. n.32, p. 207.
37. Dr. Jeffrey Bradford, "Contrasting Efforts: The British Strategic Defence Review and the United States Quadrennial Defense Review Processes", *RUSI Defence Systems*, October 2008.
38. Jack McCaffrie and Chris Rahman, "Australia's 2009 Defense White Paper", *Naval War College Review*, vol. 63, no.1, Winter 2010, p. 64.

10

Modernisation and Challenges Before Defence Research and Development Organisation (DRDO)

One of the basic challenges of modernisation of defence is to make indigenous defence research and development a vibrant activity, leading to development of modern systems and equipment equal to, if not better than, what is available off-the-shelf in the international market at high cost. Indian policy-makers adopted the policy of self-reliance almost as a strategic objective since independence, to be achieved in an incremental way, as the capabilities of the domestic industry grew.

Emphasis on inculcating a scientific spirit in finding solutions to defence problems and developing infrastructure for technology development and defence production in the quest for self-reliance, have been the hallmarks of our defence policy from the beginning.

As a result of the policy towards achievement of self-reliance, Indian defence industry today consists of 39 OFs and 8 DPSUs. At the time of independence, there were 16 OFs; and the first DPSU was formed in 1954.

One of the most important steps toward self-reliance in defence was the setting up of the Defence Reseach Organisation (DSO) in 1948, later renamed as DRDO. DRDO now has a vast network of 52 laboratories spread all over the country, which are grouped under eight major disciplines: aeronautics, armaments, electronics and computer systems, combat vehicles and engineering, missiles, special materials, naval systems, and life sciences.

The impetus to application of modern science to defence and defence research in India was given by the top political leadership, by the setting up of the DSO as early as in 1948. Dr D.S. Kothari, Professor and Head of the Department of Physics, Delhi University, assumed charge of the DSO as the Scientific Adviser (SA) to the Ministry of Defence in July 1948. Nehru had a love for science. He was quoted as saying, "Scientists are a minority in league with the future." (Quoted by A.B.Vajpayee, inaugurating the 2000 Indian Science Congress.) At that time Dr. Homi Bhabha, Professor M.S. Thacker, Director General of the Council of Scientific and Industrial Research (CSIR) and Dr. D.S. Kothari formed Nehru's inner circle. They laid the foundations for the development of science in the emerging India.[1]

The perception of defence policy-makers at that time was that rendering of scientific advice at a high level in all aspects of the military to the Defence Ministry was the main function of the Scientific Adviser. He should, therefore, be an eminent scientist. Dr Kothari continued as a Professor of Physics in the Delhi University for all his working years in the Ministry of Defence. He was the Honorary Adviser to the Defence Ministry and later to the Defence Minister. He realised and emphasised that defence science was intended to serve the defence forces.

In Kothari's view, the main function of the DSO would be rendering help in the integration of scientific and military knowledge, and its role should be advisory. For more than a decade, the DSO's major role was to make systematic study of, with investigation and research into, various branches of defence science for the purposes of planning and providing advice to the Services and assisting them on matters of scientific and technical interest.[2]

The Defence Research and Development Organisation (DRDO) came into existence on January 1, 1958, with the amalgamation of the Technical Development Establishment of the Army and Directorate of Technology Development and Production (DTDP) with the DSO. Prof. D.S. Kothari continued as Scientific Adviser (SA) to the Defence Ministry.

The formation of DRDO was at the initiative of Krishna Menon, the then Defence Minister. There was lack of support for its creation from the then Chief of the Army Staff and his Principal Staff Officers. As the DSO did not put in much effort for the navy and air force, these two Services were not interested in it. Krishna Menon had to order its creation.[3]

Soon, ten defence laboratories came into existence. The process of transformation of the DSO into DRDO took place for the purpose of undertaking R&D in hardware, software, and processes to meet the requirements of the user services.

Setting up of DRDO in 1958 entailed an increased scope of work, beyond scientific advice, to include applied research and development work. It called for lot of interface between DRDO and the Services as the users of the equipment and the production organisations as the suppliers. It became necessary to appoint a Chief Controller of Defence R&D (CCR&D) with executive responsibility.

Maj Gen B.D. Kapur was appointed as the first CCR&D, and was given the functional powers of a Secretariat officer. This underlined the importance of deputing senior military officers to DRDO with executive responsibility, not only to act as an interface between the users and DRDO scientists, but also to actively participate in policy-making. This point, soon forgotten, has now assumed new validity.

Undertaking R&D for a developing country, with a view to provide indigenously produced goods for the armed services, which had been totally dependent on imported arms and equipment, required political courage and vision, keeping in view the inadequate infrastructure. With users reluctant to induct indigenously developed and produced goods, it was not easy to give a boost to indigenous R&D. Political direction played an important part in developing defence R&D. Without it, we would not have achieved the extent of self-reliance in defence equipment and systems that we have. If we have not gone further on this route, it is also because of the absence of political direction at critical junctures of decision-making relating to defence procurement. There were instances in the past when pursuit of the indigenous route of development of specific items which seemed promising, was abandoned without any in-depth consideration of the long-term consequence on defence capability building, and opting for import instead.

Apparently, in these cases, among other things, the Scientific Advisers to the RM, have not been able, in the advisory role, to influence top level political decision-making in the context of long-term military capability building. With greater emphasis in the SA's role in delivery of equipment being entrusted to DRDO, his advisory role at the highest level of decision-making as far as science and technology are concerned, has gradually shrunk. This is the unfortunate part. This portion has to be reclaimed, if the aim is to achieve cost-effective modernisation.

To continue with history, Prof S. Bhagwantham, a renowned scientist of international repute, took over from Kothari in 1961 and held the post till 1969. He was of the view that to provide tactical advantage to the armed forces, it was necessary to be self-reliant and up-to-date in technology. Attaining self-reliance in defence required dedicated effort in several S&T areas. This kind of effort was not usually forthcoming from other S&T organisations. "To build a strong R&D base and to link it with production but, at the same time, without losing autonomy, he continued setting up laboratories."[4] By the end of 1962, there were 27 DRDO laboratories. After the exit of Krishna Menon, the process slowed down and only 6 more laboratories were set up in the next seven years till Dr Bhagwantham retired in 1969, making a total of 33 labs. There was still not adequate realisation that for projecting future requirements of weapon systems, the Services would have to be guided by DRDO.

Dr. B.D. Nagchaudhuri, the eminent scientist took over as SA to the RM, Director-General DRDO, as also Secretary to the Government of India, in July 1970. He was convinced that "DRDO must graduate from short-term responses to systems development for self-reliance in defence equipment and that the process must start from building of infrastructure."[5]

During the tenure of Prof. M.G.K. Menon (1974-78), the thrust was on high visibility projects such as development of the Main Battle Tank (MBT), aircraft engine, and missiles.

Dr. Raja Ramanna who was SA to the RM (1978-82) till he left to take over as the Chairman of the Atomic Energy Commission, took the initiative to create a separate department for DRDO, the Department of Defence R&D. Earlier, DRDO was under the Department of Defence Production.

In the subsequent phase, DRDO has been led by people from within the organisation. Dr. V.S. Arunachalam, Dr. A.P.J. Abdul Kalam, Dr. V.K. Aatre, Sri M. Natarajan, were all from DRDO. The present SA, Dr. V.K. Saraswat, is also from within the organisation.

The role of the SA to the RM as envisaged in the Business Rules was very broad. The way it was framed made it clear that, apart from offering scientific advice in all matters of defence, he was also to play a prominent role in boosting R&D in the country so that critical technologies are developed in the country to benefit the military .

There is every reason to support a broad view of the role of the SA to the RM in the development of science and technology in the country. This is for two reasons: (i) the largest amount of R&D funds of the government are routed through DRDO; (ii) this is the era of dual-use technology; in the last three decades in the West, more technologies have been borrowed by defence from the civil sector than the other way round. The SA to the RM should be able to give a boost to R&D in the entire country in developing critical technologies, with the participation of academia, Indian Institutes of Technology (IITs), Indian Institutes of Science (IIScs) and promoting public-private partnerships in delivering systems to the defence forces.

Nehru was convinced that industrialisation in the long run would lay the base for defence capability building. In this sense, he had a long-term strategy for defence. As he put in his inimitable style, "A country's defence potential is, if I may put it in some kind of equation, defence apparatus plus industrial growth plus economy of the country plus morale."[6]

Nehru gave a lot of importance to higher technical education, which led to the setting up of IITs and other institutions of learning to provide the country with trained manpower, which is a crucial aspect of capability building. Nehru correctly viewed that military effectiveness would be critically dependent on economic development, which, in turn, would significantly depend on the educational level in the country. Western scholars are now coming round to this view.

There were several instances in earlier years where, given the proper synergy and leadership, important items were developed indigenously, which did not seem *prima-facie* possible. The induction of 106 recoilless guns by the army, the potent anti-tank gun developed (based on an American sample) in the late Fifties, was one such instance.

As Maj Gen Kapur puts it, "Our designers, engineers and scientists had put their heads together and developed the gun, its complete range of ammunition, fire control apparatus and ancillaries, as also the raw material for making the gun and ammunition within the country".[7] This instance also brought home (to be quickly forgotten) how the joint dedicated efforts of scientists, engineers and production men working together can achieve what would initially appear unachievable for a country with a poor industrial base.

It also requires adequate time to develop a sophisticated weapon. Users have to, therefore, show patience. It took almost 10 years to develop the 75 mm package howitzer, a mountain gun which could be broken up into 10 mule loads, but assembled in very quick time for firing. It was again a very commendable effort and a successful one. The same was the case of the development of the Indian anti-tank grenade.

As Kapur points out, one of the important lessons learnt from these successful cases of development was: *"Between the R&D and the foreman on the shop floor there should be interpolated the 'development' or the application engineer, whose responsibility it should be to ensure that the design whilst it was being worked upon by R&D lent itself to mass production and should be modified then and there."*[8]

This lesson of resorting to 'concurrent engineering' was also soon forgotten and led to the delay, for example, in the production of the MBT Arjun in the Nineties.

In weapon development research, design and development, manufacture and inspection are all interrelated. How to organisationally unify them is the main challenge.

If this organisational challenge is taken on effectively to unify their approaches, it would be a giant step towards cost-effectiveness modernisation and timely delivery of equipment.

The problems of ego and personality clashes which may harm the prospect of indigenous development of a system need to be overcome. Top-level intervention is required in critical moments so that clashes are avoided and indigenous development effort gets a boost.

This was proved in the case of the induction of the Indian self-loading rifle, the famous Ishapore Rifle. A small arms design team at the Ambarnath Ordnance Factory, which had a fully instrumented experimental range was engaged in the project. It was taken up as an experimental project in 1958 by DRDO, led by the CCR&D, with full support of the General Manager of the Ishapore Rifle Factory.

It was still not a General Staff approved project. Conflicting requirements such as a long range with a short barrel and less weight, were indicated.[9]

Foreign weapons of similar type were obtained for trials but were all rejected by the General Staff. Ultimately, to resolve the issue, Sri S.S. Khera, the then Cabinet Secretary, was asked by the Defence Minister to work as a 'one-man Commission', to report to him as to which automatic rifle should be introduced into the army, foreign or indigenous. After several rounds of deliberations, the Cabinet Secretary recommended adoption of the Ishapore Rifle. The reasons given by him were as follows:

a. The Ishapore rifle had gone through a prolonged process of development to meet the specific needs of the General Staff which no other rifle did in detail.

b. The Ishapore rifle was designed by Indians based on our *raw materials* and, therefore, immediately available *machine tool* capacity already in the factory, which will certainly need expanding and balancing for mass production, and *jigs and tools* which shall be made in India on *our design*. To import a plant shall mean, besides expenditure in foreign exchange, the *normal 3 to 4 years' delay in setting up* the plant, import of raw materials, jigs and tools and some technical personnel.

c. It is true Ishapore is still at a pre-production stage and has some shortcomings, but given free support from the General Staff and six months, by undertaking a crash programme, DGOF and CCR&D are convinced that they could give the first production model. Within a year, we shall go into full manufacture.

d. It shall be the pride of India and the Indian *jawans* to have an Indian-designed basic weapon provided it meets the minimum operational requirements which , we believe, it does.[10]

They were finally given the permission to go into production. The CCR&D had played a crucial role in the process of decision-making.

But the intervention of the Cabinet Secretary was crucial. Most importantly, it was the RM, who wanted him to play the crucial role. As far as the Cabinet Secretary was concerned, it was the confidence about the ability of the domestic R&D, optimistic outlook and instinctive judgement about the ability to deliver, which played a positive role in this case.

What are the lessons to be learnt from this episode?

- It is difficult to arrive at such decisions through consensus. There would be conflicting points of view which cannot be reconciled. The decision-maker has to ultimately apply his judgement on the basis of whatever facts are available.
- These decisions cannot totally be based on technical aspects and requirements as projected by the users, as they are of a 'political' nature. This would be evident from the last point made in (d) above, emphasising that it would be a matter of pride for India to have Indian soldiers operating an Indian-designed basic weapon. What is required is that 'minimum operational requirements' are met to induct an Indian-designed weapon.
- The fact that the Cabinet Secretary was working as a one-man commission on behalf of the Defence Minister should not be lost sight of. This kind of delegation may not be possible always.

We should not miss an important point by concentrating on the decision process alone. As mentioned above, in the development of the semi-automatic rifle, the small arms design team called Rifle Development Team at the Ambarnath Ordnance Factory played a crucial role. There is a need for several such design teams in ordnance factories and other defence production organisations for in-house design and development of weapon systems.

Compared to the enthusiasm and initiative shown in the earlier years, the present situation is hardly encouraging.

For example, the 155mm gun system which was imported in the late Eighties, could not be replicated by reverse engineering even after more than two decades. We are still looking for imports.

This is a regressive tendency which needs to be corrected by emphasising and allocating resources to develop the in-house R&D facilities in DGOF and other production organisations, without which modernisation would not get the necessary momentum. This has been recognised by the Ordnance Factory Board (OFB) in 2008, leading to a decision to set up twelve Ordnance Development Centres (ODCs).[11] Historically, the OFB has been a captive manufacturing organisation, producing military hardware using technology obtained from DRDO or imported from Original Equipment Manufacturers (OEMs). It was recognised by the OFB that its business with the defence forces would shrink "unless the OFB, in a departure from the existing mandate of R&D, starts aggressively developing new products and upgrades."[12] It also states that the Government of India has also taken a decision in principle that DRDO should focus on development *of "core technologies i.e. original research work or for development of new products for which technology is denied, leaving the responsibility for development of new products and upgrades to the production organisation. In the backdrop of the above, OFB has decided to make R&D one of its mainstream activities and restructure its R&D set-up to assume the expected new role."*[13]

Consequently, the OFB decided to set up twelve ODCs in some of the important ordnance factories. The essential concept behind the creation of ODCs is to develop new products and upgrades in a focussed manner, bringing employees with a flair for R&D activities under an independent unit like Quality Assurance (QA) units. Heads of ODCs reports to the Member/ TS (OFB). Each ODC is manned by posting a suitable number of employees as per the work content of the respective ODCs.

It is a good step but does not go far enough. Existing employees of OFB may not be enthused to work in ODCs as these assignments may not be attractive enough. Then, R&D is a specialised activity, for which one has to have a suitable academic background and proficiency. Therefore, for manning the ODCs, one has to recruit scientists and technicians from outside who can be suitably trained in the factories. There has to be adequate investment in infrastructure for undertaking the R&D.

All this calls for sufficient investment, and the activities of ODCs need to be monitored by the Government of India as also by the Army. The Army should be a major stakeholder in these ODCs and may consider posting suitable officers in these ODCs on a tenure basis, so that operational requirements are kept in view in developing new products. In terms of capability building, there is no substitute for in-house design and development capabilities. This would also mean more investment on development of applied science and technology in each segment of defence concerned with defence capability building. It should not be confined to DRDO alone.

Economic development improves a state's ability to produce high quality military equipment. To quote Michael Beckley, "While states can purchase advanced technologies from others, only developed economies possess the technological industry and skilled workforce necessary to modernise them."[14] With concentrated attempts to develop science and technology, with the required incentive, synergistic approach and leadership ,even a developing country can disprove this kind of sweeping statement and aim at self-reliance.

Another kind of statement is made which should be treated as an argument for self-reliance for indigenous development of military systems rather than otherwise. To quote Eliot A. Cohen, even if underdeveloped states obtain the "teeth" of a technologically sophisticated military, they may not possess the "tail" needed to support it.[15]

That should mean that both the "teeth" and "tail" would have to be protected, if a system is indigenously developed with maximum possible domestic industrial support, than if the system is imported which can lead to disconnection between the "teeth" and "tail".

This problem calls for increasing technological capability in the domestic industry, both private and public. Technological capability in the country has increased in a significant way in the last two decades.

This is a very positive development because in the developed countries, militaries often rely directly on civilian equipment, supplies and techniques. "Today, the American military depends on private companies to provide logistical services and to produce information technologies, such as fiber optic-laced clothing, head-mounted computer displays, global satellite phones, impromptu wireless networks, and rugged laptop computers. Two of the most modern weapon systems, stealth and multi-spectral technologies, depend on innovative manufacturing and design technologies that reside in the commercial sector, and three-quarters of the computing power in the Aegis cruiser depends on commercial equipment. In these respects, a solid economic infrastructure enhances military effectiveness during wars, as well as in periods that precede them."[16]

The aim in the developing countries should also be to build a solid economic infrastructure, and the industrial policy, including the R&D policy of the government, should be aimed at building it. It should give equal attention to the public as well as the private sector.

Military technologies today are hard to copy because they are not stand-alone pieces of hardware. Earlier, one could maintain that one could modernise through the import route, but not any more. "Military power used to consist primarily of weapon platforms and troops; today, it comprises systems, which link weapons and troops to sensors, satellites, and command centers. Countries may be able to purchase certain aspects of these systems from abroad, but only developed states will have the supporting infrastructure necessary to assimilate state-of-art military technologies and integrate them into a cohesive, lethal whole."[17]

The above underlines the need for economic and technological development and emphasises the need for domestic R&D as an effective route towards modernisation. It is well recognised from international examples, starting with the USA, that advances made in defence related technologies in aerospace, electronics, computers and many other fields have great potential to *spin-off* technologies which make the domestic civil industries more capable and competitive. But the converse is true today. There is more of *spin-in* of civil technologies to defence to make the latter more cost-effective and affordable, rather than the other way round. This is very good reason to nurture the scientific and technology base, so that economic development gets a boost , which also helps in military capability development.

Therefore, every large import of defence systems, without looking for cost-effective domestic options, is, in a sense, a lost opportunity to improve the domestic technological base and economic development.

In defence procurement from abroad, there is now provision of "offsets". Several authorities on the subject recognise that offsets may not improve the technological capabilities of recipient country. "We find virtually no case where offset arrangements have yielded unambiguous net benefits for a country's economic development."[18]

The "offset" provision, used in a routine way, for short-term gain, cannot be the route for improving the technological development , partly because it is difficult to operationalise it in that way, and partly because it can, at best, have a limited impact in a narrow field. Therefore, "offset" provisions should not be treated as an argument for importing a system. But if imports become inevitable, then "offset" provisions should be used only for increasing the technology base in the country with a long-term vision.

There should be a roadmap for using offset provisions in a creative way.

Technological capabilities and in-house design and delopment capabilities have to be improved within the defence sector for achieving cost-effective defence and for self-reliance. Designing and integrating capabilities within the country would give us the independence to decide from which source a sub-system needs to be procured. Economic development, with higher national income, and more revenues to the government, enables it to allocate sufficient funds to the defence sector to finance such procurements on commercial terms. Importing of complete systems may appear a good short-term solution, but would not be a long-term one, as it does not lead to technological capability development nor to cost-effective solutions as it ignores existing indigenous capability.

The navy has developed in-house capabilities for design and development of ships .It has also to give attention to improving in-house scientific and technological capabilities so that it can help in the development of weapon systems to be fitted in the ships.

The concept of developing in-house design and development capability also applies to the air force. In the context of updating of the MiG-21 Bis fleet, for which we had to again turn to the Russians in the Nineties, it is observed by Air Cmde Jasjit Singh (Retd) that it would not have been necessary if the IAF had not ignored the in-house design and development capability.[19]

As he puts it, while the air force had stayed away from design and development of the aircraft and their systems, "the Indian Navy, its sister Service, established a Directorate of Warship Design, a Controller of Warship Construction, and the Weapons Equipment and Systems Engineering Establishment, all in the Naval Headquarters. It is not surprising, therefore, that the Indian Navy is well ahead of the Army and the Air Force in the indigenisation process of weapons and equipment... In 1980-82, the IAF had also integrated the navigation attack and weapon aiming system for the Jaguar called DARIN which made the Indian Jaguars far superior to those of the RAF and French Air Force. But in spite of this one-off step , the fact remains that the IAF has not shown sufficient interest in creating in-house design and development capabilities or establishing a more direct vital integration with design bureaus of HAL."[20]

HAL delivered the first MiG-21 Bis in 1978 on the basis of a licensed manufacturing agreement, and delivered 220 of them, but it still could not upgrade it on its own. The upgrade of the MiG-21 had been receiving attention since the late 1970s even as the manufacture of the MiG-21 Bis began. By the end of the 1970s, HAL's design bureau had dissipated, as after the winding up of the HF-24 project, there was no further challenging project.

In this context, it is worth mentioning that the Chinese upgraded the MiG -21 (Chinese J-7) fighter to the JF-17 Multi-Role Fighter Aircraft (MRFA), referred to as the FC1. It was designed by the Chengdu Aircraft Design Institute. Russia supplied the Klimov RD-93 turbofan jet engine for the aircraft. The RD-93 engine is a derivative of the RD-33 used by the MiG-29 fighter, which has been in service with the IAF for almost two and a half decades.

The FCI aircraft entered production in 2006. The initial order was from the Pakistan Air Force for 42 aircraft, which was signed in March 2009. China is actively looking for the export of this aircraft.[21] It appears as fairly modest per unit cost, compared to our recent acquisitions.

The high cost of acquisition per unit of the aircraft in our case, as per the present trend, given the same percentage of defence budget year after year, will mean a smaller number in the aircraft inventory, affecting the overall force structure of the IAF and its role.

The absence of a science and technology wing in the IAF prevents it from seeking cost-effective solutions to its capability building by establishing links with the design and development wings of HAL, ADA and other production units.

We may in this context, consider the experience of the US Air Force. To quote Donald C. Daniel, "A unique connectivity exists in the air force between science, technology, and transformation. From the defining moment of powered flight in 1903 to the creation of the air force as a separate service in 1947 to the present, these three elements have been continuously linked and undoubtedly remain so."[22] In the US Air Force, science and technology, which appear as a single line item in the air force modernisation budget, has typically around $1.5 billion per annum allocated to it. This comprises over 20 different programme elements. These programmes include one for basic research, and 10 each for applied research and advanced technology development. Participants include in-house scientists and engineers, universities, industry and international organisations. "The sustaining nature of the service laboratories is one of the great strengths for the Department of Defense, often serving as a launch pad for large scale activities by the Defense Advanced Research Project Agency (DARPA) and/or industry."[23]

In our case, setting up a science and technology wing in the IAF would provide much needed inputs for taking the air force projects further and provide the basis for much more fruitful collaboration than hitherto. This would also provide a basis and infrastructure for more investment in R&D, with a futuristic orientation.

In this context, it would be worthwhile to quote from the inaugural speech of the Prime Minister, Manmohan Singh, in the Indian Science Congress, on January 3, 2012: "We have to aim to increase the total R&D spending as a percentage of GDP to at least 2 per cent by the end of the XII Plan Period from the current level of about 1 per cent".

This point has been repeatedly made in the past few years which indicates the importance attached to it at the highest level of decision-making.But why then is it not happening? This point was made with lot of vehemence this time , pointing out that we are falling much behind China in this regard. This would affect our comparative position in the world on the basis of various indices. *This makes increase in investment in R&D in the country a very important strategic objective.* We have to remove the impediments, structural or otherwise, which are preventing this from happening.

It is for the IAF to take this opportunity to set up its own science and technology wing in the quest for modernisation.

The same applies to the Indian Navy, OFs and PSUs. These steps would further strengthen DRDO's aim to develop cutting edge technologies by collaborative efforts. It is clear from past experience that DRDO would be more effective in delivering critical technologies if its efforts are supplemented by the in-house efforts of the Services in science and technology so that a proper synergy develops, and top level decision-makers in Service Headquarters get the required in-house technical advice to help in their decision-making.

From the foreign policy angle, the issue of ensuring strategic autonomy in policy-making has recently been raised. Self-reliance in defence capability building has a lot to do with it. Shivshankar Menon, National Security Adviser, in a recent speech, stated, "Talk of strategic autonomy has little meaning unless our defence production or innovative capabilities undergo a quantum improvement... A country that does not develop and produce its own major weapons platform has a major strategic weakness and cannot claim true strategic autonomy. This is a real challenge for us all. "

A recent news report[24] by Nicholas R. Lombardo, quoting a SIPRI report of March 14, 2011, states that India has surpassed China as the world's largest importer of weapon systems "reflecting the nation's intent to modernize its armed forces and project military capabilities beyond the subcontinent." The same news report, referring to other sources mentions that India's Ministry of Defence (MoD) plans to spend approximately US$80 billion on military modernisation programmes by 2015, which, some analysts predict, will keep India on track to become one of the largest defence customers over the next decade.[25]

One of the points for concern would be whether this level of import of weapons and systems makes us overdependent on foreign sources of supplies and indirectly on the government concerned? It may be noted that some of the high-value items from the USA in recent years are coming on the basis of government-to-government sales.

There is also a presumption, which has sufficient basis, that importation of very sophisticated systems may not often be possible without some kind of strategic understanding with the country concerned. Import of equipment having sophisticated technology has to be permitted by the government concerned and cannot be treated only as a commercial transaction. For example, it can be recalled that after the Chinese aggression in 1962, India was desperately seeking a supersonic aircraft and showed a lot of interest in obtaining three squadrons of the F-104 from the USA. Although the United States had already given Pakistan the F-104s, the Pentagon strongly opposed the deal with India, apparently on the grounds that it would not be liked by Pakistan. The then Defence Minister, Y.B. Chavan, who went to the USA (May 1964) to give a final shape to a comprehensive five-year defence plan, with US assistance, had to return without being able to make the USA agree to supply the F-104 aircraft.[26]

It was only after the United States refused to provide the supersonic aircraft that India went in for the Soviet alternative of the MiG-21, though the offer was made earlier. The supply of the MiG-21 by the USSR from 1964 onward became possible as there was a clear breakdown of the relationship between the USSR and China.

The traditional pro-Soviet tilt in Indian foreign policy made importation of technological advanced systems from that country possible. Pakistan could get arms aid and sophisticated systems first by joining SEATO in the Fifties, and later, after the Soviet invasion of Afghanistan, by aligning with the USA to get sophisticated aircraft like the F-16, and Stinger missiles, etc.

It is significant that the observation of the NSA quoted above was made in the context of the rise of China and its strategic implications for India. He observed that the relations between India and China have elements of cooperation and competition at the same time and as long as we cooperate on common interests and stick to our internal transformations , the current relationship is expected to continue. It should be possible for us to follow policies which are in our national interest on the basis of strategic autonomy. One of the apprehensions may be that large scale imports of defence equipment, with increased dependence on Western sources, may affect our strategic autonomy.

How can the 'quantum improvement' in innovative capabilities come about to achieve 'strategic autonomy'? It does not happen overnight. Some of the existing lacunae have to be overcome.

One of the basic problems is that the government has not been able to put together a roadmap for self-reliance in defence technology. Another problem has been lack of synergy among development agencies/labs, user services and production agencies. While DRDO has developed important partnerships with private industry in selected areas, there is a lack of thrust in this regard. There are inadequate incentives for private industry to undertake R&D for specific items, in terms of clarification of what systems would be inducted by the users through indigenous sources, and in what timeframe. There is an absence of policy pronouncements and roadmaps for achieving self-reliance.

Showing their anxiety in this regard, the Standing Committee on Defence, in their report on the Demands for Grants for 2005-06 stated, "It is high time that the Government prepared a roadmap for self-reliance. The Committee strongly feels that India should not be taken as a weapons/arms market by the global suppliers and action should be visible by the end of the 10th Defence Plan and 11th Plan should be entirely devoted to self-reliance."[27]

Public-private partnerships, in a constructive way, with DRDO providing the technological input in a big way, would be the most effective way of achieving self-reliance.

The incentive for R&D and public-private partnership in this regard is closely linked with policy regarding self-reliance. In fact, these two cannot be segregated.

The private sector has made tremendous progress since the economic liberalisation of the country in 1991. Recognising this fact, the Government of India allowed the entry of the private sector in defence production, earlier reserved for the public sector. The Indian companies are now eligible to set up defence industries for manufacturing all types of defence equipment under licence. Such companies could also have FDI upto 26 per cent of the equity. The Kelkar Committee had also recommended greater freedom to the DPSUs to form joint ventures with private and multinational consortiums. The main recommendations of the Kelkar Committee included preparation of a 15-year acquisition plan, information sharing about the requirements of the armed forces with the industry, identification of the entry point for the private sector in the acquisition process, identification and fostering of the Raksha Udyog Ratna, and evolving of a policy framework to promote participation of small and medium enterprises. These are still to be achieved.

Though several Letters of Intent (LOI) and industrial licences have been issued for the manufacture of various types of defence equipment, they have been issued to major private sector players. A major player like Larsen and Toubro (L&T) has been involved in developing and supplying critical items for advanced weapon systems for almost two decades. Tata Consultancy Services (TCS) is also contributing in critical areas. There are other important players in the private sector.[28]

The question still remains as to how the small and medium enterprises, which are today the most dynamic players, can be involved in defence R&D. They have an excellent past record in developing indigenously various sub-systems for achieving self-sufficiency for producing items such as the T-72 tanks and BMPs , developing and supplying night vision goggles and many other items involving advanced technology, through their own efforts. For further advancement, they would require to be supported by the R&D effort of DRDO. They have a natural advantage as they have collaborated in the past with various institutions in the development of advanced systems. If we have to look for scientific innovation, then it has to be through widespread partnerships in taking up the challenges in critical areas, which may involve investment by the public sector in selective areas in those private firms that are prepared to take up the challenges, but are unable to make the investments. DRDO is well-placed to make such investments.

It is also clear that DRDO's role needs to 'redefined' if we have to take meaningful steps in this regard to achieve strategic autonomy.

The priority activity of DRDO, has been in the area of strategic systems, which accounts for 35 percent of the budget. Technologies, systems, products, and equipment delivered account for 30 percent. Fifteen per cent of the budget goes towards infrastructure, special facilities, ranges and equipment, works, maintenance, etc. S&T projects given to universities and academic institutions make up 5 percent of the budget. Salaries and human resource development account for 15 percent.[29]

Therefore, as far as strategic systems are concerned there is autonomy. But what are the achievements in the non-strategic items?

As per an assessment made in 2006, the value of indigenous defence systems developed by DRDO and delivered to the Services during 1995-2005 totalled nearly Rs. 13,000 crore. Firm orders from defence were available with the production agencies for an additional value of Rs. 11,900 crore to be supplied during the next five years till 2010 (including the first 20 Tejas LCA, ordered by the air force and 124 Arjun MBTs for the army). Thus, DRDO developed items in service with the armed forces during this 15-year period accounted for an acquisition value of Rs. 25,000 crore or $5.2 billion as per the then exchange rate.[30] If these items had to be imported, considering the margins in the world trade market and cost of life-cycle support to be provided by the supplier, the cost would have been several times more.

Steady progress has been made since then. For example, in the year 2010, some of the achievements of DRDO were as follows:

- Initial Operational Clearance (IOC) for the LCA Tejas.
- Roll out of the first prototype of the naval version of the LCA.
- Maiden test flight of the UAV Rustom.
- Successful test launches of the Prithvi-II (in salvo mode), Dhanush, and Agni series of missiles by the user groups.
- Delivery of the multi-barrel rocket launcher system(Pinaka), MBT Arjun, NBC recce vehicles, etc.

Production orders for the Akash missiles for two squadrons of the IAF were received and approval accorded for six additional squadrons. Approval was also accorded for the air-to-surface BrahMos missile.[31]

In 2010, the army accorded bulk production clearance to the 40 mm Under Barrel Grenade Launcher (UBGL), which enhances the firepower of the 5.56mm INSAS and AK-47 rifles.[32]

We should also take note of items developed by the defence production units in their in-house design facilities, with the support of DRDO. The advanced light helicopter and its variant developed by HAL, frigates and other naval vessels built by shipyards are leading examples.

Cumulative production value of DRDO-developed systems accepted by the Services and under production touched Rs 1,00,000 crore by the end of 2010.[33]

It goes without saying, that the strategic national capability created by DRDO and DAE in terms of nuclear weapons and missiles and other vectors to deliver them have determined India's status in the world and her foreign policy. Their impact cannot be measured by their production value. But then, what about the future prospects?

While, undoubtedly, there is steady progress in the achievements of DRDO, the question is: how can there be a 'quantum leap' towards self-reliance in cutting edge technology to enable DRDO, in collaboration with industry and academia, to develop and deliver state-of-the-art systems? The aim should be to absorb 10 percent of the defence budget by the end of the 12th Plan so that the goal, as mentioned by the Prime Minister, can be achieved as far as the defence sector is concerned. The technical challenges in the development of systems would be much more in the future than faced hitherto, because of the technologies that would require to be embedded in them, taking into account their maturity.

To quote Dr. Saraswat, "Technological development for futuristic products would require developing evolving new concepts and nascent technologies, which will fall in the scale of Technology Readiness Level (TRL) of 1-4. For example, development of nano technologies, fibre lasers, particle weapons would come under this category. This segment would require very close collaboration with domestic and international academia, and may be, small scale industries. This activity needs careful planning, strategy of development, and choice of partners in a judicious manner. Multiple paths are to be pursued in parallel for guaranteed success."[34]

Technology development of customised products would require dealing with technologies with a maturity level of 4-7. It would be prudent to involve medium scale industry and accomplished academia for collaboration in this segment.

Development of large scale systems should be based on technologies which are matured to TRL 7-10. This would require careful choice of various sub-systems. The emphasis in this segment should be on system engineering, systems analysis, simulation and modelling, detailed design, etc.[35]

This would call for "*transformation*" *of DRDO*, as the present SA to the RM recognises and adds, "Only the best will survive in this intensely competitive world. This calls for reengineering the process of R&D and leveraging our knowledge base, skill sets, industry support, international collaborations and support by academia to develop systems in a timely fashion."[36]

To play this role, DRDO needs to be redefined. The report of the DRDO Review Committee, submitted in March 2008, which was fully conscious of these challenges was, in fact, titled **"Redefining DRDO."**

In spite of all the efforts made during the last 60 years towards self-reliance, if we look at the import bill for defence procurement, it can be a cause for serious concern. It appears as if we have turned our back to the policies followed in the first decades after independence. It is necessary to take corrective actions viewed from the economy angle alone. We are going to see one of the biggest trade deficits this year. From the current trend, it would be close to $200 billion this year. This is clearly unsustainable. With such huge trade deficits and significant increase in the demand for dollars, the rupee fell by 19 per cent to the dollar in 2011; it may fall further. A higher import cost in rupee terms would fuel inflation further. The central government budget, on account of increase of expenditure on subsidies beyond budgetary provisions, on the one hand, and lower realisation of tax revenues than expected (on account of lower growth rate) on the other, has been subjected to enormous pressure in the fiscal year 2011-12. The fuel subsidy bill alone has crossed Rs. 50,000 crore, more than double the amount provided in the budget. The rising subsidy bill has compelled the government to seek Parliament's approval for spending an additional Rs. 97,800 crore for 2011-12. It would not be easy to curb the rising fuel subsidy bills without hard political decisions.[37]

Deficits are going to be much higher than contemplated when the budget was presented. The food subsidy bill would be implemented next year, but it is not clear what its net impact would be on subsidies. The prospect of economic growth this year has already been scaled down to 7 per cent. With industrial growth slowing down significantly this year, the growth prospect next year is under speculation.

In view of various pressures, the government would try to curb expenditure where it has a discretion. Defence comes under discretionary spending, where strategic perceptions determine a significant amount of expenditure, particularly under the capital head. In this background, the government may not easily agree to new commitments for high value imports of defence equipment, unless the requirements are really pressing. Already, the Union Finance Ministry has raised questions regarding the army's Rs. 65,000 expansion plan, including the threat assessment as depicted in making the proposal. The government is also taking its time in finalising the multi-billion dollar deal for procurement of the next generation fighters by the IAF, though the selection process has taken quite a bit of time to arrive at the best possible option.

The emerging message seems to be clear: for future defence acquisitions, we should depend less and less on imports and seek cost-effective solutions through indigenous efforts. But we would not compromise on technology. Domestic industry has to play a major role in developing and delivering the systems with indigenous R&D capabilities. It would also enable defence spending to promote industrial growth in a direct way.

That is why the role and performance of DRDO and defence production units call for an in-depth review to bring in the necessary reforms to increase the indigenous production capability and overcome the so-called 'strategic weakness'.

What should be the strategy adopted for the purpose? Should production of weapon platforms be the first priority?

C. Raja Mohan, the noted analyst, wrote in *The Indian Express*, dated August 12, 2011, an article entitled "Sea Change," referring to China's maritime ambitions. To quote from it,

> Beijing's much-anticipated aircraft carrier, which began its sea trials this week, is not a threat to its Asian neighbours, including India, in the short term. It will be a while before China's first aircraft carrier—that was brought as scrap from Ukraine a few years ago—is fully equipped, and the Chinese Navy masters the operational arts of one of the most complex weapon systems. This clearly shows China's ambition of projecting power in the South China Sea and beyond.

As will be seen, it is not the platform (which was bought at a nominal price from abroad) which matters . How the platform is refitted and what equipment and weapon systems are integrated into the platform, and how it is integrated with the operational strategy, are the things that matter. If it can be done indigenously, it would indicate one's technological prowess. China has a problem in selecting the right kind of aircraft for the carrier.

But we have shown an inclination to import the platforms as well as the weapon systems.

Both the aircraft carriers, the *Vikrant* and *Virat* were procured in the past from the UK. They were refitted there and the aircraft to put on them were purchased from the UK as a package deal. The same is the case with the latest aircraft carrier, the INS *Vikramaditya* (ex-*Admiral Gorshkov*). INS *Vikramaditya* had to be entirely refitted in Russia at considerable cost (with cost being revised from time to time). There was no alternative but to pay the price asked for, as the dependence in this case was total. The aircraft which would be based on them (MiG-29 K) are also being supplied by Russia. Apart from the cost aspect, we would be dependent on Russia for years to come for the maintenance of the aircraft carrier and the aircraft, which would not only be costly but also time consuming, going by past experience in other systems. Thus, there would be a sort of strategic dependence on Russia for the future maintenance of the system.

In the context of recent discussions for ushering in a Revolution in Military Affairs (RMA), many analysts have downplayed the role of platforms for getting a cost-effective solution for increasing defence capability. To quote Eliot A. Cohen, "The platform has become less important, while the quality of what it carries—sensors, munitions, and electronics of all kinds—has become critical. A modernized 30-year aircraft armed with latest long-range air-to-air missile, guided by an airborne warning plane, can defeat a craft a third its age but not so equipped or guided."[38]

This means that existing platforms and more of them, in case we have the production capability, fitted with the latest avionics and weapons systems, and guided by AWACs, can provide cost-effective solutions for increasing defence capability. This would help not only in filling the capability gaps, but also in resolving the debate regarding Quality Vs Quantity. The quantity aspect can never be neglected in the quest for quality as it would seriously affect the capability and performance of the desired roles. DRDO could have an obvious role in developing cost-effective alternatives in this quality vs quantity debate, with the help of systems analysis.

Technology Roadmap

Because of quickening of the pace of technology development in advanced countries, big gaps are occurring between the technology base for defence in the country and that available abroad embedded in various weapon platforms. If domestic industry does not come forward to imbibe these newer technologies with vigour, this would lead to further dependence on foreign sources of import. We have quoted the present SA to the RM regarding challenges of future technologies and what kind of collaboration is called for.

The domestic industry has to be made a major partner in the development and supply of sophisticated weapons in the future.

The Integrated Defence Staff, Ministry of Defence, had, some time back, made available to industry a "Technology Perspective and Capability Roadmap" to give them awareness of the capabilities that the armed forces are seeking and the technologies required to achieve these over a reasonable period of time. It enumerates the current and future desired capability over a 15-year period from 2010 to 2025 as required by individual Services as well as areas where joint capability would be the optimal choice. This document rightly observes, "It is an established fact that the future battlespace will be shaped by technology and technological superiority is going to determine the outcome of future battles. It is, therefore, essential that technological self-reliance remains our *mantra* for the future and a collective national effort be initiated to achieve this in the quickest possible time ensuring that developments in technology are commensurate with our desired military capability."[39]

It also outlines a strategy for the development of required technologies. It wants attention to be focussed on specific areas of technology. The strategy should be to ensure that "we are able to develop and transform superior technology into affordable and decisive military capability keeping in mind affordability, timeliness, dual use, technology base and *modular* design. The aim should be to adopt an approach towards procurement of weapons and systems, that is *war-fighting capability driven.* This would enable the country's R&D establishments to focus on specific capability requirements and work out appropriate technologies needed to fulfil these requirements."[40]

This is indeed a tall order. Firstly, the trend today is towards dual use technology and defence is getting more and more dependent on civil sector technology. Economic development is synonymous with technological development in all sectors of the economy. This calls for a forward looking technology policy of the government, where the private sector is provided sufficient incentive for upgradation of technology through domestic R&D. It cannot be driven by specific capability requirements of defence. The benefit to defence would be through spin-offs of technological development in the private sector.

Secondly, the concept of 'modular' design is right, but is achieved by those who are at a high level of technology development involving specialisation in various aspects of equipment design that are to be integrated later.

Thirdly, making the systems and technology to be developed 'war-fighting capability driven' would call for enunciation of the defence strategy in a manner which is still lacking in the country. The Technology Roadmap document mentions concepts like enhancing the "Strategic Reach", undertaking "Effect-based Operations" which do not automatically define what kind of systems would be acquired and in what numbers.

In our defence policy-making, we avoid laying down what kind of 'tasks' are to be accomplished by the military forces, in what type of environment and in what timeframe. Since the "Strategies to Tasks" concept is missing in our planning, it is difficult to define the capabilities required with any degree of precision.

So determining specific capabilities to be developed as part of technological development for helping in war-fighting capabilities, would be indeed difficult.

Finally, one can talk of affordable weapon systems, not of affordable technology. It has to be obtained the hard way. The document calls for identifying "critical technologies that are likely to be denied and efforts concentrated on indigenous development of these."[41] Countries deny those technologies to others, to develop which had required them to invest considerable time, effort and money, to give them a competitive edge in the weapon systems in which they are embedded. As the document itself says, "Development of defence equipment and cutting edge technology with defence application needs considerable investment in terms of time, money and human resource."[42]

How would the potential business be assessed, so that private industry is encouraged to make 'considerable investment in terms of time money and human resource' in acquiring these cutting edge technologies? Though there is no easy answer to this question, a helping hand from DRDO in making selective investments in research infrastructure in some of the promising small scale enterprises would go a long way. The R&D policy should permit this.

The 'Capability Roadmap' document turns to the 15-year Perspective Plan to provide the answer. It states, "This document identifies the shape and size of the services over the designated time period on foreseeable strategic trends..... Perspective Plans determine the capability sought by the Armed Forces which in turn drive the procurement of platforms and equipment and the technology required to attain this capability."[43]

Unfortunately, the government is yet to approve such a Perspective Plan. Even if it is approved in a general way , it would not get the assurance of financial backing for a 15-year period.

Thus, we are back to square one regarding participation of private industry in defence R&D, through the technology roadmap.

So where do we turn for undertaking work on critical technologies as enumerated in the Capability Roadmap document, which would involve considerable investment in terms of manpower and money, without certainty of the end products finding a market?

We have, per force, to turn to DRDO where the government has invested considerable resources over the years, and which has developed considerable infrastructure, and has sufficient scientific and technical manpower to play a pivotal and leadership role to undertake this kind of development in partnership with industry and the users. It has a big budget (6 percent of the defence budget) which can be used for developing these technologies in-house or in collaboration with academia or other research institutions by giving them grants. Industry can make suitable investment selectively in their infrastructure to provide critical facilities required for developing cutting-edge technologies to provide incentives.

For playing this kind of role, DRDO has to undergo several reforms, which would enable it to play a more dynamic and leadership role than hitherto. These would be dealt with subsequently.

But let us again highlight two important points brought out above in the "Technology Perspective and Roadmap" document: (a) the developments in technology should be commensurate with our desired military capability; (b) the aim should be to adopt an approach towards procurement of weapons and systems, that is *war-fighting capability driven.*

This may not be very relevant for technology development in the private sector but for DRDO these should provide essential guidelines. A decision is required as to what would be the specific capability requirements for the kind of war that would be fought.

In the context of discussions relating to the appropriate strategy for developing self-sufficiency, let us look at some issues in capability building, which have the chance of being neglected, by taking the example of design and development of the indigenous aircraft carrier. In the quest for self-reliance, the Indian Navy is acquiring the 337,500-ton Indigenous Aircraft Carrier (IAC) through Cochin Shipyard Limited (CSL), a commercial shipbuilding yard, for which a letter of intent was issued in 1999. It is expected to be commissioned by around 2017. For commercial purposes, CSL has been building ships on a competitive basis, within a fixed timeframe and cost budget. This necessitates detailed definition of the ship and its design at the time of signing the contract. For the aircraft carrier, the design is not completed at the time of contracting, but is done concurrently during ship's construction. This requires significant in-house design capability on the part of the shipyard. Since there is no previous experience of building an aircraft carrier, a lot of effort is required to build up the required capabilities.

Because of lack of experience and expertise in warship design, CFL had to sign consultancy contracts with agencies abroad, "for carrying out the detailed design and engineering of the vessel and to fill in the technology gaps in the design of the ship… As part of the technology absorption process, representatives from the yard were deputed to the premises of the consultants and vice versa on a regular basis ."[44]

As part of the preparation for building the aircraft carrier, CSL had to undergo augmentation of infrastructure facilities, which was financed by the Government of India. Some of the augmentations were in the following areas:

- Setting up of a 300-tonne gantry crane over the dry dock.
- Erection and commissioning of the CNC plasma cutting machine for cutting of plates in the hull shop.
- A plate bending roller for bending of plates.
- 150-tonne self-elevating transporters for transporting and storing of hull blocks made for the ship.
- Computerisation of 3D software.

These were completed by the yard before starting the construction process.

Welding consumables for high tensile steel were developed indigenously with the help of the Naval Materials Research Laboratory (NMRL) and the suppliers.

The shipyard, over the past few years, has encouraged development of ancillary units in the process.[45]

It is planned that IAC's air group will include the naval version of HAL's LCA that was rolled out in July 2010, where the primary role is that of the Aeronautical Development Agency (ADA) under DRDO.

It is, however, learnt that IAC's launch had been deferred due to shortfall of gear boxes and generators.[46]

A lot of expertise has been gained by undertaking this project. As indicated, a lot of investment has been made by the government in developing the infrastructure.

But the question that arises is whether the investments made meet the criteria of the cost-benefit analysis, keeping in view the future force structure of the Indian Navy, availability of resources for the navy, and the competing requirements. How many aircraft carriers would join the force in the next 15 years and what is their affordability, in the context of the overall force structure? As regards the cost, the aircraft carrier is not intended to operate alone. Different types of warships and submarines are to accompany it, depending on the mission of the carrier strike group. The cost of acquisition, is, therefore, much more than that of the aircraft alone. If we take a programme budgeting approach, to this must be added the cost of running, supporting and maintenance of facilities for the aircraft carrier and the aircraft. These would, therefore, make a heavy dent in the navy's budget. If the entire cost is taken into account, would it be difficult to maintain the contemplated force structure in terms of other surface ships and submarines? These surface ships have been designed by the Indian Navy's in-house design capabilities and defence PSUs through a collaborative approach. These have been designed to have independent and lethal capabilities, and cannot be allowed to suffer because of induction of more and more aircraft carriers. Then, new generation submarines are to join the force structure, which would have their own maintenance cost. Since we have not introduced the technique of long-term costing in defence planning (as in the UK), which takes into account the maintenance requirements, we can only speculate on the matter.

But what is important to remember is that force planning aspects have to be given utmost importance in defence acquisitions, be it through import or the indigenous route.

There has been rethinking on these matters by strategic planners by countries having aircraft carriers, on these aspects, particularly from the cost-benefit point of view. For example, the UK government has been contemplating, since their Strategic Review 1998, to replace their old carriers by two medium sized aircraft carriers. They have finally decided to go ahead with only one, which is expected to enter service in 2016. The second proposed carrier is expected to be converted to an amphibious commando ship with helicopters on board.[47]

The question then arises: if we decide not to go in for another indigenously produced aircraft carrier, or there is a considerable gap before the order is placed for the next one, is it worthwhile to try to develop indigenous capabilities? Or, would the fact that indigenous capability in this regard has been built up, guide the decision-making for acquisition of more aircraft carriers, irrespective of their affordability and impact on overall force planning? This would call for a rigorous cost-benefit analysis, a technique which is yet to be introduced in our decision-making.

The comparative cost approach should also be taken in deciding which systems would be developed in the country. If, for example, we could go in for acquiring the platform for the first three carriers from abroad as these could be acquired cheaply, could we not follow the same route for the fourth one? Developing indigenous capability is worthwhile when we want to induct sizeable numbers of the weapon system, so that the capability built up can be effectively utilised and infrastructure costs get distributed over a larger number, bringing down the fixed cost element.

It points to the fact that all kinds of capabilities should not be developed indigenously to aim at modernisation. Capability building has to be closely linked to force structure planning , which should be done through intensive strategic review, keeping in view the concept of comparative cost. Only when force structure planning indicates the need for several carriers and resources are likely to be available not only for acquiring them but also maintaining them, should one go in for such investments in infrastructure and build up the required expertise, which is more precious.

There is another aspect pertaining to self-reliance. It should not be equated with self-sufficiency. This would be clear from another recent example of design and development of a stealth ship for the Indian Navy.

On commissioning of the INS *Satpura*, the indigenous stealth ship, on August 20, 2011, Vice Admiral Malhi of MDL said, "It is not a easy job, but MDL was virtually like a marriage bureau for electrical, electronic, mechanical, software and operational integration of US gas turbine and French diesel engines, Russian and Israeli missiles, Italian naval artillery gun, and several other systems." The INS *Satpura* has Russian Klub anti-ship missiles, Israeli Barak air defence missiles, Italian 76 mm Oto-Melara rapid fire gun, Russian and Indian radars, the Indian DRDO provided the Kavach chaff firing system, and DRDL-BEL ECM and EW suites besides anti-submarine rockets and other Indian and imported sensors and components.[48]

The point is, the concept of self-reliance cannot be an all embracing one—one has to look for it "system by system". System integration must be within the country. The indigenous route should be adopted to develop the sub-systems through foreign collaboration where necessary. In one system, *at a particular time*, one can have a very high degree of self-reliance, depending on the state of technology, and in another, at a very low level, if at all. For example, in the mid-Nineties, we were self-reliant to the extent of

95 percent in the case of T-72 tanks (which were procured from the erstwhile USSR about a decade and a half ago), which were being produced in the Heavy Vehicle Factory, Avadi, under licence. But for the advanced T-90 tank, which we decided to import from Russia, the self-reliance has to gradually increase as the systems and sub-systems get produced indigenously by small and medium scale enterprises. The MBT Arjun which was indigenously designed by DRDO, had, at earlier trial stages, almost 50 percent of the value of the total system imported from outside in terms of various sub-systems. But it is regarded as a good example of an indigenously developed system. This is because the designing and system integration was done in India. *This is the most important aspect of self-reliance: the in-house designing capability and integration capability.*

With the induction of the MBT Arjun in the Indian Army and the order for a sizeable number of the tanks, it would be commercially viable to produce many of the sub-systems within the country. While aiming at self-reliance for a particular system, the commercial viability aspect has to be kept in view as many of them are to be developed and produced by small scale industries. In some cases, where the orders are small, it may not be worthwhile to pursue such a goal. It is for the users to keep this aspect in mind, as piecemeal ordering of a system may make it more difficult to reach the goal of self-reliance.

While ordering a system, one can also lay down the improvements that would be looked for in the subsequent systems, as the concept of Mark I, Mark II and Mark III, so that designing of subsequent systems carries on simultaneously and there is no time lag in undertaking the production of the next improved system as soon as the production of an earlier version ceases. Then the cooperation of private industries would come about in a big way in both developing and producing the sub-systems as well as the systems. In the quest for self-reliance, the commercial aspects have to be given major importance, which we are yet to do.

The problem, however, is that critical technologies are difficult to obtain through the Transfer of Technology (ToT) route. That is where the role of DRDO comes in: to develop the technologies that would not be available, in designing new systems as required by the users by keeping in view its abilities, and in systems integration, with a view to achieve cost-effective solutions.

There may be serious gaps in technology between what is available through import and what can be developed indigenously. In that case, the cost-effective way of modernisation is to allow limited imports and tie up with technology transfer of critical technologies, where DRDO should play a crucial role in the negotiations, particularly regarding offsets.

As an example of the scope of modernisation in a globalised world, one can quote the case of the Russo-French agreement concluded in June 2011 for the supply to Moscow of two DCNS-designed Mistral-class amphibious assault ships, which is regarded as a milestone in global defence trade. The contract marked the first sale of a major military platform to Moscow by a NATO country and Russia's largest procurement of a system which was not developed indigenously. It has been pointed out by analysts that the Mistral accord was driven by lack of an indigenous alternative. As per a report in *Jane's Defence Weekly*, the Russian Chief of General Staff is stated to have conceded that it would have taken at least 10 years to develop an indigenous solution. Putin is, however, quoted as saying that that the deal was interesting only if it was accompanied by a parallel transfer of technology. As far as Russia's international procurement strategy is concerned, Putin stated, "While certain technology and certain samples may be bought from abroad—and probably should—we have to realize that no one will sell us promising latest generation armaments."[49] So, for getting the latest weapon technology, we have to import by spending large sums of money, knowing full well that the technology will not be given. So simultaneously with import of a limited number of weapons, DRDO should aim at developing the weapons through the indigenous route, though it would be a challenging task. Joint ventures indicate the way forward.

Russia entered into a partnership with Israel in 2010 with a joint venture between IAI of Israel and Russia's OPK Oboronprom for medium-altitude and high-altitude long-endurance UAVs. This is because Russia's efforts to indigenously develop high-technology UAVs were not very successful, and a partnership with Israel was necessary to close the capability gap.[50]

Thus, joint ventures and joint development by DRDO with companies abroad having the required R&D capabilities is certainly a route to get high technology items to meet future requirements. But joint ventures would not be possible unless we have something to contribute technologically for the development of the system. We know how difficult it was to imbibe technology through the ATV route. We just could not move forward until some critical technologies were developed in the country.

Clearly, self-reliance does not mean self-sufficiency. Even the MBT-Arjun which has been recently inducted by the army, contained very important items including the power pack and other important items valued at 50 per cent of the cost initially at the trial stage, which gradually went down as indigenous sources were developed. This happened also with imported systems like the T-72 tanks and BMP-2, where licensed manufacture was undertaken by DGOF and indigenous sources gradually developed for supply of systems and sub-systems (many of them by SMEs) and ultimately, it had more than 90 percent as indigenous content in value terms. At a later stage, these can be upgraded with the assistance of DRDO. This is the step-by-step approach towards modernisation and indigenisation.

Diversification of sources of supply of technology and systems has been the strategy followed by India in modernisation of the armed forces. Whether this can also be treated as a route for self-reliance is debatable. This may also be described, as Ajay Singh puts it, as an "incremental model of self-reliance" where diversification in sources of supply is an important component, which India has attempted to follow. To quote, "The self-reliance model adopted in practice can best be described as one that fundamentally relied on diversification in the sources of weapons and military technology, while working on establishing and expanding the indigenous base for design, development, manufacture of weapons and equipment. Countries seeking to create indigenous industrial capabilities have been observed to adopt a series of sequential steps along an almost a linear path starting with repair and overhaul."[51]

In that sense, licensed manufacture can also be regarded as an important component of building indigenous capability, which can gradually increase in terms of value added and a proportion of the total system.

But the point is that if design capability is not passed on or not absorbed, then it does not lead to self-reliance. In the case of upgradation of the MiG-21, the government had to turn to Russia. HAL was inducted as a partner in the project for upgradation, almost as an after-thought. This puts into question as to how far the government policy was oriented towards the incremental self-reliance model for modernisation of defence.

If the incremental model was seriously followed, the design bureau in HAL should not have been allowed to be dissipated and much more capable aircraft meeting today's challenges could have come out as a sequential process from the assembling and progressive manufacture of a large number of MiG-21s of different varieties. As Air Cmde Jasjit Singh puts it, "On the face of it, with more than 700 aircraft manufactured in the country, there should not have been any serious difficulty to produce the LCA as originally conceived, that is, a modified MiG- 21."[52]

The original plan, as envisaged by the Air HQ in 1980, was to evolve a light and low cost fighter to replace the MiG-21 FL model, which was scheduled to be replaced beginning 1985-86. The goal was essentially to make the aircraft more capable for low level battlefield operations.[53] The Air Staff Target (AST) of the early 1980s which laid the basis for the development of the LCA called for a much more sophisticated aircraft, with very high specifications. This was way beyond the existing design capabilities of HAL at that time. This did not subscribe to an incremental model of modernisation. It led to the setting up of the Aeronautical Development Agency (ADA), as a registered society, under DRDO. This was a positive step but it should not have led to abandoning of the effort to develop the aircraft for low level battlefield operations. The user should have insisted upon it and the government ensured that it happened by making available the necessary resources.

The best human resources of HAL, having the design and development capability, were withdrawn from HAL to meet the requirements of ADA, to the detriment of HAL's capability in this regard. As a policy, HAL's design capability should not have been allowed to suffer. This has been a strategic failure as it has adversely affected capability building of the Air Force.

Again, in the case of the Gnat programme, the incremental model was not followed. "The Gnat was a great success for both HAL and the IAF. During the 1965 War, it performed extremely well, because of its mobility, its small size and its utility at the forward edge of the battle area."[54]

Eventually, 85 percent of the airframe and 60 percent of the engine was produced in the country. It also performed well in the 1971 War. It had, however, a high accident rate and its longitudinal control required much improvement. "These faults were rectified in the modified Gnat Mark I, the Ajeet, but not to the satisfaction of the IAF." The production of the Ajeet was discontinued in the late 1980s.

In the context of the HF-24, project, Chris Smith observes, "At no point, was it possible to identify a well-orchestrated attempt to weigh the views of the military, politicians and industry on the project. Instead, the progress was linear. As the project proceeded, it passed from the hands of politicians to the military and, finally, to the industry. Or to put it in another way, the politicians defined the possibilities, the military defined the problem and industry was left to find the answer."[55] But it would have been more apt to say that in our case, the military defines both the problems and possibilities, and the politicians decide on that basis. *It would have been better if the military had defined the problem, DRDO and the industry had indicated the possibilities and alternatives, and the politicians had decided among the alternatives.*

More relevant are the observations of the Aeronautics Committee appointed in November 1967 under the chairmanship of C. Subramaniam, regarding a critical assessment of the 'requirements ' as spelt out by the air force regarding weapon systems, "The purpose of the critical assessment is to ensure that the requirements are reasonably spelt out and not likely to be changed easily; that they take account of the resources; that they are moderated to the extent feasible, by the technological capability of the country… We have to deal with the changing situation. It is, therefore, important to recognise that the necessary exercises cannot be undertaken by any individual in any position. They have to be undertaken by organisations which have built up the necessary competence for the task. It is possible that the hesitation of the Ministry of Defence to explore the basis of the requirements arises from the handicap that none of the organisations has developed the competence to undertake the appropriate task."[56]

The design and development of the HF-24 "Marut" in the mid-Fifties was also not based on the incremental self-reliance model. It was a very courageous step decided upon by the political leadership of the country, as until then, the design experience of HAL had been limited to the HT-2 primary trainer. The work on the aircraft started in June 1957, under Dr. Kurt Tank, the German expert, in an attempt to meet the "ASR issued by Air HQ for an advanced combat aircraft which would be employed for both high altitude interception as well as low level ground attack duties.[57]

As Air Cmde Jasjit Singh puts it, "This, indeed, was an ambitious goal for a country that had yet to produce a jet trainer."[58] The IAF had its first squadron equipped with the Marut in April 1967. Jasjit Singh adds with pride, "When it started to fly, the HF -24 Marut attracted world attention with wonder, disbelief and jealousy."[59] The problem was that the HF-24 was underpowered. "Even though it was somewhat underpowered, once it accelerated, it was an outstanding strike aircraft of its day, which still had an enormous potential for further improvements."[60]

The high powered Aeronautics Committee headed by C. Subramaniam recommended in its report that the HF-24 Mk. I and 1R (Mk. II) should replace the Hunter and Mystere aircraft in the ground attack role, while development of the Mark III as an interceptor/air superiority fighter should be considered an essential priority.[61]

This did not happen. In the quest for self-reliance, particularly for a developing country , there is no alternative but to adopt the incremental mode, as existing capabilities in design and development are developed with great difficulty, and cannot be allowed to be whittled away.

For development of complicated and sophisticated systems, the user has to have a certain degree of patience and perseverance. Where this is shown, the results are good.

In this connection, one can mention the development of the Samyukta, the electronic warfare system, the development of which was undertaken in the mid-Nineties. For such systems, in the past, we had opted for import.

These systems are not available off-the-shelf from abroad. Foreign suppliers who have the required capability and are willing to supply them, take time to develop them as per user specifications, which differ from military to military, depending on the capability desired. If it is to be developed indigenously, it would take more time as such systems have not been developed earlier, though there are innate capabilities in the concerned DRDO labs and some sub-systems may be available from the development of other systems, which may be going on in parallel.

In this case, the army that wanted the system early, was keen on importing it. DRDO, represented by their CCR&D (Dr.V.K. Aatre, later SA to the RM) , argued for developing the system indigenously as he felt that basic capability for developing the system was available in the country. Further, DRDO labs had already developed some of the sub-systems through some other projects and were confident that if entrusted with the responsibility, would be able to develop it to the total satisfaction of the users. The problem, however, was about the timeframe. As per the initial estimate of the CCR&D, given the complexity of the system, it could take anywhere between six to seven years to develop the system, while the user was not willing to allow more than two and a half years' time for development of the system and felt there were good import options. The CCR&D was not in a position to undertake the project with this kind of timeframe. It appeared at one stage that it would be difficult to avoid the import option, though the imported system might not fully meet the SQRs. Import would also mean that we would not be able to subsequently upgrade the system as the design technology would not be parted with by the supplier nation. This was the past experience of importing such a system from an East European country, which, in spite of an understanding to this effect, did not part with the know-how. CCR&D agreed to bring down the period of development significantly.

It was to the credit of the then Defence Secretary, who after a few rounds of deliberations with close advisers, exercising his judgement, decided to recommend going ahead with DRDO's most challenging EW project.

As the project got going, the user requirements went on increasing, which is normally the case as new developments take place and there is a delay in the implementation of a project. Fortunately, with enhanced efforts, these additional requirements could be accommodated. The amount of software to be developed increased several-fold, compared to what was earlier planned for. Though there was delay in developing the system, the users remained fully engaged with the development of the system.

As it has turned out, it was the far-sighted decision by the policy-makers, the right attitude by the user and determination of DRDO, which resulted in the development of a very powerful system, probably one of the best of its kind. This involved almost ten years' of efforts in partnership with the user. The important point is that, as the development was on, user representatives could interact with DRDO scientists and introduce additional desirable features , leading to the development of a much more powerful system than what was conceived when the project was given the go-ahead. All these efforts were worthwhile as would be seen from the description of the Samyukta, as brought out below:

> The Samyukta, a land-based integrated EW joint project between the Army and DRDO, comprises 145 vehicles. Samyukta which is an integrated entity, can perform critical battlefield EW tasks such as surveillance, interception, monitoring, analysis, and jamming of all communications and radar signals. It consists of COM and non-COM segments and covers 1.5 MHz to 40 GHw. The Army has placed orders for the system. The scale of this venture is massive in terms of magnitude and capability, and the project has followed a consortium approach. Apart from DRDO and the Corps of Signal, other prominent partners are Tata, Bharat Electronics Limited (BEL), and Electronics Corporation of India Limited (ECIL).[62]

Why cannot we adopt this consortium approach in the case of development of other systems? If this approach is adopted, and users are prepared to participate in the development of the system right from the start, as well as willing to give adequate time, there could be achievements which were perhaps inconceivable at the beginning of the process. The Samyukta project is a clear example of this and provides lessons to all players. For DRDO, the important lesson is not to give up early on a project just because there are sceptical views about its success. Such views are to be overcome by persistent effort and persuasive arguments, taking the helping hand of the ministry.

Where the user is not prepared to wait and there is lack of a sense of urgency on the part of DRDO in developing a system , the development of a potentially powerful system may languish, or not take off at all. This happened in the case of the TRISHUL project, where costly systems were imported as there was delay in implementation of the project. There were lots of pressures in importing systems which did not necessarily have better features than systems under development. In view of these imports, the momentum in developing the system was lost. DRDO did not show any resistance to this decision as there were many projects in the pipeline and the user was not to be annoyed. After a decade and a half of development efforts, the project was brought down to a lower key. The political leadership that finally approved the import proposals did not keep in view its long-term effect on development of indigenous capability.

Once a system is allowed to be imported in large numbers, there would be narrow scope for induction of the indigenous system when developed, as the resources and the sanctioned force structure would not permit it. As a result, domestic industry would lose that much potential business. The loss is not so much of DRDO as of industry, both private and public.

It is necessary not only to develop a system but also put up strong arguments for its induction, taking full responsibility for delivering the system in time.

The role of the political leadership is extremely important. The HF-24 project had to be wound up in spite of having several positive features because the political and military leadership lacked the required vision.

The recommendation made by the DRDO Review Committee to set up a Defence Technology Commission (which we shall discuss below) is a step in the right direction to fulfill this requirement.

A private-public partnership takes place automatically if a challenging project, with a suitable timeframe, is awarded to DRDO that has an institutional mechanism for developing such a partnership. Involvement of the users from the very beginning of the project is essential to keep in view, all the time, the operational requirements and to promote user-DRDO-industry partnership. With this kind of partnership, the results are often beyond expectation and, more important, the systems can be improved indigenously.

This is the basic advantage of following the indigenous route in the development of complex systems. Modernisation of the armed forces today requires induction of increasingly complex systems involving development of complicated software, in which our country, having the necessary software skills, has an advantage over others. Hence, the indigenous route should be the preferred option.

If we apply the principle of comparative advantage borrowed from the theory of international economics, then India can have an important role in the global arms market, instead of being an importer.

But we should not miss an important point by just concentrating on the decision process. As mentioned above, in the development of the semi-automatic rifle, the small arms design team called the Rifle Development Team at the Ambarnath Ordnance Factory played a crucial role. There is need to have several such design teams in the OFs and other defence production organisations for in-house design and development of weapon systems. Compared to the enthusiasm and initiative shown in the earlier years, the present situation is hardly encouraging. For example, the 155mm gun system which was imported in the late Eighties, could not be replicated by reverse engineering even though more than two decades have passed. We are still looking for imports. This is a regressive tendency which needs to be corrected by emphasising on, and allocating resources for, development of in-house R&D, without which modernisation would not get the necessary momentum. Encouraging R&D in the production units and allocating significant resources for them would be an important step for correcting this regressive tendency. It has to be remembered that the biggest stakeholders in the R&D process are the production units themselves. For the Army, the best way to achieve self-sufficiency in a cost-effective way would be to encourage and monitor the R&D work in the ordnance factories, for which the initiative has already been taken by the Ordnance Factory Board. This is also true for defence PSUs. While BEL has a good R&D facility, HAL does not.

As pointed out by Air Cmde Jasjit Singh (Retd) in the context of updating of the MiG-21 Bis fleet, for which we had to again turn to the Russians in the Nineties though HAL delivered the first MiG-21 Bis in 1978 on the basis of the licensed manufacture agreement and delivered 220 of them. HAL did not have the required design bureau after the establishment of the ADA. If the IAF had not ignored the in-house design and development capability, it would have been in the forefront among the MiG-21 operating air forces. As Jasjit Singh puts it, while the Air Force had stayed away from the design and development of aircraft and their systems, "The Indian Navy, its sister Service established a Directorate of Warship Design, a Controller of Warship Construction, and the Weapons Equipment and Systems Engineering Establishment, all in the Naval Headquarters. It is not surprising, therefore, that the Indian Navy is well ahead of the Army and the Air Force in the indigenisation process of weapons and equipment... In 1980-82, the IAF had also integrated the navigation attack and weapon aiming system for the Jaguar called DARIN which made the Indian Jaguars far superior to those of the RAF and French Air Force. But in spite of the one-off steps, the fact remains that the IAF has not shown sufficient interest in creating in-house design and development capabilities or establishing a more direct vital integration with design bureaus of HAL."[63]

In-house R&D capabilities would enable better appreciation of the potential of systems under development to enable decision-makers to make professional judgements as also help in developing the systems at a faster pace by interacting with DRDO and industry.

As noted above, in the development of strategic systems, DRDO's achievements have been commendable. These systems cannot be imported or developed jointly with any other country. Nor can they be left to the operation of market forces. It is in the systems which are other than strategic in nature, and which are available in the international market, that the problems have been faced by DRDO in meeting the user needs. The user usually demands state-of-the-art weaponry; Service Qualitative Requirements (SQRs) are framed accordingly and demands are to be met in a short timeframe. There have often been time and cost overruns when indigenous routes have been followed.

But the long-term objectives of defence research in defence capability building, which is essential for providing a basis for the modernisation of the armed forces, cannot be neglected.

It is currently fashionable even in the advanced countries to follow the principles of market economics and to argue that the 'customer'—a Service officer demanding advancement of military capability—should decide what research should be done and funded. But some eminent defence analysts have shown that "none of the key weapon technologies that transformed 20th century warfare arose from a stated military requirement."[64]

We are aware that the development of strategic systems in India, on which defence research takes its pride and justifiably so, which has brought about a sea-change in defence capability, was not based on the specifications of the users. The enthusiasm shown in inducting some of them, once the development had taken place up to a point, was less than adequate.

But short-term objectives in defence capability building have also to be given due emphasis, where user requirements should play a crucial role. This calls for research planning which is a difficult exercise as it requires prioritisation of research funding across military capabilities to balance the amounts devoted to short-term and long-term objectives. This calls for a higher level policy to direct defence research balancing these requirements and prioritisation, which may not emanate from DRDO as it is under pressure to deliver items for meeting the short-term objectives. This may not also come from Defence Acquisition Council (DAC) as its main aim is to modernise the armed forces in a time-bound manner. It would be taking decisions on the basis of 'requirements' as projected by the Services, subject to whatever constraints there are.

The user's perception is different from the perception of R&D. In its effort at modernisation, it would always like to induct state-of-the-art equipment and as quickly as possible. As Dr Prahlada puts it, "Generally, users worldwide are highly focussed about their modernisation needs to keep pace with rapid technological advancements in military weapon systems and platforms. They demand immediate results and expect fast track speed of acquisition processes. They express their inability to wait for indigenously developed systems, which require longer development periods followed by detailed trials (many times more than one iteration)… A majority of users argue that most of the weapon systems and platforms must be imported to hasten up the modernisation process."[65]

It is well known that the benefits of defence research are greatest when its results appear in time to assist in undertaking a major defence equipment/ system project, thus, enhancing its cost-effectiveness in all phases of its life-cycle. This calls for judgements regarding when an increased capability will be required, what new equipment could provide that capability and how long the research itself would require.

A balance has to be maintained between 'requirement push' and 'technology push' in undertaking research. Further, a decision may have to be taken in developing a system with a view to inducting it in the face of uncertainties, in view of its future pay-offs. It may be necessary to dilute some of the specifications required by the users in order to get timely delivery, subject to further development of the system. These are very important but essential decisions which cannot be left to ad hoc decision-making, as is the present situation. The role of the Scientific Advisor, as conceived in the Rules of Business, has to be crucial in this regard. The SA to the RM has to function at a higher level than the DG, DRDO, so that his scientific advisory role gets prominence. This cannot be properly performed now, as he is also the DG, DRDO, as such, a stakeholder.

There is also the necessity of evolving 'stategic partnerships' between the MoD and defence industry, including private sector industries having expertise in the field.

In other words, we require a defence technology strategy to identify key technologies needed to support India's defence policy and indicate how these technologies are to be secured, to support key weapon systems as also evolve a development strategy.

Therefore, a need for a high policy-making body to lay down and review the policies to be adopted for defence research and development with the aim of achieving self reliance, becomes evident.

In this context, Dr Prahlada makes a distinction between "defence acquisition" and "defence procurement" and argues that "defence acquisition" means much more than "defence procurement". "Procurement" is focussed on getting a particular system or equipment for operational use, whereas "acquisition" should be focussed on acquiring the system along with the capability to carry out product improvement, design and development of

Mark II and futuristic products. It is "acquisition" in the above sense that can lead to self-reliance, while "procurement" can only lead to meeting an emergent need. For "acquisition", Prahlada argues for empowering domestic industry with total participation of R&D and manufacturing entities and the need for all stakeholders, including users, to come together, synchronising their individual organisation's policies for achieving self-reliance in modernisation of defence.

A balance has to be struck between the user's perception regarding modernisation and the need for self-reliance. That is where high level policy-making, balancing both the requirements, is called for. We still do not have such a high level policy-making body and modernisation proceeds in a piecemeal fashion through annual acquisition plans. This approach can never lead to self-reliance. There is an urgent need to enhance the role of the SA to the RM to enable him (as it was originally conceived) to give objective and scientific advice as to how this 'balancing of requirements' can be done in a cost-effective manner.

There is also the phenomenon of military-technological revolution which is, and will, profoundly affect the way wars are fought, and determine the steps to be taken towards modernisation, in which defence research and development has to play a crucial role. This also calls for enhancing the role of the SA, to give effective direction to future research efforts in order to develop critical technology, essential for modernisation.

Beginning in the early 1980s, Soviet observers led by Marshal Nikolai Orgakov, then Chief of General Staff, advanced the notion of an imminent technical revolution that would give conventional weapons a level of effectiveness in the field comparable to that of a small tactical nuclear weapon. Massed armour on the march may find itself detected and attacked by conventional missile showering anti-tank weapons. These operations may be conducted from a distance of several hundred miles and with as little as 30 minutes between detection and attack.[66] The Soviets found this development very disheartening, for their strategy depended on the orderly forward movement of massed echelons of tanks and armoured vehicles. As their information technology was not in an advanced state, they could not possibly keep up in an arms race driven by this technology.

The Soviet conception of a military-technical revolution came to the West chiefly through the US Department of Defence and its Office of Net Assessment.

The first Gulf War(Operation Desert Storm) gave a glimpse of the potential of emerging technologies and military systems. For the first time, the importance of space systems to effective military operations was demonstrated on a large scale, as also the effectiveness of precision guided munitions, the importance of the global positioning system to coordinate military operations and the value of stealth technologies.

To increase the military potential dramatically of any nation aspiring to be a major power, technologies central to the emerging military-technological revolution for developing significant numbers of military systems or munitions are needed. Exploiting this military-technical revolution should be an integral part of a long-term strategic planning process.[67]

All these are derived, in whole or part, from the revolution in information technology.

Defence planners can ignore this development at their peril as military-technological information has many implications in terms of organisational adaptation, force structure and strategic approach.

The above should be kept as a backdrop to appreciate the imperative need for technology development at a fast pace, depending on indigenous sources and expertise for weapon systems, as these cannot be imported like weapon platforms can be. It should also be kept in view that militant non-state entities who are waging a form of modern insurgency warfare, today exploit a range of technologies and capabilities that were unavailable to insurgent movements a generation ago. China has closely studied the implications of the Gulf War in undertaking modernisation of its armed forces.

Both these challenges are to be kept in view in our effort towards modernisation of the armed forces, which are to be capability-based to undertake the tasks necessary to meet these threats. The role of R&D and of the SA to the RM in particular, in giving direction to developing the portfolio of capabilities to enhance defence preparedness, would be most significant.

The Ministry of Defence constituted a committee under the chairmanship of Dr. Vijay Kelkar essentially to examine and recommend changes in the defence acquisition process in order to synergise the efforts of various stakeholders for improving the prospects of indigenous production and utilisation of resources available in both the public and private sectors, with the objective to strengthen self-reliance in defence preparedness.

In order to examine the effectiveness of R&D support provided vis-à-vis in-house research facilities with DRDO, and to ensure effective participation of the private sector in defence research, the Kelkar Committee recommended a review of the functioning of DRDO by a separate committee comprising an independent group of external experts. This recommendation was accepted by the government and an external Review Committee under the chairmanship of Dr. P. Rama Rao, former Secretary, Department of Science and Technology, was set up to review the functioning of DRDO, in February 2007.[68]

The DRDO Review Committee functioned for a year and submitted its report in March 2008.

This was the first review of its kind since the inception of DRDO in 1958. Significantly, the review report submitted in February 2008, was entitled "Redefining DRDO". The main assessment of the Review Committee pointed to doubts regarding the "appetite for products" of DRDO's indigenous R&D, which manifests glaringly in defence acquisition of hardware products. The share of the 'Make' (systems designed, developed and produced in India) category is insignificant when compared to the overwhelming share of "Buy" (which reduces itself to 'buy global', meaning outright purchase from global vendors) and 'Buy and Make' categories (outright purchase from a foreign vendor of a limited quantity, followed by licensed production in India). More worrying is the fact that DRDO now plays only a peripheral role in the process of decision-making for defence procurement.

The situation in defence production and indigenisation of components and sub-systems is substantially similar to that of defence acquisition. In the development of in-house defence technologies, participation of the private sector is at a nascent stage. Therefore, in defence research and development, DRDO, with the huge investment in infrastructure over the years made by the country, has to play a crucial role in the design and development of the weapon systems. The private sector also has a huge potential in working towards the country's technological independence, provided the right policy is followed in defence acquisition by giving sufficient importance to the 'Make' category and strengthening the interface with DRDO so that it is involved in much greater measure in defence R&D.

This change in emphasis would not come about through routine reforms of the procurement procedure. To make DRDO sufficiently responsive to the needs of the Services, structural and functional reforms would be required, and some of the basic points made in this regard are outlined below.

It is a well known fact that mission-oriented R&D can thrive only when there is a definite and significant demand for its products. Since there is no adequate demand for what is categorised as the 'Make' category in the Defence Procurement Procedure (DPP), the required incentives and challenges for R&D work are wanting. This is one aspect of the matter. The other aspect is the nature of work undertaken by DRDO and its potential to take on challenging technological tasks within its present structure, and human resources in terms of scientific and technical staff. What are its limitations and how can they be rectified? These aspects, among others, were examined by the Review Committee.

It was observed that the role of the Scientific Adviser to the RM, heading DRDO, has also shrunk compared to what was enunciated in the Allocation of Business Rules (1961).

This will become quite obvious when we consider the diminishing role played by DRDO today, in respect of the following three aspects mandated for it in Allocation of Business Rules:

- scientific research in the fields relevant to national security which would include basic research, design and development of systems and equipment;
- advice to the political leadership and the three Services on scientific aspects of weapons and platforms;
- participation in, and rendering scientific analysis of, acquisition of weapons, platforms and related technologies.

Today, as the committee noted, the share of the 'Make' category was clearly insignificant when compared to the overwhelming share of the 'Buy' and 'Buy and Make' categories. It was apparent that DRDO played only a "peripheral" role in defence procurement. It was observed that for the last five decades, DRDO had taken considerable strides in technology development and in establishing an impressive infrastructure. No doubt, it has made a definite mark with its contribution in the development of strategic systems.

In spite of this, because of several counter factors, the DRDO brand was "wilting" as observed by the committee.

To remedy the situation, several reforms, both structural and functional, were required. The committee particularly observed that a certain *trust deficit* had developed between DRDO and the Services. *Therefore, the review report proposed specific realignments to promote more organic and stronger linkages among DRDO, production and the Services.*

An important finding of the committee was that from a group of research oriented labs up to the early 1980s, DRDO has transformed itself into project-driven labs with a mandate to deliver technologies and systems. In this process, authority has come to be progressively centred at the HQ and the independence of the labs curtailed. This has hampered creativity and taking an innovative approach to development of systems. The support systems such as recruitment, finance, procurement and HRD have also become "headquarter-centric" and the contribution of labs has consequently suffered.

Recognising that the labs are the centres of activity in the domain- specific areas, the Review Committee strongly felt that there was a compelling need to restructure and reform the DRDO system to give a boost to science and technology. As per the committee, decentralisation to provide greater autonomy to the labs was the "core concept" in the proposed reorganisation of DRDO, without which there was not likely to be much improvement in the present state of things.

The Directors of the labs, the committee recommended, should be the key functionaries in the proposed decentralised set-up of DRDO. They have to play the lead role in the development and delivery of systems. The Directors should be armed with the associated freedom to make their labs strong in science and technology, underlying the technical projects assigned to them. Therefore, it is essential to recast several of the support systems like financial management, recruitment and procurement within the ambit of the labs to enable them to play a more effective role, and the Directors of the labs are to shoulder these responsibilities.

The goal, as envisaged by the Review Committee, should be for the DRDO labs to grow to become leading scientific and technical institutions within the respective disciplines in the country. A high scientific stature of the labs and notable performance are critical for them to able to attract talent in preference to other institutions in the country.

In essence, this was the main recommendation of the Review Committee, from which many other recommendations followed.

It was noted by the committee that the concept of autonomous labs has been implemented in several science agencies, with extremely good results.

The major challenge in the decentralisation process should be to create a domain specific group of labs which can come together to contribute more cohesively and efficiently to the implementation of modernisation projects and programmes which are related to their domain strength.

The labs should be grouped to form five centres dedicated to work related to naval systems, aero systems, weapon systems, EW systems and combat systems. Each such group of labs, designated as a centre, is required to be headed by an empowered senior scientist to be designated as a Director General (DG), reporting to the Scientific Adviser. *DGs in the field would not only directly interact with the users, but would also be responsible and accountable for the timely and satisfactory completion of the modernisation projects.* Unless there is accountability and responsibility for developing a product in a time-bound manner, within a given cost in the operating level, the prospects of self-reliance would be dim. This responsibility cannot be taken up by the SA to the RM, who has a much wider mandate.

In view of the crucial role to be played by the Director of the DRDO labs, the Review Committee felt that a search and selection process involving distinguished persons from outside DRDO has to be adopted to ensure the best possible choice of leaders, not necessarily to be drawn from DRDO. This is absolutely essential in the proposed scenario wherein the Directors would enjoy much greater autonomy and responsibility.

The DGs will also support and ensure healthy growth of S&T in the labs of the centres, leading to development of technologies beyond the requirement of existing projects and programmes.

The committee felt that the DGs should play a proactive role in ensuring that their centres are acknowledged as nodes of excellence in their domains, not only in the country but globally. This is required to be achieved by continuous interaction with scientific institutions and academia, through exchange of experts both within the country and abroad.

It was recommended that the DGs would also be accountable for the performance of the labs attached to them, in terms of both quality and quantity of their scientific output. The DGs would be the administrative heads of the centres or clusters and would have the assistance of specialist groups for management of the centres as also integrated Financial Advisers to render financial advice.

Therefore, empowering the Directors of the DRDO labs in an effective way and the appointment of DGs for the cluster of labs are the most crucial steps to enhance accountability and responsibility in the functioning of DRDO and to give a boost to the modernisation efforts of defence through the route of self-reliance.

If this basic recommendation is accepted, the Scientific Adviser to the RM, would no longer be required to bear the designation of DG, DRDO, as the responsibility of delivering the systems in a timely and cost-effective manner would be borne by the Directors of labs and DGs of the cluster of labs. *It was recommended, keeping in the view broader role of the SA to the RM in developing science and technology in the country with a view to effectively enhance defence capability, that he should then be designated as Chairman, DRDO, to whom the DGs would report. As Chairman, DRDO, he would then be required to evolve strategies, plans and policies for efficient working of the set-up, and oversee the functioning of the DGs.* The Chairman, ISRO, in the Department of Space, functions in this manner.

It is necessary that the SA to the RM regain the crucial role assigned to him in the Allocation of Business Rules *in "rendering advice to the Raksha Mantri and the three Services and inter-Services organisations on all scientific aspects of weapons; weapon platforms; military operations; support and logistics in all likely theatres of conflict."*

The committee also strongly felt that the governance structure and the principles underlying autonomous science institutions should be adopted by DRDO in respect of five of the labs which are strongly science-based. There should be a societal governance structure for such labs which will give them a much higher degree of functional autonomy and enable them to excel in the respective fields of science.

In the MoD, the Services, Defence Production and Defence R&D function through an independent hierarchical structure, which often leads to lack of cohesion in undertaking activities related to modernisation of defence. An apex level authority, which could be named the Defence Technology Commission (DTC), the Review Committee felt, has become an absolutely necessity to address major issues involving two or all of these branches so that the overall system is better interconnected and works more cohesively than at present.

For addressing major areas of policy, to make DRDO a really effective organisation, the Review Committee recommended the creation of an apex level authority which should be named Defence Technology Commission (DTC), to be headed by the RM.

Among other things, it would be concerned with:

(i) formulating a clear-cut self-reliance policy and setting up targets in relevant areas;
(ii) monitoring progress against the targets;
(iii) restoring the role of the SA to the RM in rendering scientific advice to the Services in the acquisition of weapon systems;
(iv) evolving a new management paradigm for jointness between DRDO and the Services as well as between DRDO and the production agencies.

The point mentioned at (iv) for setting up the DTC is of particular relevance for the modernisation of defence in an effective manner. Therefore, the DTC has become an absolute necessity to exercise overarching authority, so that development of technologies for their eventual integration into related defence systems occurs more cohesively than at present, which will provide a major boost to the modernisation of defence.

Keeping in view the critical role envisaged of the SA to the RM in Allocation of Business Rules as mentioned above, it was recommended that the SA to the RM should be the Member- Convenor of the proposed Defence Technology Commission. It would be his duty to present before the commission, among other things, reports on the international science and technology trends in general and defence technology trends in particular and in this background, his assessment of the state of national defence R&D.

In the quest of self-reliance, the DRDO's role has to be redefined. In this endeavour, the committee felt that the focus has to be on development of (a) the critical technologies denied to India; (b) technologies embedded in the systems made available during peace-time but which could be denied during times of conflict; and (c) technologies that are imported at a prohibitive cost.

DRDO has to draw up a technology roadmap to address the future needs of the Services as spelt out in the Long-Term Integrated Perspective Plan (LTIPP). The technology roadmap of DRDO should delineate different paths for different categories mentioned above.

In taking forward the modernisation plans of the Services, the need for higher levels of synergy between DRDO and Service HQ cannot be overemphasised. In fact, the interaction with the Services has to take place at all levels, starting from the working level scientists and Service officers up to the SA interacting with the Service Chiefs on a regular basis. The interaction process has to be institutionalised through clearly spelt out procedures. Whenever modernisation projects have been undertaken with DRDO and the users working together, as in several naval projects, there have been high levels of acceptance and success. The committee recommended that the structures within the DRDO HQ be created specifically to provide for joint working of DRDO scientists and Service officers. *To increase interaction and coordination, it was felt that Service officers should be posted at DRDO HQ as well. It was proposed that the post of CCR&D (Service Integration Group—SIG) be created at the level of a 3-star Service officer for a minimum period of three years, who should be supported by three 2-star officers from each Service. The CCR&D (SIG) was to be the main coordinator among DRDO, Integrated Defence Staff and Service HQ for all modernisation projects.*

On the basis of past experience, DRDO has to be entrusted with more and more complex systems to enable industry to develop a higher technology base.

Projects like the LCA led to development of some core and advanced technologies which gave the much needed boost to the relevant industry (in the case of the LCA, the aerospace industry). Some complex projects had to be undertaken which involved technologies, many of which were not available in the 1980s or subsequently (like that of the Akash project) due to denials imposed under the MTCR regime. In such cases, the developers underestimated the time required for developing critical technologies. Inevitably, DRDO had to depend on more than one DPSU as well as the private sector companies for the supply of the sub-systems and the components for the Akash project. Such agencies had to go through their own learning curves. But in the process, the infrastructure and expertise needed for future delivery of such systems had been developed, making it possible to have cost-effective modernisation through the route of self-reliance. These external economies in developing the systems indigenously have to be counted for their multiplier effect in creating a high technology industrial base, which would lead to greater self-reliance in the future.

In this context, a report on DRDO by the Parliamentary Standing Committee on Defence observed that despite handicaps, defence R&D in India managed to mature well by the mid-1980s and embarked on R&D for major weapon systems as also creating core competence in defence-critical technologies. But its performance was rated well below the expectation of the user Services in low-end technology, where foreign suppliers were available. However, in strategically important areas such as radars, sonar, electronic warfare equipment, advanced ammunition and missiles, the users were less critical of indigenous R&D.

If the structural aspects of the reforms suggested by the Review Committee are attended to, the main points of which have been outlined above, it would provide a framework for more vigorous R&D activity in the quest for defence modernisation in a cost-effective manner.

One factor which is not often emphasised but is crucial for revitalising

DRDO, is the necessity of enhancing its human resources in qualitative terms, if it has to take on daunting challenges in research, design and development of systems and equipment.

This factor was underscored by the DRDO Review Committee (March 2008) repeatedly, indicating it as the "biggest challenge" facing DRDO. If this aspect is not taken care of, the role of DRDO in defence acquisition would remain peripheral, irrespective of the structural and procedural reforms undertaken.

DRDO has around 6,750 scientists at present in its DRDS cadre, spread over 51 labs. The important point, however, is that the scientific manpower is dominated by first degree holders. The Ph.Ds in the science subjects comprise only 7 percent and Ph.Ds in engineering subjects are only 3 percent of the scientific manpower, which is particularly worrying. With M.Tech and M.Es accounting for just 29 percent, really qualified scientific manpower is less than 40 percent of DRDO scientists.

B.Scs, B.Techs, diploma-holders, M.Scs, MAs and medical degree holders account for 60 percent of the scientific manpower, who cannot be treated as assets for research. A survey indicates that 43 percent of the DRDO labs have less than 2 percent of their scientists possessing Ph.D. degrees in their respective core disciplines. A survey also indicates that the urge for acquiring higher qualification has decayed in DRDO.

If the manpower profile of DRDO in qualitative term does not show improvement soon, it would not be able to take on the challenges of developing cutting-edge technologies, no matter what the policy level pronouncements are regarding achieving self-reliance in defence procurement.

The age profile of the scientists is not encouraging either. In 50 percent of the labs, the average age of scientists in all grades is above 37 years which is much higher than is desirable.

An audit report on the Human Resource (HR) issues of DRDO drew attention to the high rate of attrition among its young scientists. The reasons identified for it were lack of professional challenges, better career opportunities elsewhere, location disadvantages, and furtherance of professional qualification.

Directed basic research is critical for the development of cutting edge technologies and systems. As the Review Committee noted, the nature of work undertaken by DRDO has changed over the years due to a variety of reasons. Some of the reasons for this are :

- priority assigned to systems integration work;
- non-availability of highly qualified research personnel in sufficient numbers to lead younger teams on a long term basis;
- lack of motivation and incentive to conduct research and publish findings.

All these factors affect the performance of DRDO.

A survey also reveals that the urge for acquiring higher qualifications is fast decaying in DRDO. These HR issues should be given priority and remedial measures are to be taken for which the Review Committee has made several recommendations.

In the terms of reference of the Review Committee, an important point was to consider measures for attracting and maintaining high quality manpower in DRDO.

Non-availability of highly qualified research personnel in sufficient numbers and lack of leadership and motivation to conduct research are the most important drawbacks from which DRDO is currently suffering.

Outside DRDO, the employment environment has changed radically during the last two decades. The inability to offer better prospects to young professionals, not just in monetary terms but also in terms of offering challenging tasks, and opportunity for improvement in academic qualifications during employment through special packages to enable them take on a higher responsibility, has made a career in DRDO less and less attractive to young scientists. This would be evident from its manpower profile, which is quite dismal.

It was also observed that young scientists get disenchanted soon after joining the labs. One of the basic reasons for this is that the component of systematic research is too low in their technical activities and the technical goals set for entry level scientists are not sufficiently challenging.

Structural and functional reform of DRDO is no doubt extremely important, but this would not be adequate to face the present-day challenge unless the HR issues mentioned above are addressed.

Offering extensive advanced training and abundant research opportunities to DRDO scientists within the country and abroad is now essential to enhance the capability of DRDO in undertaking research and development for state-of-the-art. No other step in reforming DRDO is more important than this. As the Review Committee emphasised, advanced training for constantly enhancing knowledge and continually augmenting skills is "inescapable for DRDO" to keep pace with the new scientific world order, which is increasingly dominated by knowledge-based systems.

For this purpose, the Review Committee strongly recommended establishing a Centre of Advanced Studies in Defence Sciences (CASDS) to be fully funded by DRDO. The goals of CASDS would be to raise the level of knowledge and research capability of DRDO scientists as well as foster a sense of belonging to the organisation. This was the crucial recommendation of the DRDO Review Committee to enhance the capability of DRDO in undertaking research in advanced areas of science.

Given the important role it had to play in the future, it was recommended that CASDS should be built on the lines of internationally reputed centres, such as the International Centre for Theoretical Physics, Trieste, which aims at raising the level of knowledge in advanced physics and research in the developing countries.

The faculty for the centre should be drawn not only from within the country but from elsewhere in the world for conducting short and long duration courses in speciality areas relevant to DRDO. Setting up of CASDS would also facilitate interactions and research collaboration among experts with similar areas of specialisation through the medium of national and international workshops and conferences.

As availability of resources is not a problem for DRDO, it is uniquely placed to set up this centre which will give a great boost to the advancement of science and technology in the country, which would, in turn, increase the indigenous capability in research and development, which no other step can. The setting up of the centre should be outsourced to a distinguished panel of specialists who have been associated in the past in setting up training centres of the type envisaged.

Considering the importance of the recommendation in enhancing the capability of DRDO in undertaking the challenging task in research and development, the government should take the urgent step of setting up such a panel for its recommendation in setting up CASDS.

DRDO should also make a fresh beginning on the challenging task of rejuvenating the research culture by taking the following steps:

- Allocate a significant amount of the DRDO budget for conducting basic research;
- Set up a Board of Research in Advanced Defence Sciences (BRADS) which should function in a manner analogous to DARPA, USA.

  BRADS should enunciate the policy and methodology for promotion of research. As recommended by the committee, BRADS should comprise distinguished external subject experts from different core disciplines of DRDO's interest and DGs of centres. The Chairman of the Governing Council should be an external expert of eminence.
- The present grants-in-aid of DRDO must be replaced as it is not serving the purpose. BRADS should endeavour to access and utilise outstanding human resources available in non-defence labs and universities.
- BRADS should also encourage small and medium establishments to undertake radically innovative research though a special programme.

The basic goal of BRADS should be to the enlarge the capability to integrate knowledge resources residing in various institutions of the country for the benefit of speedy implementation of modernisation programmes.

For enhancing DRDO's existing HR capability, it should be possible for DRDO to institute one-year PG-diploma courses at premier research institutes of the country which should be dedicated to DRDO scientists. The PG diploma courses in different institutions can each cater for separate specialised topics.

Deputation to do M.Tech, which is currently restricted to institutions in the country, can also be for institutions abroad for obtaining the Master's degree.

Deputation abroad for research in support of a candidate's Ph.D work should also be supported in deserving cases. Scientists should be allowed to collaborate with counterparts abroad, to the extent necessary.

In making the above recommendation, the Review Committee reiterated, in line with its central thesis, that every possible means should be adopted for raising the level of qualifications and knowledge of DRDO scientists who should be liberally encouraged to do so, especially in view of the present inadequate qualification profile of DRDO scientists.

The importance of promoting innovative research in DRDO and in other institutions through BRADS, cannot be overemphasised, as it would provide the necessary boost to science and technology in the country and make it easier to develop critical technologies in the country, which would otherwise be denied.

The training programme of the new inductees also needs to be revamped. The training schools of the Department of Atomic Energy (DAE) are proven examples of generation of competent manpower. The Indian Institute of Space Science and Technology has been set up few years ago. This can be emulated by DRDO. We have already mentioned CASDS. But the initiative should not end there, as the pool of competent manpower is to be generated for DRDO labs.

It is also necessary for the Director of the labs to ensure that the newly inducted scientists are not put in routine jobs, and take active interest in how they are shaping and motivate them. This calls for leadership responsibilities to be shouldered by comparably younger scientists than is the case today, as also organisational changes which focus attention on individual labs as centres of excellence.

Policy-makers have to give special attention to the present recruitment process of scientists which is archaic. The recruitment process is today handled through a centralised Recruitment and Assessment Centre (RAC). The disturbing feature is the undue time delay between the request by the labs and the recruit joining duty. This proves a deterrent to talented young scientists to seriously consider a career in DRDO, as also detrimental to carrying out research and development within a tight time schedule.

It is necessary to think about a decentralised recruitment procedure. The process of ad-hoc appointments of scientists as well as campus recruitment has to be resorted to in order to quicken the process of research activities.

The Directors of the labs should be empowered to spot, and induct, talented candidates in the quickest possible time, so that DRDO projects do not get delayed and, at the same time, it will enable DRDO to beat the competition for such talent. The ability of a laboratory Director to recruit talented candidates for research activities should be an important criteria for judging his performance. Regularisation of these appointments can be subsequently done through a suitable procedure.

Attractive scholarships can be offered to talented persons in highly rated institutes to pursue projects useful to DRDO.

The other aspect relates to technical assistance for conducting R&D. The Defence Research and Technical Development Cadre (DRTC), has a total strength of more than 12,000 personnel, representing 40 percent of the total manpower of DRDO, who provide technical assistance in research and development activities. They make important contributions in achieving organisational goals. A survey indicates that only a small percentage of the DRTC cadre is below the age of 40, which is not a healthy sign. Among the DRTC staff, however, there are quite a few persons holding Ph. D and M.E degrees.

While on one side there are insufficient numbers of Ph.Ds and M.Es in the scientific cadre, the qualified persons in the technical cadre, in spite of several years of experience, are unable to get promoted to the scientific cadre. This is because of promotion rules and vacancy position, leading to resentment in this important cadre.

If these aspects relating to improving the HR profile of DRDO scientists are not attended to with vigour , the other recommendations for revitalising DRDO through structural and procedural reforms are unlikely to succeed in making DRDO deliver. *Reforms in HR matters hold the key to the entire effort towards "redefining DRDO".*

In the last couple of decades, DRDO has burdened itself with the production of some of the systems developed by it. One of the reasons was the industrial milieu prevalent a couple of decades ago. But this is not the position now.

According to the Review Committee, if the DRDO is to accomplish its mandated role effectively, its role should be confined only to development of technologies. It should, however, coordinate with the production agency for productionisation of DRDO developed technologies and systems.

In case a decision is taken up for indigenous development of a system, the appropriate Production Agency (PA) has to be selected right in the beginning, which could be either a PSU, 0F or a private sector company, which will be the nodal agency to coordinate the project and be responsible for the performance of all the other concerned agencies involved in production. The PA should be associated with the finalisation of the Qualitative Requirements (QR).

Projects can also be taken up by the PA with the DRDO playing a supporting role on the R&D element required for the project, as R&D is not the mainstream activity of the PAs.

The Services, that are the users of the outputs from DRDO projects, have the ultimate responsibility in bench-marking the products and systems for acceptance. They have to play a proactive role in quick development of projects as new systems should be fielded within a short span of five years, in view of fast development of technology. The committee felt that that this can be achieved by following two interlinked concepts, namely, evolutionary acquisition and spiral development.

Evolutionary acquisition calls for the Services to accept a weapon, if it meets over "half the original staff requirement". Successive upgrades would aim to fulfill the original staff requirement.

Spiral development is a useful concept which is a method that accepts the possibility that the eventual weapon may be quite different from what the staff requirement envisaged but will still accomplish the job that was sought.

The committee felt that if these concepts get acceptance, it will enhance the acceptability of DRDO developed projects with updated versions like MkII and Mark III getting into the Services progressively, thereby markedly improving self-reliance.

In this context, reference can be made to the management process of the US Department of Defence known as DoD 5000 Defence Acquisition System which aims at providing effective and timely systems to the US armed forces. A recent significant change to the DoD 5000 involved introduction of an Evolutionary Acquisition (EA) approach. EA provides for phased and overlapping development of new technology in order to bring incremental capability to the defence forces sooner than would otherwise be possible if all the technologies needed for the final system were to be developed and integrated prior to initial production. It is stated by an eminent analyst that EA is now the preferred DoD strategy for rapid acquisition of mature technology for the user.[69]

This also explains the approach adopted by the IAF of accepting the indigenously developed products in a less demanding combat environment, as also in the support and training roles. Examples of this approach are the acceptance of the indigenous Tejas (LCA), Akash Sam, indigenous AEW project, ALH and IJT.[70]

This is the procurement philosophy that should be adopted by all the Services to achieve self-reliance in major weapon systems. The procurement procedure should reflect this philosophy.

A major issue for the Review Committee was how the interface of DRDO with industry could be strengthened to develop and deliver the weapon systems after production. It has been recommended that the identified production agency should be actively involved with physical and financial support right from the early stage of development, for which necessary incentives should be provided. The principles of concurrent engineering to enable simultaneous development of production engineering drawings and other documents to facilitate timely implementation of changes and design modification, should be adopted. Modern information technology and computer aided tools, which allow networking between DRDO labs and production agencies to facilitate concurrent engineering, should be adopted.

It was also recommended that the industry which participates during development and prototyping should be given the first option for production, after providing for sufficient safeguards for prices and quality.

At present, there is no uniform procedure for selection of an industry partner for DRDO. In many cases, the MoD nominates a DPSU, though in a few cases, large private sector entities have collaborated for prototype development and some have been able to participate in production. It was recommended that a combination of selection through tendering and selection by nomination might be followed.

The MoD/customer, along with DRDO, may pre-select a limited number of large industries based on transparent selection procedure and depending on their technical capability. All these potential partners may be involved in a preliminary feasibility study for the development of a system. Thereafter, normal limited commercial tendering may be resorted to among pre-selected potential partners and the best may be selected. This could also be a consortium.

For development of systems, sub-systems and components, DRDO may select from among pre-qualified small and medium scale industries depending on their area of specialisation and sign appropriate agreements for joint development and production.

The MoD may also want to nominate a DPSU as industry partner for certain large projects. In such cases, the DPSU may be mandated to get involved with DRDO on the project, with financial participation and physical involvement. The industry's R&D personnel should be attached to DRDO during the entire phase of development, leading to prototype and certification. Thereafter, the identified DPSU should accept the responsibility for the design rights, future upgrades, modifications and delivery of the product, to the full satisfaction of the customer.

Apart from the present type of partnership wherein DRDO collaborates with industry, the committee has also emphasised the need for a partnership where industry would take up the contract for development and make use of expertise, technology and infrastructure available in DRDO by signing appropriate collaboration agreements with DRDO. Under this procedure, industry wins the contract from MoD for development of a major platform/equipment and uses DRDO for specific technology development or sub-systems. It signs an appropriate agreement with DRDO for collaboration in the R&D phase and gives appropriate compensation to DRDO for the same. The industry partner can be a DPSU, any other PSU or a private sector industry. The process of selection would be as outlined above.

Among the types of collaboration between industry and DRDO, mention may be made of the concept of the government Owned Company Operated (GOCO) DRDO labs.

The GOCO concept is already followed by some of the DRDO labs.

In this scheme, the DRDO lab establishes the plant and machinery, test equipment, etc, within the campus of the lab and outsources the machining and fabrication of components, assembly of sub-systems, testing and allied services to an industry.

The committee felt that setting up captive manufacturing and testing services fully owned by a DRDO lab would be ideal. Small and medium scale entrepreneurs are most suited for this work.

This concept can also be extended to other services such as information technology based design, testing and analysis solutions. DRDO is finding it extremely difficult to induct and retain software engineers. IT companies in the medium scale sector can meet these demands by setting up GOCOs in the concerned labs—this has happened in some form in at least one lab. The Review Committee fully supported this endeavour and recommended that the lab Directors should be empowered to set up GOCO units for manufacturing, testing, analysis and IT services.

Joint Ventures (JVs) and international partnerships can be a very important model as in the case of the BrahMos project for DRDO, for the development of advanced military systems so that modernisation projects get accomplished faster, without DRDO having to develop all the concerned technologies This approach has several advantages: (i) it shortens the lead time for development; (ii) it enhances the indigenous capability and technological base; (iii) the present defence offset provisions in the defence procurement procedure can be leveraged to get appropriate technology from partners located abroad.

The Review Committee, however, stressed that in such JV projects, DRDO must ensure complete transfer of technology to India so that any future denials on supplies do not affect production and the support of the product to the armed forces.

The Defence Procurement Procedure (DPP) 2011 has provided a new category of an acquisition scheme called ‘Buy and Make (Indian)’, apart from existing categories. This is for encouraging procurement from Indian vendors or Indian joint venture companies having production arrangements with foreign OEMs. Such systems must have at least 50 percent indigenous content on cost basis.

A major difference between 'Buy and Make (Indian)' and 'Buy and Make' projects is that in this new category, the choice of foreign manufacturer, ToT and production arrangements is left to the Indian vendor, provided he is able to absorb the critical technologies. Likely Indian vendors are to be identified by Service Headquarters through a Request for Information (RFI). An approved Capability Definition Document (CDD) is floated to identified vendor. Vendors are then required to submit a Detailed Project Proposal (DPP) giving the details of the foreign partner, development and production roadmap with work share range and depth of technology and ToT details, indicating absorption of critical technologies. These proposals are to be examined by a Project Appraisal Committee constituted by the Acquisition Wing and those found acceptable are to be short-listed vendors. Thereafter, Requests for Proposals (RFPs) are firmed up and issued to short-listed vendors. Further processing is to be done as per the procedure in the 'Buy and Make' category.

This is no doubt a progressive step and if implemented properly can help in broadening the industrial base of the country.[71] But it is a rather cumbersome procedure and it may not be very attractive for industry to go through this, as there would be uncertainty about the business prospects. Once a detailed project proposal has been prepared by a vendor through extensive interaction with foreign vendors and others who would be associated with the project within the country , it may be rather odd to subject the matter again to tendering even though it is on the basis of short-listing. By default, it may go to a DPSU, which would serve only a limited purpose in broadening the industrial capability in the country.

In the existing procurement procedure, there have been instances of withdrawal of RFPs which indicates that there are deficiencies in the system. It is understood that withdrawals of RFPs have occurred where there they have elicited an inadequate response from vendors, resulting in either a no-bid or single bid situation or there has been error in the RFP, necessitating its withdrawal and re-issue. This not only leads to delay in the procurement of equipment required by a Service but also increase in the cost of the equipment. To quote an expert on the acquisition subject, "No-bid or single bid situations arising after issue of RFPs indicate an inadequate appreciation of the available equipment in the world/indigenous market or framing of narrow or unrealistic technical specifications or specifying unrealistic delivery schedules—all aspects that should have been properly examined prior to framing of SQRs, as specifically stipulated in the DPP. Errors in technical specification incorporated in RFPs often come to light during pre-bid exchanges between the Service Headquarters and vendors, necessitating withdrawal of RFPs. These are issues of lack of due diligence or insufficient in-depth study before framing of SQRs rather than of any procedural infirmity."[72]

There is a view that the user Service often tends to exaggerate the operational requirement and seeks the most high end equipment available. Issues of ensuring a wider vendor base, procurement from indigenous sources for self-reliance and budget issues, are not given adequate weightage. It is also pointed out that in some countries, framing of Service Qualitative Requirements (SQRs) that are a translation of capabilities into the specifications of the equipment is done by an agency separate from the user Service. It has to be accepted that the user Service must have a dominant voice in the decision-making for defence procurement. At the same time , it is to be recognised that there is a natural tendency of any Service to seek the best available without giving adequate weightage to other factors.[73]

No doubt, the Defence Procurement Procedure (DPP) 2011 stipulates that the SQRs should be broad-based and realistic. The SQRs should express the user's requirement in terms of capability desired, with minimum verifiable functional characteristics, so that its formulation does not prejudice the technical choices by being narrow and tailor-made. But the problem is how to ensure this, given the natural tendency to go for the best available, without adequate analysis of the cost and benefit aspects.

The present structure of the Acquisition Wing does not incorporate the expertise required to autonomously assess SQRs. Under the present procedure, the Service Equipment Policy Committee (SEPC) needs to scrutinise the proposed SQRs in keeping with the stipulations of the DPP, which is not evident in every case.[74]

Evolving and finalisation of SQRs is a crucial issue on which depends the strategy of procurement. As stated above, there is also now the provision in DPP 2011 of 'Buy and Make (Indian)' which, properly implemented, could be a catalyst for defence modernisation, following the route of self-reliance. If the SQR is defined narrowly right in the beginning of the process, there is no way it can be made more broad-based through a subsequent process, however elaborate the process may be. Deliberations take place in the SEPC (Service Equipment Policy Committee), and subsequently in the Services Capital Acquisition Categorisation Committee (SCAPCC), the Services Capital Acquisition Higher Categorisation Committee (SCAPCHC), with the Acquisition Wing playing the role of a nodal agency. They are all involved in the process of 'acceptance of necessity', with the final decisions taking place in the Defence Procurement Board (DPB) or the Defence Acquisition Council.

Though the process is elaborate, these are only two likely outcomes: 'Buy' and 'Buy and Make'. The option of 'Make' can hardly emerge as a viable one, as has been the experience till now. It would also be difficult to implement the latest option of 'Buy and Make (Indian)'.

Keeping in view the basic problem of a narrowly defined SQR (which has been an endemic problem in defence procurements) in the beginning of the process and with the objective of facilitating participation of industry in the process, the DRDO Review Committee recommended the conducting of *Detailed Feasibility Studies (DFS),* after operational requirements have been indicated by the Service. In conducting DFS, the lead role should be played by Integrated Defence Staff Headquarters. This important recommendation, if implemented, shows a way out of the present dilemma.

The feasibility studies are to be conducted keeping in view the Operational Requirements (ORs) indicated by the Services. *Resources should be specifically allocated for such studies and a time limit fixed for their completion.* The team for conducting such studies, it was felt, should consist of representatives of the Service concerned, the likely production agency including private organisations with the necessary expertise, quality representatives and scientists of DRDO.

The team could be headed by a representative of IDS or whomsoever they consider appropriate. Subsequent decisions are to be based on this report, so it should be a sufficiently detailed one, covering among other things:

- risk factors, such as non-availability of certain technologies which are essential for the system to be developed;
- risk mitigating initiatives, like import of technology or a sub-system;
- indigenous development of a system and agency for the development of the system;
- requirement for setting up of major testing facilities;
- in-depth review of the capabilities of the agencies identified for developing systems, indicating the timeframe required for development;
- identifying the agency that would be responsible for system integration which can be called the prime production agency;
- looking into all indigenous options for system integration.

All these aspects should be brought out in the Detailed Feasibility Report (DFR) for evaluation and clearance. *Based on the DFR, the SQR would be drafted by the Service concerned, with the participation of DRDO Headquarters. The SIG to be created in DRDO HQ as per the recommendation of the Review Committee, was to play a very important role in the whole process.*

The draft SQR is to be analysed by a committee to be chaired by the user Service comprising representatives from all agencies responsible for realising the system. The SQR will then be finalised which would define the essential and desirable parameters of the equipment, the timeframe within which the equipment is required as well as the quantities and delivery schedule.

On the basis of the DFR and SQR, evolved as indicated above, it would be possible to take an informed decision regarding development and production of an equipment through the 'Make' and 'Buy and Make (Indian)' route, with the maximum participation of the industry.

It is also to be noted that there is a clear distinction between defence research and the development of defence equipment projects though the two categories are often (misleadingly) aggregated together.

All defence research is directed towards the creation of enhanced defence capability, so it is classified as 'applied research'—an original theoretical or experimental investigation to gain new knowledge of a particular technology. The results of such applied research in any aspect of defence-related technology or operations are *generic,* and may be applied to various different equipment projects.[75] DRDO can play an important role in this endeavour. Some of the important recommendations of the Review Committee have been made keeping in view this larger role of DRDO in developing a science and technology base in the country to improve the generic capability—call it basic research or applied research.

In contrast, the development phase of a defence equipment project involves the exploitation of several synergistic technologies to create new equipment or to enhance existing equipment by applying the knowledge gained from defence research in those technologies. Development involves interactive processes of concept formulation, project definition, detailed design, testing and evaluation which are relevant *only to the new equipment being evolved.*[76]

In the Indian context, the Review Committee noted that the participation of industry during various stages of development leading to production, as well as the quality of participation, has been inadequate and requires considerable improvement. The committee puts in Phase A, the basic research and development of materials and technologies which are to be undertaken. Conceptual development has to be undertaken in Phase A keeping in view the mission perspective. The industry partner i.e. the production agency, may or may not participate in this phase, but will share its knowledge and experience. The DRDO labs have to conduct this type of research in collaboration with other R&D labs or with academic institutions

Phases B-E are specific to a particular system or equipment being developed and the production agency should get involved in all these stages to fortify DRDO's efforts and benefit the project. During the preliminary design (Phase B) and detailed design (Phase C) stages, the industry's experience and expertise in selection of materials, processes and technologies, as also manufacturability could be used for faster and more cost-effective design. A major complaint from the production agencies and users at present is about the design being carried out in isolation in DRDO labs, leading to problems of manufacturability and maintainability. This could be resolved if the industry's experience is fully utilised by the development agency during Phases B, C and D when the prototype development is undertaken. That also means that the production agency is selected before the start of Phase B.

The recommendation is that industry should work along with the R&D team, by forming joint teams facilitated by CCR&D (production coordination) along with necessary incentives, for concurrent engineering to enable simultaneous development of production engineering drawings and other documents to facilitate timely implementation of changes and design modification. Modern information technology and computer aided tools allow networking to facilitate concurrent engineering even when distance separates the engineering departments of the production agencies and DRDO labs.

These procedures will ensure timely delivery of weapons and systems to the users.

Offset provisions in the supply contract are mandated in the Defence Procurement Procedure. Offsets, if strategically used, are a very effective tool for bringing in needed technologies, which the developed countries are reluctant to share. It is important that the offset programme in defence is based on deliberate and purposeful selection of offsets to overcome the technology gap for delivering advanced systems.

Unfortunately, the offset policy is yet to really take off. We have not been able to negotiate really significant technology transfers. There are still debates about what is the proper percentage of offsets to be insisted upon and the best way to implement them.

The offset provision was first incorporated in DPP 2005 where all acquisitions under the 'Buy' and 'Buy and Make' categories having a value of above Rs.300 crore (about US $ 65 million), were required to have an offset of the value of 30 percent of the value of equipment being contracted. The provision was for direct offsets only, which can take the form of co-production, ToT, training, sourcing of parts/sub-assemblies/equipment/software to be used in the production of items contracted for procurement. (Indirect offsets generally include barter, counter-purchase, collaborative ventures and investment in industries.)

As the results from the above provision were not encouraging, the policy was modified in DPP 2006. The offset guidelines were liberalised in DPP-2009 by including a provision for credit banking. It also provided for establishment of Joint Ventures (JVs) and the Defence Offset Facilitation Agency (DOFA). The DPP 2011 modified the policy further to include civil aerospace internal security within eligible products, for discharge of offset obligations. So, to some extent, indirect offsets are provided for in the present policy.

DPP 2011 outlines a roadmap for indigenisation and improving our indigenous capability for producing critical items, thus, leading to self-reliance in specific areas.

The realisation out of this offset policy till now has been depressing. Only around $2 billion during the period 2005-10 has been realised as offsets from sub-contracting of low end products and services, repair and overall facilities, training, etc, as against a much higher target. The expected inflow of FDI, JV and long-term business partnership has not taken place.[77]

Nearly 70 percent of India's defence equipment required for modernisation is imported. Given the current rate of growth of defence expenditure, particularly for capital outlays, it has been estimated that India's imports of defence equipment in this decade could be of the order of US$100 billion, which could mean offset obligations of $ 30 billion on the basis of 30 percent offset obligations.

Establishment of JVs for systems involving critical areas of technology for development, production and marketing, including export, is a way forward. The JV arrangement with Russia for the BrahMos cruise missiles is often cited as a good model. It has a 50:50 FDI participation. For following this model, the FDI cap has to be raised from the present 26 to 50 percent. But that by itself may not lead to transfer of critical technologies.

The Review Committee highlighted the fact that a major gap in the BrahMos project is that the technology of the engine is not with India. There is a critical dependence on the overseas partner. Obtaining critical technologies even in JVs would involve hard bargaining.

As the committee recommended, the defence offset provisions have to be used in the negotiations. Clearly, the extent of offset to be insisted upon has to be higher than the present 30 percent. If it is a 'Buy and Make' contract, it may be easier to obtain these technologies than in the case of BrahMos where it was a joint development project.

There are two points regarding offset obligations as spelt out in the DPP 2011 that need to be reviewed. One is the use of 'multipliers' for calculating the offset obligations. Indian policy regarding offsets as yet is not in support of multipliers. But it should be remembered that development of technology, which involves years of efforts, is costly and provides the competitive edge to the suppliers. If one asks for the price of technologies embedded in equipment systems as part of the supply contract, and if the suppliers at all agree to quote, the prices quoted are very high. And if one is not prepared to pay the price quoted, then the technology regarding the design, etc is likely to be denied or avoided on some pretext or other. Even some industrially advanced countries agree to use multipliers for calculating offset obligations, when they import technologically advanced items. Therefore, the multipliers and the multiplier factors to be used should be seriously considered by India if we want to avail of advanced technology through the offset route.

At the same time, it is to be noted that the offset obligation of only 30 percent is on the low side. Keeping in view that the offset obligation should a combination of both direct and indirect offsets, confining it to 30 percent might not offer much possibility of import of advanced technologies if we have also to use the multiplier factor.

On the basis of practices followed by various countries, a multiplying factor between 3 to 4 for critical technologies may not be off the mark. If this kind of multiplier factor is applied, the offset policy may raise the percentage of the offset obligation much higher than it is now, in keeping with the practice some of the advanced countries. All these issues involve important policy decisions.

Need for Systems Analysis

In view of the large number of possibilities in arriving at an appropriate decision in choosing weapon systems, and the large number of assumptions that may be made, we have to develop a scientific method where each hypothesis is tested by appropriate methods. There is lot of commonality in the approach of the scientific method and the analytical technique called *systems analysis* which is used in the choice of weapons systems in the advanced countries. This is because in the choice of weapon system, the use of quantification is very important as a basis for judgements.

The need for applying systems analysis in choosing weapon systems, keeping in view their cost and effectiveness, was felt in US defence in the 1960s along with the Planning, Programming and Budgeting System (PPBS). The RAND Corporation played a pioneering role in the development of the method of systems analysis in the 1950s. Systems analysis turned 'policy' into 'programmes' by undertaking the following functions:

- defined measures of effectiveness for achieving policy goals;
- examined relevant capabilities in its entities;
- developed executable programme alternatives;
- assessed the cost-effectiveness of alternatives

The above helped in the preparation of a Draft Presidential Memorandum (DPM) for the development of the force structure in McNamara's time.

One can debate on the role of systems analysis in force structure development, but in the choice of weapon systems, its role should be crucial in achieving cost-effectiveness in modernisation of the armed forces. We have not given adequate attention to systems analysis in our acquisition policy, resulting in total disregard of cost-effectiveness studies.

Further, under the Capabilities-Based Planning (CBP), which we have adopted, the weapon acquisition policy has to widen its perspective to infuse technology and programmatic reality into planning and decisions. Decisions on systems are to be made within a capabilities context (systems perspective). So systems analysis should get a lot of importance in decision-making.

The DRDO Review Committee has given a lot of importance to the role of systems analysis and recommended that it should play a part in reshaping of the organisation. The work of a group of labs, named in the report, which intrinsically encompass the domains of modelling, simulation analysis, conceptual experimentation and software development could be integrated to carry out systems analysis. One of the labs that is engaged in operational analysis should, as per its recommendation, embark on building large scale, realistic models and simulation of conflicts, and battles to assess a variety of scenarios which, if the right judgments are made, may significantly affect the choice of weapon system. These models should encompass information from other DRDO labs. There is another multi-disciplinary group at the HQ which should have the major role of gathering technology forecasting information from the centres and autonomous labs, analysing it and presenting their analysis to the SA to the RM.

This group of labs should play a key role in scientific analysis, leading to the formulation of specifications for systems development that are appropriate for meeting field operational needs. They should also visualise futuristic scenarios and suggest technology development to be undertaken by DRDO to meet the projected future requirements of weapon systems for the armed forces.

The analytical work to be carried out by the above group would require to be determined by the proposed CCR&D (Systems Analysis). CCR&D (Systems Analysis) is required to function in conjunction with the three-star Service officer designated CCR&D (Service Integration Group) for which a separate recommendation has been made.

All the recommendations of the DRDO Review Committee hang together and reinforce each other. Therefore, a piecemeal approach or a selective approach in implementing the recommendations would not meet the basic objective of achieving modernisation through the self-reliance route.

In modernising of the armed forces, we have to keep in view the nature of wars that are likely be fought in the future. As the committee puts it, future wars would be fought in all dimensions of security. This implies that three levels of the conduct of wars—strategic, tactical, and operational—will merge into each other, especially in asymmetric warfare. Successful asymmetric warfare can endow a tactical victory, with strategic results. This would only be possible by ensuring inter-Service and inter-agency integration in a big way, which is not very evident right now. It also has different kinds of technological challenges than the conventional war, which have to be faced by DRDO.

We should also keep in view the changes that are being brought about by the revolution in warfare that has been taking place from the middle of the Eighties and its technological implications. Until very recently, platforms dominated warfare in that the newest ship, plane or tank outclassed its rivals and, in most cases, rendered them obsolete. The platform has now become less important and the quality of what it carries—sensors, munitions and electronics of all kinds—has become critical. Thus, the quality of what a platform carries would determine the outcome in a battle today, other things being a given. This is where one has to aspire for technological impendence if necessary through joint development, where DRDO has to play a crucial role.

The debate about redressing the ratio of 70:30 of the self-sufficiency index (that is 70 percent of the requirement of equipment is acquired from abroad and 30 percent from indigenous sources), is a rather sterile debate. What is important is the quality of the 30 percent which is obtained from indigenous sources. The question to be asked is: does it lead to technological independence and self-reliance so that further developments can be made on updating the equipments from time to time?

In a globalised world, as far as platforms are concerned, there is no reason why we should not take advantage of the competitive environment and allow the principle of comparative advantage to prevail. What we should aim is at self-reliance in those technologies which might be denied in a conflict situation or are very costly to obtain through transfer.

As emphasised by the Review Committee, to aspire for technological independence would require the same kind of passionate and inspiring political leadership which led to the setting up of several advanced scientific institutions within a decade and half of independence.

This is a serious lacuna which has to be corrected by DRDO. There is a need for great synergy between DRDO and the aeronautical industry for future modernisation efforts in the Indian Air Force.

On the basis of the DRDO Committee's deliberations, discussions with the Chief Executive of HAL, and senior scientists of DRDO/ADA, it has been proposed that the ADA-executive organisation in Bangalore be merged with HAL R&D.

There would be a lot of resistance to implement this recommendation because of parochial interests, but the government has to take the decision in the larger interest of modernisation of defence, as R&D is the most crucial element in the modernisation process. Our neglect in putting R&D

on a proper footing may prove to be the most important bottleneck towards achieving cost-effective modernisation.

This brings in the issue of following a proper strategy for modernisation through self-reliance.

Need for a Comprehensive Technology Roadmap Towards Self-Reliance and Setting up of Defence Technology Commission

The Review Report recommended that DRDO, in cooperation with IDS, should draw up a comprehensive technology roadmap based on the inputs received from Service HQ and in consultation with the industry. The roadmap should identify gaps in our technological capabilities and the strategy to fill them up by indigenous efforts. *This roadmap should be one of the first things which the proposed Defence Technology Commission should consider in depth for approval which would lay down the guidelines for technology development by DRDO and industry.*

Such a roadmap would also help in formulating an "offset roadmap". These offsets could be either in the shape of technology transfer, infrastructure development for R&D and for facilitating training of scientists in reputed institutes abroad, *which could be the basis for future negotiations with foreign vendors for fulfilling offset obligations.* The commission should enable DRDO to play a strategic role in driving the offset policy towards complementing its technology portfolio, as also expanding research horizons of the scientists.

It can also lay down the guidelines for industrial alliances with other countries on the basis of evaluation of joint ventures (BrahMos) and joint development (LRSAM) programmes; and decision-making on the induction of indigenous systems on a timely basis, so that the policy of self-reliance in the defence sector gets a boost.

This is why setting up of the Defence Technology Commission, headed by the RM is urgently required, as policy decisions which have implications for spending billions of dollars in a cost-effective manner, are involved. It should be kept in view that the choice of weapon systems is linked with the choice of strategies. How are these choices to be made and what kind of information is needed to make them? What are the alternative ways of achieving the strategic objectives, the alternatives that yield a specific degree of effectiveness for the least cost? These questions are to be addressed at the highest level. The rapid technological change is not only producing greatly improved weapons of familiar types but it is also presenting new possibilities in higher technology areas. This calls for long-term strategic thinking in terms of exploiting emerging technologies and developing new technologies. Without these, defence capability building would be seriously hampered in the future. These technologies cannot be imported—they have to be developed indigenously.

The need for a Defence Technology Commission, for developing a long-term strategy for the technology development in the country, which would enhance defence capability in an effective way, therefore, cannot be overemphasised.

But the issue to be addressed is why, though the Review Report (which was prepared after lot of interaction at various levels and in-depth deliberations) was submitted more than three years ago, and in spite of the fact that the MoD had set up a high level Implementation Committee, nothing much has happened. It is obvious that reform proposals of this magnitude would not be easily welcomed by existing stakeholders who are comfortable with the status quo. Then there is the issue of bureaucratic politics. The Prime Minister in his speech at the Science Congress in 2010 mentioned about the need for liberating Indian science from the shackles of bureaucratism, and has again drawn attention to this problem in his recent speech, which has to be overcome, if the goal of increasing R&D spending from 1 percent of GDP to 2 percent, is to be attained.

As far as DRDO is concerned, the way it is structured today, the way it is functioning, and because of the limitation in the HR profile, it would not be possible for it to significantly increase its spending on R&D. It is all the more difficult to do so because of the inadequate linkages with Services.

The Review Committee indicated the basic reforms which would be necessary to enable DRDO to play a more meaningful role in improving the capability in defence and in the cause of science and technology, both being interlinked. It is to be realised by the policy-makers that the base of science and technology manpower in the country is very weak. As per the R&D statistics published by the Department of Science and Technology, India has

110 researchers per million of its population, which is one of the lowest even in comparison to the developing countries. In Argentina, it is 715, in Brazil, it is 324, and in China, it is 633 researchers per million population. Even in Egypt, it is 493. How can we compete with these countries in the development of science and technology? Even the CSIR labs are suffering from shortage of junior researchers who are to provide the base for on-going research.[78] Nothing much has happened in spite of review reports pertaining to CSIR.

The decisions about the reform proposals for giving a boost to science and technology as a strategic objective before the country, have to be taken at the political level by those who are best able to assess the stakes involved. The initiative in this regard has to come from the top, as at the bureaucrats' level, there would be several hurdles, as they are comfortable with the existing system. The government has to take urgent steps for setting up a Defence Technology Commission, as conceived by the Review Committee for guiding research and development efforts towards a more cost-effective defence. It is not for DRDO alone to take steps to bring in the reforms mentioned above. It is for the Government of India to take the lead to bring about the required changes, to rejuvenate science and technology in the cause of more self-reliant defence. This would be in keeping with the vision of Jawaharlal Nehru. The task is not just of 'redefining DRDO' but also of 'reinventing DRDO', which cannot be a bottom-up process. Initiative must come from the top, as the stakes are high.

Notes

1. Maj. Gen. B.D. Kapur, *Building A Defence Technology Base* (New Delhi: Lancer International, 1990), p. 27.
2. Suranjan Pal and William Selvamurthy, "Capacity Building in Defence Science and Technology: A Perspective from the DRDO", *Strategic Analysis*, Vol. 32, No. 2, March 2008, p. 260.
3. Kapur, n. 1.
4. Pal and Selvamurthy, n. 2.
5. Ibid.
6. Nehru's address to Congress members of the Mysore Assembly, January 4, 1954.
7. Kapur, n. 1.

8. Ibid.
9. Quoted in Ibid., pp. 68-69.
10. Ibid., pp. 68-69.
11. Ref:No.295/TS/R&D/Dev. Labs, Government of India, MoD, Ordnance Factory Board, dt 4.2. 08.
12. Ibid.
13. Ibid.
14. Michael Beckley, "Economic Development and Military Effectiveness", *The Journal of Strategic Studies*, February 2010.
15. Eliot A. Cohen, "Distant Battles: Modern War in the Third War", *International Security,* Spring 1986, p. 164.
16. Beckley, n. 14.
17. Ibid.
18. Jurgen Brauer and J. Paul Dunne, *Arms Trade Offsets and Development*, January 2005, quoted by K.G. Narayanan, "Relevance of Self-Reliance in Defence Technologies", Paper presented in the International Seminar on Defence Finance and Economics, November 13-15, 2006, New Delhi.
19. Air Cmde Jasjit Singh, *Indian Aircraft Industry* (New Delhi: Knowledge World, in association with Centre for Air Power Studies, 2011), pp. 182-183.
20. Ibid.
21. http://www.sinodefence.com/airforce/fighter/fc1.asp.
22. Donald C. Daniel, "The Air Force: Science, Technology, and Transformation", *Defense Horizons*, Centre for Technology and National Security Policy, National Defense University, May 2003.
23. Ibid.
24. Nicholas R. Lombardo, "India's Defence Spending and Military Modernisation," quoting a SIPRI report of March 14, 2011, in Centre for Strategic and International Studies, *Current Issues 24.*
25. Ibid.
26. Dennis Kux, *India and the United States: Estranged Democracies 1941-1991* (National Defence University Press, 1992), pp. 229-230.
27. Para 2.13, p-24 of the Report.
28. Gp. Capt. J.V. Singh, *Transformation in Defence Logistics: Trend and Pointers* (New Delhi: Knowledge World and Centre for Air Power Studies, 2010), pp. 125-127.

29. R. Ramachandran, "DRDO : A. Better Understanding Needed", *The Hindu*, February 2, 2007.
30. Narayanan, n. 18.
31. DRDO News Letter, January 2011, carrying address of SA to RM, Dr. V. K. Saraswat, to DRDO scientists.
32. DRDO Newsletter, August 2010.
33. DRDO Newsletter January 2011.
34. Ibid.
35. Ibid.
36. Ibid.
37. Rueters, January 1, 2012, referring to interview with Montek Singh Ahluwalia, Deputy Chairman, Planning Commission, *The Indian Express*, January 12, 2012.
38. Eliot A. Cohen, "A Revolution in Warfare," *Foreign Affairs*, Vol 75, No 2, March-April 2006.
39. "Technology Perspective and Capability Roadmap", IDS, Ministry of Defence, Government of India, 2009, p. 3.
40. Ibid., p.13.
41. Ibid.
42. Ibid., p. 3.
43. Ibid., p. 3.
44. M. Jitendran, "Challenges of Engineering/ Creating Domestic Industrial Capacity for Constuction of IAC", in C. Uday Bhaskar and Shishir Upadhyaya, eds., *The Aircraft Carrier in the 21st Century* (National Maritime Foundation & KW Publishers, 2011), p. 51.
45. Ibid.
46. Quoting Admiral Nirmal Verma, in *Jane's Defence Weekly*, July 27, 2011, by Rahul Bedi, JDW correspondent.
47. A.K. Khetan, "Challenges of Carrier Design and Construction on a Limited Budget", in Bhaskar and Upadhayaya, n. 44, p. 57.
48. *India Strategic*, September 16-October 15, 2011.
49. Guy Anderson, "Russia and Mistral: The Shape of Things to Come?" *Jane's Defence Weekly,* July 27, 2011.
50. Ibid.
51. Ajay Singh, chapter on "Quest for Reliance", in Air Cmde Jasjit Singh , *India's Defence Spending* (New Delhi: Knowledge World, in association with IDSA, 2000),

p. 127.

52. Ibid., p. 184.
53. Ibid., p. 198-199.
54. Chris Smith, *India's Ad Hoc Arsenal* (SIPRI: Oxford University Press, 1994), p. 160.
55. Ibid., p. 162.
56. Subramaniam Committee Report, pp. 63-65, note 52, quoted by Smith, Ibid., p. 167.
57. Singh, n. 19, p. 127.
58. Ibid., p. 128.
59. p. 132.
60. Ibid., p. 144.
61. Ibid., p. 140.
62. Pal and Selvamurthy, n. 2, p. 260.
63. Singh, n. 19, pp. 182-183.
64. David Kirkpatrick, "The Future of UK Defence Research", *Defence and Peace Economics*, Vol 19(6), 2008, pp 479-491.
65. Dr. Prahlada, "Acquisition Focussed on Empowering the Defence Industrial Base: Indian Experience and Way Forward", paper presented in the International Seminar on Defence Acquisition, held in IDSA, July 12-14, 2011.
66. Cohen, n, 38.
67. Andrew F. Krepinevich, Jr "Keeping Pace with the Military-Technological Revolution", 1994, http: //www.issues.org/19.4/updated/krepinevich.pdf.
68. Government of India, MoD letter no RRC/01/1001/M/231/D (R&D)/2007 dated February 8, 2007.
69. Terrence Elmendorf, "A Critique of the US Defense Acquisition Process", paper presented in the International Seminar on Defence Acquisition held in IDSA, July 12-14, 2011.
70. Air Marshal A.K. Nagalia (Retd) "Categorization Options: User's Dilemma", paper presented in the International Conference on Defence Acquisition held in IDSA, July 12-14, 2011.
71. Ibid.
72. R.K. Ghose, Jt. Secretary & Acquisition Manager (AiR), "Towards an Optimal Procedural Framework—the Indian Experience", paper presented in the International Seminar on Defence Acquisition held in IDSA, July 12-14, 2011.

73. Ibid.
74. Ibid.
75. Kirkpatrick, n.64, pp. 479-491.
76. Ibid.
77. S.N. Misra, Principal Controller of Defence Accounts (Navy), "Impact of India's Offset Policy on Military Industrial Capability and Self-Reliance", paper presented in the International Seminar on Defence Acquisition held in IDSA, July 12-14, 2011.
78. Nikhilesh Jha, "The Lab in a Bubble", *The Indian Express*, January 12, 2012.

Index